A GLOBAL AGENDA

Issues Before the 48th General Assembly of the United Nations

An annual publication of the United Nations Association of the United States of America

John Tessitore and Susan Woolfson, Editors

University Press of America
Lanham • New York • London

Published by
University Press of America,® Inc.
4720 Boston Way
Lanham, Maryland 20706

3 Henrietta Street
London WC2E 8LU England

Printed in the United States of America
British Cataloging in Publication Information Available

ISSN: 1057-1213
ISBN 1-880632-08-X (cloth : alk. paper)
ISBN 1-880632-09-8 (paper : alk. paper)

Cover by Scott Rattray

The paper used in this publication meets the minimum requirements of American National Standard for Information Sciences—Permanence of Paper for Printed Library Materials, ANSI Z39.48–1984.

Contents

A GLOBAL AGENDA

Issues Before the 48th General Assembly of the United Nations

Contributors

José E. Alvarez (Legal Issues) is an Associate Professor of Law at George Washington University's National Law Center, where he teaches international law and international organizations.

Tamara Babiuk (Other Social Issues: Disabled Persons; Shelter and the Homeless), a UNA-USA Communications Intern, is a graduate of Vassar College, where she majored in international studies.

Natalie Blaslov (Other Social Issues: Children and Youth; Aging), a UNA-USA Communications Intern, has just completed a bachelor's degree at New York University, where she majored in both journalism and political science.

Frederick Z. Brown (Cambodia) directs Southeast Asian studies at the Paul H. Nitze School of Advanced International Studies of Johns Hopkins University and follows the Cambodian peace process under a grant from the United States Institute of Peace.

Brienne Cliadakis (Other Social Issues: International Year of the World's Indigenous People) is a Program Coordinator at UNA-USA.

Ivo H. Daalder (Arms Control and Disarmament) is an Assistant Professor in the School of Public Affairs at the University of Maryland and Director of Research at the University's Center for International and Security Studies. He has published many works on arms control and is the co-editor (and co-author) of *Rethinking the Unthinkable: New Directions for Nuclear Arms Control.*

Donna C. Dayton (The Status of Women), a UNA-USA Communications Intern, is completing a master's degree in government and politics, with a specialty in international law and diplomacy, at St. John's University, New York.

Haseena J. Enu (Health) served as a UNA-USA Communications Intern while studying for a master's degree at Columbia University's School of International and Public Affairs, with a specialty in human rights.

Felice D. Gaer (The Former Yugoslavia) is Director of the Jacob Blaustein Institute of the American Jewish Committee. She is the former Executive Director of European Programs at UNA-USA and served for many years as Executive Director of the International League for Human Rights.

Christopher C. Joyner (Antarctica) is Professor of Political Science and International Affairs at George Washington University, where he teaches international law and world politics.

Lee A. Kimball (Law of the Sea), based in Washington, D.C., is a specialist in international law and institutions dealing with environment and development issues.

Craig Lasher (Population) is a senior policy analyst and legislative assistant at Population Action International, a private nonprofit organization that works to expand the availability of voluntary family planning services worldwide.

Kathryn C. Lawler (Refugees) is a Research Assistant at the Refugee Policy Group, an independent nonprofit organization engaged in policy analysis and research on refugee issues.

Anthony Mango (Finance and Administration) worked for the U.N. Secretariat from 1960 to 1987. Between 1970 and 1983 he headed the secretariat of the Advisory Committee on Administrative and Budgetary Questions, and in the period 1983–87 he served as Secretary to the U.N. Pension Board. Since retirement he has done consultancy work for the United Nations.

Martin M. McLaughlin (Food and Agriculture) is a consultant on food and development policy.

Jennifer Metzger (Environment and Sustainable Development) is UNA-USA's Public Affairs Coordinator and environment columnist of the Association's quarterly, *The InterDependent.*

George H. Mitchell, Jr. (Economics and Development) is an Assistant Professor of International Politics at Tufts University, where he is a member of the Department of Political Science and of the Fletcher School of Law and Diplomacy.

Charles H. Norchi (Human Rights) is Executive Director of the International League for Human Rights. He wishes to thank Felice Gaer, SueAnne Gormley, Lara Kaufman, Caroline Zukerman, and Elke Zyern.

Edmund T. Piasecki (Redefining the U.N. Role, Africa, Central America and the Caribbean, Cyprus), a Washington-based consultant to UNA-USA, is the co-author, most recently, of "The U.N. in Disarmament," a chapter-length section of the forthcoming *Encyclopedia of Arms Control and Disarmament.*

Rebecca M. Rosenblum (Drug Abuse, Production, and Trafficking), a UNA-USA Communications Intern, is completing a master's degree at Columbia University's School of International and Public Affairs, with a concentration in Russian affairs.

Peter James Spielmann (The Middle East and the Persian Gulf) has been an Associated Press correspondent at the United Nations since 1988. Since 1989 he has also been an adjunct faculty member of Columbia University's Graduate School of Journalism, teaching U.N., diplomatic, and international affairs reporting.

John Tessitore (Co-Editor) is Director of Communications at UNA-USA.

Susan Woolfson (Co-Editor) is Managing Editor of Communications at UNA-USA.

Preface

This past year, like so many years before, millions of us sent and received those delightful greeting cards from UNICEF, bearing tidings of peace and joy. Yet the first half of 1993 brought little peace—and even less joy—to many millions of people throughout the world, people in Bosnia, in Cambodia, in Haiti, in Nagorno-Karabakh. . . . How is it, we ask, that we are finally freed of the crippling fear of nuclear holocaust only to find ourselves engulfed by raging battles such as we have not witnessed since the Second World War?

Men and women of goodwill everywhere—in the developed and developing world alike—share a sense of shock and grief as ethnic and religious hatreds fuel montrous engines of death. And they look with increasing helplessness to their own governments for the enlightened leadership that will take the world away from the abyss and direct our ever-limited resources toward the vital work of global repair.

There is so much to be done. The world cries out for economic growth, for expanded trade and industry, without sacrificing our fragile ecosystem or overlooking social needs. It calls for better health care, universal literacy, the protection of basic human rights, and so much more. And for all this—as well as for the peace without which there can be no progress—the world looks increasingly to the United Nations.

The pages that follow recount what the United Nations has been doing over the past year, told in what we believe to be clear and objective prose. It is a tale of few triumphs, a great many gains, and too many tragedies. It is, in other words, a reflection of the real world.

From time to time we do well to remind ourselves that the United Nations is an institution, not a world government, and that it must suffer the same slings and arrows of international misfortune that affect its 183 member states. Indeed, when one notes how many of its members' problems have been placed at the U.N.'s door over recent years—problems involving individual states as well as those of the collective membership—one marvels that it functions as well as it does.

And that, we think, is what emerges as the underlying theme of this volume. For irrespective of which section one chooses, the reader cannot fail to discover that the U.N. system is performing important, often heroic, work on behalf of people the world over. Thus we conclude that even in the apocalyptical light of war and famine and disease, it must be argued that mankind has *not* succumbed to the fatalistic Hobbesian vision but, rather, valiantly strives to forge order out of chaos. To this end, the United Nations has made a major contribution for nearly 50 years, and can be expected to do so for many years to come.

A word about those who have made this volume possible. To our many authors—some new to *A Global Agenda*, others veterans of one or even several earlier issues—we express our deep appreciation for their invaluable contributions and comradeship. It has been a pleasure working with each of them. And, as we have done each year for many years, we pay special tribute to the cadre of young, bright, enthusiastic interns who have given so freely of their time and energy to this project. To Tamara Babiuk, Natalie Blaslov, Donna Dayton, Haseena Enu, Lorraine Farahmand, Ian Goldberg, Kevin Fitzpatrick, Peter Fitzpatrick, Moon Lee, Michelle Lesbire, and Rebecca Rosenblum we extend our deep thanks and very warm wishes for an exciting and fulfilling future.

Finally, it is with great respect and sorrow that the editors dedicate this work to the nearly 100 U.N. peacekeepers and staff members who lost their lives in the pursuit of their duty over the past year.

John Tessitore
Susan Woolfson

New York, July 1993

I
Making and Keeping the Peace

1. Redefining the U.N. Role
By Edmund T. Piasecki

Secretary-General Boutros Boutros-Ghali has initiated an intensive debate at the United Nations and in capitals around the world on the role of the world body in maintaining international peace and security after the Cold War. In his "An Agenda for Peace" report, issued June 17, 1992, the Secretary-General offered an ambitious blueprint for aggressive action to make, keep, and "build" the peace by a United Nations freed from U.S.–Soviet obstructionism and deadlock. The report proposes a dramatic expansion in the U.N.'s capacity to respond to the qualitatively new threats to the peace prompted by the collapse of a global order founded on East-West divisions; and it demands a significant commitment by member states to provide the increased financial and operational support necessary for such a task and to revise existing funding and budgeting procedures accordingly. Only a small fraction of the Secretary-General's many recommendations have been implemented, and he has already revised some of his more controversial ideas. As the debate continues, mounting financial worries and the difficulties encountered by current U.N. operations raise the question of whether or not the Organization is already overstretched and therefore unable to assume new functions.

Changing Realities

"An Agenda for Peace" attempts to codify and expand adaptations the United Nations had already made to meet changing demands for its services. As originally envisioned, peacekeeping enabled the United Nations to play a small but vital role in the maintenance of peace and security by containing regional conflicts until political settlements could be reached. Prevented from taking action to reverse aggression by U.S. and Soviet vetoes in the Security Council—279 of them through 1990—the United

Nations sought to limit the effects of "proxy wars" fought by superpower surrogates by stationing lightly armed forces between warring states with the consent of both sides. These "interpositional" forces were provided only limited mandates—usually the monitoring of compliance with a cease-fire accord—and operated under narrow "rules of engagement" that permitted the use of force only in self-defense. The deployment of the U.N. Transition Assistance Group (UNTAG) to Namibia in 1989 ushered in a "second generation" of peacekeeping, the Secretary-General has argued, and paved the way for the large, complex, and expensive operations of the 1990s. In guiding Namibia from trusteeship to independence, the United Nations undertook not only a military mission but also extensive humanitarian and even electoral responsibilities.

Demands for this type of operation have increased with the outbreak of ethnic tensions and secessionist pressures long held in check by Cold War confrontation. The massive abuses of human rights and the humanitarian crises that often accompany these upheavals have modified traditional notions of sovereignty and reinforced the belief that the international community has a "right" or even a "duty" to intervene without prior consent. Disputes between states and interpositional peacekeeping have given way to intrastate conflicts and comprehensive efforts to restore peace, protect human rights, promote democracy, and support economic and social development. "An Agenda for Peace" is geared toward increasing the United Nations's capacity to launch such efforts and to modify the structure and function of an organization accustomed to dealing only with sovereign states and internationally recognized governments.

The Secretary-General argues that the function of peacekeeping should no longer be simply the maintenance of the post-conflict status quo. He broadens the concept to include actions to be taken before and during, as well as after, a resort to arms to forestall violence, encourage a speedy end to hostilities, and consolidate the peace. According to the Secretary-General, the United Nations should more vigorously pursue "preventive diplomacy," including an early resort to traditional political tools such as confidence-building measures, good offices, and fact-finding missions. These steps are generally popular as a quick, cheap, and relatively easy response to incipient crises that offers good return on investment. Early warning systems, to the extent they are limited to interagency cooperation in collecting, analyzing, and disseminating relevant information (as on impending humanitarian crises), are also generally supported, but the use of sophisticated technologies (satellite monitoring, for example) raises financial and security concerns. Preventive deployment of military observers to "hot spots" around the globe, authorized for the first time in December 1992 (Resolution 795 on the expansion of the U.N. Protection Force (UNPROFOR) to Macedonia), remains an extremely controversial option. At the request or with the consent of the state or states in question, such action could provide an important symbolic presence of the international community in regions of instability, serving to deter actual aggression. Civilian monitors deployed recently in South Africa (UNOMSA) to discourage acts of political violence have been regarded as generally effective and may serve as models for similar deployments in other countries suffering extreme civil unrest.

During a conflict, the Secretary-General recommends the use of "expanded peacekeeping" techniques, especially the exercise of limited force to protect the supply and delivery of humanitarian relief. The Security Council has already done so in ex-Yugoslavia, mandating UNPROFOR to take control of Sarajevo airport and establish relief "corridors." It took even stronger action in Somalia by empowering the Unified Task Force (UNITAF) to use "all necessary means" to fulfill its humanitarian mandate. Disarmament and mine clearance are also often necessary to guarantee the provision of relief to affected populations; UNOSOM II in Somalia has been mandated to undertake both tasks. Sanctions can also be effective peacekeeping tools, the Secretary-General says, including the "no-fly zone" established over Bosnia and the oil embargo imposed on violators of the Cambodian peace agreement [S/Res/792 (1992)].

After the cessation of hostilities and the demobilization of troops, U.N. peacekeepers have increasingly engaged in "peacebuilding" activities aimed at democratization, national reconciliation, and development. In El Salvador the United Nations has overseen a purge of human rights abusers from the military and has begun assisting in the distribution of land to demobilized soldiers on both sides of the conflict. It will oversee elections there and in Mozambique, and has already done so in Angola and Cambodia. Between October 1991 and March 1993 the United Nations received more than 35 requests from member states for assistance in holding or observing elections. The emergence in the post-Cold War period of the "failed nation state"—struggling badly against the tide of democratization and free market economics—may imply long and costly peacebuilding efforts to completely reestablish governmental and societal institutions. Somalia and Haiti may be candidates for such "third-generation peacekeeping" or, alternatively, some new type of U.N. conservatorship or trusteeship. Afghanistan, Cambodia, Ethiopia, Liberia, and Sudan could be added to the list.

The Use of Force

The heart of the Secretary-General's report—and the proposals that received the most attention—related to the use of military force. Boutros-Ghali called for the conclusion of special agreements under Article 43 of the Charter by which member states would agree to place armed forces at the disposal of the United Nations on a permanent standby basis. Such forces would serve a valuable deterrent function, he argued, and could be effective against lesser military powers. The Secretary-General also proposed the establishment of "peace enforcement units" to restore and maintain cease-fires in the event of resumed hostilities. Member states, for their part, have traditionally objected to either a U.N. "standing" army or a rapid deployment force, due largely to their lack of confidence in U.N. command and control capabilities and fears that such forces might be used for purposes inimical to their individual interests. In October 1992 the Collective Security Project of the United Nations Association of the USA unveiled its own proposal for a three-tiered force. It would consist of a small standing-ready force under U.N. command; a larger rapid deployment force, numbering several tens of thousands of troops from units earmarked for the purpose in national armies; and an even larger contingency force, pledged by a wide range of member states [*Partners for Peace: Strengthening Collective Security for the 21st Century*].

A somewhat related proposal, requesting member states to inform the United Nations of the number of skilled military personnel (logistic units as opposed to observers or infantry troops) they were prepared to make available on short notice for peacekeeping operations, received the qualified endorsement of the Security Council. On October 29 it issued a statement encouraging compliance with the request "subject to overriding national defense requirements and the approval of . . . Governments" [A/24728]. By the spring of 1993, Boutros-Ghali was urging member states to commit themselves in advance to provide "blocks" of operational capability in accordance with standard force structures worked out in the Secretariat. Such standby agreements would ease national planning and budgeting, he maintained, while allowing the Organization to field more effective operations in a shorter period of time.

Regional Organizations and Burden-Sharing

To meet the increased demands placed on it in the post-Cold War era, the United Nations would also have to cooperate more closely and more frequently with regional organizations and establish a division of labor with them. The Security Council, for its part, encouraged them to undertake early warning, preventive diplomacy, peacebuilding, and, "where appropriate," peacekeeping [S/25184, 1/29/93]. In ex-Yugoslavia, the United Nations was providing peacekeeping capabilities while the European Community pursued peacemaking efforts. Were a peace plan to be adopted and implemented there, the United Nations would likely cede operational control to NATO, whose forces would form the core of a U.N. peacekeeping operation estimated to require as many as 75,000 troops. The United Nations was also cooperating with the Organization of American States (OAS) in Haiti, but for the most part regional organizations lack the capacity, experience, and funding to be effective partners in the near term.

Securing adequate financial resources has become a crucial issue at a time when the United Nations is maintaining 13 operations and more than 63,000 military and civilian personnel in the field. The cost of such a massive international presence climbed to over $3 billion in 1992, three times the U.N. regular budget and four times the previous highest annual figure. Arrearages have also ballooned, to $1.48 billion as of April 30. To cover the start-up costs for new operations (or expansions of existing missions), Boutros-Ghali reprised a recommendation of the former Secretary-General for the establishment of a revolving peacekeeping reserve fund. The General Assembly agreed [A/Res/47/217] and set the level of the fund at $150 million, but as of June 1993 it contained only $35 million [data supplied by Unit for Peacekeeping Matters, 7/1/93]. Other more controversial proposals were not even seriously entertained: the assessment of interest on late contributions, authorizing the Secretary-General to borrow commercially, and establishing a $1 billion peace endowment fund. Nongovernmental sources of funding were considered a threat to General Assembly control in budgetary matters and were particularly unpopular: taxes on international arms sales and air travel and the solicitation of contributions from private foundations, businesses, and individuals.

Restructuring and Reform

In addition to funding, the staffing and command and control capabilities at Headquarters remain woefully inadequate. Incredibly, overseeing the design and implementation of increasingly large and complex operations falls to some 12 full-time officials in the Secretariat, although the Office for Peacekeeping Operations has been upgraded to department level and a permanent planning unit is to be established. An operations center will also be brought on-line to provide secure voice and data communication with forces in the field around the clock. The Secretary-General has decided to appoint a Senior Police Advisor, but has not yet acted on a proposal to elevate his military advisor to under-secretary-general-level and provide him with a general staff and real operational capacity. The General Assembly, for its part, has suggested transferring the Department of Administration and Management's Field Operations Division, which helps prepare budget estimates for existing and proposed operations, to the peacekeeping department.

Structural changes in the Secretariat have also renewed calls for reforms on the intergovernmental side, particularly an expansion in the membership of the Security Council. Germany and Japan have endeavored to strengthen their credentials for permanent membership by participating in peacekeeping efforts despite constitutional restrictions. In its first-ever contribution of personnel to a U.N. operation, Germany donated flight crews to reconnaissance missions over Bosnia in April and promised to send a transportation and support battalion (with a small number of armed infantrymen) to Somalia in early June. Japan, which had contributed civilian election monitors to UNTAG, supplied 75 civilian police, 8 military observers, and a 598-man engineering battalion to the U.N. Transitional Authority in Cambodia (UNTAC). The Clinton administration, for its part, has announced its support for permanent membership for both countries [*The New York Times*, 1/30/93]. While the General Assembly has considered the "Question of equitable representation on and increase in the membership of the Security Council" since 1979, the debate on the item in 1992 was much more substantive and urgent than in the past. The Secretary-General is to submit his first report on the question to the 48th Session [A/Res/47/62].

Debate on "An Agenda for Peace" is likely to be ongoing in several different bodies. The Security Council has established an ad hoc committee on the matter, and the General Assembly has formed an "informal, open-ended Working Group." The General Assembly also considered the item in its plenary session [A/Res/47/120] and approved a relevant resolution from its Special Committee on Peacekeeping Operations [A/Res/47/71].

2. The Former Yugoslavia

By Felice D. Gaer

The continuing conflict in the former Yugoslavia, the carnage in Bosnia-Herzegovina, the tragic spectacle of 3.5 million new refugees and internally displaced persons, and reports of "ethnic cleansing" carried out through systematic forced expulsions, terror, and massacre, as well as through rape and torture in detention facilities and camps, have challenged the conscience of the world and the capacity of the United Nations to respond. In fact, to date the Yugoslav case has illustrated what the United Nations *cannot* do when the parties to a massive conflict do not agree to seek peace and when the Organization's most powerful member states remain ambivalent about how to stop it.

A Global Agenda: Issues Before the 47th General Assembly of the United Nations tracked the conflict in the former Yugoslavia and the U.N.'s role in finding a political solution to it up until July 1992. That earlier article demonstrated the conflict's change in status at the world body—from civil war threatening international peace and security to full-fledged state-against-state aggression—once Croatia, Slovenia, and Bosnia-Herzegovina were admitted to the United Nations as independent countries in May 1992. It reported that the United Nations had coordinated its actions to be supportive of—even subordinate to—the European Community, which had been assigned the responsibility of working out a compromise political settlement to the conflict. To underline this point, the sizable U.N. peacekeeping operation sent to former Yugoslavia (the U.N. Protection Force, or UNPROFOR) was headed by a military figure. In mid-May 1992, as UNPROFOR was almost fully deployed, the plan's problems were becoming evident from the Secretary-General's reports to the Security Council [S/23900, 5/12/92], which noted ongoing violence and ethnic cleansing and problems in demilitarizing the conflict area as well as the "pink zones" of Croatia—sites formally outside the truce perimeters but, in fact, active conflict areas in Serb-dominated regions of Croatia. When *Issues/47* went to press in early July, the siege of Sarajevo was well under way, U.N. Security Council Resolution 757 had established economic and other sanctions against Serbia, and—with world attention now trained on Bosnia—the United Nations began its effort to open Sarajevo airport for humanitarian purposes. But the world's attention was also drawn to the visible limits of traditional U.N. peacekeeping in the face of aggression and brutality. As one news source commented: "U.N. peacekeepers have become a cover for Western inaction" [*The New York Times*, 5/12/92].

By May 1992 the U.N. Secretary-General had already reported that "**ethnic cleansing**" was not an effect of the conflict but its actual goal. Under this policy, civilians were targeted for abuse on the grounds of their national, ethnic, or religious origin. The abuses were taking place particularly in Bosnia-Herzegovina and parts of Croatia—abuses by Serbs against Muslims in Bosnia and by Serbs against Croats in Croatia. And although there were some actions by Muslims and Croats to cleanse their own areas of Serbs, U.N. and private observers agreed that these were mostly reactions to Serb policies and not the result of well-planned, coordinated, and funded policies.

Back then, in the summer of 1992, some observers were saying it was urgent to stop aggression by one state (Serbia) against another (Bosnia-Herzegovina), to restore the pre-conflict borders, punish those responsible for war crimes and human rights violations, prevent further "ethnic cleansing," and enable the refugees to return home. If the international community reacts firmly to this conflict, some argued, the effect might be not only to end the conflict in Bosnia-Herzegovina but also to discourage other minority disputes in the region from turning into ethnic warfare. Still other observers maintained that a ground war could do little to stop the conflict and that humanitarian aid to the civilian victims of the war was the No. 1 priority. Officials often argued that there was only a single set of alternatives: to enter the conflict militarily—deemed a "quagmire" from which it would be impossible to extricate U.N. or other foreign forces—or to do little more than express moral outrage and provide humanitarian assistance to the victims of the conflict who managed to stay alive. Undeterred by such arguments, still others continued to search for more varied options the United Nations could pick up.

The **siege of Sarajevo**—and providing humanitarian relief to the city's hundreds of thousands of inhabitants—has remained a major focus of attention of the United Nations: The U.N.'s success in opening the Sarajevo airport did not solve the problem of delivering humanitarian relief. In the face of continuing political and military roadblocks to delivering that aid, many observers call for the use of military force to support humanitarian efforts in Sarajevo and elsewhere in the former Yugoslavia.

Despite the fact that private organizations began chronicling human rights abuses and atrocities fairly early on, and despite the massive, telltale outflow of civilians from Bosnia, human rights concerns did not figure prominently in discussions among the Security Council's permanent five until August 2, 1992, when *New York Newsday* reporter Roy Gutman (later to win a Pulitzer Prize) supplied a pathbreaking report on Serbian-run concentration camps in northern Bosnia. When ITV cameras brought images of emaciated Bosnian prisoners into the living rooms of diplomats and ordinary citizens alike, the world community was stirred into action. The words and photos revealed what many on the ground—including U.N. officials—had preferred to keep quiet and perhaps wanted to hide: that massive atrocities, including killings at the camps, were being perpetrated all around them. Soon the Security Council would express its dismay over violations of the humanitarian laws of war and the United States would succeed in its call for an unprecedented emergency session of the U.N. Commission on Human Rights.

At that session, which met in Geneva on August 13, the Commission appointed a Special Rapporteur to report on such violations. In early October the Security Council appointed a Commission of Experts [S/Res/780] to examine evidence of war crimes, and in February and May 1993 it took steps to establish an ad hoc war crimes tribunal on the former Yugoslavia [S/Res/808 and 825]. To date, however, the Commission of Experts has been seriously hampered by the decision to fund its activities through the current U.N. budget and by the very modest task force assigned to support its work.

In the summer of 1993, the world is still awaiting word of how the Security Council intends to put an end to the aggression against a U.N. member state and the policies of ethnic cleansing and genocide against Bosnian Muslims.

In April 1993, during one of the few Security Council debates opened to comment by states that do not sit on the 15-member body, Third World countries and a sprinkling of Western ones articulated their concern over where U.N. policy was heading. Bosnia's U.N. Ambassador, Muhamed Sacirbey, called for a lifting of the arms embargo against Bosnia's Muslims so they could defend themselves if others would not and called for still other military measures to neutralize the Serbs' heavy weapons and interdict their supplies, asserting that the international community has a legal obligation to stop aggression and genocide. "Obviously," he said, "that is the reason why certain members of the Council avoid the use of these two words. It is tragically comical how resolutions and statements are drafted that describe the acts but so faithfully and meticulously omit the damning words." Then, referring to the August 1992 E.C./U.N.-sponsored International Conference on Former Yugoslavia (ICFY, or London Conference), which attempted to negotiate a political settlement, he observed: "It has become a priority to recharacterize the problem to suit the solutions that were being offered instead of modifying the solutions to actually address the unavoidable problem" [S/PV.3201, 4/19/94, pp. 6–7].

At the same meeting, Amini Moumin, Representative of Comoros, articulated the **frustration of the nonaligned, and especially Islamic, countries** when he asked the Security Council whether "its members, particularly its permanent members, in all honesty and in clear conscience, [could] look straight into the eyes of the 50,000 raped women of Bosnia and Herzegovina and into the eyes of the children and parents and say they have done all they could do to stop the savagery of the Serbs?" Putting diplomatic tact aside, he addressed each of the permanent representatives. To France and the United Kingdom he said: "Your countries' hesitation . . . is difficult to comprehend." To Russia he advised: "The cold war is over—gone. . . . I am sure the people of Russia do not wish to be identified with people who practice mass rape of women and small children for political goals, as the Serbs do." Addressing China, he noted its long-standing opposition to the use of force by the United Nations but asked it to "think again and consider what is happening." Turning to the United States, he said: "Without American leadership nothing can be achieved," adding that small nations and especially those of the Islamic faith were encouraged by "President Clinton's firm stand on the question of Bosnia and Herzegovina," and he urged America to live up to its principles [S/PV.3202, 4/30/93, pp. 13–21].

These frustrations reflected the sense of powerlessness and helplessness felt by most Third World states and others as they had watched the world body try to cope with the conflict in the former Yugoslavia. They had seen peacekeeping forces sent to Croatia in spring 1992, with a largely traditional mandate, and to Bosnia-Herzegovina in the summer, with a mandate to deliver humanitarian aid. Then, in August 1992, they had seen the U.N. begin a major peacemaking initiative, the ICFY, under the direction of the Co-Chairmen of the London Conference's Steering

Committee: former U.S. Secretary of State Cyrus Vance and former British Foreign Minister Lord David Owen. The Vance–Owen peace conference initiatives (see "Peacemaking Efforts" below) took center stage from November 1992 through May 1993.

The two diplomats pressed all the parties to the conflict to work out a comprehensive peace plan for the entire former Yugoslavia, based on the principles agreed to in London. As the world watched, the negotiators talked to—or shook hands warmly with—leaders branded "war criminals" by nongovernmental organizations and even by the then U.S. Secretary of State Lawrence Eagleburger. On press and TV, former detainees recounted the atrocities they had witnessed or been subjected to themselves, and the bombardment of civilian enclaves increased.

When Vance and Owen made public their comprehensive and complex plan, it was simplified and castigated by the press, and even by incoming officials of the new U.S. administration, who declared it unworkable and unenforceable. Many commentators, and even Bosnian government spokesmen, declared that the plan rewarded ethnic cleansing, and the participants in the negotiations used the media to complain of being pressured to accept the plan. The negotiators, for their part, pointed out that the plan was based upon, and reaffirmed, the London principles: territorial integrity, no state-within-a-state, no acquisition of territory by force, the reversal of ethnic cleansing, and maintenance of the highest international standards of human rights protections. The government of each of the ten sectors in a decentralized Bosnian state would be headed by a representative of one ethnic group but would include representatives of the others.

By April 1993 the much-criticized plan was recognized as the best overall settlement the international community could offer, and all but the Bosnian Serbs had signed the last aspects of it: the map and an agreement on interim arrangements for Bosnia-Herzegovina. The Security Council's Resolution 820 of April 17 commended the peace plan, recommitted the Council to achieving a complete reversal of ethnic cleansing, and set forth an array of stiffer economic sanctions to take effect in nine days if the Serbs failed to sign the plan and stop military attacks. The sanctions, under Chapter VII of the U.N. Charter, were to be enforced by "such measures . . . as may be necessary."

Intense pressure was placed on the Bosnian Serbs by the negotiators, whose hand was strengthened by Resolution 820 and also by the much-publicized U.S. efforts to gain support for lifting the arms embargo and for limited air strikes against Serbian supply lines. Even Serbian leader Slobodan Milosevic, his economy beginning to feel the pinch of sanctions, joined in pressing the Bosnian Serbs to endorse the Vance–Owen plan. Though negotiators offered additional concessions to the Serbs,

Bosnian Serbs called a "referendum" in the ethnically cleansed territory they controlled. Predictably, the plan was rejected.

Many Third World states had come to believe that, with the Bosnian Serbs as the only "obstacles" to Vance–Owen, stronger international action—including military force—would be brought to bear against the Serbs. They were to be disappointed. Shortly thereafter, the threat of U.S. intervention evaporated, as top American officials declared they had been unable to convince Europeans to support military measures, and the Belgrade government retreated from its promise to bring additional pressure against the Bosnian Serbs. All the while, massive military battles were in progress, the always tenuous Croat-Bosnian alliance in Bosnia broke down dramatically, and a seeming land-grab was on for territories "promised" by the Vance–Owen plan.

It was in this context that the United States suddenly decided to **recast the situation** once again. At the end of May, U.S. Secretary of State Warren Christopher declared the conflict a *civil war*—"a problem from hell"—and thus not a case of state-versus-state aggression. Furthermore, he removed, or leveled, distinctions between the Muslim victims and Serb aggressors by asserting that there are "atrocities on all sides, which makes this problem extremely difficult" [*Newsweek*, 5/24/93]—although reports compiled by international human rights monitors, including the U.N.'s own Special Rapporteur and the U.S. State Department, have noted that the vast majority of abuses are directed against the Bosnian Muslims by the Serbs and are carried out in a systematic fashion.

With this U.S. redefinition, the Clinton administration called for a more muted response than the one it had advocated earlier. Instead of urging concerted international military action against an aggressor's genocidal policies, the new Secretary of State argued for a more moderate response to a conflict in which there was putatively no strategic interest, only a humanitarian one. Where Christopher had earlier been consulting with European governments about adopting the administration's "lift and strike" plan—lifting the arms embargo against the Bosnian Muslims and conducting artillery strikes against selected Serbian targets—he was now calling for a strategy of "constrict and constrain"—involving the strengthening of a combination of measures already in place and a variety of ideas under consideration for some time but never fully implemented. The Security Council received letters from the ambassadors of five countries that agreed to the **"new" policy** (Russia, Spain, the United Kingdom, France, and the United States) advising the Council that they had adopted a Joint Action Programme that saw the following as "the most productive immediate steps" [S/25829, 5/24/93]:

1. Provide humanitarian assistance for the people of Bosnia-Herzegovina and insist that all parties allow humanitarian aid to pass without hindrance.

2. Rigorously enforce the economic sanctions imposed by the U.N. Security Council against Serbia and Montenegro in accord with Resolution 820. Insist on withdrawal of Bosnian Serb troops from territories occupied by force before the sanctions will be lifted.

3. Watch to see whether the Belgrade authorities live up to their promise to seal borders between Serbia and Bosnia, helping to put pressure on the Bosnian Serbs to accept the "Vance–Owen peace plan" [details of the plan are provided in a later section].

4. Adopt a U.N. resolution on the concept of "safe areas" in Bosnia-Herzegovina. The United States declared that it was prepared to join forces with the other signatories in helping to protect UNPROFOR forces in the event they are attacked and such action is requested.

5. Continue to enforce the no-fly zone in Bosnia.

6. Support rapid establishment of the War Crimes Tribunal, so that those guilty of atrocities may be brought to justice.

7. Build a durable peace through a negotiated settlement in Bosnia-Herzegovina, drawing on the Vance–Owen process and on intensified international cooperation. Implement mutually agreed parts of the Vance–Owen peace plan.

8. Agree that Croatia should be put on notice that assistance to Bosnian Croatian forces engaged in their own variety of ethnic cleansing and in attacks against Bosnian Muslims could result in international sanctions against Croatia.

9. Strengthen efforts to contain the conflict and prevent the possibility that it will spill over into neighboring countries.

10. Stress that aggression against the "Former Yugoslav Republic of Macedonia" would have grave consequences. Support an increase in the international presence there in consultation with the authorities in Skopje, Macedonia's capital.

11. Encourage a larger international monitoring presence in Kosovo, which is considered a tinderbox because the province's overwhelmingly ethnic Albanian population desires independence from Serbia. (The Security Council does not support their quest.)

12. Encourage greater international monitoring in the Serb-populated areas of Croatia. Work for the renewal and strengthening of UNPROFOR's mandate and for cease-fires, and pursue dialogue as a means of settling problems.

The Serbs viewed this program as indicating the weakness of the West and as a statement that force would not be used in Bosnia by the United States or others. It seemed, in fact, to embolden the Serb forces, which began to attack several of the "safe" areas in Bosnia that the Security Council had identified as meriting special protection because of the presence of many Muslim civilians who had fled to these enclaves.

On June 4, 1993 the Security Council adopted Resolution 836 to secure these areas, in the process opening the door to any "necessary measures" by national or regional organizations that might wish to lend UNPROFOR a hand. But here, as elsewhere, there was little to back up the Council's rhetoric. UNPROFOR could now reply to bombardments and air power could be used, but the Secretary-General could not obtain troops to police and protect the safe areas. He reported that his military advisors felt that 36,000 troops were needed, but he now recommended a "light option" of 7,600 troops. On June 18, 1993, when the Council authorized such an increase, Hungary bemoaned the U.N.'s "passive and minimally credible deterrent" and expressed the hope that, at a minimum, the new forces would protect people and end grave abuses in the "safe areas." France, on the other hand, termed this the "only realistic option," while the United Kingdom emphasized that it was only a step in the right direction, designed to help the humanitarian effort. Brazil contended that this would do nothing to help the convoys delivering aid and called for a political solution. Pakistan and Bangladesh offered troops, and the Secretary-General accepted the presence of Third World forces from Muslim countries in embattled areas of Bosnia. Soon after, the Security Council called on the Secretariat to revive and revise its six-month-old report on providing monitors on the Serb-Bosnian border to prevent transshipment of banned goods [S/Res/838, 6/10/93].

In mid-June, in the midst of these developments, President Milosevic of Serbia and President Tudjman of Croatia proposed a new plan that would partition Bosnia into three sectors: Serb, Croat, and Muslim. In view of long-standing rumors that the two leaders aimed to divide Bosnia-Herzegovina between them, this was understood by most commentators to be a proposal to allow neighbors to absorb most of Bosnia-Herzegovina. This flew in the face of the London Conference and the Vance–Owen plan, both of which were predicated on the principle that the territorial integrity of Bosnia would be preserved.

Lord David Owen, meeting with these leaders and Bosnian President Izetbegovic, and then separately with the remainder of the Bosnian collective presidency (three Serbs, three Croats, and one Muslim)—reportedly in the dead of night on June 16—promptly declared the Vance–Owen plan "dead" [*International Herald Tribune*, 6/18/93]. Owen's former co-negotiator, Cyrus Vance, who had retired in May and was replaced by Thorvald Stoltenberg, was reportedly dead set against a three-way ethnically based partition [*The New York Times*, 6/21/93], expressing concern that this would in fact reward and legitimize ethnic cleansing. But as the days passed and criticism mounted, Lord Owen stated—to widespread skepticism—that the plan, as proposed by Milosevic and Tudjman, would ensure that the Bosnian state continued as a "federal republic," with three ethnically based republics. To a BBC-TV interviewer's query whether this meant that "might is right," Lord Owen replied: "I don't like it, but then I have to live in the world as it is. . . . The situation on the ground is deteriorating hour by hour . . . and that's what makes me feel that we have to . . . get a settlement as quickly as we can" ["On the Record," 6/20/93].

On the heels of this new plan, the U.N.'s World Conference on Human Rights, meeting in Vienna, called on the Security Council to lift an arms embargo that, the conferees argued, prevented Bosnia-Herzegovina from exercising its right to self-defense. The Security Council took up a draft resolution on this subject in public session on June 29: The resolution failed to carry because it could not muster the minimal nine votes. (The United States and five Third World countries voted in favor and, while none of the members opposed the resolution, the other permanent members, still other East and West Europeans, and Brazil abstained.) The extensive debate that followed unleashed criticism akin to that heard at the April 17 Security Council meeting cited above, with the Bosnian representative asking particularly pointed questions of the French, British, and Russian ambassadors.

Members of the Council argued against lifting the arms embargo, declaring that it would raise the level of violence, put the negotiating process in jeopardy, endanger civilians in the safe areas, hinder humanitarian aid deliveries, cause the withdrawal of UNPROFOR, and admit that the Security Council had failed. In a sweeping reply to these arguments, the Venezuelan Ambassador, who had traveled to see the "safe havens" in Bosnia as part of a Security Council team, countered that only Bosnia-Herzegovina was negatively—and thus unfairly—affected by the embargo; the others (the Serbs and Croats) were well supplied. Further, the negotiating process had already been jeopardized—indeed replaced—by the Milosevic-Tudjman proposal for partition and its seeming endorsement by Lord Owen (who, said the Ambassador, had denounced Izetbegovic because he, "like Benes, like Churchill, like De Gaulle, like the valiant people of Leningrad, did not agree to surrender"). Why, the Ambassador argued, defend a process in which Lord Owen has switched the rules, provoking the division of the Bosnian government? As to harming the "safe areas," the world has already seen the United Nations leave them "definitely safe for committing all kinds of crimes and attacks." Yes, the Serb attacks might well be speeded up by lifting the arms embargo, which is why the United Nations should neutralize Serb heavy weaponry. Humanitarian assistance would be hindered, but its purpose, after all, has been to help people survive while steps are taken to end the conflict. It continues to be used, wrongly, in place of those political efforts. UNPROFOR should be given a proper mandate or be withdrawn. It cannot go on to protect only humanitarian convoys and not people. As for the defeat of the Security Council, said the Ambassador, "no one can deny that the aggressors have been progressively defeating this illustrious body." Although one can decide not to help a state, it is all the more reprehensible "to deny it its natural right to self-defence." Recalling that the Council and the United Nations recognized the independence and territorial integrity of Bosnia-Herzegovina, Venezuela called upon the Council to be consistent and shoulder the responsibility it had assumed [S/PV 3247, pp. 121–31].

On June 30, the day after the Council refused to lift the arms embargo, it adopted Resolution 847 extending UNPROFOR's mandate until September 30 and calling for a 2,750-person addition to the force.

UNPROFOR and Its Mandate

The United Nations is the only international organization with a sizable presence in the former Yugoslavia, consisting of its **24,197**-person **peace-keeping force (UNPROFOR)** and staff of the U.N. High Commissioner for Refugees (UNHCR), a leading humanitarian agency. In June 1993, UNPROFOR was authorized to add nearly 11,000 troops. Its military, police, and civilian officers hail from 34 countries (17 in the "West European and other" group and 4 in Eastern Europe) and were stationed mainly in four ethnically mixed sectors of Croatia (Eastern and Western Slavonia and Krajina) that have been named "**U.N. Protected Areas (UNPAs)**." These are areas in which Serbs constitute a majority or substantial minority and intercommunal tensions previously led to armed clashes.

UNPROFOR's original mandate was to oversee the maintenance of a cease-fire, the demilitarization of the conflict areas in Croatia, and an easing of ethnic tensions by ensuring equitable law enforcement in areas in which there was armed conflict and by facilitating the return of refugees and displaced persons. This mandate has been broadened several times: to include the "pink zones" that abut the UNPAs [S/Res/762]; to control entry of civilians into the UNPAs [S/Res/769] (yet to be implemented); and to monitor the demilitarization of the Prevlaka Peninsula [S/Res/779]. Initially, too, UNPROFOR's mandate was said to be an "interim measure," pending a permanent settlement.

Although UNPROFOR was intended to deal with the problematic territories of Croatia, the United Nations decided to put the Forces' headquarters in Sarajevo, the capital of Bosnia-Herzegovina, in what was then considered a largely symbolic effort to deter conflict in that ethnically diverse republic. But as the situation in Bosnia deteriorated sharply, the United Nations deployed about a thousand UNPROFOR peacekeepers at Sarajevo airport, with the aim of reopening the facility for the purpose of receiving and distributing humanitarian aid. Later, some 7,500 more troops were assigned to protect the deliveries of humanitarian aid in Bosnia-Herzegovina [S/Res/770 and 776], provided and paid for by NATO member states. Somewhat after that, UNPROFOR was mandated to monitor a "no-fly zone" [S/Res/781 and 786], prohibiting military flights in Bosnia-Herzegovina. And in December 1992, UNPROFOR sent a detachment of 700 to Macedonia for the **U.N.'s first deployment of peacekeepers to *prevent* the outbreak of conflict** [S/Res/795]—a concept found in Secretary-General Boutros-Ghali's "An Agenda for Peace." On June 18, 1993, an additional 7,600 troops were authorized to protect the "safe areas" in Bosnia-Herzegovina, and on June 30, 2,750 more were authorized to monitor later Serb-Croat agreements [S/Res/844 and 847]. Furthermore, the U.S. government agreed to provide another 300 troops as part of a preventive deployment in Macedonia. As of early July, it had yet to be decided whether the troops would serve under U.N. command or under a joint U.S.-U.N. command.

UNHCR, the U.N.'s "lead agency" for international humanitarian relief efforts in the former Yugoslavia, is providing relief and protection to some 3 million refugees and displaced persons while attempting to facilitate their return to their homes. Many of those to whom UNHCR staff are attempting to deliver food, medicine, and shelter live well beyond Sarajevo airport—some in areas of Bosnia-Herzegovina that have been cut off from such assistance for months.

Other U.N. and international agencies active on the ground are the **European Community Monitoring Mission**; a small group of long-term monitors from the **Conference on Security and Cooperation in Europe (CSCE)** deployed in such troubled Serbian areas as Kosovo, Vojvodina, Sandjak, and Macedonia; and other U.N.-related operational agencies, prominently UNICEF and WHO.

In attempting to manage and resolve the conflict in former Yugoslavia, the United Nations has concentrated on six areas:

- Peacekeeping efforts, involving the deployment of UNPROFOR
- Peacemaking efforts, aimed at a political settlement of the conflict
- Delivery of emergency humanitarian aid to refugees and civilian victims of the conflict
- Human rights monitoring and enforcement
- Strengthening economic and other sanctions against "Yugoslavia" (Serbia and Montenegro)
- Consideration of other military enforcement measures

Peacekeeping Efforts, Involving the Deployment of UNPROFOR

As noted above, the mandate of UNPROFOR has been expanded and adapted several times. Originally designed as a traditional peacekeeping operation in which third-party (here U.N.) troops keep the parties to the conflict apart and the fighting from flaring up again, the forces were given limited responsibilities and the **usual rule of engagement: Fire only when fired upon**. The mandate's grandiose language about protecting the human rights of all minorities was little more than rhetoric. What did suggest the untraditional nature of the conflict the forces were dealing with was the fact that they would be **deployed in "inkblot" fashion in the Croatian enclaves dominated by Serb forces**. There was no "front line" or truce line to be monitored, and none of the plans to form the operation took account of the "sovereignty" issue per se, since recognition of Croatia came well after the plan was formulated and agreed to by the parties. The UNPAs were located along the old republican borders of Croatia, but their status seemed undetermined—and the Croats were later to argue that recognition settled the sovereignty issue and that the UNPAs were part of Croatia. Local Serbs went on to argue that if Croatia could exercise self-determination and secede from Yugoslavia, the self-styled "**Serbian Republic of Krajina (RSK)**" could do the same. U.N. officials reported that the situation was further complicated by the Serb consolidation of the RSK *under* U.N. "protection"; and Croatia noted that, other than removing from the region the heavy weaponry and forces of the Yugoslav National Army, the U.N. plan had not demilitarized the UNPAs but, rather, had had the effect of enabling the consolidation to take place. Former fighters donned new uniforms, called themselves border police, and continued the struggle—and nowhere more so than in the **pink zones**, which had been formally acknowledged as part of Croatia but were often Serb-dominated.

So it was that the pink zones, which for political reasons were kept outside the U.N. Protected Areas, remained "live" conflict zones.

The United Nations was not only concerned about local complicity in carrying out the policy of ethnic cleansing in Serb-dominated areas of Croatia but also about the materials that were being transported across these borders between the UNPAs in Croatia and Serbian or Bosnian territory, in violation of both the economic sanctions and the arms embargo. This led to a request to expand UNPROFOR's mandate to include the power to conduct **immigration and customs controls** on the border. On August 8, 1992, the Security Council authorized 800 new members of UNPROFOR to exercise such border control functions. The Secretary-General cited his "misgivings" about further deployment of resources in the region but acknowledged that, without this extra step, the entire effort and investment in Croatia would be undermined.

Ironically, this plan never became operational, and the whole question of enforcing the various sanctions that had been adopted by the Security Council was part of the "new" Joint Action Programme being worked out in spring 1993. After the Bosnian Serbs' referendum in which the Vance–Owen plan was rejected, Serbian authorities, who had said they would accept U.N. border guards to monitor the sanctions, disavowed the idea altogether, claiming it would violate their sovereignty. In mid-June, however, the Security Council asked for an updated assessment of how to employ border monitors.

In the past, U.N. peacekeepers have been more or less successful in monitoring the separation of conventional military forces, verifying withdrawals of forces from combat, monitoring or supervising elections, and mediating transitions—when all sides to the conflict agree on their desirability. The peacekeepers have not been successful, absent an overall settlement, at restoring government authority that has been undermined by civil unrest, and equally unsuccessful at monitoring borders to detect illegal flows of weapons or people. These **traditional failings of U.N. peacekeepers** have been on display in the operation in former Yugoslavia.

The traditional tools and rules of engagement (fire only when fired on) do not work in the absence of a peace desired by all, and most assuredly do not work in the midst of an ongoing war, as in Bosnia-Herzegovina. Further, by demonstrating its inaction in the face of ethnic cleansing during the initial deployment of UNPROFOR in spring 1992, the force **lost the trust of the inhabitants of areas in which it was deployed**; and the same is true in Bosnia, where the mandate is restricted to the delivery of humanitarian aid but where UNPROFOR has allowed itself to be intimidated and kept from carrying out its functions, often by a few "solo" operators. In a situation without civil order, the peacekeeping forces need more authority—a stronger and clearer mandate, particularly when it comes to resisting the kinds of intimidation, maltreatment, and abuses that go on around them (and are sometimes directed at them).

Much of the debate that has taken place behind Security Council doors in 1993 (and in the media and elsewhere, for that matter) has reflected on the need for a stronger mandate for the UNPROFOR forces. Indeed, the peacekeepers themselves seem to have become hostages. When Secretary-General Boutros-Ghali tried to remove them from Sarajevo in spring 1992, he was severely chastised by the Security Council. Yet, a year later, his own report to the Security Council on renewing the mandate of UNPROFOR in Croatia after June 30 [S/25777, 5/15/93] sets forth three options: to withdraw the force, in view of Serb noncompliance; to approve enforcement action to force Serb compliance; or to leave UNPROFOR in place with no change of mandate but with limited enhancement of its military capacity. Stating that the only justification for the latter would be "the high risks associated with the other two" options, the Secretary-General made no recommendation, requesting the advice of his newly appointed special envoy, Thorvald Stoltenberg.

In another report [S/25993] at the end of June, however, the Secretary-General concluded that continuation of UNPROFOR in Croatia and Bosnia-Herzegovina was indispensable: It would prevent the resumption or escalation of the conflict, provide a breathing space for the continued efforts of the negotiators, and support essential humanitarian assistance to victims of the conflict. Focusing on the UNPAs, he called for a review of the local Serb cooperation with the U.N.

Inch by inch, the Security Council has moved to enhance the peacekeepers' mandate. Resolution 836 authorizes UNPROFOR to react more forcefully in the Bosnian safe areas. It asks member states to contribute more troops, and it extends the mandate of UNPROFOR in Bosnia so that the U.N. forces will be able to deter attacks against these areas, promote the withdrawal of military or paramilitary units other than the Bosnian government army, and occupy some key points on the ground. The resolution also authorizes UNPROFOR, acting in self-defense, to use force in response to bombardments against the safe areas, armed incursions into them, and deliberate obstruction of food and medical convoys headed their way. It allows member states or regional organizations to use air power in and around the safe areas, and it affirms that safe areas are a temporary measure and that the primary objective is to reverse the advances made by arms and allow people to return to their homes. (This last was meant to reassure the Bosnian Muslims and the nonaligned countries, both of whom feared that safe areas would become open jails, with U.N. forces serving as the prison guards.)

It seems apparent, however, that changes and advancements are being made, on average, six months after they are first discussed or recognized as useful. Often, decisions to upgrade the mandate and the actions of the peacekeepers are not implemented in their entirety, as with the border guards. Speeding up the full implementation of the actions called for and strengthening the UNPROFOR mandates will no doubt be a key element in future decisions and actions on the ground.

Peacemaking Efforts, Toward a Political Settlement of the Conflict

From the outset, the U.N. endorsed the efforts of the **European Community (E.C.)-sponsored Conference on Yugoslavia** to work out a political settlement to end the conflict. The U.N. peacekeeping plan, agreed to by all parties to the conflict, was described as an "interim arrangement" that would create the conditions making possible the negotiation of an overall settlement. Secretary-General Boutros-Ghali emphasized the distinction between "peacemaking," conducted by the European organization, and "peacekeeping," conducted by the United Nations.

By summer 1992, the Conference on Yugoslavia, chaired by Lord Carrington of the United Kingdom, was badly stalled. The E.C.'s London Agreement of July 17, establishing a cease-fire in Bosnia-Herzegovina, had called on the U.N. peacekeepers of UNPROFOR to supervise all heavy weapons. After a highly publicized disagreement, in which the

U.N. Secretary-General questioned the appropriateness of such U.N. action and the process by which it had been decided, the Security Council endorsed his assessment that conditions were not yet ripe for the United Nations to take on this role. But it also emphasized the importance of a political settlement by urging a "broadening and intensifying" of the Conference on Yugoslavia, and it called too for greater cooperation between the Secretary-General and the E.C. in such political negotiations.

The London Conference

At the end of August 1992 the British government called for a new, widened international meeting on Yugoslavia. Quietly, the U.N. abandoned the Secretary-General's earlier position and decided to play a substantial role in this new, joint peacemaking initiative with the E.C.

The London Conference brought all the parties and factions together. Of the lengthy list of principles they adopted concerning the conflict, two were preeminent: territorial integrity and the need to protect minority rights and other human rights. The Conference also established a permanent negotiating structure—the **Steering Committee of the ICFY, chaired by Cyrus Vance for the United Nations and Lord David Owen for the European Community**—and soon set up a small headquarters in Geneva, with staff borrowed from the two organizations.

On the positive side, the London Conference was not only successful in bringing the parties together, including representatives of the Bosnian government and of the Bosnian Serbs and Croats, but also in obtaining promises by President Slobodan Milosevic of Serbia to end ethnic cleansing and promises to inspect and close the detention camps in northern Bosnia and elsewhere. It took measures to toughen the sanctions, provided for a stronger U.N. presence in the delivery of humanitarian aid, and agreed to send U.N. monitors for the Serb-Bosnian border. In addition, the United Nations and the European Community agreed to speak as one. Furthermore, the London Conference began the negotiating process later associated with the "Vance–Owen plan."

Still, observers were quick to note that, while the Conference was taking place, the shelling of civilian targets in Bosnia had intensified. There were no guarantees in the Conference framework that commitments would be kept; and there were no concrete decisions about the future of almost 3 million refugees and internally displaced people—or about establishing a war crimes tribunal, which nongovernmental organizations had been calling for. In fact, many observers charged that the London Conference, coming so soon after the shocking revelations of atrocities in northern Bosnia, diverted attention from these matters and even gave the false impression that progress was being made (at the Conference, Bosnian Serb leader Radovan Karadzic had stated, incorrectly, that all civilians were released from the camps), nor was there a resolution of Macedonia's status. And if territorial integrity was one of the principles affirmed by the Conference, the Vance–Owen plan spoke of "no unilateral changes of borders," while the ICFY tried to gain acceptance of the firmer assurance that "All parties would respect international frontiers." The latter won out when the phrase "unless changed by mutual agreement" was appended—with the effect, some have suggested, of opening the door even wider to the possibility that one or another party, negotiating from a position of strength during de facto negotiations, could obtain the territory it had seized by force.

The Vance–Owen Peace Plan

The ICFY set up six Working Groups that began intense and continuous meetings and negotiations very soon after London: (1) Bosnia-Herzegovina: cessation of hostilities and constitutional options; (2) humanitarian issues, including delivery of aid, assistance to refugees, and release of civilian detainees from detention camps; (3) ethnic and national communities and minorities (with subgroups on Kosovo, Macedonia, Vojvodina, Sandzak, and Serbs in Croatia); (4) succession issues arising from the emergence of new states of the territory of the former Yugoslavia, including citizenship and state property; (5) economic issues (with six expert subgroups to inventory assets and liabilities of the former Yugoslavia and reconstruction needs); and (6) confidence and security-building and verification measures, addressing military issues.

The Conference turned its attention to human rights and humanitarian issues, proposing norms for the future constitutional structure of Bosnia-Herzegovina and suggesting a constitutional court, a human rights court, ombudsmen, minorities protections, and ratification of international human rights treaties. Later, it proposed an "international human rights monitoring mission" for the country, to provide more data and more accessible redress for victims.

Early agreements with leaders of Serbia and Croatia reaffirmed the London principles and other understandings. Key among them was reaffirmation of the inviolability of existing borders and establishment of a "quadripartite mechanism" to advance the return of refugees in Croatia's U.N. Protected Areas. Leaders condemned ethnic cleansing and promised once again that all civilian detainees would be freed and detention centers closed.

The negotiators reported to the Security Council in November and convened a ministerial session of the Steering Committee in December. Again, principles were reaffirmed. This session heard reports of "grievous human rights violations," continued ethnic cleansing, and mass rape. Support for the establishment of an international criminal court to try war criminals was voiced.

The Co-Chairmen stressed that their priorities were an end to hostilities and a constitutional settlement. Mr. Vance noted "there are no serious alternatives to a negotiated political settlement." He explained that incentives were available to those who cooperate in the peace negotiations and warned that additional "costs will be borne by those who do not." Responding to the calls to use military options, Vance noted that, as of mid-December, UNPROFOR had not found any breaches of the no-fly zone, which prohibits using fixed-wing aircraft in support of combat operations. He pointed out that military measures by the U.N. would endanger personnel already on the ground, including humanitarian aid workers. Noting that proposals for safe havens had been made, he and Lord Owen expressed reservations about any policy that would contribute to ethnic cleansing. Seeking leverage, the Co-Chairmen now called on the Security Council to toughen the monitoring and enforcement of sanctions. To forestall policies they deemed harmful to their negotiations, they asked that enforcement of the no-fly zone proceed if and only if there were genuine infringements.

In January, after the Serbian presidential elections, the negotiators convened the three sides—for the first time since London—for peace talks in Geneva. There they unveiled their "plan" for the future of Bosnia and Herzegovina, in which the country would be divided into ten ethnically mixed provinces, with the dominant nationality spelled out for each. A detailed map, a set of constitutional principles, and other relevant data were circulated.

Criticism of the Vance–Owen plan mounted quickly. Officials of the incoming U.S. administration suggested that the plan was not tough enough, and that the arms embargo had to be lifted and the no-fly zone enforced. Winter, devastation, continued conflict, and the Clinton administration prodded the negotiators to press for prompt agreement to their plan, which consisted of a draft delimiting proposed provincial boundaries in Bosnia, a constitutional framework, and terms for monitoring the end of hostilities. The Bosnian Croats accepted the package in mid-January and the Bosnian government agreed to the constitutional principles, but the Bosnian Serbs, headed by Radovan Karadzic, refused to agree to either the principles or the map. The negotiators made it clear that there could be no "state-within-a-state" by which Bosnian Serbs could act as an independent international entity. The sessions broke up and, before the next was convened, Bill Clinton was inaugurated and hostilities broke out between Croatian and Serb forces at Maslenica bridge and in the UNPAs.

Later, Bosnian President Izetbegovic declared he could not support the plan because it would reward ethnic cleansing. Karadzic said he would put the map to a vote among the Bosnian Serbs. The Clinton administration began conducting a widely announced policy review. On February 3 another round of talks began, this time in New York. Enforceability of the plan became a dominant issue. Negotiations on the map continued. The Bosnian government pointed out that its legitimacy as a state was in effect being destroyed because it was being treated as just another party to the negotiations.

On February 10, U.S. Secretary of State Warren Christopher set forth the new U.S. administration's plan. Affirming the reasons why resolution of the conflict was important to Americans, he explained that the United States would appoint its own envoy to the peace talks, would consult first and closely with the Russian Federation (which later appointed *its* own envoy to the talks), and without endorsing the plan, offered to search for ways to strengthen the Vance–Owen process. The map continued to be the main sticking point, and neither the Bosnian Serbs nor the Bosnian government signed the plan.

In late March, at still another round of talks, the Bosnian Serb position "hardened appreciably" on the political aspects of an overall settlement. In contrast, the Bosnian government negotiated acceptable terms on the governance of Sarajevo and agreed to the map. The Bosnian Serbs were now isolated and identified as the sole obstacle to peace. This was the time when the Americans began pressing for limited military strikes. Enforcement of the no-fly zone was approved [S/Res/816, 3/31/93], and brutal Serb attacks on the Muslim enclave of Srebrenica gripped the world's conscience, leading the Security Council to declare the town a "safe area" [S/Res/819, 4/16/93]. Stepped-up sanctions were approved, to go into effect automatically in nine days if the Bosnian Serbs did not sign the agreement.

Lord Owen began further diplomatic efforts to get President Milosevic and others to bring pressure on the Bosnian Serbs to sign. The Serb "Assembly" called for a "popular" referendum. Lord Owen succeeded in arranging a meeting in Athens at which Karadzic, under intense pressure from Milosevic, signed the provisional map and agreement on interim arrangements.

When the Bosnian Serbs rejected the plan absolutely, many were poised for a military response. Yet shortly afterwards, American pressure simply evaporated. As *New York Times* columnist Anthony Lewis, writing on June 21, recalled the situation:

> At a crucial point this spring, President Clinton failed to support the Vance–Owen plan, apparently believing the cantonal arrangement would leave Bosnia too weak. He said he wanted to use air power . . . and lift the arms embargo. But Mr. Clinton did not press his position on the Europeans: did not lead. When they said no, he gave up his proposal and agreed instead for a plan for U.N. forces to protect six

> Muslim "safe havens." . . . Having put down Vance–Owen as not strong enough, he opted for something distinctly weaker.

Although Lord Owen has pronounced the plan dead, it lives on. Governments have called for its step-by-step implementation.

Looking back on the Vance–Owen plan, the strongest argument in favor of it was always the *principles* on which it was said to be based. Yet there were many who viewed its proposed outcome—ten provinces, whose ethnic leadership would be determined in advance—as de facto rewarding of ethnic cleansing. In fact, the plan was more complicated than that.

The more essential question is whether the plan could have been enforced. Could an international community that allowed its peacekeepers in Croatia to be harrassed and intimidated by Serb militiamen be counted upon to do better in Bosnia? Could the international community send enough military and civilian experts into a post-settlement Bosnia, and for a long enough period, to translate the complex principles and proposals of the Vance–Owen plan into reality? Could military personnel help reconstruct a severely shattered civilian society and assure that perpetrators of gross atrocities would be punished—or at least be disqualified from holding office in the civilian successor state?

The *process* by which the plan was developed and pressed on the parties has evoked rather little commentary. It is clear that the negotiators had a very pro-active view of the process, came up with their own proposal, and used the media to announce their plans, rather than revealing them in diplomatic meetings, in order to bring public pressure on the parties. Vance and Owen used whatever tools the Security Council and its permanent members would give them: threats of economic and even military sanctions, threats of a war crimes tribunal, threats of public opprobrium. But these were not very strong tools. They lacked credible enforcement. Key Security Council governments publicly disavowed military intervention as an option, repeatedly expressed as their prime worry the safety of *Western* military presonnel rather than the victims of the conflict, and disagreed among themselves. The Security Council's own indecision and slowness to take steps that could have strengthened the negotiators left the latter with little to work with other than their own talents. When Serbian officials threatened to strike back against U.N. troops or, worse, West European targets, some West European governments were quick to declare the military option unworkable.

Delivery of Humanitarian Aid to Refugees and Civilian Victims

As the Bosnian situation deteriorated in the spring of 1992, the humanitarian crisis in the former Yugoslavia became a major concern of the Security Council. By May 12, the Secretary-General reported, over 520,000 persons had been displaced in Bosnia-Herzegovina alone, confirming instances of **forcible deportation** in which individuals were made to sign documents stating that their departures were voluntary. Later, Boutros-Ghali clarified the importance of focusing on the humanitarian situation. "For some of the parties," he said, "the **infliction of hardship on civilians is actually a war aim,** as it leads to the desired movements of populations from certain areas. Therefore there appears to be a predisposition to use force to obstruct relief supplies" [S/24000, 5/26/92]. Already aid shipments had been commandeered and relief workers harassed and some even killed.

At the end of May 1992 the Secretary-General put the number of people needing emergency relief at 300,000 to 400,000 [ibid., para. 7]. At the end of July, following her five-day visit to the former Yugoslavia, **U.N. High Commissioner for Refugees** Sadako Ogata estimated that 1.8 million were now homeless, that about 10,000 more were fleeing every day, and that 800,000 people were trapped by the fighting, many without food or medical help [UNHCR, "Emergency Report: Displacement in Former Yugoslavia," 7/27/92]. (Later in the year UNHCR began speaking of nearly 3 million refugees and displaced persons.)

Mrs. Ogata stated that the crisis had advanced far beyond expectations only three months earlier and that "reports of atrocities abound." Calling an emergency conference in Geneva for July 29, she hoped to mobilize the international community to assist in both short- and long-term aid [ibid.].

Not many weeks before, the U.N. had established a security zone and installed UNPROFOR peacekeepers to reopen and run **Sarajevo airport** for the purpose of receiving and distributing humanitarian aid shipments. But the carnage continues in areas not far from the airport: Sarajevo's civilian population and infrastructure have since become a regular target of Serb heavy weapons.

Mrs. Ogata was named Chair of the ICFY's ongoing working group on humanitarian issues, and UNHCR found itself the principle relief agency in the former Yugoslavia—a role it had never played before in a conflict situation. UNHCR has also become the principal agency concerned with providing humanitarian and "preventive" protection for several million refugees.

One result of the August 13, 1992, Security Council decision to "take all measures necessary" to facilitate delivery of humanitarian aid to Sarajevo and elsewhere [S/Res/770] and the September 14 decision to enlarge UNPROFOR in Bosnia [S/Res/776] is that some 8,500 UNPROFOR troops (donated by NATO countries) are now deployed in Bosnia for this purpose. And, indeed, the delivery of humanitarian aid has often seemed the primary concern of the United Nations in the region—a fact that has generated criticism by, among others, key international aid workers themselves (and none more pointedly than UNHCR's courageous special envoy, José Maria Mendiluce). As this criticism was summed up in *The Washington Post* on June 4, 1993, by the normally taciturn operations coordinator of the International Committee of the Red Cross, Urs Boegli, writing in his personal capacity: "Throughout the Bosnian conflict, humanitarian organizations have been used to fill a political vacuum left by the world community. Relief workers are being asked to throw wheat flour at political problems. . . . Humanitarian organizations should be part of an overall response, not a substitute for political policy." One of the risks, he writes, is that "meaner antagonists," armed with nuclear weapons rather than mere artillery, will challenge the international community in other states nearby, alluding to some of the states of the former Soviet Union.

UNHCR has identified four priorities in addressing the humanitarian situation in the former Yugoslavia: enhance respect for human rights and humanitarian law; strengthen efforts to prevent or contain displacement; provide temporary refuge and material assistance for those in need of international protection; and create the conditions that will encourage refugees and displaced persons to return home. At the July 1992 refugee conference in Geneva, Mrs. Ogata noted that "the policy of establishing ethnically pure zones—'ethnic cleansing'—lies at the heart of this conflict." Having called attention for some while to the "horrifying atrocities" related by refugees—"systematic expulsions, forcible relocations, assassinations and other forms of persecution . . . for no other reasons but . . . national, ethnic, or religious origin"—she now called for a new humanitarian "counteroffensive" to prevent the expulsions.

High Commissioner Ogata has explained that such a humanitarian counteroffensive for the former Yugoslavia would require sizable funding to purchase, obtain, and distribute desperately needed relief supplies; an expansion of the airlift to include ground convoys throughout Bosnia; a greater degree and kind of logistical support (trucks, staff, warehouse space, etc.) so that thousands of tons of relief supplies could be brought in and distributed; guaranteed safe passage for relief workers attempting to reach those in need; and temporary international protection for the refugees, including housing and accommodation centers for displaced persons before the onset of winter.

The **needs of Bosnians outside Sarajevo** have been enormous, and UNHCR has tried to increase its deliveries of goods into all regions. At present, U.N. officials must negotiate the safe passage of each convoy (and they do the same, at least initially, where other land or air routes are concerned). They need wider guarantees of safe passage for humanitarian convoys. The sight of U.N. convoys being intimidated by lone Serb gunmen conveys a sense of the impotence of the international community and increases the scorn with which many in former Yugoslavia treat the United Nations.

Most countries have refused to accept large numbers of refugees from the conflict, and it is for this reason that the idea of **safe havens,** located in or near Bosnia and guarded or protected by foreign (read U.N.) military forces, received more consideration as a means of aiding the displaced than might otherwise be the case. The refuge afforded the Kurds in Iraq after the Gulf War supplies a model. Opposition to the idea by refugee officials and others centers on the belief that, by forming such safe havens, they will become collaborators in the policy of ethnic cleansing. Some observers also point to the complexity and danger of providing military protection for such an entity within the conflict area.

The idea of establishing safe havens for the civilian victims of the conflict in Bosnia had been formally recommended as early as November 1992, when Tadeusz Mazowiecki, Poland's first post-Communist Prime Minister and the man appointed Special Rapporteur on human rights in former Yugoslavia, presented a report at the first emergency session of the U.N. Commission on Human Rights. A variety of organizations and commentators later called for such action in the name of saving lives. The International Committee of the Red Cross, initially critical of such a plan, subsequently suggested the conditions under which safe havens might operate (including assurances of free movement in and out so that the zones would have nothing in common with prison camps). But the Security Council's most influential governments resisted the idea on the grounds that the safe areas would have to be defended by ground forces, who might be in a particularly vulnerable position, and that the establishment of such enclaves would help to solidify, and might even cooperate in, the reprehensible policy of ethnic cleansing. (This same argument had been used by Western governments when faced with the prospect of an influx of refugees from the conflict.) By mid-1993, however, it was the nonaligned countries on the Security Council that were most resistant to the idea of safe havens, which they saw as a means of avoiding such action as the lifting of the arms embargo to allow the Bosnian government to fight back.

The concept was adopted bit by bit, and with compromises on the terms and conditions of the safe havens. In Resolution 819 of April 16, 1993, Srebrenica was declared a safe area, although the only action to enforce this took the form of a call for increasing the UNPROFOR presence there and for dispatching a fact-finding mission of Security Council members themselves. In the weeks that followed, the Vance–Owen peace plan was rejected by the Bosnian Serb party to the conflict and Serb attacks against the other enclaves grew bolder, and on May 6 the Security Council declared Sarajevo and five other towns to be safe areas as well [S/Res/824]. To keep them safe, the resolution authorized the presence of a mere 50 additional U.N. Military Observers, who were also asked to monitor the humanitarian situation in those areas. It was only with the adoption of **Resolutions 836 and 844** in June that the Council **put teeth into its earlier declarations.** Yet, as with so many other U.N. resolutions on former Yugoslavia, it remains to be seen whether enforcement actions of any significance will follow.

The Bosnian government was skeptical about the concept of safe havens but agreed to go along if the areas included the "economic environment" of each town as well as the town itself; if the "blue ways" (U.N.-controlled roadways open to all) were opened, connecting these areas with other areas of Bosnia; and if heavy armaments were withdrawn from the protected zone. It also called for U.N. monitors on the Bosnian border and for a lifting of the arms embargo [Reuters, 6/7/93].

Refugees

The conflict in the former Yugoslavia has produced some 3.5 million refugees and displaced persons, and hundreds of thousands more could join them at any moment. Over 625,000 refugees or displaced persons are now officially registered in Croatia, 430,000 in Serbia, and more than 1.5 million in Bosnia-Herzegovina. Just over half-a-million former Yugoslavs have been able to obtain refuge abroad, all but a fifth of them in Germany, Austria, Hungary, Switzerland, and Sweden. So large is Croatia's population of refugees and displaced persons that 20% of the state budget, it says, is devoted to their care and maintenance; and it has refused to accept additional refugees, except those in transit. **The closing of the border of Croatia**—country of asylum for Muslims fleeing Bosnia-Herzegovina—has created an obstacle to their effort to seek asylum, placing them in peril of their lives.

Some "ethnically cleansed" people report that they have been required to sign papers stating that they are leaving voluntarily and still other documents stating that they are turning their houses over to the local authorities. Only with receipts in hand testifying to their "agreement" with these conditions will they be permitted to leave. Muslims who flee ethnic cleansing in Bosnia-Herzegovina are apt to encounter Serbian military and paramilitary forces, bandits, minefields, and certain "technical" restrictions.

Those who try crossing bridges to reach U.N. Protected Areas have encountered Serb obstacles on both sides of the border. UNPROFOR soldiers have **returned some asylum-seekers to Bosnian territory** because of Croatian opposition to their presence in the place of asylum. But the problems persist even when those who flee have found "refuge": The Serbs in Bosnia have repeatedly demanded that the U.N. civilian police monitors turn the refugees over to them, and the monitors reject all such requests, but on one occasion armed men kidnapped the refugees and spirited them back to Bosnia. UNHCR, with only a few staff at each UNPA, is nonetheless asked to observe the entry of the refugees, and its representatives state that they must resist becoming a "border police" that checks documents for the Croatian government.

Muslim refugees in Croatia cannot leave the republic if they lack the proper registration documents, which are also needed to obtain visas to third countries. Moreover, lacking official status, they reportedly are unable to obtain hospital care and other services available to Croats. And under an agreement between Presidents Franjo Tudjman of Croatia and Alija Izetbegovic of Bosnia-Herzegovina, **men of draft age** are subject to being sent back by the Croatian government—and are unable to obtain the support the government makes available to refugees and displaced persons.

Some of those released from Bosnian detention centers have been permitted to enter Croatia in transit to third countries. Although considered priority cases, spaces for them were relatively slow to open up.

Refugees and displaced persons in the former Yugoslavia have two basic needs: humanitarian aid (in the form of shelter, food, medicine, and the like) and security. A number of U.N. Security Council resolutions have authorized **military escorts for the delivery of humanitarian aid and the clearing of detention centers**, if requested by the International Committee of the Red Cross. Some 6,500 soldiers have been provided for the specific purpose of escorting such convoys.

The Serbian refugees now in these UNPAs have reported that organized violence drove them from their homes in Croatia (Zadar and Biograd, etc.) and that they would like to return or, in some cases, receive insurance or other restitution for the properties they have lost. It has been reported that Croats prevent Serbs from returning to their homes by listing their names in the newspapers as enemies of the state and by opening criminal proceedings against them.

Muslim forces have been engaged in combat with Croatian forces in Bosnia, undermining what had been an alliance, and the situation deteriorated sharply in spring 1993 when the Bosnian Serbs rejected the Vance–Owen peace plan. Reports of ethnic cleansing by Croats against Serbs and Muslims against Croats were common in May and early June, reportedly because each party was jockeying for control of territory "allotted" to it under Vance–Owen.

UNPROFOR's mandate in the UNPAs includes responsibility for overseeing the eventual return of the displaced population to their homes. Croatian authorities have identified 274,000 Croats who once lived in UNPAs but now live in other parts of Croatia, and UNHCR counts 87,000 (presumably Serbs) from Croatia who live in UNPAs. Certainly conditions in the UNPAs and the pink zones offer none of the safety that would permit the return of the traditional inhabitants; in fact, the houses of those who might return are being blown up and robbed, most commonly at night, when there is no patrolling by the local constabulary. Human rights monitors have received documentary evidence that, in some cases, local Serb officials sanction the looting and dismantling of abandoned Croatian houses in the UNPAs and pink zones.

Up to 14,000 local paramilitaries in the UNPAs who were to be disarmed under the Vance–Owen plan were transformed into "**border police**," who receive no police training and perform no police functions but continue to use their weapons and to maintain an atmosphere of danger in the zones.

UNHCR has reported that there are still perhaps 100,000 **mines** in Sector South UNPA alone, and evidence that more are being laid in the villages near the confrontation line. And even with the U.N. presence, ethnic cleansing continues. Local authorities of the self-proclaimed Serbian Republic of Krajina have warned that no refugee can return without their explicit permission, and some observers believe that recent actions against Croats and their property are intended to serve as warnings of what will happen on a larger scale if efforts to return were to move ahead without "Krajina's" agreement.

Parties to the conflict in the former Yugoslavia have utilized food, medicine, water, and electricity as weapons against the civilian population. Serbs in Krajina complain bitterly of the hardships created by Croats who deny them such necessities. Croats, for their part, cite cases of the Serbs' refusal to provide utilities to Croatian areas, but efforts at restoring utilities on a reciprocal basis have made only modest progress. In Bosnia-Herzegovina the siege of towns selected as military targets or slated for "cleansing" is routinely accompanied by a cutoff of utilities and services.

Human Rights Monitoring and Enforcement

Reports on the killing and torture of civilians in Croatia by combatants in the conflict were compiled by nongovernmental organizations and discussed in U.N. human rights bodies, but no action was taken on them until the **special emergency session of the Human Rights Commission in August 1992**, following press reports about Bosnian concentration camps and ethnic cleansing.

Officials of the U.N. High Commissioner for Refugees based their reports of mass killing and ethnic cleansing on refugee accounts, but, lacking any explicit mandate to take action against such atrocities, UNHCR had referred to these reports only in general terms at its own emergency meeting in Geneva the previous month. UNHCR continues to highlight the need for governments and the international community to reaffirm the importance of human rights protections when attempting to address the root causes of such conflicts.

Over the years, the United Nations has attempted to establish human rights standards, educate citizens about their rights, conduct fact-finding on human rights abuses, and promote government accountability for their actions. Fact finding is perhaps one of the U.N.'s most important human rights activities, and another is its effort to mobilize the international community against gross violations of those rights. The U.N. Commission on Human Rights has had long experience in such activity, but the Security Council has been reluctant to address such matters, on the grounds (most often cited today by China and members of the Nonaligned Movement) that human rights is not a security issue but a domestic one and should be addressed only within the Commission on Human Rights.

As will be indicated below, the distinction has been growing weaker, with peacekeeping plans now likely to include a human rights component and the atrocities themselves likely to be viewed as security threats. Nonetheless, the Council tends to hide behind the figleaf that it is appropriate for it to consider violations of the humanitarian rules of war but not of human rights norms in general. And it continues to make this distinction even when arbitrary executions and torture, to cite two examples, appear on both lists.

Indeed, one of the jobs of **UNPROFOR's civilian police monitors** is to assure nondiscrimination and the protection of human rights in the areas it patrols. UNPROFOR is assigned to monitor reports and, if warranted, forward them to local authorities, who are supposed to take steps to correct the problem or to prosecute those charged with abuse of human rights. The U.N. Secretary-General has reported to the Security Council on UNPROFOR's activities to protest and end forced expulsions and ethnic cleansing in Croatia; in June and July 1992 he stated that an UNPROFOR initiative aimed at bringing charges against 11 ringleaders of such action in the UNPAs in Croatia had stalled, pending action by local authorities. On July 27, in an attempt to characterize the human rights situation, the Secretary-General stated that "from the very outset, UNPROFOR has been faced with a situation in the UNPAs where terrorist methods such as physical abuse, coercion, harassment and even killings have been used to force non-Serb families to leave their homes" [S/24353, 7/27/92]. He noted that in the Serbian territories of Croatia in which the mass expulsions had been particularly blatant, UNPROFOR's "intense patrolling and control at checkpoints" had put a stop to them, but not entirely. UNPROFOR found that, when non-Serbs were targeted for expulsion and harassed by local residents in Sector East, the homes were "occupied immediately, in an organized manner, which indicates the involvement, or at least the acquiescence, of the local authorities."

UNPROFOR also noted actions of a similar kind in other Serb-controlled areas of the UNPAs and stated that in areas under Croatian control there was "frequent looting and destruction of the houses of Serbs who have left these areas over the past year" [ibid.].

Lamenting the lack of major improvement, the Secretary-General said that, without "the strongest action at the highest levels of government, UNPROFOR will not be able to eradicate the intolerable practices of so-called 'ethnic cleansing.' " Citing the "direct link" between this situation and the fact that so many Serb refugees have come into the UNPAs from other parts of the country, UNPROFOR's Force Commander identified their actions as "part of a concerted effort to change the ethnic composition of these areas." To combat this the Force Commander sought, and on August 7, 1992, received the authority, to prevent nonresidents of the UNPAs from entering the territories and fomenting trouble.

If implemented, such border control functions might forestall future abuses. But there is still a need to document abuses, make the findings public, and ensure that those responsible will be punished so as to deter others from doing such things.

By and large, when the Security Council has addressed the human rights aspects of the crisis—which it has done since the situation in Bosnia-Herzegovina began to deteriorate—it has done so in gingerly fashion and usually in the context of monitoring the humanitarian laws of war, notably the provisions of the Geneva Conventions of 1949. In mid-May 1992, when the war in Bosnia had spread and refugees were streaming out bearing tales of ethnic cleansing, the Security Council called publicly for "an end to forcible expulsions" and to other attempts at changing the ethnic composition of former Yugoslavia [S/Res/752].

Although as early as mid-June 1992 the Secretary-General reported to the Security Council about the lawlessness UNPROFOR faced in the UNPAs (see above) and adjacent pink zones, even citing early ethnic-cleansing incidents, the Council addressed the problem as a primarily peacekeeping issue. In Resolution 762 of June 30 it authorized the creation of a "joint commission" to help restore Croatian authority in the pink zones but did not address the real problems on the ground. (That commission, which met nearly eight times between the summer and winter of 1992, failed to achieve any tangible results.)

In Resolution 764 of July 13, 1992, the Security Council made specific reference to humanitarian law and to the Geneva Conventions of 1949, and affirmed that **persons "who commit or order the commission of grave breaches of the Conventions are individually responsible in respect of such breaches."**

Among U.N. officialdom during the early summer of 1992, it was the U.N. High Commissioner for Refugees, Sadako Ogata, who was the most vocal about the need to address the human rights situation in Bosnia, although she spoke her piece outside the U.N.'s formal structures.

In a presidential statement on August 4, two days after *Newsday* carried Roy Gutman's reports on **Serbian-run concentration camps in northern Bosnia** and ITV cameras carried pictures of Bosnian prisoners, the Security Council requested that the International Committee of the Red Cross (ICRC) and other organizations be given immediate and full access to the camps to investigate conditions in them, and it called on states, intergovernmental organizations, and nongovernmental organizations to provide directly to the Council any information they might have about violations of international humanitarian law. In the case of the ICRC the order presented some difficulty at first, since the Red Cross is normally given access to prisons only because it operates on the basis of confidentiality and the promise that its findings will not be published. (The Council's statement reiterated Resolution 764's reminder to combatants that persons "who commit or order the commission of grave breaches of the [Geneva] Conventions are individually responsible" for such breaches.)

There began a major initiative, lasting several months, to visit and empty the prisons of civilians who had been detained arbitrarily and maltreated or worse. The camp at Trnopolje emptied first, but it was only between November and December 1992 that sizable numbers of detainees were released from Manjaca and from the notorious camp at Omarska. Ex-detainees revealed that just before the media had been allowed into the camps, many of the most brutally treated detainees were transferred out and into other camps.

In the summer of 1992 too had come the U.S. call for an unprecedented emergency session of the U.N. Commission on Human Rights, which met in Geneva on August 13. On the very same day, the Security Council adopted two parallel resolutions. Resolution 770 (adopted with abstentions) called on states to take "all measures necessary"—not excluding the use of armed force—nationally or through regional organizations, to facilitate delivery of humanitarian aid. Here, the Security Council formally demanded that the ICRC and other relevant humanitarian organizations be granted "unimpeded and continuous access to all camps, prisons, and detention centers" and that all detainees therein receive humane treatment. Resolution 771, adopted unanimously that evening, condemned outright any violations of international humanitarian law, including ethnic cleansing, which it mentioned by name, and reaffirmed that those who commit or order grave breaches of the Geneva Conventions are to be held responsible for them. It demanded an end to breaches of humanitarian law and, in an important move, called on states and, "as appropriate," international humanitarian organizations (especially the ICRC) "to collate substantiated information on violations of humanitarian law in former Yugoslavia," requesting the Secretary-General to make this information available to the Council.

Some observers and the press saw this as a reaction to their clamor for an international war crimes tribunal to investigate abuses and bring those charged to trial. Even earlier, on May 30, the Russian Federation had suggested setting up an international commission to punish those responsible for "slaughtering civilians" and asked the Security Council to work out a set of criteria so that the Secretary-General could automatically trigger Council consideration of sanctions of those responsible for the bloodshed. But at the time no other government was prepared to pursue any such proposal aimed at prosecuting and halting human rights violations.

At the U.N. Commission on Human Rights emergency session in August, a **Special Rapporteur** was authorized to study and report within two weeks on the situation in former Yugoslavia, drawing upon the many resources of the U.N.'s Centre for Human Rights.

The Special Rapporteur's mandate included fact-finding and documentation of past and present violations, and it was accompanied by the request that he focus on finding solutions aimed at *preventing* further abuses. Since then, Special Rapporteur Tadeusz Mazowiecki has interpreted his mandate broadly and has seen as urgent the need to protect potential victims. It is not surprising, therefore, that he was the first to call publicly for safe areas. Nonetheless, by May 1993, few of his recommendations had been implemented. Even his request that his own human rights monitoring staff be located in the former Yugoslavia fell victim to bureaucratic and interagency conflicts. The first three monitors, sent only in April 1993, promptly undertook a first-hand study of the situation in several of the safe areas. In June, Serbia banned his aides from its territory.

In his own report after a first visit to the region on the heels of the August 1992 London Conference, Mazowiecki recommended that all heavy weaponry in Bosnia-Herzegovina be neutralized and placed under UNPROFOR, that the results of the London Conference be strictly implemented, and that authorities in the area disarm irregulars under UNPROFOR supervision. He recommended further that the United Nations advise authorities in various parts of Bosnia that it is their duty to safeguard the civilian population and that they would be held accountable for perpetrating *or tolerating* violations of humanitarian and human rights laws, and he called on the authorities to abandon the policy of ethnic cleansing. Echoing the Security Council and the London Conference, he insisted that the acts associated with the forceful departure of civilians (forfeiture of their property and the like) cease and desist. He cited the danger that such policies as ethnic cleansing might spread to the Kosovo, Sandjak, and Vojvodina regions of Serbia; called for the creation of new international mechanisms to monitor human rights there; and called as well for U.N. cooperation with the Conference on Security and Cooperation in Europe (which had already agreed to send some monitors to those regions).

Mazowiecki also made the early and critically important recommendation that UNPROFOR be used more effectively to deter human rights violations, calling for an increase in the size of the U.N. force and, most notably, an expansion of its mandate—geographically, by being permitted to cover all of Bosnia-Herzegovina; substantively, by being given explicit authorization to react to human rights violations it encounters; and, also substantively, by being asked to collect information and receive complaints about human rights violations that occur even in such territory in which it presently has no mandate.

The Special Rapporteur went on to call for full access of civilian police monitors to places of detention, and asked that their mandate specify that they send their findings not only to local police authorities (who had been ignoring them) but also to judicial authorities. Mazowiecki, himself a political prisoner during Poland's martial law period, sought (unsuccessfully) to visit the notorious prisons and their civilian detainees during this first visit. He called for giving the ICRC access to all detainees at all prisons, regardless of their size, and he added a call for the establishment of a special investigative mission to determine the fate of thousands who disappeared after Vukovar and other incidents.

Turning to broader themes, Mazowiecki began what was to become a continuing feature of his reports: a focus on the problem of freedom of information. Rather creatively, but apparently too much so for most U.N. officials, he called for the establishment of an independent, or U.N.-run, information agency outside the control of local authorities. The aim would be to support local media, "providing they disseminate objective information" to create mutual confidence. (Mazowiecki failed, however, to explain who would determine just what constitutes "objective information.") His main aim, however, was to suggest the need for a body that provides for the systematic gathering of documentation—this well before the Security Council's establishment of the Commission of Experts. Finally, to aid in coordinating his work with that of other international and multilateral bodies, he called for the basing of a number of staff in former Yugoslavia.

According to Mazowiecki's mandate, he was to return to the region repeatedly and report regularly. His second report, dated October 27, 1992, was critical of Croatia's position vis-à-vis the entry of additional refugees. Commenting on reports that UNPROFOR personnel in the UNPAs were sending refugees back to Bosnia, he declared it "extremely regrettable that UNPROFOR has to violate the principle of non-refoulement" and demanded that Croatia stop sending Bosnian refugees of military age back across the border. He revealed the evidence of the mass grave near Vukovar and asked that the Secretary-General warn all parties against tampering with mass graves or with evidence of war crimes.

Then, focusing on prevention, the Special Rapporteur suggested that further efforts at exhuming the graves be carried out under the auspices of the Commission of Experts itself. He concluded that a number of emergency actions had to be taken. One of these was that safe havens be found for people whose lives are in acute danger (e.g., the would-be refugees streaming to the former detention camp at Trnopolje), in the belief that when it is a matter of cooperating in ethnic cleansing or saving lives, the choice must be to save lives. The Special Rapporteur noted, critically, that very few European governments had accepted refugees from the conflict, and he urged governments to respond promptly and adequately to UNHCR and ICRC efforts to help the refugees. He called for the setting up of security zones and for actions by the republics' governments to help save civilian lives. Continuing in a humanitarian mode, he called for an increase in humanitarian assistance to benefit any and all citizens of former Yugoslavia who might need it and for opening humanitarian relief corridors in Bosnia-Herzegovina as a matter of priority.

Mazowiecki's third report was presented to the 47th General Assembly only weeks later, on November 17. Its conclusion was that ethnic cleansing continues and in some regions has intensified, and that there seems to be no lack of examples of arbitrary executions, attacks against homes and places of worship, and hostage-taking in Bosnia-Herzegovina, not to mention the UNPAs. The victims, he noted, "are primarily Moslem and Croat civilians," and so flagrantly are these policies carried out that it suggests the international community can do nothing to stop them. This, he advised, undermines the credibility and authority of international institutions, which cannot afford to allow the London agreements to be systematically ignored or violated. Finally, he stated that Serb authorities in control of Bosnia-Herzegovina "bear primary responsibility for the policy of ethnic cleansing" there. However, he noted, the Yugoslav National Army, and the leadership of the Republic of Serbia in particular, also share responsibility.

In February 1993, Mazowiecki presented a fourth report to the Commission on Human Rights after traveling to Slovenia and Macedonia to complete his investigations of human rights conditions in the former Yugoslavia. Offered here were the findings of a team of medical experts he had dispatched to examine the reports of **mass rape** that had surfaced at the end of 1992, and there were recommendations of ways to aid the trauma victims. In mid-May 1993 there was a fifth report, by a team of field staff, concerning conditions in the enclaves designated "safe areas." The Commission on Human Rights continues to adopt resolutions addressing the situation and has endorsed many of the Special Rapporteur's recommendations.

War Crimes Commission and Tribunal

The London Conference set forth a number of principles and understandings about the human rights/humanitarian situation and the emptying of the detention camps. In Resolution 780 of October 6, 1992, the Security Council agreed to set up a **Commission of Experts** "to examine and analyze the information submitted" on violations of the humanitarian laws of war and to undertake its own investigations, study those of others, and submit its conclusions to the Secretary-General. This was widely viewed as the first step toward establishing an international war crimes tribunal on former Yugoslavia. But the Commission, consisting of five jurists, disappointed many by moving slowly and by lacking the capacity to undertake its own investigations owing to a shortage of staff, expertise, and resources. By January 1993, when it issued a first, preliminary report, it had done nothing more than undertake a perfunctory review of the issues, identifying topics and types of violations that merited further study. Human rights organizations complained that the Commission was diffident; Commission members explained that their task was primarily evaluative.

As a result of the efforts of U.N. Special Envoy Cyrus Vance, the Commission did, however, undertake a preliminary **investigation of a mass grave near Vukovar** in December 1992, with assistance from a nongovernmental organization. The team identified the site as the likely grave of 175 wounded Croatian soldiers who had "disappeared" from the hospital at Vukovar when it fell to Serbian forces.

On February 22, 1993, as a result of a French initiative, the Security Council agreed to establish an **ad hoc international criminal court** to "prosecute persons responsible for serious violations of international humanitarian law" and called for a complete study of the matter [S/Res/808]. Detailed and scholarly works about structures and statutes to govern the tribunal flooded the Secretary-General's office, and in May he offered his recommendations on this score [S/25704 and Add.1]. On May 25 the Council approved his report [S/Res/827], which called for 11 judges and a staff of more than 370 others to consider crimes committed since January 1991.

Some observers, including a number of professors of international law, argue that the process of accumulating evidence (much less evidence that would meet court standards) is so difficult, and the effort to ensure due process for all the accused so formidable, that such a tribunal will try very few cases. Adding to such pessimism is the problem of obtaining custody of those accused. Two nongovernmental organizations, the Centre for Constitutional Rights and the International League for Human

Rights (ILHR), however, have already filed civil claims against Radovan Karadzic, the Bosnian Serb leader.

Reports surfaced in early August 1992 that the United Nations knew about the abuses in Bosnia-Herzegovina and about the detention camps well before they made newspaper headlines, and this has been confirmed by U.N. officials. The explanation given for this by UNPROFOR officials was that their mandate did not include protecting human rights. Nongovernmental organizations, unwilling to let the matter stop there, have questioned the general reticence of international agencies to publicize such violations, noting that information has been abundant [see, e.g., ILHR, preliminary findings, 11/92].

The United Nations has likewise been unsuccessful in getting local authorities to take immediate measures to reestablish control over the army and paramilitary forces, punish those guilty of human rights violations, or adopt measures to prevent further violations. The troubled areas of Bosnia-Herzegovina are no less plagued by abuse and lawlessness than they were before the United Nations turned its attention to them, suggesting the limits of exhortation alone.

Strengthening Economic and Other Sanctions Against Yugoslavia (Serbia and Montenegro)

The **arms embargo** called for under Security Council Resolution 713 of September 25, 1991, was the first sanction against the former Yugoslavia approved by the international community. But it was not until Resolution 757, adopted on May 30, 1992, that the U.N. undertook other significant sanctions. Stating that "all parties bear some responsibility for the situation," 757 condemned the authorities in the "Federal Republic of Yugoslavia (Serbia and Montenegro)" for failing to comply with Resolution 752, which had demanded that all parties put a halt to fighting and to outside interference in Bosnia and Herzegovina. During the debate, members noted that the "authorities" in Belgrade bore the *primary* responsibility for the situation and were, in fact, the aggressor.

Acting under Chapter VII of the Charter ("with respect to threats to the peace, breaches of the peace, and acts of aggression"), the Council adopted **wide-ranging sanctions** against Yugoslavia, **affecting trade** (only food and medicine for humanitarian purposes would be allowed); **air transport** in and out of the country; **all sport, cultural, and scientific contacts**; and **the size of diplomatic staffs.**

The Security Council assigned the job of supervising compliance with the sanctions to a committee, which has asked governments to report on measures taken to assure compliance, called upon both governments and individuals to supply information about noncompliance, and adopted a formal procedure for filing requests to send commodities other than medicine or emergency food [U.N. press release SC/5422, 6/18/92]. Although generating a great deal of paper, this last is generally viewed as an ineffective and remote enforcement mechanism. Both NATO and the West European Union (WEU) subsequently sent ships to monitor commerce in the Adriatic, but with orders simply to monitor, not intercept, shipments that might violate the sanctions.

Although the sanctions did have the effect of squeezing the Serbian economy, they were being routinely flouted, and by November 1992 their failure was too obvious to ignore. In Resolution 787 of November 16, the Security Council, acting under Chapters VII and VIII ("regional arrangements") of the Charter, called on states to use **"such measures . . . as may be necessary" to halt maritime shipping to inspect cargoes, and destinations**, and implement Resolutions 713 and 757. That November resolution went on to **prohibit transshipment of petroleum and energy byproducts** (and some additional items), to be lifted only on a case-by-case basis, and requested state reports on measures taken to implement the resolution. By citing Chapter VIII, it opened the door to cooperation with NATO, WEU, and the Conference on Security and Cooperation in Europe (CSCE) in enforcing the sanctions.

It fell to the nonaligned members of the Council to push for stronger enforcement measures. Cape Verde, Djibouti, Morocco, Pakistan, and Venezuela pressed the permanent members and other colleagues to tighten sanctions if the Serbs failed to comply with the Vance–Owen peace plan. Resolution 820 of April 17, 1993, dealt with this issue and called for the Security Council's Sanctions Committee to begin reporting publicly on violations. Once the peace plan was accepted, said the resolution, sanctions could be modified.

Now the **Sanctions Committee** began to issue guidelines and information about its expectations. The Croatian government went so far as to circulate a list of towns and villages, so no one could argue that they had no idea of just where their goods were headed. Earlier the Croatian government had provided the Council with documentation about the pumping of oil in UNPA Sector East and its transshipment to Serbia under the eyes of U.N. monitors.

For a while in the spring of 1993, when Serbia was backing the idea of the Bosnian Serbs signing the Vance–Owen peace plan and the United States seemed ready to begin military strikes, Serbia appeared to accept the prospect that U.N. (or NATO or U.S. military) personnel might be quartered in barracks along the borders of Serbia and Montenegro, where they would maintain perimeter checkpoints, with a close eye on the Bosnian–Serbian border. But once the plan was rejected and the United States publicly abandoned the air strike option, Serb leader Milosevic declared that the presence of such monitors would violate Serbian sovereignty and that he was unalterably opposed to deploying them.

Romania, Bulgaria, and other neighbors have asked for help in enforcing the embargo, and the United States has called upon the countries of the region to step up their monitoring of the embargo. But as reports of atrocities continue and the refugee flow continues unabated, concerned nations, organizations, and individuals have grown impatient with economic sanctions, viewing them as slow-working and insufficient, and calls for military intervention are on the rise.

Consideration of Other Military Enforcement Measures

In September 1992 the United Nations began to implement an arms embargo, effective for all parts of the former Yugoslavia. Nearly a year later, monitoring (if not enforcement) is carried out in the **Adriatic**, although there are reports of considerable transport of prohibited goods along the Danube River. Additionally, as indicated by the UNPROFOR experience in Serb-dominated areas of Croatia, there is little or no control of interrepublic (that is, intra-former Yugoslavia) arms transfers. Some observers have criticized the arms embargo for preventing the Bosnians and others from defending themselves against the heavily armed Army of Yugoslavia and the Serb militias. Leaders of Bosnia-Herzegovina, and prominent Westerners, such as Britain's Margaret Thatcher, have called publicly for **lifting the arms embargo against Bosnia** and have asked that the United Nations or third parties provide arms to the Bosnians directly. The issue was brought, unsuccessfully, to the Security Council on June 29. The arguments presented were summarized above.

Some observers, including leading U.S. officials, continue to doubt that **military force** can be used effectively in former Yugoslavia, noting the complexity and difficulty of the situation in Bosnia-Herzegovina. A number of observers have drawn attention to the fact that in World War II the German army had more than a dozen divisions tied up in Yugoslavia; and today the former Yugoslavia is one of the most militarized areas of Europe: Under Yugoslavia's defense strategy, all males were issued weapons and trained in guerrilla warfare for the local defense. Furthermore, the country was a major arms manufacturer, and its arms factories are reported to be functioning still. Citing such factors, world leaders say that they are reluctant to commit ground forces to the Bosnian conflict because they are apt to find themselves in a "quagmire" from which it is difficult to escape.

In discussions of military enforcement options available to the United Nations, observers have pointed to several other means of enforcing economic and other sanctions or assisting in the delivery of humanitarian aid. Prominent among these is the threat of air strikes within Serbia itself. Advocates of such an option have argued that strikes could be aimed at key transport routes into Bosnia, including roads and bridges, as well as at arms factories, aircraft, and the like. Some observers note that while this is not an ideal enforcement weapon, it would diminish Serbian superiority in weaponry, is less likely to injure civilians, and would send the message that further attacks will be forthcoming if nothing is done to change the situation.

Another widely discussed alternative, requested earlier by Bosnia, is to begin limited air strikes against Serbian heavy-artillery positions above Sarajevo, with the hoped-for effect of decreasing the level of random violence against civilians in Sarajevo—but perhaps also causing considerable collateral damage in heavily populated areas, critics of the proposal point out. Still others have recommended using fighter aircraft and ground attack escorts to open up humanitarian corridors or establish safe areas to ensure the delivery of humanitarian relief. Although a no-fly zone was endorsed and all necessary measures to enforce it authorized, there has been little aerial activity.

According to estimates, ground-based military actions would require from 15,000 to 500,000 troops, depending upon military and political factors as well as upon terrain. It is noted that the Serb government has threatened to retaliate against U.N. forces and those of individual governments involved in the attacks if Serbian targets were to be chosen. Such a turn of events would necessitate additional military deployments to protect U.N. humanitarian and peacekeeping forces—or might lead the Secretary-General to withdraw U.N. forces from troubled areas. It is indeed a question whether the world body can bring the conflict to a peaceful conclusion and aid the refugees, the displaced, and other victims in returning to their homes.

3. The Middle East and the Persian Gulf

By Peter James Spielmann

Iraq

Iraq continued its defiance of the Security Council, the Western allies, and particularly U.S. President George Bush into 1993, leading to a brief but intense flare-up in hostilities that some called Gulf War II.

Iraq, already facing virtual partition into a Kurdish northern zone, Baath Party-ruled midsection, and Shiite south, had decided to test the resolve of the Security Council and the unity of the Gulf War coalition by breaching the "no-fly zones" in the north and south that are patrolled by U.S., French, and British warplanes.

The concept of such zones had evolved from a series of events after Baghdad's surrender to the allies at the end of February 1991. These events, launched by the rebellion of Kurds and Shiites in the north and south of Iraq, brought a furious counterattack by the Iraqi Army, which precipitated the flight of hundreds of thousands of Kurds to the borders with Turkey and Iran. **Security Council Resolution 688 of April 1991** labeled this surge of refugees a "threat to international peace and security" and went on to condemn Iraq's repression of its civilian population and specifically criticized its treatment of the Kurds.

China, threatening a veto, blocked the Council from using the **Charter's Chapter VII** ("Action with Respect to Threats to the Peace . . .") to enforce this "humanitarian" resolution, which it viewed as an intrusion into Iraq's internal affairs—a breach of the national sovereignty that the U.N. Charter pledges to respect. Other nations argued, however, that the situation in Iraq's north and south had gone beyond a strictly domestic affair when Kurds crossed the border and began pouring into Turkey and Iran by the thousands. As the debate continued, there was **discussion about setting aside the concept of national sovereignty** and taking action when governments are found to commit or permit egregious violations of the International Covenants on Human Rights, the Universal Declaration of Human Rights, and numerous other U.N. conventions.

The 47th General Assembly assailed Iraq for its "massive violations of human rights," naming "orchestrated mass executions and burials, extrajudicial killings, including political killings," especially in the Kurdish north and Shiite south, and condemned the Iraqi practice of torture—of children as well as of adults [A/Res/47/145]. The 53-nation U.N. Human Rights Commission, meeting in Geneva in March 1993, condemned Iraq for a policy of widespread terror and executions and opened an official examination of reported atrocities [Associated Press, 3/11/93].

One ongoing attempt to provide a safe haven for the **Kurds massed at the Turkish border** has been Operation Poised Hammer, inaugurated in mid-1991 with the dispatch of U.S., British, and French troops to set up relief camps while allied warplanes kept Iraqi military flights out of the skies above the 36th parallel. Today, the north of Iraq has evolved into a quasi-Kurdish state, where Iraqi Kurds hold their own elections to choose a parliament and prime minister [*The Christian Science Monitor*, 1/25/93].

In August 1992, following reports of Iraqi air raids and artillery shelling of the **Shiites in the southern marshes**, the United States, United Kingdom, and France declared a **no-fly zone** in southern Iraq and began enforcing it below the 32nd parallel, though the Security Council never endorsed the idea [ibid., 9/1/92]. The Council's Resolution 688 on the Kurds had in fact said nothing about an air-exclusion zone or about military intervention at all; and Baghdad argued that the no-fly zones enforced by the three countries had no legal basis in any Security Council resolution. The U.N. Legal Department later agreed that 688, cited by the United States, United Kingdom, and France for the establishment of the zones, was humanitarian in intent and not enforceable, since it did not cite Chapter VII of the U.N. Charter [Associated Press, 1/21/93], under which rubric a decision is mandatory and may be followed up by military action.

On December 27, 1992, Baghdad attempted to exploit potential divisions between the lame-duck administration of President Bush and the new administration of President-elect Bill Clinton by sending MIG warplanes into the southern no-fly zone. The planes were intercepted by U.S. F-16s, and one of the MIGs was shot down [*The New York Times*, 12/28/92]. As the old year gave way to the new, Iraq also moved antiaircraft missiles into the southern no-fly zone [ibid., 1/5/93].

During the same period, Baghdad announced that, since it was unable to control its own air space in the no-fly zones, airplanes carrying U.N. Special Commission inspectors to Iraq would have to file flight plans for approval. When Iraq barred a flight of U.N. Special Commission weapons inspectors in early January, the stage was set for direct confrontation with the Security Council and the allies [*The Washington Post*, 1/11/93].

During this December–January period too, Iraqi troops in civilian garb made numerous raids across the Kuwaiti border to retrieve **weapons left behind in the Gulf War** and now stored in U.N. arms depots. Silkworm surface-to-surface missiles were among the munitions seized by the Iraqis, who pushed past the unarmed military observers of the U.N. Iraq–Kuwait Observer Mission (UNIKOM) [ibid., 1/11/93]. Although the scavenging raids were not considered a major threat in themselves, they heightened tensions between Washington and Baghdad.

Tension gave way to blows on January 13, when Britain and France joined the United States in **air raids against antimissile sites and their radar bases in southern Iraq**. About 80 warplanes blasted these sites, backed by about 30 support planes [*The New York Times*, 1/14/93]. A **second raid**, on January 17, was more ambitious: U.S. Navy ships fired 40 Tomahawk cruise missiles at the Zaafaraniya industrial complex in a Baghdad suburb—a site the Special Commission had visited and identified as a precision computer-aided tool shop capable of making crucial components for Iraq's banned nuclear weapons program. The attack brought mixed results, including a propaganda coup for Saddam Hussein's government, when one of the American "smart bombs," perhaps crippled by antiaircraft fire, missed its target and slammed into Baghdad's Rashid Hotel as a CNN camera crew filmed the onslaught from a window. According to Iraq, two civilians were killed [ibid., 1/19/93].

In a **third wave of air raids** the following day, allied bombers returned to southern Iraq, blasting radar sites at Nawaf and Samawa and damaging a building at Tallil air base. In the northern no-fly zone, allied warplanes attacked Iraqi air defense radar sites and an airfield near Mosul. Iraq said the raids killed 21 people [Associated Press, 1/18/93].

On the very next day, January 19, Iraq—in the hope that the incoming Clinton administration would reevaluate U.S. policy on the no-fly zones—announced that, as a **goodwill gesture**, it would not fire on U.S. warplanes unless they attacked first and would let U.N. Special Commission weapons inspectors fly into Iraq on their own planes and on their own flight plans [*The New York Times*, 1/20/93]. But the mounting death toll in Iraq and the damage wrought by the cruise missile attack in the industrial area outside Baghdad had a **fraying effect on the allied coalition**. London and Paris distanced themselves from the attack, and Moscow severely criticized it, saying "the reaction was not in proportion" to the Iraqi provocation. Many Muslim nations that had helped drive Iraq's troops out of Kuwait, among them Turkey, Egypt, and Saudi Arabia, questioned why the Security Council and the allies were so aggressive in punishing an Arab country while doing nothing to back up its resolutions on Israel and only very little to curb the far more vicious and destabilizing assault by Orthodox Christian Serbs on the Muslim-led government of Bosnia-Herzegovina [*The Christian Science Monitor*, 1/15/93, 1/20/93; *The New York Times*, 1/20/93].

Indeed, as 1993 wore on, the five permanent Security Council members' concern about Iraq was eclipsed by the war in Bosnia. The most telling evidence of this is the drop-off in the contributions that have kept U.N. guards posted in the Kurdish region of northern Iraq; and by May, about 100 of the 300 guards sent to reassure the 750,000 or so Kurds in that area, and protect the relief convoys bringing food and medicines to them, had been withdrawn [Associated Press, 5/13/93]. It seemed just a matter of time before all were sent home.

Baghdad's cooperation with the Security Council's demands for dismantling its **nuclear, biological, and chemical weapons programs and demolishing its missiles with a range greater than 150 kilometers** (about 90 miles) remained grudging and limited. Reporting mixed progress was the **U.N. Special Commission** charged with overseeing the elimination of Iraq's capacity to produce weapons of mass destruction under the **Security Council's Resolution 687 of April 1991**, which had set the terms of the cease-fire in the Gulf War.

The Commission's experts had no problem when working with Iraqis to set up a chemical weapons-destruction plant at Iraq's main al-Muthanna munitions dump at Samarra, about 60 miles northwest of Baghdad—at least partly because this military site contained over 100,000 corroding barrels of nerve and mustard gas, and huge stacks of bombs and shells, many of them leaking, and Iraq would have had to dispose of them anyway [*The Christian Science Monitor*, 6/23/92]. Germ warfare had also been a fear of the allies during the Gulf War, although it too never materialized, and Iraq has since turned over samples of bacteriological warfare agents it had developed, saying these were for defensive purposes. The U.N. Special Commission, however, remains convinced that Iraq was looking toward the development of a site for producing such weapons [ibid.].

The most protracted standoff with the Iraqis began in July 1992 with the Special Commission's attempt to search the Agriculture Ministry in Baghdad for some documents it believed would provide **clues to the foreign suppliers of components for Iraq's ballistic missile programs.** On July 5, Iraqi forces blocked the inspectors' access to the building, saying that as a top government ministry it was exempt from search. White U.N. jeeps remained parked outside the building for three weeks as an end to the standoff was sought. In a compromise, the search was allowed, but the inspectors who carried it out were from countries other than those whose military forces participated in the anti-Iraq coalition during the Gulf War. A German led the team, which finished its inspection on July 29 without finding any trace of such documents. Special Commission head Rolf Ekeus said he had "well-founded reasons" to believe the documents had been in the building [*The New York Times*, 7/30/92].

The pursuit of evidence indicating the scope of Iraq's nuclear weapons programs has lost nothing of its cat-and-mouse quality as Baghdad continues to withhold a complete list of its suppliers, arguing that the request is in **violation of its sovereignty** and that to comply would be to compromise its commercial relationships with the foreign companies. The International Atomic Energy Agency (IAEA), which is working with the Special Commission in this weapons area, has collected soil and water samples from sites throughout Iraq so that later samples will show whether they had been irradiated or heated by a secret nuclear site. IAEA expert Maurizio Zifferero said that analyses "tend to indicate" there have been no nuclear activities since the Gulf War [ibid., 2/1/93].

Iraq also continues to reject Special Commission and IAEA **long-term monitoring of its industries with potential military uses,** as required by Security Council Resolution 715 of October 1991 [Secretary-General's Report to the Security Council, S/25620, 4/19/93].

Baghdad dug in its heels when the Special Commission sought to set up remote-controlled cameras at two former missile test sites to make sure that Iraq does not reactivate its ballistic missile program. The cameras were to be placed at Rafih, 45 miles southwest of Baghdad, and at Yam al-Azim, 45 miles to the south. But Special Commission inspectors left Baghdad on July 5 empty-handed after a month of trying to gain Iraq's cooperation [Associated Press, 7/5/93].

The Security Council warned Iraq it would suffer unspecified "serious consequences" if Saddam Hussein's government continued to reject the monitoring [Security Council statement, 6/18/93]. Only eight days earlier, U.S. President Bill Clinton had given the green light for a U.S. Navy pounding of Saddam Hussein's intelligence headquarters in Baghdad with cruise missiles because the Iraqi government allegedly plotted to kill former President George Bush.

These shows of noncooperation have led the Security Council to vote "no change" during its periodic reviews of the **economic sanctions** placed on Iraq since the invasion of Kuwait in August 1990. Currently, only food, medicines, and other humanitarian goods may be imported, but Iraq, prohibited from exporting its oil—virtually the country's only source of foreign exchange—is financing some purchases by selling off its gold reserves [Associated Press, 7/6/93].

Iraq continues to refuse **to sell $1.6 billion in oil under strict U.N. supervision**, claiming that such oversight is an intolerable violation of its sovereignty [for background, see *A Global Agenda: Issues/47*]. The funds, to be placed in an escrow account, would go toward paying for U.N. programs in Iraq, such as those to monitor and destroy the country's weapons of mass destruction, and for the humanitarian aid supplied to the Kurds and Shiites. Already weary of Baghdad's resistance in October 1992, the Security Council voted 14–0, with China abstaining, to seize some of the **proceeds of Iraqi oil sales deposited on or after the August 1990 invasion** of Kuwait to pay for U.N. programs and some war reparations [Associated Press, 10/2/92; S/Res/778]. Iraq had an estimated $5 billion in assets overseas that were frozen by the Security Council, but not immediately seized, after the invasion. The seizure of the oil funds marked the **first time the Security Council has impounded a nation's assets.**

Economic sanctions continue to strangle the Iraqi economy, although most of the major damage done by the Gulf War has been repaired. Food rationing continues, the black market flourishes, inflation clips along at 3,000% annually, and monthly incomes have plunged from the prewar average of $320 to about $7, virtually eliminating the Iraqi middle class [*The Christian Science Monitor*, 1/29/93].

Iraq's Deputy Foreign Minister, Tariq Aziz, told the Security Council in November 1992 that continuation of the sanctions amounts to "genocide" against the Iraqi people [*The New York Times*, 11/24/92]. At that meeting and in subsequent contacts with the West, Iraqi diplomats have argued that they have complied with most of the Council's demands and that the sanctions should be relaxed proportionately—a notion that the Security Council has rejected repeatedly.

The sanctions have helped de-fang Iraq's military machine and have increased dissent among the country's citizenry, although Saddam Hussein's security apparatus has so far guaranteed that there is no significant opposition to his rule. U.S. **President George Bush**, who had vowed that sanctions would not be lifted while the Iraqi President remained in power, left office in January 1993 without having seen that goal accomplished. But Washington was not relying on sanctions alone to topple

Saddam. President Bush's National Security Advisor, Brent Scowcraft, told reporters that the United States had a covert policy of encouraging the Iraqi leader's ouster, and that one attempt, apparently involving Iraqi officers, came "pretty close" to succeeding until Saddam's security thwarted it [*The Washington Post Weekly*, 1/25–31/93].

The **Clinton administration** announced that it would scale back, but not abandon, those covert action plans [*The New York Times*, 4/11/93].

Iraq, for its part, apparently plotted to avenge itself on Bush.

Kuwait invited Bush and his former Secretary of State, James Baker, to a three-day gala celebration of thanks in Kuwait City in April 1993. But as Bush was arriving on April 14, Kuwaiti security forces arrested 14 Iraqis and two Kuwaitis and charged them with attempting to kill Bush with a car bomb.

In the trial that began June 5 in Kuwait, a 36-year-old Iraqi told the court that Iraqi intelligence agents sent him to Kuwait to detonate a car bomb in a Toyota Land Cruiser during Bush's visit or, failing that, to strap explosives around his waist and detonate them in a suicide attack. Another defendant pleaded guilty to accepting explosives from Iraqi intelligence to plant in shops around Kuwait. [Associated Press, 6/5/93].

But even before the trial ended, President Clinton concluded that the Iraqi government had schemed to kill Bush—an act of attempted international terrorism—and that Saddam Hussein must have approved the plan [*The New York Times*, 6/29/93].

The response was swift: on June 27, the U.S. Navy fired 23 cruise missiles at the Iraqi intelligence agency headquarters in Baghdad as vengeance for its part in the plot [ibid., 6/27/93]. Sixteen of the missiles hit their target, but several fell into residential neighborhoods nearby, killing eight Iraqis, according to Baghdad [ibid., 6/28/93]. President Clinton later said that the timing of the attack—early on a Sunday morning—was intended to avoid casualties.

Later that day, U.S. Ambassador to the U.N. Madeleine Albright told an emergency session of the Security Council that investigators from the U.S. Justice Department and the Central Intelligence Agency had examined the car bomb. The forensic experts concluded that the same people had built key components for that device and the Iraqi bombs previously recovered in other attempts at terrorist attacks, including the remote-controlled detonator, the circuitry and wiring, the blasting cap, and the plastic explosives.

Iraqi Ambassador Nizar Hamdoun replied that a U-2 spy plane from the U.N. Special Commission had flown over Baghdad "for espionage operations in preparation for the American attack on Iraq," and said Kuwait had concocted a "false story" about an assassination plot against Bush that Washington had used as an excuse for its missile attack. But other Security Council members delivered pointed statements denouncing terrorism and generally supported the U.S. attack as a proportionate response to the Iraqi assassination plot [Security Council press release 5657, 6/27/93].

The Arab–Israeli Conflict and the Occupied Territories

The U.S. and Soviet-chaired Arab–Israeli peace talks that began in 1991 [see *A Global Agenda: Issues/47*] limped along through 1992—a year that saw domestic elections in Israel and the United States, and the deportation by Israel of 415 Palestinians, triggering Arab demands for their repatriation. By the summer of 1993, there were still few signs of progress.

Throughout the 1980s, various attempts to convene peace talks foundered on the demands of the Palestinians for a homeland and the unwillingness of Israel's right-wing Likud leadership to give up an inch of the Occupied Territories. But the outbreak of the Palestinian *intifadah* (Arabic for "uprising," or "shaking off") forced Israel to consider Palestinian demands for self-rule in the West Bank and Gaza, and the Palestine National Council—the PLO's parliament-in-exile—recognized Israel's right to exist, breaking the long-standing deadlock.

Peace talks convened in Madrid in October 1991, then shifted to Washington for several sessions. But national elections in Israel set for July 1992 put in doubt the future of Likud Prime Minister Yitzhak Shamir, and the United States elections set for November 1992 left in question the tenure of President Bush and Secretary of State James A. Baker, the architects of the new peace talks. The delegates mostly grappled with procedural questions until the new cast of characters emerged.

In July 1992, Israel's Labor party prevailed over Likud, replacing Shamir with Yitzhak Rabin. Labor espoused a "**land-for-peace**" line that was compatible with **Security Council Resolution 242 of 1967**, although the new Prime Minister was not necessarily committed to bargaining away *all* occupied lands.

Rabin signaled his willingness to negotiate seriously by halting the **construction of new Jewish settlements in the occupied West Bank and Gaza Strip**, a population policy that had been a key tactic in Likud's effort to increase the Jewish presence in the Occupied Territories, thereby assuring their future as Israeli lands [*The New York Times*, 7/20/92]. This policy shift also enabled Washington to begin releasing **$10 billion in loans** over five years that had been **frozen by the U.S. Congress** in protesting the Likud settlement campaign. The loans had been approved to help Israel resettle immigrant Jews from the former Soviet Union [*The Washington Post*, 8/11/92].

Israel and **Syria** began dancing around the idea of a partial Israeli withdrawal from the Golan Heights—where about 12,000 Israelis have settled—in exchange for a peace treaty. Syria insists on return of all of the Golan, and there the matter rested as the November U.S. elections approached.

Barely a month after Democrat Bill Clinton defeated Republican George Bush, three Israeli soldiers were shot to death in the Gaza Strip, bringing to 11 the number of **soldiers killed in the Occupied Territories in 1992**—equal to the total for the previous four years—and Israel took draconian measures in response. The Gaza Strip was sealed off while soldiers searched for the killers, a step that Arabs regard as a form of collective punishment outlawed under the **Fourth Geneva Convention on the treatment of civilians in time of war** [*The New York Times*, 12/9/92]. Israel continues to maintain that the 1949 conventions do not apply to the Territories, which it says it does not occupy but "administers," after having freed them from Arab military occupation in the 1967 Arab-Israeli War.

The West Bank was sealed off a week after the Gaza Strip's closing, when the **fundamentalist Islamic group Hamas** kidnapped an Israeli border patrolman and demanded the release of imprisoned Sheik Ahmed Yassin, the founder of this militant movement [*The New York Times*, 12/15/92]. The Sheik was not released and the policeman was found slain [*The Christian Science Monitor*, 12/16/92].

Israel detained for questioning over 1,000 members of Hamas and of Islamic Jihad (a smaller, allied group) and on December 17 **banished 415 of the Palestinians** to an area north of the Israeli-declared "security zone" in southern Lebanon. Most of the deportees were said by the government to be associated with Hamas or other fundamentalist Islamic groups committed to Israel's destruction [*The Christian Science Monitor*, 12/18/92] and were accused of instigating recent terrorist activities in the Occupied Territories [*The New York Times*, 12/18/92].

The move polarized the parties to the Mideast peace talks, with Arabs demanding Security Council action against Israel and refusing to resume peace talks until the Palestinians were repatriated. On December 18, the **Security Council** passed **Resolution 799** demanding the "immediate" return of the deportees. Israel dug in its heels and said that any "new measures" to enforce that resolution could jeopardize the peace talks [*The New York Times*, 1/9/93].

New U.S. Secretary of State Warren Christopher began lobbying Israel for a compromise solution to the standoff, and he warned Jerusalem that it would have to show some flexibility if the United States was to defend Israel against a new PLO-sponsored draft resolution in the Security Council that would impose sanctions on the Jewish state. Lebanon still refused to accept the men, contending that to do so would imply recognition of the legitimacy of Israel's expulsion order [ibid., 12/18/92]. By late January 1993, Israel had allowed more than two dozen of the Palestinians to return for medical care and conceded that several had been deported in error, but nearly 400 remained in exile. As snow fell, they were huddled in a makeshift tent camp at Marj al-Zohour. Cameras recorded the scene, adding to the public relations embarrassment for Israel.

Israel finally accepted a compromise engineered by Christopher, agreeing to bring back 101 of the deportees immediately and cut the sentences of the others so they could return by the end of 1993 [*The New York Times*, 2/2/93]. Christopher then contended that this **compromise formula** was consistent with the Security Council resolution demanding the "immediate" return of the men, and said no Council action was justified [ibid.].

In a highly unusual move, the Security Council's President, Ambassador Ahmed Snoussi of Morocco, met informally with the PLO, Arabs, Israelis, and other concerned delegations, with the result that the Council agreed to accept the U.S.-Israeli compromise as legitimate and consistent with the Council's Resolution 799 of December 18 and to drop the PLO-sponsored draft resolution that would have imposed sanctions on Israel. All this was done behind the scenes, so that there was no official debate, vote, documents, or any record of the deal. The PLO's Permanent U.N. Observer, Nasser Al-Kidwa, called the arrangement "meaningless" [ibid., 2/13/93].

The exiled Palestinians maintained their solidarity, and none accepted the offer to allow 101 to go home. The peace talks remained stalled for additional weeks while Arab countries held a series of meetings to decide how far to push the issue. In the end, Arab delegations decided not to lose the chance of making progress in the peace talks and, at a meeting in Damascus, agreed to return for a ninth round of talks beginning April 27 [Associated Press, 4/21/93].

The United States began pressing the Arabs to agree to continuing negotiations and even to step up their pace. As a confidence-building measure, Israel agreed to allow the **return to the West Bank of 30 Palestinians who had been exiled for nonviolent organizing** well before the *intifadah* began [*The New York Times*, 4/30/93]. None of the returnees were among the group of Hamas and Hizbollah members languishing in southern Lebanon.

The **ninth round of talks**, marking 18 months since negotiations began, took place during three weeks in April and May 1993, but ended without signs of movement by either side. The United States tried, but failed, to get the Arabs and Israelis to sign a two-page document outlining the principles of transition to Palestinian self-rule in the Territories [*The New York Times*, 5/14/93]. Both sides broadly agree to a five-year, two-step process that aims at setting up an interim Palestinian administration in the third year.

The atmosphere at the talks deteriorated when the Palestinians, protesting an Israeli crackdown on Palestinians in the Occupied Territories, suspended participation in the separate working groups on water resources, human rights, and other specific issues, and then reduced the size of their delegation at the main talks from 11 to three. The only point of agreement was that all parties would meet again for a tenth round.

The tenth round of talks also fizzled in June as the Palestinians elevated the status of Arab east Jerusalem—which Israel captured in the 1967 war—to the top of their agenda.

The Palestinians demanded that east Jerusalem be included in the area where self-rule is established, becoming the capital of their state. Israel vows never to give up Jerusalem, which it designated its capital after annexing the eastern sector, and opposes even discussing its status [Associated Press, 7/5/93]. The talks recessed until October.

In another attempt to warm relations, Arab nations quietly dropped their long boycott of foreign companies doing business with Israel but still refuse to trade directly with the Jewish state until a peace accord is reached. Kuwait announced that it and other Arab nations had let the boycott instituted in the 1950s lapse, primarily so that they could buy goods and services only available from companies that also did business with Israel [*The New York Times*, 6/9/93].

In the course of the five-and-a-half-year-old *intifadah*, at least 1,125 Palestinians have been **killed in clashes** with **Israelis**, and 139 Israelis have been **slain by Arabs**. During the same time, more than 741 other more Arabs had been **killed by fellow Palestinians** on suspicion of collaborating with Israel or of prostitution, drug dealing, or violations of hardline Islamic beliefs.

The **47th General Assembly** followed in the footsteps of previous sessions by adopting several resolutions condemning Israeli security practices aimed at suppressing the *intifadah* in the Occupied Territories, which were labeled "grave breaches" of the 1949 "Geneva Convention relative to the Protection of Civilian Persons in Time of War as well as of other relevant conventions and regulations" [A/Res/47/70A–C]. In its annual resolution on "The Situation in the Middle East," the Assembly once again called for Israel's withdrawal from "occupied Arab territories," including **Jerusalem** [A/Res/47/63A–B]. The once-divided city of Jerusalem was seized by Israel in the 1967 Arab-Israeli War and declared the nation's capital; the Israeli government has repeatedly said it will never give up Jerusalem as its capital.

Although the United Nations has had only a marginal role in the Arab-Israeli peace talks [see *A Global Agenda: Issues/47*], the General Assembly welcomed the process and stressed again that the core of the Mideast conflict is "the Question of Palestine" [A/Res/47/64A–E]—a fact that has been highlighted by the events of the past year.

Lebanon

Persistent sectarian strife and public disorder kept Lebanon in a state of virtual anarchy for more than a decade after the **outbreak of the Leba-**

nese civil war in 1975. In the last three years, however, the government of **President Elias Hrawi,** backed by the Syrian Army and Arab mediators, has made significant strides in restoring order in most of Lebanon.

Still **partly occupied by Israel and Syria,** Lebanon took several small steps in 1992 to extend its control over even more of the country. But these measures remained tentative because Beirut's fragile new government still cannot afford an out-and-out clash with the country's disaffected Maronite Christians or with Israel or Syria.

The first parliamentary elections in 20 years were held in three rounds in August and September 1992, despite Christian objections that it was impossible to hold free and fair elections while thousands of Syrian troops remain in the country [*The New York Times*, 8/24/92]. Predictably, the **Christians boycotted the polling,** resulting in an upsurge of parliamentary seats for the pro-Iranian Islamic fundamentalist Hizbollah (Arabic for Party of God) [ibid., 8/26/92].

The Hizbollah and another **anti-Israel Shiite faction, Amal,** took 22 of 23 contested seats in the third round of balloting, resulting in a **128-member parliament dominated by Muslim interests.** Christians were guaranteed half the seats in parliament, but, due to the boycott by the Maronite groups, the Christians who were elected to occupy them were those who ran as independents or with Muslim backing. Amal ended up controlling 18 seats—the largest bloc—and the Hizbollah 12 seats [ibid., 9/9/92].

The increasing strength of the **Hizbollah** helped increase the influence of one of its patrons, Syria, with its 35,000 soldiers in eastern Lebanon. Lebanon's President Hrawi met with Syrian President Hafez al-Assad after the elections to discuss a Syrian pullout. The meeting on September 12 coincided with U.S. State Department pressure on Syria to withdraw all its troops from Lebanon except those in the Bekaa. This troop withdrawal was among the terms of the **Taif accord** of October 1989 that ended Lebanon's civil war—although the two-year deadline set by Taif was now past [ibid., 9/13/92]. (Syria had sent 40,000 troops to Lebanon in 1976 under an Arab League peacekeeping mandate to try to end the factional violence of the civil war, but they were soon drawn into the conflict and lost any chance to serve a peacekeeping role.)

Some weeks after the September meeting, the Syrian government announced that it would not withdraw its troops until other provisions of the Taif accord were fully implemented, including the scrapping of the 49-year-old tradition of assigning Lebanese government posts along religious lines [*The New York Times*, 11/23/92]. Under the current system, the president is a Maronite Catholic and the prime minister a Sunni Muslim. Since it is widely believed that the Muslim population has grown much more quickly than has the Christian population, true proportional representation would amount to a Muslim takeover of Lebanon.

Syria's Defense Minister went on to say that "to talk about Syrian redeployment is tantamount to treason" at a time when Israel continues to occupy Lebanese territory [ibid.], referring to the six-to-nine-mile deep, 50-mile-long buffer zone that Israel has carved out of southern Lebanon in an attempt to cut off cross-border guerrilla raids and rocket attacks. Both Israel and Syria consistently link any withdrawal on their part to countermoves by the other party.

Israel and the Hizbollah tested each other in **southern Lebanon** in November 1992. The 5,000-strong Shiite militia force fired dozens of rockets into northern Israel and ambushed Israeli troops in and around the buffer zone, and the Israelis upped the ante by massing troops and artillery at the border, ready for a full-blown invasion reminiscent of 1982. But Israel suddenly and without public comment drew down its reinforcements. Both sides apparently decided it was better to carry on with their war of attrition than to allow the conflict to escalate [*The New York Times*, 11/16/92].

Syria declared that the Iranian-armed, financed, and trained Hizbollah is not a militia, which would be required to disarm under the Taif accord, but a resistance movement trying to oust the Israelis from southern Lebanon. The Lebanese government has gone along with that position, reflecting the degree of influence that Damascus has on Beirut [ibid., 11/14/92].

Israel also manages to control some areas of southern Lebanon through its proxy militia force, the South Lebanon Army.

Clashes between these contending forces were supposed to be prevented by the presence of the **U.N. Interim Force in Lebanon (UNIFIL)**, sent to restore Lebanon's sovereignty in the south in 1978 after an Israeli incursion. Although Israel withdrew from most of southern Lebanon in 1985, skirmishes between the Israelis (or the SLA militia) and the Hizbollah (or the Palestinian guerrillas) break out regularly. UNIFIL's nearly 6,000 peacekeepers can do little to halt the guerrilla raids or Israeli counterattacks, since its mandate bars it from using force.

Since 1978, 186 UNIFIL soldiers have been killed—29 of them in the period November 1992–June 1993 [data supplied by U.N. Field Operations Division, 7/1/93].

Iran

After the Gulf War ended and Iraq was out of the spotlight, the West began to look again at Iran and ask if it deserved full acceptance by the family of nations. On one hand, Iran had cooperated fully with the U.N. **economic embargo of Iraq** during and after the Gulf War: Widespread smuggling across the two nations' long border could have rendered the sanctions useless. But many Western leaders still harbored reservations about Teheran's respect for civil, political, and human rights, and they worried about signs that Iran might be developing a nuclear weapons program, as had its nemesis, Iraq. Many countries also worried about Teheran's support for Islamic guerrillas and terrorists, such as its backing of Hizbollah in Lebanon.

Ever since the Ayatollah Ruhollah Khomeini's Shiite Islamic revolution toppled Shah Reza Pahlavi, a reliable Western ally, many Western nations have looked upon Iran's theocratic state as the most dangerous long-term threat in the Middle East. This fear has been shared by the Saudi and Jordanian monarchies and the oil-rich Gulf states, such as Kuwait, all of whom helped bankroll Iraq in its 1980–88 war with Iran. In August 1990, Kuwait came to regret having helped build up Baghdad's military machine.

Now that Iraq's expansionism has been curbed, Gulf states are worried about Iran's appetites. Teheran has already laid claim to three small islands in the Persian Gulf near the Strait of Hormuz, through which a fourth of the world's oil supply is shipped. The islands—**Abu Musa, Greater Tunb, and Lesser Tunb**—were jointly administered for two decades by Iran and Sharjah, one of the sheikdoms that later joined the United Arab Emirates (UAE). In spring 1992, Iran began expelling some UAE residents of Abu Musa, where Iran has a naval garrison. Iran's ally Syria was among the eight Arab nations that joined in criticizing the annexation attempt, but Teheran denounced the statement [*The New York Times*, 9/13/92]. Iran's Foreign Minister, Ali Akbar Velayati, later indicated that Teheran sought Abu Musa as an exclusive naval base to counterbalance the post-Gulf War defense alliance between the United States and the Arab states of the Gulf Cooperation Council [*The Washington Post*, 10/12/92].

Gulf states and oil-importing nations alike had further cause to worry when Iran bought a Russian diesel-electric Kilo class **submarine** in 1992, becoming the first Gulf state to have a sub. Teheran is believed to be buying two more, which could give it even more control over the Strait of Hormuz. This comes on top of the Iranians' $7 billion spending spree in 1988, after the end of its war with Iraq, when it bought tanks, missiles, MIG-29 interceptors, and Sukhoi ground-attack warplanes [Associated Press, 11/23/92].

U.S. Secretary of State Warren Christopher signaled the shift in concern when he called Iran an "international outlaw" and "a dangerous country" for its alleged support of international terrorism and attempt to develop nuclear and other weapons of mass destruction. "Iran is one of the principal sources of support for terrorist groups around the world," Christopher said. U.S. intelligence agencies believe Iran could have a working **nuclear weapon** by the end of the decade [*The New York Times*, 3/31/93]. Iran's U.N. Ambassador, Kamal Kharrazi, denied that Teheran has a nuclear weapons program or wishes to develop one [Associated Press, 4/30/93].

Iran's **human rights practices** have been scrutinized by the U.N. Commission on Human Rights for years, and the 47th General Assembly condemned Teheran for allowing widespread torture and for rampant executions, failure to safeguard the rights of the accused, oppression of members of the Baha'i faith, and placing restrictions on the press as well as on freedom of expression, thought, and opinion.

The West is still rankled by the late Ayatollah Khomeini's *fatwa*, or religious decree, authorizing the slaying of **Salman Rushdie** for purportedly blaspheming Islam in his book *The Satanic Verses*. Not only does the decree still stand, four years after it was issued, but an Iranian foundation has raised the bounty on Rushdie's head to $2 million [*The New York Times*, 11/3/92]. During a speaking engagement in Washington, Ambassador Kharrazi rejected any idea that Iran might be willing to drop the edict, saying that it was not an Iranian government order but a religious matter. Rushdie is considered an apostate, he said, and "the sentence of an apostate man is death based on Islam" [Associated Press, 4/30/93].

UNRWA

The U.N. Relief and Works Agency for Palestine Refugees in the Near East (UNRWA) was founded in 1949 to provide humanitarian aid to some 750,000 Palestinians who became refugees as a result of the 1948 Arab-Israeli War. Today the agency extends a wide range of welfare services to some 2.5 million eligible Palestinian refugees in the Middle East, about a third of whom live in refugee camps. It provides education to 350,000 Palestinian students in Jordan, Lebanon, Syria, and the Occupied Territories; and it supplies shelter materials, emergency medical supplies, and food relief to more than 108,000 Palestinians it classifies as "special hardship cases."

UNRWA's regular and emergency operations for 1993 were budgeted at $327 million, with almost all of the funds and supplies taking the form of voluntary contributions by donor countries. But their donations fell $28.5 million below the budget, and the agency is constantly challenged to find the best ways of utilizing its limited resources to serve its large and quite needy constituency.

The agency's staff of 2,300 often face grave dangers in the field. Since June 1982, 26 staffers have been killed in Lebanon alone [UNRWA Annual Report, A/47/13].

Since the start of the *intifadah* in December 1987, UNRWA has had to overcome extreme difficulties in meeting emergency needs for food, water, and medical care in the refugee camps of Gaza [U.N. press release DH/85/88 and the UNRWA Public Information Office publication *UNRWA 1991/92*]. At least seven staffers alleged to be Israeli collaborators have been killed since the start of the uprising; and at any one time, Israel is usually holding in detention a dozen or two UNRWA staffers suspected of being rioters or guerrillas. From July 1991 to June 1992, Israel detained 61 staffers, 10 of whom were still being held at the end of the reporting period [UNRWA Annual Report]. UNRWA has repeatedly protested what it believes is Israeli harassment of its staff in the Occupied Territories. Israel responds that the arrests and detentions are justified on grounds of national security.

4. Africa

By Edmund T. Piasecki

Making and keeping the peace in Africa confronts the United Nations with uniquely difficult challenges. On a continent subject to prolonged droughts and already heavily dependent on international food aid, armed conflict is often accompanied by the imminent threat of mass starvation. To restore peace and stability, the United Nations must not only mediate and often help implement cease-fires and final settlements, it must also provide humanitarian relief to affected populations, often numbering in the millions. The undeveloped and often heavily damaged infrastructures in these poor and war-torn countries make the delivery of such relief a difficult undertaking even with the cooperation of all parties to a conflict. In the absence of effective central authority, as in Somalia, or in the case of the Sudanese government's deliberate policy to deny access to U.N. relief workers (officially reversed on December 5 under international pressure), reaching those in need becomes extremely dangerous if possible at all.

Ethnic, tribal, and religious rivalries throughout Africa also hinder dispute settlement and humanitarian relief efforts. Class and race-based hatreds between government and rebel supporters in Angola have complicated U.N. attempts to monitor compliance with a peace agreement there, and deep distrust between the predominantly Muslim north of Sudan and the Christian and animist south have fueled a ten-year civil war in that country and produced a "silent famine." The situation in the Sudan and—before Boutros-Ghali helped bring it to the world's attention—Somalia illustrate another problem: the tendency of the international community to ignore conflict and hunger until they have reached crisis proportions. Furthermore, once consensus exists for international action, the response is often hampered by competing claims on increasingly scarce U.N. resources. The December 1992 peace agreement in Mozambique remains unimplemented due to the U.N.'s inability to find states willing to commit troops.

Lacking the financial and operational capacity to deploy the large and heavily armed forces increasingly in demand in Africa and elsewhere, the United Nations has designated major military powers to act under its authority on a temporary basis. After restoring order in Somalia, the U.S.-led Unified Task Force was succeeded by a sizable U.N. operation, UNOSOM II. To handle less pressing crises, the world body has requested regional organizations to do their part. In Liberia the Security Council has declared an arms embargo on the combatants and appointed a Special Representative, but has left enforcement of the November 1990 cease-fire to the 15-member Economic Community of Western African States (ECOWAS). Similarly, the Security Council has so far refused a request from parties to the conflict in Rwanda to join the Organization of African Unity (OAU) in monitoring compliance with the cease-fire of March 1993 and deploying observers along the border with Uganda. When it did agree to dispatch some 50 monitors to South Africa, the United Nations requested and received participation from the OAU, the European Community, and the Commonwealth states.

South Africa

The United Nations has assumed a more active and high-level role in facilitating an end to political violence in South Africa and promoting negotiations to establish the democratic, nonracial, and united state that the Organization has long demanded. Deeper U.N. involvement in these questions came in response to requests from **South Africa President F. W. de Klerk** and **African National Congress (ANC) President Nelson Mandela** for international assistance in halting a wave of politically motivated killings and restarting bilateral talks on arrangements for a transition from white minority rule. For the ANC the move was a logical extension of General Assembly efforts to dismantle the system of apartheid, or racial separation; for the government, it represented new-found trust in the world body derived from the United Nations's demonstrated ability in Namibia to function effectively and impartially in matters pertaining to South African national security. In agreeing to consider the questions of violence and peaceful settlement in South Africa, the Security Council signaled a shift in international concern from the moral outrage of apartheid to the threat that ongoing political instability poses to peace and security. The need to protect progress made in reversing institutionalized racism and in opening up multiparty dialogue returned South Africa to the top of the international agenda.

The period of civil unrest that engulfed the country after Mandela's release from prison in February 1990 had claimed the lives of more than 6,500 South Africans by mid-1993, most as a result of black-on-black violence between the ANC and its archrival, the **Inkatha Freedom Party (IFP)**. After the massacre in June 1992 of some 40 men, women, and children in the black township of Boipatong, allegedly by members of the

IFP with police support, Mandela had broken off talks with the government over the outlines of a new, nonracial constitutional order. Accusing de Klerk of sponsoring or at least condoning the violence, Mandela demanded more effective action to stop the killings. The government denied direct or indirect involvement and refused to honor the 14 conditions for resumption of the talks issued by the ANC (including the election of a constitutional assembly, the establishment of an interim government, and the release of all political prisoners).

Following consultations by the Secretary-General with both Mandela and South African Foreign Minister Roelof (Pik) Botha, reportedly regarding a visit by the Secretary-General to South Africa or the deployment of up to 500 U.N. monitors there [*The Christian Science Monitor*, 7/3/92], the **Organization of African Unity** on June 23 called for an urgent meeting of the Security Council to consider a U.N. role in creating conditions conducive to the resumption of negotiations. In response to an official request from the **Group of African States**—an informal caucus group of the General Assembly—for Security Council action on the OAU recommendations, the Council convened to debate the matter on July 15. Citing a threat to regional peace and security, the Council condemned the violence, strongly urged the government to take immediate measures to stop it, and called upon all parties to cooperate in that effort. The Secretary-General was also invited to appoint a Special Representative to consult with all involved parties and recommend measures to stop the bloodshed and encourage the resumption of talks. Significantly, the Security Council also decided to "remain seized of the matter," signaling its intent to go beyond the imposition or maintenance of sanctions (the United Nations had imposed a mandatory arms embargo and a voluntary oil embargo on South Africa in 1977) to active and long-term dispute settlement [S/Res/765 (1992)].

The Secretary-General moved immediately to appoint **Cyrus Vance**, the former U.S. Secretary of State, as his representative. Vance arrived in South Africa on July 22 for a ten-day mission as the ANC was gearing up for "mass actions" scheduled for August 3. To prevent further violence and help relieve the atmosphere of extreme distrust, the Secretary-General deployed ten U.N. monitors to promote compliance with the provisions of the **National Peace Accord** governing such protests. (The Accord, signed by the government, the ANC, the IFP, and others in September 1991, established "codes of conduct" for political parties and organizations as well as for the security forces.) While the United Nations had previously deployed election and human rights monitors in numerous instances, the monitors in South Africa were the first specifically authorized to observe and report on political protest.

In his report of August 7 on the Vance mission, the Secretary-General recommended first and foremost that the international community support the activities of a government-appointed body, the **Commission of Inquiry into Public Violence and Intimidation**, known as the **Goldstone Commission** after its chairman, Justice Richard J. Goldstone. Since its establishment in October 1991, the Goldstone Commission has investigated numerous specific instances of violence, and has proposed practical steps to the government and political leaders to prevent future incidents and to defuse tensions. It is said to have kept the death toll from rising even higher and to have contributed to the maintenance of the negotiating process. Goldstone himself is credited with having convinced de Klerk to accept regional and international involvement during the transition period [*The Christian Science Monitor*, 2/10/93].

The Secretary-General further recommended "strengthening" the National Peace Accord and the bodies established by it. Under the Accord, the National Peace Committee is charged with monitoring the implementation of provisions aimed at promoting community reconstruction and development and resolving disputes over the interpretation and alleged violations of the codes of conduct. The National Peace Secretariat establishes and coordinates the work of the Regional and Local Dispute Resolution committees, which report to the national committee. The Secretary-General specifically suggested the dispatch of 30 additional U.N. monitors to assist the Secretariat personnel in observing demonstrations, marches, and other forms of mass action and monitoring compliance with the codes of conduct.

Finally, the Secretary-General called for the immediate and unconditional release of all political prisoners and proposed the dispatch of U.N. fact-finding missions to South Africa on a quarterly basis. Under Resolution 772, the Security Council called upon the government and all political parties to implement the Secretary General's recommendations, authorized the deployment of observers, and invited other international organizations to do the same [8/17/92].

On September 9 the Secretary-General announced the formation of the **U.N. Observation Mission in South Africa (UNOMSA)** and dispatched an advance team of 13 on September 11. By the end of October, UNOMSA had established a presence in all 11 regions of the country, with deployment weighted toward the black townships outside Johannesburg and the Zulu-dominated areas in Natal province, where 70% of the violence was occurring. UNOMSA had reached its full complement of 50 (increased at the discretion of the Secretary-General from 30) by the end of November. The U.N. monitors were joined in October by 17 observers from the Commonwealth states and 14 from the European Community. The OAU sent 11 more observers in November.

Although the chairman of the National Peace Committee had called the peace accord a "dismal flop" in September [*The Washington Post Weekly*, 9/14–20/92], the Secretary-General reported in December that the presence of

UNOMSA had "significantly enhanced and reinforced the structures under the National Peace Accord" and had had a "salutary effect on the political situation in general" [S/25004, 12/22/92]. Several members of the mission were assigned to assist the Goldstone Commission along with full-time legal experts provided by the United Nations and the European Community. The level of violence continued to rise in some locales, however, and ten more observers were scheduled to be sent.

Following up on the Security Council's request for quarterly updates, the Secretary-General appointed two Special Envoys and dispatched them in separate missions during September and November 1992. Reporting in December on the results of these efforts, the Secretary-General noted unanimous support in South Africa for multiparty negotiations leading to free elections and a democratic constitutional order. While talks in the existing negotiating forum, the Convention for a Democratic South Africa (CODESA), had ended in deadlock in May, there was little agreement on an alternative. The parties were also far apart regarding matters of participation, agendas, and timing with respect to multilateral discussions. The Secretary-General, for his part, underscored the importance of "inclusiveness" in any future arrangement and expressed "guarded optimism" about the prospects of a negotiated settlement.

Through informal contacts begun in late July 1992, the ANC and the government had reached provisional agreement on many of the conditions governing a resumption of formal bilateral talks between them. On September 26, **Mandela and de Klerk met** for the first time since June and agreed to a **Joint Statement and Record of Understanding** covering constitutional questions as well as measures to improve the atmosphere for negotiations and decrease the likelihood of violence.

Both sides recorded their support for the election of a democratic constituent assembly, which would function as a constitution-making body as well as the "interim/transitional" parliament. They further agreed to the establishment of an "interim/transitional government of national unity," i.e., the inclusion of de Klerk's National Party in a cabinet dominated by the ANC, which would function according to a previously agreed-to "constitutional framework/transitional constitution." Left unspecified were preparations for the elections and post-interim arrangements, i.e., the authority under which elections would be held and an interim constitution drafted, and whether there existed the need for a second round of elections following the adoption of a nonracial constitution. As recommended by the Vance mission, the government pledged to release all political prisoners by November 15, 1992 (it had already freed 150 of over 400 held), and also accepted the proposals of the Goldstone Commission regarding fencing and policing for migrant worker hostels—

frequent sources of violence—and prohibitions on the carrying and public display of "dangerous" weapons.

Calling these steps "a most welcome development," the Secretary-General concluded that they had effectively removed the cause of deadlock in the CODESA process and helped clear the way for renewed multilateral negotiations [A/47/574, 11/6/92; S/25004, 12/22/92]. On the basis of the Joint Statement and Record, the ANC decided on September 30 to return to formal bilateral talks with the government.

Fearing domination of the ANC in a black majority government, other political parties staked out their own positions regarding the resumption of multilateral talks. **Chief Mangosuthu Gatsha Buthelezi,** President of the IFP, rejected the Joint Statement, especially its prohibitions on "cultural" weapons (e.g., spears), refused to be bound by agreements negotiated by the ANC, and on September 27 announced his withdrawal from any constitutional discussions. The Secretary-General's repeated attempts to convince him to support the agreement were unsuccessful. The IFP struck a deal in December on the outline of a new multilateral negotiating forum with representatives of three of the ten "independent homelands" set up under apartheid and two white parties from the far right. The militant **Pan Africanist Congress of Azania (PAC),** which had broken away from the ANC in 1959, agreed to its own joint statement with the government on October 24, but formal talks were not resumed due to PAC's unwillingness to renounce violence on the part of its military wing, the **Azanian People's Liberation Army (APLA).**

In advance of their resumed bilateral discussions, the ANC and the government offered competing timetables for the implementation of the constitutional arrangements contained in their Joint Statement. Long committed to the holding of multiracial elections before the end of 1993, the ANC approved on November 18 a five-phase transition plan—covering the drafting of an interim constitution and elections through the adoption of a nonracial constitution and the complete dismantling of apartheid—that envisioned a fully functioning democratic government within two years. In a major strategy shift, the ANC proposed as part of the plan to extend the government of national unity for a five-year period beyond the adoption of a new constitution, i.e., to delay a second round of elections and share power with the National Party for an indeterminate period, estimated between seven and ten years [*The New York Times, The Christian Science Monitor,* 11/20/92].

While welcoming the proposal, the government sought to underscore its own commitment to majority rule and reaffirm that a complete transfer of power was still far off. On November 26, de Klerk announced a timetable that did not contemplate elections before April 1994. He argued that at least 16 months would be required to complete bilateral talks, convene and conclude multilateral negotiations, establish executive transitional councils (empowered to draft an interim constitution and oversee elections), and register voters [*The New York Times*, 11/27/92]. The ANC's insistence that elections be held in 1993 stalled further progress at formal bilateral talks December 2–4, after which the parties reaffirmed their commitment to resume multilateral negotiations as soon as possible.

The stage was set for practical deal-making, driven as much by economic necessity as by political expediency. Whereas constitutional talks had stumbled through numerous delays and bouts of mutual recrimination, nearly four years of severe recession and the worst drought in decades had combined to produce unemployment rates topping 40% and extremely low domestic and foreign investor confidence [A/47/22-S/24663, 11/6/92]. In proposing an extended government of national unity, Mandela and the ANC conceded that full majority rule would only alienate the predominately white business community, promote capital flight, and invite economic collapse. The government, in welcoming the national unity concept, admitted that it provided the stability and legitimacy necessary to end political uncertainty and violence. De Klerk and the National Party were holding out, however, for constitutional guarantees on a permanent power-sharing arrangement and a loose federal system that gave the regions significant political authority over the center. In four rounds of talks through February 1993, the government would bargain away these demands but win assurances of its status as the junior partner in a five-year coalition.

By February 12, Mandela and de Klerk had reportedly reached tentative agreement on most issues, though both sides denied having struck a deal. De Klerk was said to have made a significant concession on the question of federalism, agreeing to leave the task of defining regional authority to the elected constitutional body but winning support for the inclusion of regional representatives in it. Mandela apparently gave way on a veto power for the coalition members; the president of the national unity government would be required to obtain a two-thirds vote of approval from his cabinet on certain questions. To prepare for multilateral negotiations, the government and the ANC also reportedly pledged to hold a planning conference to sell the power-sharing plan to other political parties [*The Washington Post*, 2/13/93, *The New York Times*, 2/18/93].

Delegates from 26 political parties attended the Multi-party Planning Conference held March 5–6, 1993, including the rightist Conservative Party and the far-left Pan Africanist Congress, neither of which had attended the earlier CODESA meetings. Only the Conservatives abstained on a procedural resolution according to which the delegates agreed to reconvene the yet-unnamed multiparty forum, successor to CODESA, for substantive negotiations on constitutional questions and the ANC–National Party power-sharing plan no later than April 5 [A/48/123-A/25495, 3/31/93; *The Washington Post*, 3/7/93]. According to de Klerk's timetable of November 26, multilateral talks were to conclude agreements on the **outline of the transitional constitution**, the establishment of the **Transitional Executive Council**, and the formation of an **Election Commission** before the end of May 1993. The council and the commission, multiparty bodies empowered to supervise state media and security forces during campaigning, were to be instituted before the end of June. By the end of September the transitional constitution would be enacted, and election rules and regulations were to be formulated and promulgated before the end of October. Elections for the Constituent Assembly/Constitution-Making Body are scheduled for April 1994 [Permanent Mission of South Africa press release No. 12/93, 3/22/93].

Despite the success of the ANC and the government in restarting multilateral negotiations, violence continued unabated throughout the spring of 1993. The death toll since Mandela's release, the legalization of the ANC, and government steps to dismantle apartheid stood at more than 9,000. The assassination on April 10 of Chris Hani, secretary-general of the South African Communist party and a leading proponent of peaceful change, set off the most violent protests in years, leaving eight dead, causing millions of dollars in property damage, and inviting censure from the Security Council. Negotiations continued, however, and on May 7, delegates to the multilateral talks issued a declaration of intent to decide within a month the exact date for elections. Once that occurs and the transitional council and its subsidiaries are established, Mandela has promised to call for the lifting of the remaining international sanctions against South Africa. U.S. Secretary of State Warren Christopher pledged U.S. assistance in this regard, announcing on May 21 his intention to work with the Group of Seven industrialized democracies "to help South Africa re-enter the global economy" [*The Washington Post*, 4/11/93, 5/8/93, 5/22/93].

Angola

A year after signing the "Peace Accords for Angola" in May 1991, **President José Eduardo dos Santos** and rebel leader **Jonas Savimbi** were cooperating fairly well with each other and the United Nations in bringing an end to 17 years of civil war. Despite an atmosphere of tension and mutual suspicion, both sides were honoring the cease-fire they had declared as part of the accords, and U.N. military observers were verifying the concentration and disarming of the rival armies. On May 20, 1991, U.N. police and civilian observers began monitoring voter registration in preparation for the country's first multiparty elections in September. At the close of the registration period on August 10, 4.86 million Angolans had registered to vote, 92% of those eligible. While demobilization was going less smoothly, dos Santos and Savimbi pledged on September 7 to dissolve their forces by September 27 and to form a government of national unity in the post-election period. It was hoped that this effort at reconciliation between the ruling and formerly Marxist **Popular Movement for the Liberation of Angola (MPLA)** and the fiercely anti-Communist rebels of the **National Union for the Total Independence of Angola (UNITA)** would place the peace process firmly on track.

The United Nations had taken a considerable risk in expanding the mandate of **the U.N. Angola Verification Mission (UNAVEM)**—originally deployed to oversee the withdrawal of Cuban troops from the country under a December 1988 accord—to monitor compliance with the Angolan peace agreement. The new operation, **UNAVEM II**, had no authority under the agreement to actually demobilize troops or organize elections. The former task was left to the Angola Joint Verification and Monitoring Commission (CMVF), consisting of military personnel drawn from both government and rebel forces, and the latter task to the National Election Council (NEC), made up of representatives of all political parties. UNAVEM II was simply to verify the compliance of the CMVF with the peace agreement and certify the fairness of the elections by monitoring all phases of the electoral process—registration, campaigning, voting, and tabulation of the results—directed by the NEC.

In addition to the narrowness of its mandate, UNAVEM lacked firepower and size. Unlike peacekeeping forces, UNAVEM II contained no armed troops and would be unable to either deter or contain violence despite threatening conditions on the ground, i.e., an uneasy truce and delays in demobilizing some 120,000 government and rebel soldiers. The mission was also quite small, owing to government concerns that the U.N. presence not violate national sovereignty. Even at full strength, UNAVEM II's 350 military and 126 police observers and its civilian contingent of 83 political/electoral observers were hard pressed to carry out their duties in a country of 10 million, nearly the size of Western Europe. While the success of all peacekeeping operations is dependent on the willingness of parties to an agreement to implement an accord in full and on time, this was especially the case with UNAVEM II.

Of all the flaws in UNAVEM's mandate and the peace agreement itself, the inability of the United Nations to force the pace of demobilization and ensure its completion by election day proved most damaging. By September 17 only half of the government's Popular Armed Forces for the Liberation of Angola (FAPLA) and a quarter of UNITA's Armed Forces for the Liberation of Angola (FALA)—rivals in the struggle that ended Portuguese colonial rule in 1975—had been demobilized. In addition, many of the 40,000 disarmed FAPLA personnel waged violent protests against the government's failure to provide promised transport, food, and employment. Efforts by the U.N.'s World Food Programme (WFP) to supply food and civilian clothing to newly demobilized military personnel on both sides and transport them from U.N.-monitored assembly points quelled the disturbances somewhat, but UNAVEM was helpless to restore order in the absence of a national military or police presence.

Both UNITA and the government, the Secretary-General would later charge, had failed to take agreed-upon steps to create the conditions necessary for democracy to take hold in Angola. Although the peace accords provided for the establishment of the Angolan Armed Forces (FFA), a 40,000-man force to be drawn equally from demobilized FAPLA and FALA personnel and placed under joint command, it numbered no more than 10,000 troops in mid-September due to delays in demobilization. Only with the dissolution of both armies on September 27—two days before elections and with the active intervention of the United Nations—was the FFA established and UNITA military leaders sworn into command positions. Even then, no provisions were made for the disarming of combatants not chosen for the FFA. The accords also provided for the training of a politically neutral national police force, but UNITA had allowed only 642 of its supporters to become members, charging that the government was more intent on creating anti-riot police units under its direct control. The government, for its part, accused UNITA of stockpiling weapons near assembly points and maintaining its military authority over some 20,000 demobilized FALA personnel [*The Christian Science Monitor*, 9/24/92].

The Elections

During the period of active campaigning, from August 29 through September 28, UNAVEM reported no "major" violence, and Angola seemed to shift quickly from a one-party state controlled by the MPLA to a pluralistic democracy with 18 legalized and registered political parties. Similarly, voting took place over two days beginning September 29 under conditions, the United Nations said, "which could generally be described as peaceful and orderly." Turnout topped 91% of registered voters, but distorted reporting in the government-run media claiming a dos Santos landslide led UNITA and six other parties to complain on October 3 of "widespread, massive, and systematic irregularities and fraud" [S/24858, 11/25/92].

In an attempt to preserve the peace process and to prevent UNITA from rejecting the election, U.N. diplomacy shifted into high gear. The Secretary-General contacted Savimbi several times, appealing for his cooperation in an investigation of the charges, and the U.N.'s **Special Representative for Angola, Margaret Anstee**, interceded with dos Santos for an extension on the announcement of the results. After the withdrawal of 11 UNITA generals from the FAA on October 5 in protest against the alleged cheating, the Security Council, in declaring itself "gratified" by the calm atmosphere prevailing during the vote and the high turnout, decided to send an ad hoc commission of its members to Angola to demonstrate strong international support for the full implementation of the peace accords [S/24623, 10/6/92]. Following meetings with dos Santos, Savimbi, and others, the commission reported on October 13 that both leaders had promised to prevent violence and resolve their differences through dialogue and peaceful means. It warned that "any resumption of armed confrontation will meet with the strongest condemnation of the international community" [U.N. press release SG/1961, 10/14/93].

Press reports, unconfirmed by the United Nations, alluded to attempts by South Africa, a longtime backer of UNITA, to mediate a power-sharing arrangement between the sides and help establish a provisional government. The "winner-take-all" elections, the absence of guarantees on broad political participation in the resulting government, and the failure to provide for a period of transitional rule were considered major weaknesses in the peace accords [*The New York Times*, 10/15/92; *The Washington Post*, 10/16/92].

At the conclusion of its two-week investigation, conducted with the assistance of UNAVEM, the NEC announced on October 17 that dos Santos and the MPLA had defeated Savimbi's UNITA party in the presidential race by 49.57% versus 40.07% and in the legislative contest by 53.74% against 34.1% [S/24858, 11/25/92]. That same day, Anstee issued a statement in which she ascribed the election's "irregularities" to human error and inexperience. Having found no evidence of fraud or of irregularities significant enough to have altered the outcome, the Special Representative declared the elections "generally free and fair" [U.N. press release SG/1966, 10/19/92]. As neither major presidential candidate had received more than 50% of the vote, a runoff election was to be held within 30 days. Heavily favored to win in preelection polls, UNITA immediately denounced Anstee for alleged partiality, and death threats were received against her and UNAVEM personnel. The possibility of a second election soon vanished under a rising tide of violence.

Armed clashes in the Angolan capital of Luanda spread to the country as a whole, as UNITA remobilized and began seizing control of vast stretches of the countryside. Having just approved the report of its ad hoc commission on October 19 [S/24683], the Security Council issued another statement on October 27, calling on both sides to abide by their commitments under the peace accords and requesting that they honor their promises to open a dialogue and allow the second round of elections to go forward [S/24720].

With the expiration of UNAVEM's mandate period on October 30, the Security Council also authorized the operation for another month and requested long-term recommendations from the Secretary-General regarding the maintenance of a U.N. presence on the ground [S/Res/785

(1992)]. The very next day, the heaviest fighting since the signing of the peace accords broke out in Luanda and quickly engulfed all the major cities. Left with few soldiers still under arms, the government called out its paramilitary police and began distributing weapons to civilians. Thousands of UNITA supporters were reportedly killed in Luanda and other cities as a result. After the personal intervention of the Secretary-General and the coming into force of a cease-fire early in the morning of November 2, the government retained control in the capital and other population centers, but UNITA had occupied at least 57 and perhaps as many as 97 of Angola's 164 smaller towns.

A glimmer of hope for reviving the peace process appeared on November 26, when the United Nations succeeded in bringing the parties together in the city of Namibe for their first meeting since the resumption of hostilities. Both sides reaffirmed the validity of the peace accords, promised to maintain an effective cease-fire and halt all offensive movements, and agreed on the need for greater U.N. involvement in Angola [S/24996, 12/21/92]. In extending the mandate of UNAVEM two additional months, the Security Council welcomed these pledges, urged the government and UNITA to immediately act on them, and strongly appealed to both sides to agree on a clear timetable for the full implementation of the original accords [S/Res/793 (1992)]. The dialogue was immediately broken off, however, after the UNITA seizure of two northern cities, Uige and Negage, on November 29 and its refusal to complete the partial withdrawal it effected from these cities on December 4.

There were some positive political developments during this period that gave reason to hope for a timely resumption of direct talks. The government had offered cabinet positions to UNITA in a new "Government of National Unity" on December 2, and UNITA had decided on December 8–9 to nominate supporters for the posts, take up its 70 seats in the National Assembly, and return its generals to the FAA. Both sides had also agreed in principle to a broader UNAVEM mandate and a larger force deployment, including armed troops. In a statement by the president on December 22, the Security Council endorsed the Secretary-General's attempts to exploit the common interest in a continued U.N. presence as the basis for face-to-face meetings between the leaders under his auspices. It also agreed with him on the need for "early evidence" from both sides that the continued commitment of scarce U.N. resources in Angola was justified [S/25002].

While unable to agree on a venue for the joint meeting with the Secretary-General, dos Santos and Savimbi were considering indirect negotiations between their senior military leaders when another round of fierce fighting, centered this time on Lubango, erupted on January 3, 1993. To find a solution to the ongoing problems at Uige and Negage, which the government insisted had to precede a resumption of the political dialogue, both sides agreed to convene face-to-face military talks on new cease-fire arrangements and immediately follow them with political negotiations. They further agreed to hold the meetings under UNAVEM auspices in Addis Ababa on January 16–17, but Savimbi backed out at the last minute, demanding that military and political talks be held simultaneously, not sequentially. The meetings in Addis Ababa remained "in suspense."

Meanwhile, heavy fighting had spread to at least ten provincial capitals and appeared to constitute, in the words of the Secretary-General, "a planned offensive to drive UNITA from the main cities." Despite the loss of Benguela and Lobito, where it allegedly massacred some 3,500 civilians before withdrawing in mid-January, UNITA increased the number of municipalities under its control to 105 and seized the oil-producing center at Soyo, 180 miles north of Luanda, on January 20. Already in control of diamond production in the northeast valued at $1.5 billion, UNITA stood to gain some $2 billion annually if it could retain the city [*The Christian Science Monitor*, 1/21/93]. Citing unprecedented UNITA control over major population centers, reports of thousands of civilian deaths, and numerous human rights violations on both sides, the Secretary-General stated in his report of January 21: "To all intents and purposes, Angola has returned to civil war and is probably in an even worse situation than that which prevailed before the Peace Accords were signed in May 1991" [S/25140].

Against a background of full-scale warfare, UNAVEM's monitoring and verification functions were becoming increasingly irrelevant. The fighting had forced the abandonment of 45 of 67 observation posts around the country at an estimated loss of $5.2 million in vehicles and equipment; and as the mission's mandate neared expiration, the Secretary-General presented the Security Council with three options: maintain UNAVEM's current strength and attempt to reoccupy all 67 posts; reduce the posts to six and decrease manpower accordingly; or confine the operation to the capital, reduce staff correspondingly, but retain the capacity to deploy observers outside the city if necessary. The Secretary-General recommended the last option—including a reduction in forces to 30 military and 6 police observers and 28 civilian staff—and the Security Council agreed. It extended the mission's current mandate through April 30 and stated its willingness to "substantially" increase the U.N. presence in Angola should progress in the peace process warrant.

While offering this incentive, the Security Council also denounced noncompliance with the peace accords in its harshest language to date, citing UNITA for particular censure. It strongly condemned persistent violations of the accords by the rebels, breaches of international humanitarian law on both sides, and attacks against UNAVEM personnel. The Council also demanded an immediate cease-fire and the release of some

20 foreign nationals taken hostage by UNITA in Soyo [S/Res/804 (1993)]. The convening of cease-fire talks in Addis Ababa on January 28 received only a passing mention, and the discussions, characterized in the press as "wary but polite" broke down after three days without agreement. The hard-pressed government was reportedly seeking an immediate cessation of hostilities, while UNITA, in control of two-thirds of the country, insisted on strong international monitoring arrangements before agreeing to a truce. The rebels were also said to have demanded the immediate disbandment of the "special" police and civilian "vigilante" groups [*The Washington Post*, 1/29/93; *The Christian Science Monitor*, 2/3/93].

Renewed Talks

The war had taken a particularly nasty turn, as Cold War ideologies faded and tribal, racial, and class-based rivalries reasserted themselves. According to international relief workers quoted in the press, both sides had engaged in systematic killings and "pogroms" of civilian political opponents since the resumption of hostilities in October. Government riot police and MPLA-armed civilians had allegedly targeted members of the Ovimbindu tribe, strong Savimbi supporters making up the poorest 35% of the population, and UNITA was said to have directed its attacks against whites, mixed-race Angolans, and "intellectuals" in the middle and upper classes [*The Christian Science Monitor*, 2/3/93; *The Washington Post Weekly*, 2/8–14/93]. Renewed warfare also hindered the delivery of humanitarian relief by blocking access to affected populations, further weakening the country's already heavily damaged infrastructure and halting the removal of some 12 million landmines. The displacement of more than a million people from their homes and the disruption of agricultural production resulted in **acute food shortages and threatened widespread famine**. Warning of a "Somalia situation," the World Food Programme estimated that 1.5 million Angolans faced imminent starvation, a number that could double by September [*The Washington Post*, 2/26/93, 3/22/93].

Refusing to participate in a second round of talks in Addis Ababa scheduled for February 26, UNITA concentrated on consolidating its gains in the field. On March 8 it scored the most decisive military victory in the renewed war, capturing the central highlands city of Huambo, 300 miles southeast of Luanda. The 56-day battle for control over Angola's second largest city was estimated to have cost more than 10,000 lives, mostly civilian, and constituted the bloodiest single engagement of the entire war. These losses increased to over 20,000 the number of Angolans killed since October but added only marginally to the 300,000 casualties already suffered between 1975 and 1991. Savimbi immediately called for new talks (the United Nations had called off the negotiations at Addis

Ababa on March 1) and insisted they take place in Geneva without Anstee, the Special Representative [*The Washington Post*, 3/8/93, 3/9/93].

Concerned with the continued loss of life and the growing humanitarian tragedy, the Security Council increased its criticism of UNITA while praising the government's support for U.N. mediation. It reiterated its strong condemnation of UNITA's ongoing violations of the peace accords and attacks on U.N. personnel (including verbal attacks on the Special Representative), and it repeated demands for an immediate cease-fire and early evidence of real progress in implementing the peace agreement. The Security Council called for increased humanitarian relief assistance to Angola and invited the Secretary-General to organize and convene a meeting between the parties "at the highest possible level" before April 30, the expiration date of UNAVEM's current mandate period [S/Res/811 (1993)]. On April 6, Anstee announced that the government and UNITA had agreed to meet in Abidjan, Côte d'Ivoire, on April 12 under her chairmanship and the auspices of the United Nations [U.N. press release SG/1993, 4/6/93].

The four-point agenda for the talks would include arrangements for a cease-fire, completion of the peace accords, national reconciliation, and the future role of UNAVEM. Reasoning that action on the last item would place him in a better position to make appropriate recommendations on the mandate and strength of the mission, the Secretary-General requested the Security Council to extend UNAVEM II's current mandate through the conclusion of the talks and up to May 31. He had earlier moved to reduce its strength to 75 military observers, 30 police officers, and 49 civilian staff, a somewhat larger force than he had previously thought advisable [S/25690, 4/29/93]. The Council granted the extension on April 30 and declared its support for the current talks [S/Res/823 (1993)].

Despite opening in an "excellent climate," the talks themselves failed to advance beyond consideration of the first agenda item on the cease-fire. Perhaps seeking to preserve its military gains, UNITA offered an immediate truce and subsequent negotiation of conditions for a permanent peace. The government for its part, sought guarantees on the delivery of humanitarian assistance, including UNITA's cooperation in rebuilding bridges and clearing mines. By mid-May the parties had agreed in principle on rebel representation in all levels of the government, but talks broke off May 21 over UNITA's insistence that it not be required to assemble its forces for demobilization before U.N. peacekeepers could be fully deployed to protect them, especially against the government's anti-riot police [*The Washington Post*, 4/14/93, 5/12/93].

To reward dos Santos for embracing democracy, cooperating at the talks, and inviting UNITA representatives to participate in the government, **the United States** established formal diplomatic relations with Angola on May 19, 1993. Washington had refused to recognize the country's independence from Portugal after the MPLA seized power and cancelled free elections in 1975. The move was also a dramatic and public punishment of Savimbi, who had been supported by the Reagan administration financially and militarily as a freedom fighter against Soviet expansionism in the Third World. While President George Bush had promised to recognize the government resulting from the September elections, delays in holding the required runoff election postponed a final decision on the matter to the early days of the Clinton administration. Clinton, for his part, had hoped to continue to delay recognition as an incentive to Savimbi to moderate his behavior. While normalizing ties with the new government sends a strong signal that the United States stands behind democracy in Angola and throughout Africa, it is unclear what effect, if any, the decision will have on efforts to settle a conflict no longer driven by the imperatives of the Cold War [*The Washington Post*, 5/20/93, 5/23/93].

Mozambique

A two-year effort by the government of Italy to mediate an end to the civil war in Mozambique was reaching its culmination in the summer of 1992 with the negotiation of two accords, providing for deeper international involvement in feeding the hungry and U.N. guarantees on a final peace agreement. In the **Declaration of Rome on the Principles of Humanitarian Assistance**, signed July 16, **President Joaquim Chissano and the leader of the Resistência Nacional Moçambicana (RENAMO), Afonso Dhlakama**, granted U.N. and Red Cross relief workers their first unlimited access to displaced persons and refugees since the outbreak of hostilities in 1978. The government and RENAMO further agreed to guarantee political freedom and personal security for all citizens and accepted a U.N. role in monitoring a pending cease-fire and elections in their Joint Declaration of August 7 [S/24406, 8/10/92]. The declarations would form integral parts of a General Peace Agreement both sides pledged to conclude by October 1.

Africa's longest running conflict, the civil war in Mozambique was in part an internal response to the political oppression of the Marxist government that seized power after the country gained its independence from Portugal in 1975. But its length and ferocity were ascribed to support for RENAMO from white-controlled governments, first Rhodesia and then South Africa, which sought to destabilize the regime and deny bases and sanctuary in the country to guerrillas fighting white rule in southern Africa [*The New York Times*, 10/15/92]. By 1992 the war and a two-year drought—the worst of the century—had claimed the lives of more than 600,000 Mozambicans, displaced between 3 and 4 million, and driven 1.8 million to seek refuge in neighboring states, primarily Malawi and South Africa. Destruction and hunger were widespread, hampering international relief efforts; and the total breakdown of agricultural production in the territories under RENAMO control had reportedly been decisive in forcing the rebels to the negotiating table [*The Christian Science Monitor*, 12/16/92].

Under the **General Peace Agreement**, signed with some delay on October 4 [S/24635], the government and RENAMO agreed to effect a cease-fire by October 15, separate and concentrate their forces within a month, and demobilize all combatants within six months. Elections were scheduled to take place no later than October 15, 1993. The United Nations was asked to oversee the cease-fire and the troop demobilizations, monitor elections, and coordinate the delivery and distribution of humanitarian assistance. It would do so in part by chairing the Supervisory and Monitoring Commission to be set up under the Agreement and its two subsidiary bodies: the Ceasefire Commission and the Commission for the Reintegration of Demobilized Military Personnel. The United Nations would also be required to deploy a large peacekeeping force to carry out its military, electoral, and humanitarian responsibilities.

Based on an October 9, 1992, report by the Secretary-General [S/24642], the Security Council approved the proposed appointment of an "interim" Special Representative to Mozambique and the dispatch of a U.N. military observer mission of up to 25 personnel to initiate the implementation of the peace accord [S/Res/782 (1992)]. A "token" force, the observer mission would establish an immediate U.N. presence on the ground pending the submission of an operational plan for a larger force. Boutros-Ghali named **Aldo Ajello**, an Italian national and the Assistant Administrator of the U.N. Development Programme (UNDP) his **Special Representative** on October 13, and he and 21 observers arrived in Mozambique on October 15.

Despite their pledges under the Agreement, the parties had not met to reach agreement on the composition of the supervisory commissions, and RENAMO was said to be committing "major" violations of the cease-fire. The U.N. observers were refused permission to investigate these incidents, and the Security Council called for an immediate halt to them and full cooperation from both sides with the Special Representative [Statement of the President of the Security Council, 10/27/92, S/24719]. Ajello was successful in arranging the first face-to-face meetings between government and RENAMO representatives since the signing of the peace accords, and on November 4 he appointed the states members of the Supervisory and Monitoring Commission and its subsidiary bodies. Meanwhile, the government had initiated further military action aimed at retaking territories seized earlier by RENAMO forces.

In urging the Security Council to approve his operational plan submitted December 3 [S/24892], the Secretary-General underscored the need to bring the still unstable military situation under control and to complete the demobilization process before elections were held. He referred to "recent experiences elsewhere" (the renewal of hostilities among still-armed combatants in Angola after U.N.-monitored elections in late September) and argued that at least 5,500 troops would be necessary to avert a similar outcome in Mozambique. The Secretary-General also requested approximately 2,000 civilian staff to oversee elections and the provision of humanitarian relief. With an estimated cost of $332 million, the operation would be the U.N.'s third largest peacekeeping effort to date after Cambodia and Yugoslavia. (The deployment of UNOSOM II in Somalia in April 1993 moved the Mozambique operation to fourth place.) On December 16 the Security Council established the **U.N. Operation in Mozambique (ONUMOZ)**, authorized its activities through October 31, 1993, and requested the Secretary-General to report no later than March 31, 1993, on its progress [S/Res/797 (1992)].

Under the Secretary-General's plan, 354 U.N. observers in the Military Division of ONUMOZ would monitor the concentration of some 110,000 government and RENAMO combatants in 49 assembly areas around the country as well as the activities of separate observer teams dispatched by each side. The U.N. observers would also oversee the disarming and demobilization of all assembled troops; and with the assistance of a civilian "technical unit" cooperating with ONUMOZ's humanitarian component, the observers would provide food and other support to facilitate the troops' reintegration into civil society. In addition to the observers, the military component would consist of five infantry battalions of 850 personnel each to implement another key aspect of the peace accords: the monitored withdrawal of some 5,000 Zimbabwean and Botswanan troops who had assisted government forces in maintaining control over four vital "transport corridors" linking landlocked countries to the north and west of Mozambique with the Indian Ocean. Once these foreign contingents had withdrawn, ONUMOZ would have to guarantee security for humanitarian convoys using the transport corridors, especially the strategic Beira road and the rail lines, until a new Mozambican Defense Force could be deployed to do the job.

ONUMOZ's 148 electoral officers were charged with verifying the impartiality of preparations made for the legislative and presidential elections. They would be joined by 1,200 international observers during the actual voting to determine the legitimacy of the election results. The electoral officers would specifically monitor the activities of the National Elections Commission and help guarantee the accuracy of rolls of eligible voters as well as respect for political freedoms and fair access to the media for all political parties. The officers would also participate in public education efforts and report periodically on the election campaign to the Secretary-General through his Special Representative. Finally, the entire Electoral Division would observe voter registration, the voting itself, and the tabulation of results, and would report to the national authorities or itself investigate any irregularities uncovered or communicated to it. UNDP would support ONUMOZ in providing "technical assistance" throughout the electoral process.

The **U.N. Office for the Coordination of Humanitarian Assistance (UNOHAC)** would constitute the humanitarian component of ONUMOZ. Headed by the U.N.'s Humanitarian Affairs Coordinator, UNOHAC's 16-member staff would oversee the activities of both the World Food Programme (WFP) and the Red Cross as well as some 160 nongovernmental relief agencies already active in Mozambique. Both donor agencies and nongovernmental organizations (NGOs) would be represented on UNOHAC's Humanitarian Assistance Committee, chaired by the Coordinator. UNOHAC would also supply food and supplies to the Military Division's technical unit for the reintegration of demobilized soldiers [*United Nations Operation in Mozambique*, DPI/1326, 1/93].

Implementation of the Peace Agreement

Donor support for rehabilitation and relief operations in Mozambique has been strong over the last several years, allowing the country to escape the political and economic chaos that has affected Somalia since 1991. Two special international pledging conferences convened following the cease-fire were particularly successful. Donors pledged $620 million toward economic rehabilitation and reform programs (Mozambique renounced Marxism and central economic planning in 1990) and $140 million in food aid at a World Bank-sponsored conference held December 9–10 1992 in Rome. They promised $308 million more for refugee resettlement, military demobilization, and election monitoring at a December 15–16 conference, also held in Rome and organized by the Italian government. Through mid-December 1992, Mozambique had already received 550,000 tons of food through similar appeals by the United Nations and regional bodies [*The Christian Science Monitor*, 12/16/92].

The cease-fire had also eased food distribution problems and, combined with an end to the drought, promoted the repatriation of Africa's largest refugee population. Progress by RENAMO in de-mining roads in the interior allowed for the first WFP food deliveries to former rebel-held territories in late January 1993. Heightened security and the prospects of a good harvest also encouraged 100,000 refugees to return from Malawi by early February [*Africa Recovery*, 12/92–1/93]. In addition, the cease-fire paved the way for the biggest repatriation effort ever undertaken by the **U.N. High Commissioner for Refugees (UNHCR)** in Africa. Under a $30 million three-year program announced March 15, UNHCR expected to facilitate the return of some 1.3 million Mozambicans, perhaps 500,000 of them in the first year alone. However, the presence of some 2 million landmines in the country and the destruction of roads, bridges, health facilities, and schools presented significant challenges to prompt repatriation and the full reintegration of returnees [U.N. press release REF/1018, 3/16/93].

Despite the durability of the cease-fire, the implementation of the military aspects of the peace accords fell badly behind schedule, endangering the holding of elections by the specified date. While the Secretary-General placed the "main responsibility" on the government and RENAMO, the press alluded to the U.N.'s preoccupation with events in Yugoslavia, Cambodia, and Somalia [*The Christian Science Monitor*, 2/9/93]. The General Assembly's Fifth (Administrative and Budgetary) Committee was so dissatisfied with the preparation and deployment of ONUMOZ that it recommended "an urgent review of the current procedures to enable the proper and timely launching of such missions in a cost-effective and efficient manner" [A/C.5/47/L.32].

The Secretary-General, for his part, cited government delays in circulating a new election law as the grounds for rescheduling the elections. He maintained that many of the timetables for implementing various aspects of the peace accords were "unrealistic" and said that his delay in deploying observers—fewer than 100 were on the ground by the end of January 1993 [ibid.]—was due to "deep distrust" between the parties and their "reluctance" to begin concentrating and demobilizing their forces. Boutros-Ghali also criticized the government and RENAMO for failing to honor their commitments to guarantee the observers' freedom of movement and implied that government intransigence, not U.N. negligence, was responsible for the lack of a negotiated "status of forces" agreement for ONUMOZ, delineating standard guarantees of unannounced access for U.N. peacekeepers. Without such an agreement, observers were forced to notify the government in advance of their intended destinations, severely reducing the effectiveness of their monitoring and verification tasks. Finally, the Secretary-General admitted that consultations with troop contributors begun in September 1992 were still ongoing, but asserted that several states had only recently fulfilled their earlier pledges to place contingents at the U.N.'s disposal [S/25518, 4/2/93; U.N. press release SC/5589, 4/14/93].

As the Secretary-General had argued, disagreements between the government and RENAMO were holding up demobilization and the deployment of U.N. observers. In particular, the parties had been able to agree on only 12 of the 49 assembly points called for in the peace accords [*Africa Recovery*, 12/92–1/93]. But the Secretariat's submission of late and incomplete budgetary information on ONUMOZ to the General Assembly delayed budgetary approval until March 16 and held up deployment. The Secretary-General is authorized to expend only 10% of the estimated cost of a peacekeeping operation before its budget is approved by the General Assembly. Furthermore, the Fifth Committee had recommended appropriating only $140 million for ONUMOZ, sufficient to cover expenditures through June 1993, not through the end of the mandate period in October. In addition, the Committee requested the Secretary-General to submit revised and detailed cost estimates for the operation by July 1 before it would agree to appropriate the balance of the estimated cost. Considering the Special Representative's reported assertion that elections might not be held before May 1994 [*The Christian Science Monitor*, 2/9/93], the Secretary-General may face an uphill battle in convincing the General Assembly that ONUMOZ will be worth its total cost.

Regardless of what the General Assembly may decide to do, the Security Council is still firmly behind the Secretary-General's efforts in Mozambique. It did, however, "stress its concern" about the delays and difficulties encountered and "strongly urge[d]" the parties to finalize the timetable for the full implementation of the General Peace Agreement, including the concentration and demobilization of forces and the elections. The Security Council took similar action regarding guarantees on ONUMOZ's freedom of movement, and requested the Secretary-General to report back by June 30, 1993 [S/Res/818 (1993)].

Somalia

The lateness of the international response to the civil war in Somalia and the devastation wrought by the fighting itself hampered efforts throughout 1992 to restore stability and deliver emergency humanitarian assistance to a country that was already among the world's poorest and least developed. When the United Nations made its first attempts in January 1992 at implementing an effective cease-fire and providing food, shelter, and medical attention to the starving and displaced, 12 months of warfare had resulted in widespread hunger and the near-complete destruction of the rudimentary infrastructure that had existed. The breakdown of central administrative authority—in fact the complete absence of a national government—compelled the United Nations to negotiate security arrangements for the delivery and distribution of aid with various warlords, militia leaders, and clan elders who exercised what control there was over territory and the use of military force.

Insecurity remained a serious problem despite these efforts. A U.N.-mandated embargo on the import of arms had done little to stem the proliferation of weapons throughout the country, and the prevalence of heavily armed gangs looting supplies and robbing relief workers constituted a serious impediment to the effective provision of food and medicine, especially to the most afflicted populations of the interior. Unchecked violence, drought, and famine also contributed to massive population flows, both within and across national borders. The extent of the need within Somalia—and the inability of Somalis themselves to assist the United Nations in meeting that need—confronted the Organization with qualitatively new challenges in terms of emergency relief, dispute settlement, and rehabilitation.

Deployment of UNOSOM

On June 23, 1992, Secretary-General Boutros-Ghali announced that the principal warring factions in Somalia had agreed to the initial deployment of what would become by year's end the largest and most complex U.N. peacekeeping operation to date. **So-called interim President Ali Mahdi Mohammed** and his chief rival, **General Mohammed Farah Aidid**, agreed to accept 50 unarmed U.N. observers to monitor compliance with a March cease-fire covering the capital city, Mogadishu. Stability in Mogadishu—with its port facilities, international airlinks, and connections by road with the rest of the sprawling country—was vital to the overall relief effort.

Despite this progress, the United Nations had lost valuable time in saving the lives of 1.5 million Somalis it estimated were in imminent danger from malnutrition and disease and the 3 million others it said were at risk. The cease-fire monitors were not fully deployed until July 23, three months after the Security Council had established the **U.N. Operation in Somalia (UNOSOM)**, of which they were a part [S/Res/751 (1992)]; and the Secretary-General was not able to announce agreement on the deployment of the 500 "security personnel," approved "in principle" at the same time, until August 12. Donated by Pakistan and airlifted to Somalia by the United States, the security units were mandated to protect U.N. relief workers, equipment, and supplies within Mogadishu and to escort relief convoys through the city and its immediate environs. Following their arrival on September 14, the first Pakistani troops began to take up positions at food distribution centers but were prevented from fully deploying at the port or from securing the airport—essential for the quick delivery of food to the interior—by the particular subclan occupying the area.

To facilitate an expansion of the cease-fire beyond Mogadishu and the provision of relief to the country as a whole, Boutros-Ghali recommended in his report to the Security Council of July 22 a "comprehensive, decentralized and zonal approach" to the interrelated problems of security and hunger in Somalia and a significant expansion in the mandate of UNOSOM. His plan called for the establishment of four separate "operational zones"—in the northwest, the northeast, the central region (including Mogadishu), and the south—and the implementation within each of a consolidated program of activities, including humanitarian relief, cease-fire monitoring, the demobilization and disarmament of regular and irregular forces, and the promotion of "national reconciliation." In approving the establishment of the zones on July 27, the Security Council also underscored the urgent need to accelerate the delivery of assistance and requested the Secretary-General to consider the airlifting of food and supplies directly to the most affected populations [S/Res/767 (1992)].

In his report of August 24, 1992, the Secretary-General concluded that the airlift operations currently undertaken by the World Food Programme (WFP), UNICEF, and the International Committee of the Red Cross (ICRC) were in need of strengthening. Since March, WFP and UNICEF had been able to bring in only 1,300 metric tons of food and medical supplies by air, while deliveries by sea by WFP and the ICRC since January 1992 had totaled almost 120,000 metric tons. (Food requirements for the period from July 1992 to June 1993, however, were placed at 500,000 tons.) Boutros-Ghali recommended targeting the drought-stricken areas in the central and southern regions of the country for deliveries by air but stressed that these flights could not substitute for overland convoys. He also proposed establishing a "preventive zone" along the Somali-Kenyan border for special deliveries of food and seeds by the Office of the U.N. High Commissioner for Refugees (UNHCR) to benefit the 280,000 refugees gathered there in search of food and security [S/24480].

The Secretary-General emphasized that delays in the provision of relief were caused not by any lack of donor assistance but by general lawlessness and looting at food delivery and distribution points and even from docked ships and airport storage facilities. To help ensure the arrival of assistance transported by road beyond Mogadishu, the Secretary-General requested the Security Council to authorize four additional security units for UNOSOM, each numbering up to 750 troops. Two were to be deployed immediately around Bossasso on the northeast coast and adjacent to the preventive zone in the southwest; the others, intended for Berbera on the northwest coast and the port city of Kismayo in the southeast, would be deployed upon agreement "of those concerned." Boutros-Ghali also proposed the establishment of separate UNOSOM headquarters for each of the four operational zones approved by the Security Council in July but did not consider the deployment of cease-fire monitors outside Mogadishu feasible under the current circumstances [ibid.].

In its Resolution 775 of August 28, the Security Council endorsed the proposals regarding airlift and expanded headquarters and authorized the additional security forces. It also approved on September 8 the proposed deployment of a further 719 personnel constituting three logistical units, bringing the total authorized strength of UNOSOM to 4,219.

An intensified program of airlifts—or, for isolated towns, airdrops—had begun August 17 under the auspices of the WFP. By September 14 more than 1,500 tons of food had been delivered within the central and southern "hunger zone" [U.N. press release WFP/829, 9/15/92]. That same day the **Under-Secretary-General for Humanitarian Affairs, Jan Eliasson**, announced preliminary agreement on a "100-Day Action Program for Accelerated Humanitarian Assistance for Somalia" to meet the demands for food and non-food assistance from mid-October 1992 through mid-January 1993. Combining the services of the six U.N. agencies and programs active in Somalia, the $82.7 million plan called for massive infusions of food aid and supplementary feeding by WFP and UNICEF; the provision of basic health services, including a measles immunization campaign and maternal and child health care by UNICEF and WHO; and the supply of clean water, sanitation, and hygiene on an urgent and temporary basis by UNDP.

In the longer term, UNDP was also to assist in the reestablishment of essential services, including water supply, electric generation, and waste disposal as part of the overall effort to promote rehabilitation, employment, and stability. Also under the 100-Day Program, UNICEF would provide shelter materials, blankets, and clothing to internally displaced families; and UNHCR would combine these supplies with deliveries of food, seeds, and tools to prevent further refugee outflows and promote repatriation along the Somali border with Kenya. FAO would also undertake seeds and tools projects along with livestock health programs, including the delivery of animal vaccines, to aid in the long-term rehabilitation of the agricultural and livestock sectors at the core of the Somali economy [U.N. press releases IHA/469, 12/14/92; IHA/462, 10/13/92].

Heavily reliant on ground transport, the implementation of the 100-day program depended on the swift deployment of the **additional security units** authorized under Resolution 775. While deliveries by air had increased significantly in early October (Canada, Germany, and the United States had commenced airlift operations to the interior in support of ongoing WFP flights), potentially much larger deliveries by road were still stymied by opposition to further U.N. troop deployments, particularly from General Aidid and his supporters. In fact, the entire security situation in Somalia deteriorated badly during October and November.

Aidid withdrew his acceptance of U.N. troops for Kismayo and Berbera; and UNOSOM observers in the capital were hijacked and robbed, apparently by troops loyal to Ali Mahdi. The Pakistani troops, which finally secured the Mogadishu airport on November 10, came under heavy fire three days later, believed to be directed at them by Aidid's forces, and a WFP cargo ship was shelled in the port on November 24, reportedly by the Ali Mahdi faction. The Secretary-General also reported that relief agencies had been forced to pay "protection money" and "bribes" in order to guarantee the safety of their supplies and their 400-or-so civilian personnel. By late November the United Nations had gained the necessary consent for the deployment of additional security units only at Bossasso. Regarding the implementation of the 100-Day Program, the Secretary-General concluded that, "while massive amounts of relief supplies have been readied in the pipeline, . . . the humanitarian assistance that reaches its intended beneficiaries is often barely more than a trickle" [S/24859, 11/27/92].

In informal consultations held November 25, the Security Council agreed with the Secretary-General that the current situation was "intolerable" and that, to "create conditions for the uninterrupted delivery of relief supplies to the starving people of Somalia," it should consider a resort to the provisions of Chapter VII of the Charter governing the use of force. For his part, Boutros-Ghali set out five options for future action, including the continued deployment of UNOSOM to its authorized strength of 4,200 troops or the complete withdrawal of the operation. He dismissed the first as inadequate, and in rejecting the second he argued that more troops and a proper mandate (including wider rules of engagement) could overcome the current difficulties. Concerned that a U.N. "show of force" in Mogadishu, the third option, might not succeed in guaranteeing cooperation and unimpeded access to all parts of the country, the Secretary-General recommended a "country-wide enforcement operation," undertaken either by member states under the authorization of the Security Council (the fourth option) or by the United Nations itself. He stated his preference for an operation under U.N. command and control, if "feasible," but reported that **U.S. Secretary of State Lawrence Eagleburger** had informed him on November 25 of **U.S. readiness to "take the lead"** on implementing option four [S/24868, 11/31/92].

Reminiscent of the language it had adopted in 1991 to reverse Iraqi aggression in Kuwait, the Security Council on December 3 authorized the Secretary-General, the United States, and other troop contributors to "use all necessary means to establish a secure environment for humanitarian relief operations in Somalia" [S/Res/794 (1992)]. The resolution placed troops under U.N. auspices but "unified" command and control, and requested that the states involved coordinate the activities of their military contingents with the United Nations. The Security Council asserted what authority it had over the operation with respect to monitoring and reporting. It established an ad hoc committee to oversee the implementation of the resolution and invited the Secretary-General to detail UNOSOM liaisons to the unified command. Troop-contributing states were requested to report within 15 days on their participation in the operation and periodically thereafter. Finally, the Security Council emphasized the temporary and limited nature of the unified force's mandate by requesting the Secretary-General to draft a plan on the implementation (or revision) of UNOSOM's mandate following the withdrawal of the force.

Operation Restore Hope

Under the authority granted him in Resolution 794, President George Bush directed the execution of "Operation Restore Hope" on December 4, projected to involve 28,000 U.S. personnel and the more than 10,000 troops pledged by some 20 countries to the **"Unified Task Force" (UNITAF).** Concentrating on the hardest-hit areas in the south and center of the country—and constrained by Bush's informal pledge to have the troops home by Inauguration Day—U.S. planners proposed a limited, four-phase operation involving the establishment of a multinational presence in eight population centers. After securing the port and airport in Mogadishu as well as the airstrip at Baledogle, troops would push north and west to take control of relief centers at Baidoa, Oddur, Belet Weyne, and Gialassi. They would also drive south to occupy Kismayo and Bardera and secure the land corridor from Bardera to Baidoa. In the final phase of the operation, responsibility for security and the delivery of humanitarian relief would be gradually transferred to a U.N. peacekeeping force [S/24976, 12/18/92]. Even with the exclusion of the entire northern half of the country from the UNITAF operational plan, Pentagon officials estimated that its full implementation would require at least 60 days [*The New York Times*, 12/4/92].

After an unopposed landing in Mogadishu on December 9, the first U.S. troops immediately secured the port and airport and by December 16 had reached Baidoa, 160 miles west of the capital. The arrival there of a 20-truck relief convoy from Mogadishu on December 20 marked the opening of the first of six major relief supply routes to be established by U.S. and UNITAF forces [*The Christian Science Monitor*, 12/21/92]. With the assistance of Belgian, Canadian, French, and Italian troops, the last relief zone at Belet Weyne was secured on December 28. But sporadic fighting and looting continued in Mogadishu (despite a December 11 cease-fire) as well as in those parts of the country not under direct foreign control. On December 18 the U.S. command indicated that it might soon abandon its policy of disarming only those Somalis clearly threatening its troops and authorize the confiscation of all weapons not voluntarily surrendered in exchange for cash or other compensation [*The New York Times*, 12/18/92, 12/19/92].

The question of disarmament became a major point of contention between the United States and the United Nations in discussions of when and under what conditions the transition from UNITAF to a reorganized UNOSOM would occur. In his follow-up report to the Security Council, called for in Resolution 794 [S/24992, 12/19/92], the Secretary-General argued that the U.S.-led force should not withdraw before at least bringing heavy weapons under international control and disarming lawless gangs. He also pushed for an expansion of UNITAF operations to northern Somalia to address the humanitarian needs there and ensure that weapons and gangs were not temporarily moved into the area from the south pending the departure of U.S. troops. The United States, determined not to prolong its presence in Somalia by undertaking such dangerous and time-consuming tasks, argued that the United Nations should replace UNITAF as soon as possible with a heavily armed force provided with rules of engagement sufficiently broad to protect humanitarian activities under prevailing security conditions. Such a force, the Secretary-General claimed, was beyond the current capacity of the United Nations to manage and finance. Differences over what constituted a "secure environment" and U.N. insistence that UNITAF's success also be measured against demonstrable improvements in the humanitarian and political situation delayed the development of a specific and concrete transition plan.

Some progress was made on both political and security issues at the U.N.-sponsored Informal Preparatory Meeting on Somali Political Reconciliation, convened January 4, 1993, in Addis Ababa. Representatives of 14 Somali "political movements" (factional leaders) signed agreements on January 8 providing for an immediate and binding cease-fire throughout the country and, pending a final settlement, the concentration of heavy weapons and the disarmament of militias under UNITAF and UNOSOM supervision [S/25168, 1/26/93]. They also agreed to convene a national reconciliation conference on March 15 and provide inventories of weapons to the U.N. forces.

In response to numerous sniping incidents and occasional interfactional clashes, U.S. troops had already stepped up efforts to seize and destroy arms caches in Mogadishu. Relying on random tips and limited sweeps of the city rather than undertaking a comprehensive disarmament campaign, they had nevertheless collected a sizable arsenal by mid-February: 1.27 million rounds of light ammunition; more than 129,000 rounds of heavy ammunition; 2,255 small arms; and 636 heavy weapons, including tanks, mortars, grenade, rocket, and missile launchers, and even surface-to-air missiles [*The New York Times*, 2/16/93]. The United States was also taking the lead in organizing local police forces, planning for the deployment of some 3,500 police in Mogadishu alone. Some 300 unarmed officers had already been fielded in the city and 300 more in Kismayo, with U.N. financial support [*The Washington Post*, 1/30/93].

The humanitarian situation had improved dramatically since the arrival of UNITAF, though theft, looting, and extortion remained problems. By January 20 some 40,000 tons of relief supplies had been brought through the port of Mogadishu, including 8,000 tons of medicines, seeds, tools, and veterinary supplies. Kismayo's port, closed at the end of September by factional fighting, had also been reopened. "Humanitarian Operations Centers" had been established in Mogadishu and Kismayo as well as in the interior at Belet Weyne, Oddur, Bardera, and Gialassi to coordinate activities between UNITAF and U.N. and NGO relief workers. Escorted road convoys had delivered 25,000 tons of food, with the remainder either airlifted or airdropped [S/25168].

Increased security and the expiration of the 100-Day Plan on January 19 moved the United Nations to unveil a new "Relief and Rehabilitation Program" for Somalia on March 4, de-emphasizing emergency food aid and concentrating on longer-term reconstruction. The $166.5 million effort covered ten "core" activities, including reestablishing local administration and regional police forces; encouraging the return of 800,000 refugees and a million internally displaced Somalis; developing systems for basic health care and public education; increasing the availability of potable water and sanitation and creating public works jobs; and expanding outputs in the agriculture and livestock sectors of the economy and promoting "food security" [U.N. press release IHA/479, SOM 11, 3/4/93]. Donor countries agreed to fund only $130 million of the program, however—mostly for food self-sufficiency, job creation, and public education—pending increased security for relief workers and progress toward a political settlement [*The Washington Post*, 5/14/93].

Growing restless with a humanitarian mission largely accomplished, and disillusioned by their inability to solve the larger security problem in the absence of a peace agreement, U.S. troops accelerated their withdrawal begun in the final days of the Bush administration. From a high of 25,800 in mid-January (less than originally projected due to unexpectedly large contributions from more than 30 other U.N. member states), the size of the U.S. contingent in UNITAF had fallen to 16,000 by the end of February and the number of non U.S. troops had risen to almost 15,000. Frustration was also growing among U.S. military planners with the slow progress in developing transition arrangements to a U.N.-led operation. Finally, in his report of March 3 [S/25354], the Secretary-General announced May 1 as the target date for the "formal transfer of command" from UNITAF to what would be called **UNOSOM II**. His report detailed the deployment of a large and expensive peace-enforcement operation, the first of its kind under U.N. command, with a broad mandate and unprecedented U.S. participation.

Authorized under Chapter VII of the Charter and not subject to the approval of any Somali faction, UNOSOM II would combine the limited humanitarian mandate of UNITAF with more general security functions and expand the international presence in Somalia to the entire country. In addition to protecting U.N. and nongovernmental personnel, facilities, and equipment (pending the establishment of a new Somali police force), UNOSOM II was to monitor compliance with cease-fires, especially under the Addis Ababa agreements of January 8; respond with force if necessary to violations or threatened violations of those agreements; seize small arms of irregular forces; and assist in repatriation activities and the removal of "many hundreds of thousands" or perhaps "millions" of landmines. The 20,000-man military component of the operation would also oversee the implementation of the disarmament provisions of the Addis Ababa agreements by maintaining control over heavy weapons surrendered by organized militias and establishing "transition sites" for the concentration of factional fighters and separate "cantonment sites" for the storage of their personal arms.

The United States would contribute to an 8,000-man logistical unit for UNOSOM II—the first U.S. troops to serve under U.N. command, albeit in noncombat roles—and position an additional 1,000 troops offshore as a rapid reaction force. This force, to be deployed if necessary, would remain under U.S. command. The transition from UNITAF to UNOSOM II would take place gradually, area by area, as rehabilitation and political reconciliation progressed. After assuming operational control at headquarters, the United Nations would begin deploying its forces throughout the country. Once the United Nations had consolidated its control and fully deployed its forces, UNOSOM II would begin enforcing the cease-fire and assisting local authorities in reestablishing and maintaining law and order. When a national police force was able to take over the latter duties, the remainder of UNITAF would withdraw. The cost of the operation, including a civilian staff of 2,800, was estimated at $856 million for the first six months [U.N. press release SC/5573, 3/26/93].

In approving the deployment of UNOSOM II on March 26 [A/Res/814 (1993)], the Security Council requested the Secretary-General to submit as soon as possible his recommendations for the establishment of Somali police forces at all levels. The Secretary-General was also to issue progress reports on the operation's activities at 90-day intervals to allow the Security Council to conduct a formal review of UNOSOM II by the conclusion of its first mandate period on October 31, 1993. With further commitments from the international community to maintain security and promote reconstruction in hand, 15 factional leaders signed the Agreement of the First Session of the Conference of National Reconciliation in Somalia at Addis Ababa on March 27, after 13 days of on-and-off talks. The agreement calls for the disarmament of the factional militias within 90 days and establishes a 74-seat Transitional National Council to serve as an interim government in advance of elections in 1995. Arrangements were also made for autonomous councils on the regional and local levels, the drafting of a provisional constitution ("charter"), and the establishment of an independent judiciary [U.N. press release SG/SM/4953, SOM/18, 3/29/93; *The Washington Post*, 3/28/93].

The turnover of command took place without incident or fanfare on May 4, just two days behind schedule. The last 340 U.S. servicemen attached to UNITAF had departed the previous day, leaving behind 3,625 of their colleagues in communications and other support roles until replacements could be found. Another 1,381 U.S. personnel in the quick reaction force, officially counted among the 21,521 UNOSOM personnel already deployed, would remain "indefinitely." U.N. sources indicated that the operation would likely remain in Somalia at least two years. Already by mid-May, significant progress had been made in fulfilling one of the conditions for UNOSOM's withdrawal: the building of an effective police force. In Mogadishu alone 2,840 policemen were directing traffic, controlling crowds, and protecting feeding centers; 2,000 more were performing similar duty in other major cities [*The Washington Post*, 5/5/93, 5/17/93].

Aside from reports on the U.S. troop withdrawal and occasionally on the efforts of UNOSOM II, media coverage of Mogadishu was relatively light during the last days of May. Peaceful disarmament remained a priority for U.N. peacekeepers as they confiscated rifles, submachine guns, grenades, and other weapons.

The relative success of Operation Restore Hope lent credence to the idea that the "[United States] could go into Somalia quickly, get out quickly and turn it over to the U.N." [*Newsweek*, 6/21/93]. Thus, Somalia became the litmus test for determining whether the U.S. could "help keep peace in the world" without having to do it all by itself [ibid.].

The resolve of the international community to bring peace to Somalia was stiffened by the events of June 5, when a group of Pakistani U.N. peacekeepers was ambushed while inspecting an arms dump where Aidid's military stored their weapons. The incident sent a tremor through the international community that would be felt for weeks. Three military inspections had been carried out successfully that day, but at one location—adjacent to a radio station sympathetic to the Aidid regime—the inspectors were ambushed by sniper fire. As later reported, the radio announcers stirred up public sentiment against the peacekeepers with reports that the U.N. troops were ready to seize the station. The U.N. forces were then surrounded by a mob of angry demonstrators led by a group of women and children, the gunmen behind them. According to Jamsheed K. A. Marker, Permanent Representative of Pakistan to the United Nations, the Pakistani troops held their fire until "they were physically overwhelmed by Aidid criminals and brutally murdered and mutilated." The troops had been operating under instructions of extreme self-restraint. Nevertheless, the rules governing engagement were clear: Troops are authorized to fire upon armed gunmen regardless of whether they are hiding in crowds [minutes of a press conference by Jamsheed K. A. Marker, 6/15/93].

Civilian demonstrations around the inspectors became more violent and were mirrored by similar eruptions at U.N. headquarters in Mogadishu. Later that day, according to a U.N. report, a Pakistani Army unit was caught "in a carefully prepared 3-sided ambush" while driving to investigate another incident in the capital city. The soldiers were pinned down for two-and-a-half hours by sniper fire but were later rescued by a contingent of U.S. troops.

The events of June 5 meshed together into an ugly picture of the Somali warlord: Aidid had staged the incidents in a deliberate attempt to discredit the U.N. forces by inciting them to fire on unarmed civilians. The Pakistani force was targeted by Aidid because it was regarded as vulnerable and inadequately equipped.

In condemning Aidid's premeditated attacks, the Security Council reaffirmed its "commitment to assist the people of Somalia in re-establishing conditions of normal life" [S/Res/837, 6/6/93]. Further, it pledged to continue the fight to restore law and order and to contribute to humanitarian relief, reconciliation, and political settlement. Invoking Chapter VII of the U.N. Charter, which authorizes the use of force, the Council demanded that "all Somalia parties including movements and factions comply fully with the commitments they have undertaken . . . on implementing the cease-fire" [ibid.].

All told, the June 5 attacks killed 22 Pakistani soldiers and 15 Somalis and wounded 54 Pakistanis and 3 Americans [*The New York Times*, 6/16/93]. The following week saw Mogadishu in a state of shock and uncertainty; preparing for a likely U.N. retaliation, dozens of nonessential U.N. relief workers fled to Nairobi, Kenya, while Somalis also began evacuating women and children from the city.

By June 14, Somali storage sites, rocket launchers, and one of Aidid's radio stations had been hit in three successive retaliatory strikes by American gunships and attack helicopters. Yet military strategists encountered a number of problems that compromised the effectiveness of the operation: a lack of proper equipment for ground soldiers and the intricacies of communicating with a multilingual force of 1,400 troops with varying degrees of military training. When the Arabic-speaking Moroccans backing the Urdu-speaking Pakistanis were pinned by Somali gunfire, they had to rely on hand signals to communicate with U.S. officers.

General Aidid sought to prevent U.N. retaliation by using women and children as human shields, with the result that many were caught in the crossfire. U.S. cameramen filming a daylight attack on June 13 witnessed a rocket hitting a tea stall, just short of its military target, wounding 12. These incidents, in addition to the razing of a Digfer Hospital operating room, killing several patients, did little to validate the claim of Adm. Jonathon Howe, Special Representative for Somalia, that the attack was a "surgical strike." Still, unfazed by Somali chants of "Down with Clinton," Maj. David Stockwell, a U.N. spokesman, pledged to continue the attacks [ibid., 6/15/93].

Some relief agencies have become concerned that the initial goal of military intervention—to allow humanitarian operations to continue unimpeded—has been supplanted by the military objective of removing Somalia's warlords from power. Aided by vituperative statements issued by Radio Mogadishu against the United Nations and the United States, Aidid has been able to portray U.N. peacekeeping forces as oppressive and evil. Conversely, Aidid's image among many Somalis borders on the messianic: In the words of his daughter, "[Aidid] is the Gandhi of Somalia, and everyone loves him. He is a man of peace who has always fought for peace" [*Newsweek*, 6/28/93].

Aidid responded to the U.N. attacks by requesting a cease-fire and offering to negotiate with U.N. officials. Admiral Howe warned that no negotiations would take place until Aidid agreed to disarm his troops and end the campaign of violence against U.N. forces. Empowered by Security Resolution 837, Howe reaffirmed the authority of the UNOSOM II forces to investigate, arrest, and detain those individuals responsible for the armed attack, including Aidid himself [*The Economist*, 6/19/93].

U.N. officials have some reason to be optimistic. In northern Mogadishu important political developments have improved the prospects for disarmament. Warlord Ali Mahdi, Aidid's main rival, has allowed the U.N. control over his heavy artillery. In Kismayo, a city still rent by rival factions—one aligned with Aidid, the other with Mahdi—leaders of both factions have agreed to disarm [*The Christian Science Monitor*, 6/18/93]. Observers in the north have also reported that neither gunmen nor heavy artillery can be spotted in the streets.

Regarding the proposal to arrest General Aidid, the question arises what to do with him when he is caught. To arrest Aidid under the U.N. flag would set a precedent. Who, then, would be responsible for setting up the tribunal? Should the trial take place in Somalia, which has no independent judiciary, or should an independent court be convened? These and other question must be resolved as the U.N. prepares to expand its traditional role in peacekeeping to include peace enforcement.

5. Central America and the Caribbean
By Edmund T. Piasecki

The governments of the five Central American states came closer in 1992 to achieving their ultimate goals of peace, democracy, and development, with a formal cessation of hostilities in El Salvador, the building of a free market economy in Nicaragua, and the initiation of substantive negotiations aimed at settling the region's remaining conflict in Guatemala. The General Assembly applauded these efforts at its 47th Session, as it has annually since the signing of the **Esquipulus II Agreement** in 1987, in which the states of the region committed themselves to a policy of reconciliation and peaceful settlement of disputes [A/Res/47/118].

The processes of national reconciliation and economic reconstruction now under way in El Salvador and Nicaragua may result in increased international attention to the region's longest running and bloodiest conflict, the civil war in Guatemala, which has already claimed 120,000 lives over the past three decades. Stepped-up competition for scarce foreign aid and investment along with heightened scrutiny of a deplorable human rights record have already pushed the right-wing government and its left-wing guerrilla opponents toward greater flexibility in the negotiations that opened in April 1991.

Nicaragua

By the fall of 1992, Nicaragua had made significant progress in overcoming the political, economic, and social upheavals wrought by eight years of civil war. Following U.N.-monitored elections in April 1990, a democratic government had been installed in a peaceful turnover of power after 12 years of leftist Sandinista rule. Some 24,000 U.S.-backed rebels, or "contras," had been disarmed, again under international supervision, and the government had reduced the size (if not the influence) of the armed forces from 96,000 to 17,000 men. Government-sponsored "disarmament brigades" had also collected nearly 50,000 weapons from civilian hands. Even inflation, which by official estimates had reached 55,000% in 1991, had been reduced to zero, according to government figures. Nicaraguan President Violeta Barrios de Chamorro could claim in her September 21 address to the General Assembly to have met what she called the country's main challenges: reestablishing peace, introducing democratic rule, and ending hyperinflation [A/47/PV.4].

Progress on the remaining problems, however, was likely to be less dramatic and far more difficult. Reactivating a stagnant economy laboring under an IMF structural-adjustment program and 40% unemployment would be heavily dependent on continued high levels of foreign assistance. Although the U.S. had been a major donor of such assistance, the Bush administration had stopped disbursement of a $731 million, two-year aid package in June, reportedly under pressure from conservative Republicans in Congress dissatisfied with continuing Sandinista control of the army and national police and delays in returning properties confiscated during Sandinista rule [*The New York Times*, 9/3/92]. Facing payments by the end of the month to the international financial institutions whose cooperation was vital to the continued pursuit of economic stabilization [*The Economist*, 9/12/92], Chamorro appeared before the General Assembly in an effort both to encourage the release of U.S. funding and appeal for additional multilateral assistance.

Reintegrating demobilized rebels and soldiers into economic and social life and dealing with recurring outbreaks of violence by rearmed contras and Sandinista soldiers were not problems that macroeconomic restructuring and stabilization could necessarily solve. By the fall of 1992 the "recontras" had organized themselves into small but well-supplied and disciplined units, demanding the ouster of Sandinista party members from the government and an end to the "systematic" murder of former rebel leaders. Capable of mounting frequent attacks on military targets in the agriculturally strategic northwest, the groups constituted a minimal security threat but placed a constant strain on scarce government resources. The 600-or-so insurgents adamantly refused government offers of cash, vehicles, and land, arguing that ongoing disputes over property rights denied them the proof of ownership they needed to obtain credit and agricultural loans [*The Washington Post*, 11/15/92]. Demobilized Sandinista soldiers were themselves rearming and taking retribution against large landowners for government rollbacks of confiscations authorized under the former regime.

The social fabric of the country was further strained by a series of earthquakes and a tsunami, which had struck Nicaragua's Pacific coast on September 1, inflicting some $20 million in damage and leaving 150 dead and 16,000 homeless [*The Economist*, 9/12/92]. In response to these losses and the strains of postwar political and economic transformation, Nicaragua requested that a new item be inscribed on the General Assembly agenda, "International Assistance for the Rehabilitation of Nicaragua: Aftermath of the War and Natural Disasters." Under a resolution carrying the same title, the General Assembly requested the Secretary-General to provide "all possible assistance to support the consolidation of peace" and specified as priority areas the settlement of displaced and demobilized people and refugees, land ownership and land tenure in rural areas, direct care of war victims, mine clearance, and the restoration of the productive areas of the country. The Secretary-General was further requested to report on the implementation of the resolution at the 48th Session [A/Res/47/169].

Although the U.N. system was doing what it could to aid in the national reconstruction effort, Nicaragua remained the second poorest country in the hemisphere after Haiti. The World Bank had given the country access to the funds of the affiliated International Development Association, which deals exclusively with the world's poorest nations, and the U.N. Development Programme (UNDP) had agreed to treat Nicaragua as it would a least-developed country without requiring its official reclassification into that category [A/C.2/47/SR.8]. The economy grew at a rate of 0.5% in 1992, after eight years of decline, and the government had been successful in persuading the major donors in the Paris Club to forgive 75% of its foreign debt, but a serious balance of payments deficit persisted. The United States was due three-quarters of the $600 million owed [*The Washington Post*, 2/8/93].

The government, for its part, was taking steps to address the "culture of violence" and the conditions of extreme poverty that had contributed to economic instability and civil unrest. Within the framework of the 1987 Esquipulus II Agreement, Nicaragua was cooperating with other Central American countries in eliminating illegal traffic in weapons and facilitating the removal of some 130,000 landmines throughout the country [A/C.1/47/PV.18]. The government had arrived at measures to provide a legal solution to the problem of property rights through broad-based debate in the Forum for National Consultation, and had established a Ministry of Social Affairs to deal with the most pressing needs of health, education, housing, and unemployment. Nicaragua had also established a national education program on human rights with the assistance of the European Community, opened an Office of the Attorney General for Human Rights, empowered the Ministry of the Interior to monitor the observance of international standards by the police, and introduced the topic into police and military training programs [A/C.3/47/SR.44].

Noting such progress, the United States released $54 million of the $104 million of unspent aid on December 4, 1992, earmarking $40 million to replenish Nicaragua's foreign currency reserves, pay oil-import fees, and meet obligations to the IMF, the World Bank, and the Inter-American Development Bank. Funds were also designated for strengthening democratic institutions and respect for human rights [*The New York Times*, 12/5/92].

Despite President Chamorro's efforts to promote the rule of law and redress social grievances, 1993 does not appear to be the year of sustained economic recovery, social harmony, and political stability that she had hoped. Inflation rose to 9% in January, and the number of unemployed or underemployed climbed to 53% of the population. Clashes continued between rearmed rebels and government forces along the Honduran border, fed by the availability of an estimated 30,000 weapons [*The Washington Post*, 2/8/93]. And the President's attempts to consolidate what she termed the political center—by engineering the removal of the right-wing UNO coalition from control in the National Assembly and by placing Sandinista deputies in leadership positions—precipitated an ongoing political crisis that threatens to recall her from power [*The Christian Science Monitor*, 1/12/93, 3/2/93]. With the parties that had backed her election now in opposition, President Chamorro retains a mere one-seat majority in the legislature, owing to the support of her former political opponents.

Although Nicaragua has been the third largest recipient of U.S. foreign aid over the last three years, receiving more than $1 billion since the elections of April 1990, congressional critics charge that human rights abuses, corruption, and de facto Sandinista control of the government through the army and the police continue unchecked [*Congressional Record*, 4/2/93, p. S4371]. Action to institute a judicial review process for some 18,000 outstanding property claims and initiate a compensation system of government bonds for displaced owners [*The Washington Post*, 2/23/93] has resulted, critics say, in the return of only one property to a U.S. citizen. The Clinton administration nevertheless announced its intention on April 3 to release the remaining $50 million in U.S. assistance, citing Nicaragua's ongoing cooperation with the Organization of American States in an assessment of the human rights situation throughout the country, the suspension of police officers accused of human rights violations, and the establishment of arbitration procedures governing the disposition of expropriated property [ibid., 4/3/93].

El Salvador

The cease-fire declared February 1, 1992, between the government of El Salvador and its rebel opponents continued to hold throughout the spring even as both sides were falling seriously behind schedule in complying with other key aspects of the Peace Agreement they had signed January 16 in Mexico City. Residual suspicions between the parties and the unrealistically tight timetable for implementation contained in the accords were holding up the numerous reforms promised by the government and the demobilization of the guerrilla forces of the **Farabundo Martí National Liberation Front (FMLN)**. "Deeply concerned about the many delays," the Security Council issued a presidential statement on June 3, 1992, urging "good faith" efforts to implement the peace provisions in full and "by the agreed time-limits" [S/24058]. Through consultations opened in May between the government and rebel leaders under the mediation of officials from the **U.N. Observer Mission in El Salvador (ONUSAL)**, arrangements were finalized June 12 for the adjustment of several dates specified in the original timetable [S/23999/Add 1, 6/19/92]. The peace process, scheduled to culminate October 31, 1992, in the complete demobilization of the FMLN and a formal cessation of hostilities, appeared to be back on track.

The revised timetable, issued June 17, covered the core security aspects of the Peace Agreement, including the concentration of all forces in designated locations; the disarming and demobilization of some 8,000 rebel fighters in 20% increments; the deployment of a new National Civil Police force to replace the government-controlled National Police; and the abolition of the National Guard and the Treasury Police, heavily implicated in human rights abuses. Post-conflict issues were also addressed, among them the legalization of the FMLN as a political party, the finalization of social and economic programs to facilitate the reintegration of former rebels into civilian life, and the verification of an FMLN inventory of land occupied by rebel sympathizers in the former zones of conflict. But the revisions upset the delicate balance in the Peace Agreement between the gradual implementation of governmental reforms and the phased demobilization of rebel combatants, resulting in further disagreements and delays.

Under the original timetable the government was to have implemented certain key reforms—especially the provision of land to former guerrillas and the deployment of an independent police force—before the FMLN had affected the complete disarmament and demobilization of its forces. The new schedule still obligated the FMLN to fully dismantle its military structure completely by October 31, largely at the insistence of the government, but pushed the deadlines for governmental action on land reform and civilian policing—expensive and complicated undertakings—well beyond that date. The unwillingness of the FMLN to dissolve itself as a military force before the government had addressed the property and human rights concerns at the heart of the conflict required the U.N. to reestablish the balance between rebel and government action foreseen in the peace accords through additional adjustments to the timetable.

The First and Second Revisions

The government and the FMLN largely abided by the revisions through June and July, concentrating the bulk of their forces by June 26, nearly two months behind the original schedule. (Some 200 guerrillas remained outside the designated assembly points, however.) On June 30 the first contingent of more than 1,600 rebel fighters turned over 220 weapons to U.N. peacekeepers and left the safe zones [*The New York Times*, 7/26/92]. ONUSAL issued them identity cards confirming their civilian status and the government provided food, clothing, and cash as promised, but the distribution of land to former rebels awaited the settlement of the entire land-tenure problem. Because U.N. and Salvadoran officials regarded the number of arms surrendered as unrealistically low, ONUSAL requested the handover of additional weapons to approximate 20% of the known FMLN arsenal. Arguing that the first contingent consisted largely of "support personnel" who had generally been unarmed, rebel leaders nevertheless agreed to surrender more weapons at a later date.

The government passed legislation abolishing the National Guard and the Treasury Police in late June, three months later than originally agreed, and on July 30 declared the FMLN a "political party in formation," a step toward its legalization. But difficulties in finding permanent headquarters and sufficient funding for the new National Public Security Academy, rescheduled to open by July 15, continued to delay the training of the National Civil Police force. In addition, the government refused to abandon the practice of transferring demobilized Guard and

Treasury personnel to the National Police and had even attempted to win senior positions for them in the security academy, despite strong objections from ONUSAL. Regarding rebel compliance, the United Nations had raised serious questions as to the accuracy of an FMLN inventory of arms submitted in February and an expanded inventory of occupied land submitted in June. Using what leverage it had over the peace process, the FMLN ignored the July 31 deadline for the disarming and demobilization of the second 20% of its forces—though it complied on August 18 with ONUSAL's request for additional weapons from the first disarmament phase—and further adjustments to the timetable became necessary.

Following a visit to El Salvador by then Under-Secretary-General for Peacekeeping Operations Marrack Goulding, a second revised timetable was agreed upon August 19, again retaining October 31 as the date for the complete reintegration of FMLN personnel. On August 31 the six-month training program got under way for the first 622 recruits at the police academy, and the government demobilized the first of five U.S.-trained rapid-deployment battalions—instrumental in the counterinsurgency campaigns waged against rebel guerrillas—slated for elimination under agreed-upon reductions in the country's armed forces. In early September the **Commission on the Consolidation of the Peace (COPAZ)**, consisting of equal government and FMLN representation with a U.N. observer, began verifying the ownership of some 4,000 properties in former zones of conflict on the basis of the June inventory [*The Christian Science Monitor*, 9/4/92]. The government dismantled a second rapid-response unit and began dissolving the third on September 22, while the FMLN completed the disarmament and reintegration of a second rebel contingent on September 24. But the FMLN's rejection of a government-proposed land-transfer program covering demobilized soldiers as well as former guerrillas threatened to delay the entire peace process once again.

After receiving technical advice from the Food and Agriculture Organization (FAO), the IMF, and the World Bank, the **Secretary-General dispatched Marrack Goulding and his Special Representative to Central America, Alvaro de Soto,** to San Salvador on September 28 in search of a compromise solution. On October 13, Boutros-Ghali presented both sides with a proposal meeting government demands for the inclusion of former soldiers in a land-distribution scheme and satisfying rebel concerns that the ownership rights of current landholders in the former conflict zones (i.e., FMLN supporters occupying land in territories previously under rebel control) be formalized and evictions from these properties prohibited. The FMLN and the government accepted the proposal on October 15 and October 16, respectively, and the land distribution program, originally scheduled for full implementation by July, was set to start.

The Third Revision

Having suspended the disarmament and demobilization of its personnel on September 30 in protest over the land-distribution problem, the FMLN had again fallen behind schedule for the reintegration of its forces into civilian life. Meeting the October 31 deadline for the formal cessation of hostilities no longer appeared feasible. On October 23 the Secretary-General proposed to both sides a third, and he emphasized final, adjustment to the original timetable under which the reintegration of the remaining 60% of rebel forces would commence October 31 and proceed in three phases to completion on December 15. The FMLN accepted the revisions on October 26, subject to their acceptance by the other side, and disarmed and demobilized a further 1,500 personnel by October 31.

The government, however, announced on October 28 the suspension of its program for restructuring and reducing the armed forces called for in the accords and conditioned its resumption on the submission of a complete weapons inventory by the FMLN. It also raised questions about the new dates offered for the implementation of the recommendations of the **Ad Hoc Commission on the Purification of the Armed Forces,** charged under the Peace Agreement with identifying army officers to be "purged" from the service for suspected human rights violations.

To reach an accommodation with the government on these matters, the Secretary-General sent Goulding and de Soto once again to San Salvador on October 30. After seven days of negotiations, the government accepted the Secretary-General's proposal in full, including the December 15 deadline, but stipulated that reductions in its forces would proceed only upon the receipt of explicit confirmation by the United Nations that rebel weapons had been inventoried, collected, and destroyed. This marked the first time that the United Nations had allowed one side to condition its compliance with specific provisions of the Peace Agreement on corresponding action from the other side. The FMLN was to submit a final weapons inventory and concentrate its weapons in the safe zones by November 30 and begin their destruction on December 1. The government was to notify the Secretary-General by November 29 on the "administrative decisions" necessary to implement the purge of army officers. The peace process, the Secretary-General said, was "entering an especially delicate phase" [S/24805, 11/13/92].

In the meantime the Secretary-General had asked the Security Council for a one-month extension of ONUSAL's mandate through November 30 to verify the implementation of the final steps toward a cessation of hostilities. The Council granted the request on October 30 by adopting Resolution 784 and requested him in turn to submit recommendations on the mandate and staffing required to oversee compliance with the Peace Agreement through December and beyond.

While the Security Council was voting and negotiations over the third timetable were still under way, the government officially initiated the national land-transfer program on October 31, signing with the FMLN an agreement to hand over two state-owned properties to demobilized rebels and the current peasant occupiers. Under the Secretary-General's October 13 plan, plots of 3.5-to-12 acres would be distributed to 7,500 former guerrillas, 25,000 peasant families who had supported the rebel cause, and 15,000 demobilized soldiers. Problems are expected throughout the implementation process, as the government currently holds only a third of the 407,000 acres to be distributed, and $85 million will be required to purchase the balance from private landowners [*The New York Times*, 10/18/92]. Continued land seizures by rebel supporters have also raised tensions in the former zones of conflict, and the FMLN has requested a halt to that practice.

By the end of November, progress achieved in implementing the peace accords had allowed the Secretary-General to reduce the strength of ONUSAL by some 100 personnel, and approximately 100 more were scheduled for withdrawal in January 1993 following the complete demobilization of rebel forces. ONUSAL would be further reduced by 300 after the National Civil Police became fully operational in early 1994. In extending the operation's mandate for six months through May 31, 1993 [S/Res/791 (1992)], the Council underscored its concern about anonymous threats appearing in Salvadoran newspapers aimed at FMLN leaders, politicians, and U.N. personnel as the date neared for the purge of human rights violators in the army.

Final Demobilization and the Cessation of Hostilities

On November 29 the government duly issued the administrative decisions it had promised the Secretary-General regarding the removal of military personnel named by the Ad Hoc Commission. Immediately following Boutros-Ghali's December 1 announcement that the government was in compliance with this provision of the peace accords, the FMLN completed the demobilization of 1,300 more guerrillas [*The Washington Post*, 12/2/92], whose reintegration had been suspended on November 28. This fourth contingent brought to more than 6,000 the number of FMLN combatants disarmed and demobilized since the start of the reintegration process in June. Those still retaining their arms were the best-equipped, most battle-hardened veterans constituting the core of the rebel force.

The FMLN also submitted a final inventory of its weapons shortly thereafter, reportedly increasing by 16% its previous tally of 4,500 arms and including surface-to-surface missiles for the first time [*The New York Times*, 12/2/92]. Destruction began December 3, and the Secretary-General announced December 8 that the inventory had been analyzed and "found satisfactory" [U.N. press release SG/SM/4873, CA/69, 12/8/92]. On the same day, the government completed the demobilization of the third and most notorious of its rapid-deployment battalions, Atlacatl, implicated in numerous atrocities, including the 1981 massacre at El Mozote and the 1989 slayings of six Jesuit priests and two others. According to unofficial estimates, the government had reduced the overall size of the armed forces in the preceding 12-month period from 62,000 to 41,000 men [*The New York Times*, 12/9/92].

Difficulties in convincing mid-level rebel commanders to comply with the fifth and final phase of disarmament and demobilization delayed U.N. certification of the complete reintegration of FMLN combatants until 6:40 p.m. December 14 [ibid., 12/15/92]. After some 1,800 guerrillas surrendered their weapons and 55 surface-to-air missiles to ONUSAL, the Supreme Electoral Council registered the FMLN, no longer an "armed political group," as a legal political party [*The Washington Post*, 12/16/92]. In ceremonies held December 15 to mark the "National Day of Reconciliation," the Secretary-General declared: "The armed conflict in El Salvador has come to an end." "Many steps [had] been taken toward achieving" democratization, and respect for human rights was being "gradually consolidated," he continued, but "the reunification of Salvadoran society [was] still not within reach" and remained a "long-term goal" [U.N. press release SG/SM/4811,CA/71, 12/15/92].

After spending over $5 billion to support the government in its 12-year war, most of it in military assistance and grants, the United States sent then-Vice President Dan Quayle to the ceremonies to announce plans to forgive 75% of El Salvador's debt to Washington for economic and food aid. The $456 million deal will reportedly reduce government debt repayments by $19.3 million in 1993 and may facilitate access to additional foreign credits for the national reconstruction effort. The United States is also the largest donor to the National Reconstruction Plan, endorsed by the General Assembly on December 18 [A/Res/47/158], promising $250 million of the $800 million pledged to date [*The New York Times*, 12/16/92; *The Christian Science Monitor*, 12/18/92].

The Purge of the Armed Forces

Controversy and rumor had surrounded the work of the three-man Ad Hoc Commission on the Purification of the Armed Forces since it had submitted its report to Boutros-Ghali and El Salvadoran President Alfredo Cristiani in late September. Although the recommendations of the Commission as well as the timing and method of their implementation remained officially confidential, the media had speculated widely on the number and names of army officers subject to removal or reassignment, the dates by which the government was to take such action, and the means through which it would protect the identities of those implicated. By one accounting, the Commission had cited a total of 110 officers of the rank of lieutenant colonel and above and had recommended 76 for immediate dismissal and 34 for transfer from command positions [*The Washington Post*, 1/1/93, 1/4/93]. Press reports also held that the "administrative decisions" adopted by the government on November 29 called for the dismissal or transfer of one group of officers in December and that a second set of decisions, to be issued at the end of that month, would take effect in January and cover the remaining personnel. It was believed that the identities of officers to be purged were to be disguised by mixing their names with those of other officers subject to regular retirement or routine transfer.

Cristiani had reportedly fought hard during the negotiations in November over the third revised timetable for a delay in the implementation of selected recommendations, arguing that certain officers had to be retained permanently and others temporarily to oversee ongoing reductions in the armed forces and help guarantee the army's compliance with other aspects of the accords. The U.N. mediators rejected these claims, and the army leadership began to complain publicly that the Commission had failed to make or substantiate specific charges and had denied purged officers due process. (The Commission made its decisions on the basis of broad criteria: an officer's demonstrated respect for human rights, his professional competence, and his ability to function effectively in the postwar army [*The New York Times*, 11/5/92].) In direct talks with FMLN leaders throughout December, Cristiani reportedly offered additional land and increased financial support for demobilized rebel combatants in return for an agreement permitting some 34 officers nearing retirement to continue their service until eligible for pensions. The talks broke off without an agreement, and, facing an army high command threatening "individual acts of insubordination," the President failed to include the names of any of the implicated officers in the "general order" issued December 31 [*The Washington Post*, 1/1/93].

The Secretary-General responded immediately and directly. The personnel decisions announced by the government "do not conform to the recommendations of the Ad Hoc Commission," he said in a January 1 statement, and the government "has not complied with its commitment" under the peace accords [U.N. press release SG/SM/4891, CA/74, 1/4/93]. According to press sources, Cristiani was seeking to bring the government into compliance by winning U.N. approval of modifications he had made to certain recommendations of the Ad Hoc Commission and the phasing of others over several months.

In a set of secret administrative orders made public on January 4, copies of which were delivered to U.N. Headquarters the following day, Cristiani had reportedly implemented the Commission's recommendations in full regarding the 34 officers believed to be subject to transfer from command positions but was said to have dismissed only 23 of the 76 others presumed slated for ouster. Of the remaining 53 officers, Cristiani had removed 38 from active duty, the press said, placing them "at the disposition" of the armed forces and allowing them to receive pay and to acquire the time in service required to retire with full pensions. The President had also reportedly retained the final 15 officers permanently, transferring 7 to foreign postings and allowing 8—including Defense Minister Rene Emilio Ponce and his deputy, Juan Orlando Zepeda—to remain in office through the end of his current term in 1994 [*The Washington Post*, 1/6/93].

In a January 9 letter to the Security Council, the Secretary-General revealed for the first time that the Ad Hoc Commission had recommended action against 103, not 110 officers. One had already left active service, the Secretary-General said, and of the remaining 102 officers, 76 were to be discharged, as had been reported, and 26 transferred. As of January 1 the government had dismissed 23 officers, the number mentioned by the media, and reassigned 25. The Secretary-General also confirmed that 38 other officers nearing retirement had been placed on "leave with pay," and another officer had been permitted to remain on active duty until retiring on March 1.

The Secretary-General considered the government in full compliance with its obligations regarding the transfers and dismissals and said the measures taken with respect to the other 39 officers complied "broadly" with the recommendations of the Ad Hoc Commission. He also corroborated press reports on the status of the remaining 15 officers and stated that government actions taken in that regard "do not comply" with the recommendations and "are thus not in conformity" with the Peace Agreement. The Secretary-General urged "early action to regularize the positions" of those officers [S/25078]. President Cristiani, however, had already announced his refusal to consider "major" changes in his implementation of the recommendations. The Security Council expressed its "concern" over these developments and "strongly" urged the government to play its part in completing the process of peace-building and national reconciliation [S/25257, 2/9/93].

Even as it stalled on purging the army, the government moved to disband a fourth immediate-reaction battalion on January 6 and submitted an official request on January 8 for U.N. monitoring of the presidential, legislative, and municipal elections scheduled for May 1994 [S/25241, 1/26/93]. The Security Council welcomed "with satisfaction" this request as well as the intention of the Secretary-General to recommend its acceptance by expiration of ONUSAL's current mandate period in May [S/25257, 2/9/93]. But the FMLN, for its part, had failed to meet the extended

January 29 deadline for the destruction of its weaponry, and the Security Council responded once again with concern and urged compliance [ibid.].

The Report of the Commission on the Truth

While President Cristiani had some control over the removal of military personnel implicated in human rights abuses by the Ad Hoc Commission, he could do little to prevent the **Commission on the Truth** from carrying out its mandate to name the army and FMLN officials it believed responsible for the most heinous acts committed in the war. Since January, 1993 the President had reportedly sought support from other Central American governments as well as from the "Friends of the Secretary-General" involved in the peace process—Colombia, Mexico, Spain, and Venezuela—in an effort to have the names of individuals removed from the Commission's report. Failing that, the President requested a delay in its publication until after the elections, arguing that "extremist elements" would exploit the information at the expense of national stability [*The New York Times*, 3/2/93, 3/12/93].

Already recommended for dismissal from the army and believed to figure prominently in the findings of the Truth Commission, General Ponce submitted his resignation as defense minister to President Cristiani on March 12, reportedly under heavy pressure from the United States. That same day, U.S. officials had announced the withholding of $11 million in military assistance for El Salvador, pending the full implementation of the recommendations of the Ad Hoc Commission [*The Washington Post*, 3/14/93]. To prevent the loss of additional senior officers in the wake of the Truth Commission report, the President moved quickly to request the National Assembly to declare a general amnesty for all those to be named in it [*The New York Times*, 3/15/93].

Upon the release of the report on March 15 by the three commissioners—**Belisario Betancur**, former President of Colombia; **Thomas Buergenthal**, Professor of Law at George Washington University; and **Reinaldo Figueredo**, former Foreign Minister of Venezuela—the reasoning behind the amnesty request became clear. Of the 18,000 victims of violence on which the Commission had gathered information, 60% were found to have been killed, abducted, or "disappeared" by army personnel, 25% by the security forces affiliated with the army, 10% by right-wing death squads with army participation, and only 5% by members of the FMLN. In 211 pages of text and more than 600 pages of annexes, the Commission reported in depth on some 32 of the most notorious and heinous cases of abuse perpetrated between 1980 and July 1991 [English-language "Summary" of the Report of the Commission on the Truth; *The New York Times*, 3/16/93].

It recommended the immediate removal and suspension for life from any military or security post of more than 40 senior officers—including

Ponce and Zepeda—for their roles in either ordering or concealing the killings of six Jesuit priests, their cook, and her daughter on November 16, 1989. It cited the army's Atlacatl Battalion for the massacre of over 200 peasants in the village of El Mozote on December 11, 1981, and found that the President of the Supreme Court had impeded the investigation of the killings. The Commission also found that the late Major Roberto D'Aubuisson, founder of the ruling ARENA party, had ordered and planned the assassination of Archbishop Oscar Arnulfo Romero on March 24, 1980, and cited the former head of the National Guard, General Eugenio Vides Casanova, in the cover-up of the murder of four American churchwomen on December 2, 1980.

The Truth Commission also held the FMLN responsible for more than 400 killings and 300 disappearances, including the assassinations of at least 11 civilian mayors. It cited the entire General Command for ordering those assassinations, and especially the commandantes of the People's Revolutionary Army—the most violent of the five factions constituting the FMLN. Among those named were Joaquín Villalobos, regarded as the chief military and now political strategist for the rebels. The Commission recommended that those cited on either side be barred from holding public office for ten years.

The report contained extensive proposals for follow-up action as well as political, military, and judicial reform. It called for stronger civilian control of the military and a special investigation of death squads, which it said remained "a potential menace." Labeling the current system for the administration of justice "highly deficient," the Commission refused to recommend judicial proceedings against human rights violators until reforms were implemented, including the resignation of the current Supreme Court and the establishment of a truly independent judicial council to oversee the functioning of the entire judicial system. To promote national reconciliation, the Truth Commission also recommended the payment of compensation to the survivors of victims and the establishment of a special fund for this purpose to be financed by 1% of all foreign aid received.

Arguing that "There can be no reconciliation without public knowledge of the truth," the Secretary-General reminded government and FMLN leaders of their obligations to implement the recommendations in full [U.N. press release SG/SM/4942, CA/76, 3/15/93]. The Security Council also underlined the need for compliance and the role of the recommendations in preventing a recurrence of violence, creating confidence in the peace process, and stimulating national reconciliation [S/25427, 3/18/93]. But the National Assembly's approval on March 20 of a government-backed amnesty over the strong objections from the center and left placed the implementation of any of the recommendations in serious doubt. The Assembly had specifically rejected an attempt to link the measure with commitments to remove implicated army personnel and adopt judicial reforms [*The New York Times*, 3/21/93]. Admitting that the amnesty was, "strictly speaking," an internal affair, the Secretary-General nevertheless requested the government to inform him "how and when" it proposed to implement the recommendations of the Truth Commission in light of developments [U.N. press release SG/SM/4950, CA/77, 3/24/93].

The amnesty may not only protect many senior officers from dismissal but may also free more junior personnel imprisoned for carrying out acts of violence on their orders. Two officers serving 30-year sentences for the murder of the six Jesuits were released under the amnesty on April 1, and the National Guardsmen jailed in the killings of the four American churchwomen may also be freed. But continuing U.S. pressure was forcing the government to at least follow through on its implementation of the recommendations of the Ad Hoc Commission. General Zepeda announced his resignation from the Defense Ministry on March 25, and President Cristiani finally agreed to place all 15 of the officers he had sought to retain on "leave with pay" by June 30 and to retire them from the military by December 31. In doing so, the Secretary-General reported to the Security Council on April 2, the government would bring itself into "broad compliance" with the relevant provisions of the Peace Agreement [*The Washington Post*, 4/1/93, 4/3/93]. On July 1, Cristiani presided at a high-profile retirement ceremony for Zepeda, Defense Minister Ponce, and 16 other officers, apparently marking the completion of the purge process mandated by the Ad Hoc Commission [*The Washington Post*, 7/2/93].

Haiti

The United Nations has begun to play a more active role in restoring democracy in Haiti after the failure of regional efforts to gain the return to power of exiled **President Jean-Bertrand Aristide**, overthrown in a coup on September 30, 1991. Aristide, the country's first democratically elected head of state since the ouster of the dictator Jean-Claude Duvalier in 1986, served just eight months in the office he had won with 68% of the vote in **U.N.-monitored elections** in December 1990. While the General Assembly had joined the Organization of American States (OAS) in condemning the coup, demanding Aristide's reinstatement and supporting a voluntary trade embargo on the Caribbean island-nation, the United Nations had left responsibility for resolving the crisis largely to regional actors. But the collapse of two OAS-engineered accords between the deposed President and the military-controlled government in Port-au-Prince, continued reports of massive human rights violations against Aristide supporters, and the threat of a renewed exodus of Haitian boat people bound for the United States increased pressure for effective U.N. intervention by the fall of 1992.

Support for a Joint Settlement

For its part, the OAS had at least been successful in gaining access to the island for a high-level mission in August 1992, led by OAS Secretary-General João Baena Soares and including a U.N. representative, to provide the international community with its first direct look at the human rights situation in Haiti since the coup and the effect of the regional embargo on the humanitarian situation there. Baena Soares had also managed to initiate indirect negotiations between personal representatives of President Aristide and the de facto Prime Minister, and won approval from them on September 10 for the dispatch of an 18-member OAS observer mission to promote respect for human rights and facilitate the distribution of humanitarian assistance. But in his report to the General Assembly on November 3, Boutros-Ghali passed on the conclusions of the OAS that the year-old embargo had been "largely ignored" by states outside the region and had "failed to provide the desired effect." The observer mission, he also noted, continued to be confined to the capital city at the insistence of the Haitian authorities and was thus unable to execute its mandate effectively [A/47/599].

Other evidence was mounting in support of more aggressive action by the international community. A recent **U.N. Commission on Human Rights investigation** cited by the Secretary-General described a "pattern of gross and widespread" abuses since the coup, and the Secretariat's Department of Humanitarian Affairs reported to him on a national economy "in a state of free fall," with growing malnutrition, a deteriorating health situation, and a breakdown in public education. Of greatest concern to neighboring states, especially the United States, were data supplied to Boutros-Ghali by the office of the U.N. High Commissioner for Refugees (UNHCR), which placed at 38,315 the number of Haitians attempting to flee to southern Florida by boat since September 1991. After interception by the U.S. Coast Guard, some 27,000 had been returned "by force" to the island and only 11,617 had been admitted as asylum seekers. While providing assistance to nearly 6,000 returnees, UNHCR "deplored" the U.S. government's decision of May 24 to repatriate all detainees immediately without determining whom among them might qualify for protection as legitimate political refugees [ibid.].

U.S. policy on Haiti was changing to favor a quick political settlement and the return of President Aristide once it was determined that the tide of refugees could not be stemmed by any other means. Summary repatriation had had some deterrent effect but raised serious legal questions and invited international criticism. Attempts to target the embargo against the military leadership—exempting light industry, which employs thousands of poor Haitians, and excluding economically vital oil deliveries on the list of prohibited items—did nothing to redress the grinding poverty compelling many to flee, and actually eased pressure on the government to negotiate an end to the crisis. And raising the level of U.S. humanitarian assistance to $70 million in fiscal year 1992 had little effect in the hemisphere's poorest country, offering at best a short-term inducement to stay put. Campaign pledges by then-Governor Bill Clinton to grant temporary asylum to all Haitians intercepted at sea and the end of hurricane season in October resulted in further increases in the number of those fleeing the island. Some 700 had been repatriated that month, and the threat of a massive exodus loomed.

Finally, the more conciliatory poses struck by the parties to the dispute themselves made a negotiated settlement seem practicable for the first time. According to press accounts, members of the Haitian High Command had realized that the continued lack of meaningful concessions on their part would lead to a perpetuation or even a strengthening of the embargo and economic chaos that they could not possibly hope to control. Rejection of serious negotiations, it was said, also threatened the withdrawal of U.S. offers to preserve the current leadership of the armed forces after the restoration of democracy. On the other side, representatives of President Aristide had reportedly promised to guarantee, as part of a political settlement, the safety of those who perpetrated the coup and their supporters against violent reprisals by either the restored government or individual Haitians [*The New York Times*, 11/6/92, 11/26/92].

The General Assembly played its role in encouraging greater U.N. involvement in Haiti by requesting the Secretary-General in late November "to take the necessary measures" to assist in finding a solution with the cooperation of the OAS [A/Res/47/20]. At the same time, it supported OAS calls for an increase in humanitarian assistance to the country, and urged member states to refrain from supplying military equipment or petroleum for the use of the police or the armed forces, items not specifically included in the original embargo. In response to the resolution, the Secretary-General appointed a **Special Envoy for Haiti** on December 11, naming **former Argentine Foreign Minister** (and President of the 45th Session of the General Assembly) **Dante Caputo**. The Secretary-General of the OAS also named Caputo as his Special Envoy on January 13, 1993.

The International Civilian Mission

The Special Envoy launched the new U.N.–OAS initiative by holding a first round of talks from December 17 to 22 with Aristide in Washington; with his representatives and the Army High Command in Port-au-Prince; and with the "Friends of the Secretary-General" on the situation in Haiti—Canada, France, the United States, and Venezuela—in New York [A/47/908, 3/24/93]. Regional players offered demonstrations of their strong support for Caputo's efforts. On December 19 the OAS pledged to increase the size of its civilian presence in Haiti substantially and to foster closer cooperation with the United Nations, and even the Security Council if necessary. In the United States, the outgoing and incoming administrations exhibited an unusual level of cooperation in issuing a January 6 joint statement urging "all sides to be flexible in their positions and to be responsive to the entreaties of the United Nations and the OAS" [*U.S. Department of State Dispatch*, 1/25/93]. In the meantime, the number of Haitians picked up at sea had remained at 700 a month through November and December, with over 5,000 repatriations carried out since May. Unnamed senior U.S. officials cited in the press estimated that as many as 200,000 more Haitians could depart the island soon after the inauguration of then President-elect Clinton [*The Wall Street Journal*, 12/22/92; *The New York Times*, 12/31/92].

After further talks with Caputo, President Aristide was prepared to open negotiations on the settlement of the crisis under the joint mediation and supervision of the United Nations and the OAS. In a January 8 letter to Boutros-Ghali, Aristide requested the deployment of an "international civilian mission" by both organizations to monitor respect for human rights in Haiti and promote a reduction in the level of violence. He also requested the Special Envoy to initiate a dialogue among all the concerned parties aimed at securing agreements on the naming of a prime minister to lead a "government of national concord," the rehabilitation of national institutions (including judicial reform, the "professionalization" of the armed forces, and the separation of the police from them), the provision of international technical assistance for reconstruction, and a system of "guarantees" to ensure compliance. In return for such agreements and the deployment of the observers, Aristide promised even before his return to office to work toward the gradual lifting of the embargo and the mobilization of international financial assistance in rebuilding Haiti's economy [A/47/908]. According to the media, there were indications that the President would also drop his insistence on punishment for participants in the coup that ousted him [*The New York Times*, 1/14/93].

Caputo's additional consultations in Washington with Aristide, the Secretary-General of the OAS, and officials of the U.S. Department of State, including Secretary of State-designate Warren Christopher, resulted in "an understanding on a framework," according to the United Nations, for the opening of actual negotiations and the possible dispatch of the joint mission [U.N. press release SG/SM/4901, HI/8, 1/14/93]. On January 17, at the close of two days of meetings in Port-au-Prince with the Special Envoy, **Commander in Chief of the Haitian Armed Forces Gen. Raoul Cédras** and **nominal Prime Minister Marc Bazin** "accepted in principle" the proposed U.N.–OAS dialogue and observer mission. Boutros-Ghali informed President Aristide by letter the next day of the U.N.'s willingness to participate in the joint mission, now officially named the **Interna-**

tional Civilian Mission to Haiti [A/47/908], and Caputo set about drafting an operational plan for its deployment. U.S. Assistant Secretary of State for Inter-American Affairs Bernard W. Aronson, quoted in the press, called the agreement "a very important breakthrough" and said it might constitute "the beginning of the end of the Haitian crisis." Washington also made an initial pledge of $1 million toward the estimated $1.5 million monthly cost of maintaining the observers, said to number up to 500 [*The New York Times*, 1/18/93, 1/22/93].

President-elect Clinton seized the opportunity presented by the framework accord to announce on January 14 a temporary extension of the Bush administration policy of summary repatriation, reportedly fearing an exodus of as many as 150,000 Haitians on or about Inauguration Day. In a taped radio address broadcast directly to Haiti, Clinton emphasized the move was only temporary, pending the outcome of negotiations, and promised to increase the number of U.S. offices and personnel in the country assigned to process applications for political asylum [ibid., 1/15/93].

Despite "serious consequences" threatened by Caputo should the government and the army renege on their pledges—and a reported offer of $50 million in U.S. nonlethal military aid to the Haitian High Command in return for its cooperation in reaching a settlement with Aristide [*The Economist*, 1/23/93]—both General Cédras and Prime Minister Bazin publicly renounced their agreements with the Special Envoy shortly after his departure. Bazin in particular rejected terms in the U.N.–OAS operational plan guaranteeing unlimited, unaccompanied, and unannounced travel for the observers throughout the country [*The New York Times*, 1/29/93].

Following consultations with Secretary of State Christopher and OAS officials in Washington, reportedly over the possibility of blockading all shipments of oil and arms to the Haitian military, Caputo returned to Haiti on February 2 to be met by angry crowds of government-organized protesters and a long list of demands, including the right of the government to revise the operational plan. According to press reports, the government conditioned its continued cooperation with the overall settlement effort on effective international recognition of the de facto regime and an immediate lifting of the embargo. It also sought to limit the size of the joint mission to 100 observers, restrict their movements, and remove any observer at will [*The New York Times*, 2/5/93; *The Washington Post*, 2/5/93]. After reaffirming the prerogatives of the United Nations and the OAS to decide on the size, composition, and procedures of the mission, Caputo returned to New York on February 4, where Boutros-Ghali strongly condemned the violence against his representative [SG/SM/4922, HI/9, 2/5/93].

Heavy diplomatic pressure and strong public pronouncements in support of the mission prompted the government and the army to reconsider their positions. On February 5, Boutros-Ghali declared a four-day deadline for agreement by Bazin and Cédras with the terms of the mission as formulated by the Special Envoy. He telephoned Secretary of State Christopher to request a clear U.S. statement on the matter and considered, were the U.N.–OAS terms to be rejected, either recommending the General Assembly withdraw from the mission or approaching the Security Council for a mandatory and global embargo. Christopher, for his part, pledged that "those who hold illegal power [in Haiti] will not prevail," and President Clinton promised "a more vigorous course" should the government refuse to cooperate. Visiting Canadian Prime Minister Mulroney, long active in the regional OAS effort on Haiti, proposed "hard action . . . at the appropriate time" [*U.S. Department of State Dispatch*, 2/15/93; *The Washington Post*, 2/6/93, 2/10/93]. On February 9, just within the four-day deadline, Caputo announced that an agreement had been reached for the deployment of the mission.

Deployment of the Mission

Terming the deployment agreement the "first effective step" toward a solution to the crisis, the Secretary-General had won a formal one-year commitment from the Haitian government guaranteeing the safety and unencumbered movement of the observers, with none of the conditions or restrictions previously proposed. Prohibitions against violations of the Haitian constitution and national sovereignty were, however, included as concessions to Bazin. Urging quick deployment and negotiations on the remaining political issues, Secretary Christopher pledged a U.S. contribution of at least $2 million to the mission. The first group of 40 OAS observers, including 15 Americans, arrived in Port-au-Prince on February 14 without incident and had successfully deployed outside the capital within a week. On February 15, Boutros-Ghali dispatched a three-man team of human rights experts to Haiti to make recommendations to him on the structure and organization of the mission once fully deployed [U.N. press releases SG/1982, HI/10, 2/9/93, and SG/1985, HI/11, 2/22/93; *The Washington Post*, 2/10/93, 2/15/93].

Despite hopes that an international presence in the country would help reduce both illegal departures by sea and requests for U.S. asylum, the refugee problem remained critical throughout the first half of 1993. Interdictions and repatriations declined modestly to 500 during January, but applications for asylum rose dramatically to more than 100 per day. The new U.S. administration, despite its promises to the contrary, had effected only minor increases in staff to screen such applications to determine whether an applicant faced a "credible fear of persecution" and could be issued a refugee visa for entry into the United States. Only 179 visas had been approved by mid-February, allowing those Haitians to present further proof that their fear of persecution was "well-founded" and qualified them for permanent residency as political refugees. So-called "economic refugees" were excluded from receiving temporary or permanent visas. In early March the administration announced plans to spend $5 million on strengthening the screening program in Haiti, including the establishment of immigration offices in the provinces, to accelerate the process and help prevent the public exposure and harassment of applicants [*The Christian Science Monitor*, 2/1/93; *The New York Times*, 3/2/93, 3/7/93].

Human rights and refugee advocacy groups have raised **legal challenges** to the practice of summary repatriation, and the Clinton administration has been placed in the awkward situation of having to defend in court a controversial policy of its predecessor. In a case heard by the Supreme Court on April 3, administration lawyers argued that protections under U.S. and international law prohibiting the return of asylum seekers without conducting initial interviews on their refugee status did not apply to aliens who had not yet entered the United States. They further argued that the policy was necessary to save the lives of Haitians attempting the perilous 600-mile journey and that the President was within his legal authority to issue and implement the executive order of May 1992 without court review. In June 1993 the Court issued its decision, upholding the administration's position.

Efforts to Settle the Political Crisis

By March 25, 103 OAS observers had arrived in Haiti and established local offices in eight of the nine Haitian provinces [U.N. press release HI/13, 3/25/93]. With that operation on track but U.N. participation still pending General Assembly approval, negotiators turned their attention to working out agreements on the return of President Aristide to power, the appointment of a compromise prime minister, and conditions for a general amnesty. In an effort to expedite the talks, Aristide requested the United States to set a firm date for his reinstatement and impose tougher sanctions on the de facto government, including rescinding the visas of the coup leaders and their supporters, freezing their personal assets in the United States, and deploying the U.S. Navy to halt shipments of oil to Haiti. President Clinton turned down the requests in a face-to-face meeting with Aristide on March 16, but did commit the United States to cover about a fifth of the costs of a $1 billion multilateral reconstruction program for Haiti, to be implemented once the political crisis had been resolved [*The Washington Post*, 3/17/93].

Caputo returned to Haiti on March 22, and by March 27 the press was reporting that an agreement was near calling for the immediate resignation of General Cédras and the return of Aristide within six months. As representatives of Clinton's National Security Council and the U.S. military pressured the government and the High Command to finalize the accord, the administration was reportedly planning to hold an international pledging conference on April 6 in Washington aimed at funding a massive program for building a modern infrastructure in Haiti and establishing democratic institutions. Talks broke off March 31, however, apparently over the difficulties in securing a firm pledge from Aristide for an amnesty. In addition to support for economic revitalization and democratization, the United States was also reportedly contemplating sending a small number of military advisors to help professionalize the armed forces and instill respect for civilian authority in its leadership [*The New York Times*, 3/28/93, 3/30/93; *The Washington Post*, 4/14/93].

In preparation for the next round of talks, Caputo was believed to have extracted a major concession from Aristide designed to close the deal on the President's return to power. Aristide had agreed not only to grant a limited amnesty covering political crimes, the press said, but also to forswear criminal proceedings against any member of the armed forces and to refrain from blocking legislation intended to insulate soldiers from civil actions initiated by private citizens. In exchange for these commitments from the President, General Cédras and other top generals had reportedly agreed in March to resign their posts. But in four days of talks concluding April 17, the army had apparently balked, concerned that Aristide could not be held to his promises. The implementation of U.S.-backed plans announced in May to deploy some 1,000 police monitors in addition to human rights observers might provide the guarantees needed to cement an agreement [*The Washington Post*, 4/15/93, 4/17/93, 5/13/93].

Despite this setback, the General Assembly adopted a resolution on April 20 approving U.N. participation in the civilian mission to Haiti and the recommendations of the team of experts dispatched in February, authorizing the immediate deployment of U.N. observers to join those of the OAS already in the country, and requesting the Secretary-General to submit periodic reports on the activities of the mission and a comprehensive review of its progress no later than September 1993 [A/47/L.56, 4/13/93]. Under the team's recommendations, the United Nations would provide half of the 260 observers needed, and the mission would establish a total of 13 local offices throughout the country—one for each department, with the balance concentrated in the largest and most violence-prone regions—staffing them with 12 observers initially and 20 when recruitment permitted [A/47/908]. Although the joint mission cited continued abuses by the armed forces in its first public assessment of the human rights situation in Haiti, the observers were said to be effective in facilitating the release of those wrongfully detained and preventing a resort to violence at public events they monitored [*The Washington Post*, 5/6/93].

Failure of Talks and Imposition of New Sanctions

A sixth round of talks centering on the deployment of a multinational police force convened May 22 but concluded three days later without an agreement. Accompanied by senior U.S. officials and backed by a threat of tighter international sanctions on the Haitian regime, Caputo had reportedly offered the force as a guarantee against reprisals by Aristide supporters aimed at military and civilian supporters of the coup. In addition to this protection, the package deal was also said to offer a lifting of the embargo and a general amnesty for human rights abusers in return for the High Command's agreement to restore Aristide to power and resign from office [*The Washington Post*, 5/25/93]. With political talks at a standstill, the human rights situation reportedly was also deteriorating, despite the deployment of some 150 U.N. and OAS monitors by the end of May [ibid., 5/30/93]. Concern was mounting that gradualist, carrot-and-stick diplomacy had damaged the credibility of the international community as an effective defender of democracy and human rights in Haiti, while encouraging the de facto regime to continue its stalling tactics and outlast efforts to oust it.

On June 4 the United States announced a set of political and economic sanctions against those it considered responsible for blocking serious talks on a peaceful solution. The measures barred the entry into the U.S. of some 100 military, government, and civilian opponents of Aristide and froze the assets of 83 individuals (including Prime Minister Bazin and General Cédras), the central bank, and other financial entities. These individuals and entities were also banned from conducting any commercial business in the United States. (It was reported, however, that most of the assets in question had already been transferred out of the country.) Also on June 4, Bazin announced the replacement of four ministers in his cabinet, perhaps an attempt to convince U.S. officials of his independence from the military. But Bazin's reported failure to consult with the army in advance of the announcement resulted in his own resignation on June 8 and even tighter control of the government by the High Command [ibid., 6/5/93, 6/9/93].

The United States was also successful in winning unanimous Security Council approval of a worldwide oil embargo on Haiti on June 16 [S/Res/841]. In taking that action, the Council also directed that Haitian assets overseas be frozen beginning June 23, should the regime fail to initiate serious negotiations on the return of Aristide to power. Council members appparently dismissed concerns that the imposition of binding international sanctions in the absence of a civil war or a direct threat to international security might set a precedent for similar action elsewhere. Diplomatic sources quoted in the press believed the embargo would be respected, due primarily to the smallness of the Haitian oil market and the low return and high risk to those still willing to service it. Nevertheless, the Haitian regime had reportedly stockpiled a three-month supply of oil, convinced that international pressure would ease and petroleum imports resume before the depletion of the reserves on hand [ibid., 6/18/93].

By the middle of June, the international sanctions had managed to convince Cédras to meet with Aristide on Governor's Island in New York to discuss the formation of a new government and the establishment of an international police force to protect against further violations of human rights. In a note sent to Caputo on June 23, Cédras spoke of the need to return Haiti "quickly and viably to the concert of nations" [*The New York Times*, 6/26/93]. A former Haitian official close to Cédras accounted for the change in policy noting that the General had become "increasingly worried" over his ability to hold onto power and was concerned only to "save his skin" [*ibid.*]. Consequently, his wish for political amnesty embodied in his statement, "I have not accepted, and will not accept, that one single member of the army be removed," became the dominant issue—if not the stumbling block—of the talks.

The first week of talks achieved little as Cédras remained resolute over the point of political amnesty for himself and his officials. However, on the morning of Saturday, July 3, General Cédras announced that the U.N. mediators had succeeded in reaching a proposal that was acceptable. The plan, calling for his resignation but providing for the reassignment of his fellow conspirators, was signed by Cédras shortly after 11 a.m. However, Aristide delayed his commitment, worried about the safety of his supporters in Haiti in the interim. Tired and frustrated, Caputo muttered to a reporter, "He will have to answer to history. I am fed up" [ibid., 7/3/93]. Eleven hours later Aristide yielded after repeated assurances from the international community that they would ensure the accords were respected.

According to the Associated Press, the U.N. plan outlines a number of meetings between Haiti's political parties, to take place in Washington, to "lay the ground work for the new government." The selection of a new prime minister will be followed by a comprehensive program of economic stability. The international package, aimed at "jump-starting" the economy, will cost an estimated $1 billion and will focus on sanitation, road building, and well digging [ibid., 7/5/93].

The U.N. plan also recommends that an international advisory group be convened to aid in the formation of an independent police force, divorced entirely from the military. Until recently the military and the police force had been a symbiotic force accountable only to the government. Under the U.N. plan the police force will find its new role restricted to protecting civilians and to maintaining basic law and order. Similarly, the military will be removed from politics and, ultimately, will take its command from the democratically elected government. Some diplomats, however, are still concerned that the coup conspirators—with the exception of Cédras—will not be punished (though some will be demoted and reassigned); and in light of the 21 months of brutal political repression and hunger since the coup, many wonder whether letting these men go unpunished will leave intact sufficient opposition to Aristide to result in yet another coup. This last point has been especially worrisome to the 35,000 Haitians who have sought political asylum in the United States since President Aristide was overthrown. Dante Caputo perhaps best captured their concern when he expressed his hope that "[the parties involved] are not going through all the trouble [they've] been through for one day of victory. . . . To be considered a success, this has to be something lasting" [ibid.].

6. Cambodia

By Frederick Z. Brown

Throughout the year the Cambodian peace process was a major preoccupation of the United Nations. In May 1993 that process reached a major milestone when the first genuine popular elections in Cambodia's history took place. More than 90% of Cambodia's 4.25 million voters cast ballots in a demonstration of political enthusiasm that exceeded the most optimistic expectations of U.N. officials in Phnom Penh. In a stunning upset, opposition parties received half the votes, beating the government's **Cambodian People's Party (CPP)** handily. The U.N. Security Council urged all Cambodians to accept the results of the elections. **Prince Norodom Sihanouk** declared himself Prime Minister and formed an interim coalition government of opposition and government parties, but in a surprise move he announced on June 3 that he was leaving the government, which would now be in the hands of a son, **Prince Ranariddh,** and the incumbent government of **Prime Minister Hun Sen** [*The New York Times*, 6/4/93]. At the time of writing, the question of peace in Cambodia remains an open question.

The Paris Conference

On October 23, 1991, the **Paris Conference on Cambodia** adopted a series of historic documents—the "Agreements on a Comprehensive Political Settlement of the Cambodia Conflict"—designed to bring peace to a country torn for decades by internal strife and massive external intervention [U.N. Department of Public Information, DP/1180-92077, 1/92]. While few diplomats from the 19 nations attending the conference claimed that the Cambodia conflict was definitively settled, the Agreements laid out a plan of action that, if followed in good faith by the Cambodian parties and supported by the international community, would create a Cambodia at peace, with a pluralistic political system and the prospects of a viable economy.

The key was to be the Agreements' *comprehensive* nature. The **Khmer Rouge**, who had ruled Cambodia brutally from 1975 through 1978 as the government of Democratic Kampuchea (D.K.), would be included: Better to have the Khmer Rouge inside the tent than on the outside spitting in, the logic went. Their inclusion was also imperative if China, with its history of support for the Khmer Rouge (and a veto in the Security Council) was to give genuine support to the Agreements: Without China there would be no settlement of any sort.

The Agreements created the **U.N. Transitional Authority in Cambodia (UNTAC)**, a peacekeeping organization given greater power over a sovereign government than any U.N. mission before it. UNTAC was commissioned to deal with the **four competing Cambodian factions**: the Khmer Rouge's Party of Democratic Kampuchea (PDK); the current State of Cambodia Government (SOC) installed by Vietnam in early 1979 and its People's Party of Cambodia (PPC); FUNCINPEC (the acronym in French for "National United Front for an Independent, Neutral, Peaceful and Cooperative Cambodia"), Prince Norodom Sihanouk's party headed by his son Norodom Ranariddh; and the KPNLF led nominally by Son Sann, a former Cambodian prime minister. For a period of a year-and-a-half leading up to supervised nationwide elections in May 1993, UNTAC's mission was to oversee the political transition of Cambodia to a new governmental structure and the beginning of economic and social rebirth.

Cambodian sovereignty rested in a 12-member Supreme National Council (SNC)—six members from the SOC and two from each of the three other parties—under the guidance of Prince Sihanouk. UNTAC placed international civil servants in the SOC ministries of defense, foreign affairs, public security, information, and finance in order to establish these ministries' impartiality during the transition. According to plans, UNTAC civil police would work with the SOC to ensure protection of civil rights for all Cambodians, and UNTAC human rights and information components would educate the population about democratic procedures in preparation for the elections organized and supervised by UNTAC's election component.

Sihanouk, once Cambodia's ruling monarch and possibly its future president, was the linchpin, attempting to bridge bitter political differences with his Khmer compatriots while coping with the cruel physical realities of a devastated society. Whether or not his presence was actually helpful was the subject of dispute; his absences for months at a time, pilgrimages to North Korea, and constant changes in attitude toward UNTAC created grave doubts as to Sihanouk's reliability. **Yasushi Akashi**, a former Japanese diplomat and senior U.N. official with peacekeeping experience, had been appointed in December 1991 to direct the joint military-civilian UNTAC effort. Among his extensive powers during the transition was the authority to make law when the SNC reached an impasse.

The October 23, 1991, Agreements included compromises and ambiguities in addressing the deadlocks over political principle and practical implementation that could not be broken in Paris. These came back to haunt Mr. Akashi and his UNTAC peacekeepers in their first full year on the ground in Cambodia, particularly with regard to the comprehensive nature of the plan and the Khmer Rouge's refusal to cooperate in its core provisions.

The Khmer Rouge's attitude, as displayed in the actions of the PDK, called into question the Paris Agreements' basic premise: that the Khmer Rouge could become part of the solution to the Cambodian problem rather than remaining a source of discord and armed threat. Foreign observers in Phnom Penh made different assessments of the Khmer Rouge threat. Some maintained that the Khmer Rouge leadership was split, that recruiting of fresh guerrilla fighters was difficult, that most Cambodians remembered the horrors of 1975–78 and would not support the PDK, and that the Khmer Rouge high command was content with making money on the Thai border. Other observers saw the Khmer Rouge military capability (consensus estimate: 10,000–15,000 combat troops in small units, well equipped and firmly led) as still formidable, with its units able to roam virtually at will in many areas supposed to be under the SOC's control. The Khmer Rouge, some believed, would never consent to join in a process that was unlikely to result in its gaining power through the ballot box, and thus would conduct guerrilla war against whatever government was elected in May 1993. The observers who took this pessimistic view considered their beliefs vindicated by the actions of the PDK during the climactic weeks before the May 23–28 elections.

By September 1992, UNTAC was fully deployed in Cambodia, with 15,900 peacekeeping troops, 3,600 civilian police, and about 3,000 civilian administrators and election officials. The estimated cost was $1.9 billion, not counting $600 million for the repatriation and resettlement by the U.N. High Commissioner for Refugees of 325,000 Cambodians living in camps in Thailand.

UNTAC's military responsibility in the **first phase of the peace plan** was to supervise a cease-fire between all four Cambodian parties, to verify the withdrawal of Vietnamese troops (which had taken place in September 1989) and the cessation of external arms supplies from all sources, and to begin clearing millions of mines littering the countryside. Also in Phase One, UNTAC had the responsibility to canton and disarm the parties' armed forces and then demobilize 70% of these forces. The success of other aspects of the plan (the election, a new constitution, creation of a government) would ultimately depend upon this important first step of standing down the armed forces of the hostile factions.

Phase One was to have been completed by June 30, 1992. The SOC and the two non-Communist parties complied adequately with this requirement, but as the year progressed, it became clear that the PDK was refusing to cooperate. In his Special Report to the United Nations, Mr. Akashi put the PDK on notice, stating bluntly that the continued refusal of the Khmer Rouge to grant UNTAC personnel access to the zones it controls or to commit its forces to cantonment as called for in the Agreements threatened to undo the Paris accord [S/24090, 6/12/92]. While the Phnom Penh regime had cantoned (or given "temporary agricultural leave" to) 20% of its armed forces, and the Sihanoukist and Khmer People's National Liberation Front forces had furloughed proportionately more, the PDK had refused any cantonment or disarmament and denied UNTAC access to its base areas for strength assessments. In time, UNTAC suspended further cantonment by the three other parties in order to avoid a military imbalance that might precipitate further fighting [S/24578, 9/21/92].

By year's end there had been numerous instances of PDK forces firing on UNTAC helicopters and mining roads leading to PDK base areas. A dozen UNTAC military personnel had been wounded in ambushes and minings, all believed to be PDK-inspired. In early December 1992, PDK forces seized six UNTAC soldiers in Kompong Thom province north of Phnom Penh and accused them of spying; they were released several days later. The incident demonstrated dramatically the PDK's hostility to UNTAC's presence and the impasse that was then developing.

Defining the impasse were two PDK allegations:

- that UNTAC had not created the neutral political environment called for by the Paris Agreements, with the effect that the Phnom Penh regime's administrative and police apparatus exerted a degree of control over Cambodian life that made fair political competition for other parties impossible; and
- that the continued presence in Cambodia of hundreds of thousands of Vietnamese "settlers" or soldiers in disguise made fair elections impossible. The PDK demanded that *all* Vietnamese, however defined, be expelled, and it refused cooperation in Phase One until this was done.

Rejecting the demand that the peace process be delayed until these charges were resolved in favor of the PDK, the Security Council, on October 13, 1992, voted unanimously that the Cambodian elections go forward in May 1993 with or without PDK participation [S/Res/783]. The resolution called on **Indonesia and France**, the co-chairs of the Paris Conference, to try once more to convince the PDK to canton and demobilize its forces, to permit UNTAC access into PDK-controlled zones, and to join in the election process. The resolution did not suggest the use of force to obtain compliance but held out the possibility of economic sanctions if cooperation was not forthcoming. The resolution authorized further consideration of a "consultative administrative body" to advise the Supreme National Council, a concept suggested by Japanese and Thai mediators to tighten control over the Phnom Penh regime's ministries during the pre-election period. And in an important move to stabilize Cambodia's struggling economy, the resolution invited the international community to make reconstruction aid (as differentiated from shorter-term "rehabilitation" assistance) available immediately rather than wait for an elected government to take office in mid-1993.

The PDK's demands had already been the subject of extended discussions between the PDK and the Paris Conference co-chairs beginning in early 1992. Subsequent negotiations led by Thailand and Japan also failed to budge the PDK, which repeatedly refused to address the substance of various proposals to modify the SNC structure within the framework of the Paris Agreements. Regarding the presence of Vietnamese, the United Nations has found no evidence of foreign forces still on Cambodian soil, at least in the areas to which it has had access. While admitting that "the issue of foreign residents and immigrants is a matter which deeply concerns many Cambodians," the United Nations declared that this was "a matter for discussion between the future government of Cambodia and the Governments of neighboring countries" [Report of the Secretary-General on the Implementation of Security Council Resolution 783, S/24800, 11/15/92]. A last-ditch attempt at a ten-nation conference in Beijing, November 7–8, 1992, failed to produce any compromise in the PDK's position on either of the points fundamentally at issue [*The New York Times*, 11/9/92].

With the PDK obstructionism and UNTAC's conciliatory efforts documented, the Security Council adopted a resolution that prepared implementation of the next stage of the Paris Agreements [S/Res/792, 11/30/92]. The resolution's key provisions

- confirmed that elections for a constituent assembly would be held no later than May 1993 and ordered UNTAC to hold them in all areas to which UNTAC had access as of January 31, 1993;
- instructed UNTAC to make contingency plans for a presidential election at the same time;
- demanded that the PDK fulfill its obligations under the Paris Agreements;
- called on "those concerned" to cut off petroleum supplies to the PDK;
- threatened to freeze PDK assets outside Cambodia if it continued to obstruct the peace process;

- supported the SNC's earlier ban on export of logs, gems, and minerals from Cambodia and requested "neighboring states" to respect this moratorium;
- suggested another meeting (the first was held in June 1992) of countries providing economic assistance to Cambodia to review the current state of the Cambodian economy.

The terms "those concerned" and "neighboring states" in the November 30 resolution referred mainly to Thailand. One of the most sensitive issues facing the United Nations was how to halt the lucrative timber and gem trade in western Cambodia conducted by the PDK in concert with Thai businessmen, including the Thai military. Neither the United Nations nor Thailand's traditional friends wished to place additional strains on the fledgling government of Prime Minister Chuan Leekpai by demanding that Thailand enforce an embargo against PDK warlords that would threaten the rice bowls of influential Thai military and business interests. But the resolution's polite wording did not disguise a central fact: The PDK's ability to defy the United Nations and threaten the stability of Cambodia indefinitely rested largely on commerce with Thailand.

The creation of a "neutral political environment" also proved to be difficult, if not impossible. Although UNTAC representatives were involved in many aspects of Cambodian life, control of the administrative machinery of Cambodia remained with the central government to a greater degree than had been expected by the drafters of the Paris Agreements. Thus, in the competition for domestic political power, the Phnom Penh regime has had a built-in advantage against its political foes.

The SOC retained many of its Marxist-Leninist characteristics and was often uncooperative when its self-defined vital interests were affected by legitimate UNTAC application of the Paris Agreements. FUNCINPEC (which managed to open its first provincial office in the western city of Battambang only on September 30, 1992) and the KPNLF were hindered in their efforts to organize politically. KPNLF organizers were harassed and several were reportedly killed in early 1992 while attempting to organize or open offices in the provinces. SOC harassment of these parties reached a peak in November and December 1992, then slacked off in response to UNTAC pressure. In the first quarter of 1993, as the political campaign prepared to kick off, the intimidation and other acts of harassment by the SOC diminished, but not before markers had been laid down to the electorate clearly indicating the perils of voting for the opposition.

Anti-Vietnamese sentiment continued to be a ticking time bomb. PDK accusations that a million Vietnamese remain in Cambodia as soldiers in disguise or as "settlers" usurping Khmer lands were exaggerated, but hatred of the Vietnamese is deeply embedded in Cambodian society and has political resonance. Much of the PDK's appeal in the countryside is based on its image as a champion of Cambodian nationalism. A sizable ethnic Vietnamese or mixed-blood minority has lived in Cambodia for many decades. Thousands more Vietnamese have entered the country recently to find work in Phnom Penh and eastern Cambodia; some have established themselves in fishing villages around the Tonle Sap. Taking advantage of anti-Vietnamese sentiment, the Khmer Rouge, in March 1993, executed 27 Vietnamese fisherman and their families in cold blood in Siem Reap near the Tonle Sap. Another score were murdered in separate incidents during April, and by May tens of thousands of Vietnamese "boat people" fleeing the violence were perched in the lower reaches of the Mekong River south of Phnom Penh.

One element of the Khmer Rouge's strategy at the beginning of the peace process was to draw out the effort as long as possible on the theory that the international community would, in frustration, withdraw support from the expensive UNTAC operation. Beginning in March 1993, however, direct attacks against UNTAC units became more and more frequent. The Japanese and Bulgarians were singled out for special pressure, no doubt capitalizing on the already skittish Japanese public concerning overseas peacekeeping operations. On May 3, 300 Khmer Rouge guerrillas attacked Siem Reap town, killing 9 and wounding 21 in the largest such operation since the signing of the Paris Agreements. On May 5 several hundred rounds of artillery were fired at UNTAC's Chinese and Polish units in Kompong Thom. The next day 13 persons were killed and 34 injured during an attack on a train in Battambang, and the Khmer Rouge attacked UNTAC positions in Kompong Speu.

Following this spate of violence, Cambodia experienced two weeks of relative calm. However, reports made public May 19–20 indicated that fighting had once again resumed between government soldiers and the Khmer Rouge, limited to areas in the countryside where voting was scheduled to take place [*The New York Times*, 5/21/93]. On May 21 two Chinese engineers serving in a detachment under UNTAC were reported killed and seven others wounded, following a day in which the unit was subjected to heavy shelling by Khmer Rouge forces [Note by the President of the Security Council, S/25822, 5/22/93]. In response, the Security Council issued a stern warning to those parties resorting to violence in the hope of subverting the peace process [ibid.].

Anticipating an escalation in Khmer Rouge activity in the final days before the election, U.N. officials put on a brave face. According to a captured Khmer Rouge document, the organization's objective "is to conduct a strategic offensive in the countryside and to open up a battlefield in Phnom Penh in order to capture popular strength. Initially we will capture it politically. From politics we will move on to organization and from organization to action" [*Far Eastern Economic Review*, 12/10/92].

The United Nations' approach until January 1993 was to give the PDK every chance to participate in the peace process *as defined by the Paris Agreements*, a process that had been accepted by all the Cambodian parties after torturous negotiations. If the PDK chose unequivocally to be an outlaw, only then would it be treated accordingly by the international community. Despite criticism from outside observers impatient to see the PDK crushed at once (as advocated in early 1992 by some French military figures, for example), Mr. Akashi pursued this approach doggedly. He chose his moments of confrontation carefully, while dealing with the PDK in strict accordance with the Agreements. Yet he was also accused of favoring the SOC as the only practical vehicle for bringing off a valid electoral process that would vindicate U.N. efforts and allow UNTAC to depart Cambodia more or less on schedule.

UNTAC's voter registration campaign yielded a potential electorate of 4.25 million voters, about half of Cambodia's entire population, including 325,000 refugees returned from camps in Thailand. As the May 23–28 elections approached, two major uncertainties loomed: how many voters would be intimidated by the PDK's threats to disrupt the electoral process and therefore refuse to vote; and would the CPP's strong-arm tactics against FUNCINPEC result in a CPP victory at the polls that did not reflect the political will of the Cambodian people? More than 200 persons had died during election campaign violence, about two-thirds attributable to PDK attacks. However, on the first day of the election it became clear that the Cambodian people would not be cowed by threats and that they were determined to exercise their right to vote. By May 28, in a stunning display of collective political courage, more than 90% of the electorate had voted [*Far Eastern Economic Review*, 6/3/93]. At the last moment, the PDK announced it would not attack polling places, although in Battambang, Siem Reap, Kompong Cham, and in several other provinces Khmer Rouge shelling forced closure of some polling places. By and large, however, the actual voting period was not severely disrupted, and the Cambodian voters came forth in numbers that astounded UNTAC's most optimistic forecasters.

The results of the polling were even more remarkable. In a major setback to the Phnom Penh government, FUNCINPEC won approximately 45.5% of the vote to the CPP's 38.2% (and Son Sann's Buddhist Liberal Democratic Party's (BLDP) 3.8%). Given the proportional representation system by province established by the Paris Agreements, this translated into a 120-person constituent assembly made up of 58 FUNCINPEC and 51 CPP members, 10 from BLDP, plus 1 from Moulinaka—an offshoot of FUNCINPEC, which immediately pledged to support Ranariddh. [*Asian Wall Street Journal*, 6/3/93].

The CPP's initial reaction was to angrily demand new elections in key provinces (Kompong Chhnang, Prey Veng, Phnom Penh city, and Battambang) where the government party had lost. The CPP's charges that "irregularities" and "UNTAC prejudice" had slanted the elections in favor of FUNCINPEC were rejected by Mr. Akashi as groundless. Privately, UNTAC officials said that any meddling in the electoral process had been overwhelmingly perpetuated by the CPP.

On June 3, Prince Sihanouk announced that he would immediately form an interim coalition government with himself as prime minister and head of the armed forces. His son Prince Norodom Ranariddh, head of FUNCINPEC, and Hun Sen, Prime Minister of the SOC, would be deputy prime ministers. FUNCINPEC had won the allegiance of the Cambodian voters but had no army or administrative capacity to govern. The CPP/SOC had clearly lost the confidence of the people yet retained whatever administrative power existed in the country, as well as an army of more than 100,000 men, plus police and other internal security organs.

Prince Sihanouk's bold move reflected a harsh political reality: that the SOC refused to relinquish power and that FUNCINPEC clearly was ill-equipped to assume it. This move also went directly counter to the Paris Agreements' insistence on a democratic electoral process reflecting the will of the Cambodian people, and it denied Ranariddh the primacy that the election had given him. It was received less than enthusiastically by UNTAC; and in the face of criticism from several Security Council permanent members, Sihanouk withdrew his plan, leaving the Cambodian political scene in shambles. On June 4, Prince Chakrapong, another of Sihanouk's sons, who had joined the SOC as a deputy prime minister, announced formation of a sessionist government comprised of Cambodia's seven easternmost provinces along the Vietnamese border—a move that met with little favor in any quarter and showed dissension within the ranks of the CPP. By mid-June the Constituent Assembly had begun its work; but despite the successful election, the Cambodian problem was still far from a permanent settlement. Also left unresolved was whether the Khmer Rouge could be incorporated into the Cambodian polity so as to avoid another civil war.

7. Cyprus

Edmund T. Piasecki

There had been hopes at the United Nations of settling the 30-year-old conflict between ethnic Greeks and Turks in Cyprus by the end of 1992, but the good offices mission of the Secretary-General continues well into 1993, and the effort to conclude negotiations between the predominantly

Greek Cypriot Republic of Cyprus and the **Turkish Cypriots** in the north has encountered new difficulties.

At the same time, the **U.N. Force in Cyprus (UNFICYP)** that patrols a 180-kilometer buffer zone between the north and south of this Mediterranean island must begin making do with 28% fewer troops, and greater cuts to come. UNFICYP, which dates back to 1964, is the only U.N. peacekeeping mission to rely solely on voluntary contributions from member states—contributions that have traditionally fallen short of the sum needed to reimburse the troop-contributing countries.

The Set of Ideas

Conditions looked right for a settlement in the spring of 1992, when the Security Council gave formal approval to a "**Set of Ideas**" that former Secretary-General Javier Pérez de Cuéllar had drafted at the outset of the current peacemaking effort in 1990 and that have since been expanded to 100 paragraphs by his successor, in consultation with the parties [S/Res/750 (1992)]. The package is based on, and attempts to put into practice, the principles of settlement reaffirmed by the Security Council since the 1970s and accepted, at least rhetorically, by all the parties to the dispute: that Cyprus will exercise a single sovereignty; that the two communities will be political equals in a bicommunal and bizonal federation; and that union in whole or in part with foreign powers, partition of the island, or secession from the federation will not be permitted.

All sides are in general agreement on five of the eight issue areas ("headings") contained in the Set of Ideas: overall objectives, guiding principles, security and guarantee issues, transitional arrangements, and economic development and safeguards. Turkish Cypriots are particularly concerned about two other headings—on constitutional aspects of the proposed federation and on displaced persons—while the Greek Cypriots are concerned about a third—on territorial adjustments.

Only 18% of the total population, the Turkish Cypriots seek a new constitutional arrangement with firmer guarantees of political equality between the two communities and have stalled efforts to facilitate the return of Greek Cypriot displaced persons and refugees to their homes in what the Turkish Cypriots consider the Turkish Republic of Northern Cyprus. The latter is recognized diplomatically only by Turkey. The United Nations seats the Greek Cypriot-controlled Republic of Cyprus, located in the south, as the island's legitimate government.

The government Cypriots, for their part, have argued that the Turkish Cypriot sector in the north is a product of military aggression and "occupation" by another country (Turkey), both of which are prohibited under the U.N. Charter. Turkey invaded the island in 1974 in response to a coup led by Greek army officers and what it termed the continued oppression of the Turkish minority since the civil unrest of December 1963. The Turkish Cypriots now control some 38% of the island, and the Greek Cypriots, with the support of the government of Greece, are demanding the return of more than the "29-plus percent" of territory the Turkish side has insisted on keeping.

Proximity Talks and Direct Negotiations

In an effort to settle these outstanding issues and maintain momentum toward an overall framework agreement, the new U.N. Secretary-General, Boutros Boutros-Ghali, directed his representatives to initiate further talks with both Cypriot sides as well as with Greece and Turkey in early May 1992. Given the Security Council's stated intention of becoming directly involved in the peacemaking effort—which it had reaffirmed as recently as April 10, 1992, in its Resolution 750—the representatives consulted informally on the nature of the upcoming discussions with the President of the Council and other interested members [U.N. press release SG/SM/4745, 5/6/92].

After briefings from his representatives on their endeavors since mid-May, the Secretary-General opened "proximity talks" at U.N. Headquarters—the first phase of intensive negotiations on the Set of Ideas that the Security Council had requested in Resolution 750. He characterized as "constructive and helpful" the total of five separate meetings he had held with the leaders of both communities between June 18 and June 23, and requested both sides to maintain a media blackout on the substance of their discussions [U.N. press release SG/1935-CYP/1152, 6/23/92].

Reporting orally to the Security Council on June 24, the Secretary-General said the talks had focused on the issues of territorial adjustments and displaced persons and that both sides had agreed to resume indirect negotiations on July 15. He also announced his intention to initiate direct talks between the parties by convening a "joint meeting" of the leaders at an appropriate time, and he reaffirmed his commitment to chair the "international high-level meeting" endorsed by the Security Council as the mechanism through which an overall framework agreement would be completed. In a "Statement of the President" issued on July 13, the Security Council called the resumed talks a "determining phase" in the Secretary-General's good offices mission and requested him to provide an "ongoing assessment" of his progress [U.N. press release SC/5437, 7/13/92].

Three weeks into the second round of indirect negotiations, the Secretary-General met informally with the Security Council and told of his plans to recommend face-to-face talks "in the days ahead" [U.N. press release SG/SM/4790, 8/7/92]. Both Greek and Turkish Cypriot leaders accepted the invitation to "joint meetings" under his auspices on August 12, where territorial adjustments and displaced persons were again the focus, and consideration was given to the Secretary-General's suggestions on both matters. In the course of four meetings ending August 14, the participants succeeded only in drafting an agenda for future talks (final agreement on displaced persons would come first, followed by constitutional arrangements and only then territorial adjustments and other matters) and in agreeing to "pause for reflection" until October 26 [U.N. press release SC/5459, 8/26/92].

The negotiations received negative reviews in some quarters. *The Economist*, using such terms as "failure" and "no positive progress" to describe both the proximity and the joint talks, argued that the Turkish Cypriots had now realized two long-sought objectives: face-to-face meetings with the other side and a delay in the consideration of territorial adjustments. As for the Greek Cypriots, the magazine went on to say, three of its five leaders had found the talks so worthless that they were not planning to attend the resumed session in October. To no one's surprise, the Secretary-General put a more optimistic spin on developments, claiming in his report to the Security Council of August 21 that the issues of displaced persons and territorial adjustments had now been brought "to the same level of clarity" as had the other six topics.

In the course of direct negotiations on the Set of Ideas, the Secretary-General had argued that territorial adjustments should be negotiated in terms of "precise areas," not "percentages," and he presented the proposed territorial adjustments to both sides in the form of a map. Pointing out that the proposals would reduce Turkish Cypriot-controlled areas to 28.2% of the island, leaders of that community continued to insist on a 29-plus % settlement. On the matter of displaced persons—160,000 Greek Cypriots and 45,000 Turkish Cypriots—the Turkish Cypriot side accepted the principle of the right of return and the right to property but denied that its own people were obliged to vacate all premises originally owned by the other side, offering financial compensation instead. The Greek Cypriots, for their part, opposed "massive confiscation" of the property of displaced persons and proposed long-term leasing as an alternative. Reviewing the progress to that point, the Secretary-General appeared to believe that an early settlement was possible if the Turkish Cypriots demonstrated the necessary willingness to compromise on the territorial issue; proposals already on the table, he said, offered "reasonable arrangements" to address the problem of displaced persons [ibid.].

The Security Council too put a positive spin on the outcome of negotiations. Welcoming the Turkish Cypriot acceptance of the rights of return and the right to property, as well as the "narrowing of the gap" on territorial adjustments, the Council endorsed the Secretary-General's map and agreed that "the Set of Ideas as an integrated whole has now been sufficiently developed to enable the two sides to reach an overall agreement." This late-August resolution called for "uninterrupted negotiations" in the talks, to commence on October 26, and stated its expectation that an agreement would be reached by the end of 1992, making 1993 a "transition period." On the off chance the October talks failed, the Secretary-General would identity the reasons and suggest an alternative course of action [S/Res/774 (1992)].

The Restructuring of UNFICYP

During the prenegotiation phase of the 1992 talks, the attention of the Secretary-General and the Security Council turned once again to UNFICYP, whose mandate was due to expire on May 31. The increasing dissatisfaction of troop-contributing countries with the operation's financing arrangements and the refusal of the Security Council to revise them had placed the six-month mandate renewal—not to mention the future of the operation—in some jeopardy.

Voluntary payments to the UNFICYP Special Account have never been sufficient to reimburse troop contributors for one-third of the total cost of their troops in each six-month mandate period, as had been agreed upon. By May 31, 1992, when the U.N.'s indebtedness to past and present troop-contributing countries reached $192.7 million, these states had been reimbursed only through June 1981. Just the previous December the Security Council had refused to change the operation's funding from a voluntary to an assessed basis, and it was then that three of the eight UNFICYP troop contributors began hinting at plans to withdraw some or all of their personnel. In granting the Secretary-General's request for a mandate extension through December 15, 1992 [S/Res/759 (1992)], the Security Council took the unprecedented step of requesting him to consult with the troop-contributing countries and submit "specific proposals" on restructuring the Force in light of the threatened withdrawals.

On a provisional basis the Secretary-General recommended—as the "least bad option"—absorbing the reductions by decreasing from four to three the number of battalions in the Force and the number of deployment sectors [U.N. press release SC/5418, 6/12/92]. But he strongly advised against scaling back UNFICYP's present broad mandate and argued instead for an increase in the number of troops "on the line," i.e., those with actual patrol duties. This could be accomplished, the Secretary-General hoped, through increases in troop contributions from states remaining in the operation or through reductions in headquarters and support staff. Were it necessary to decrease the number of line troops, Boutros-Ghali warned, UNFICYP would have to be provided some "rapid reinforcement capability" to handle crisis situations.

In the report requested in Resolution 759 [S/24581, 9/21/92], the Secretary-General revealed that not three but five contributors were contemplating reductions in forces, that none would agree to delay its withdrawals pending the conclusion of the current round of negotiations, and that UNFICYP's rapid-response squadron would be eliminated completely. As a result, the Secretary-General concluded, the number of observation posts on the buffer zone and the frequency of patrols would be reduced and the response time to incidents would increase even after the proposed restructuring.

The Failure of Joint Talks

On October 23, Secretary-General Boutros-Ghali held informal consultations with the five permanent members of the Security Council on the joint meetings scheduled to open three days later. (It was later revealed that representatives of the Secretary-General had held preparatory meetings in the area with all the concerned parties from October 9 through October 22.) The Council fully endorsed the Secretary-General's negotiating approach and promised to give his efforts "every support" [U.N. press release SG/1968, 10/26/92]. The joint talks, delayed for two days, began on October 28 and adjourned November 11, five months and 59 meetings after the opening of "intensive negotiations" the previous June but without completing an overall framework agreement. Negotiations were set to resume in early March 1993 [U.N. press release SG/SM/4853-CYP/1157, 11/12/92].

The New York Times was quick to call this second round of talks "unsuccessful" and a "setback" for Boutros-Ghali [11/12/92]. *The Economist* agreed that the talks had "failed," adding that, "As usual, nothing has been agreed on" [12/14/92]. It reported that the Greek Cypriot side had accepted the Secretary-General's map and Set of Ideas as the "basis of discussions," while the Turkish Cypriots had rejected them out of hand and were "dressed down" by the Secretary-General. The "impasse" was ascribed to the reluctance of the Security Council, and particularly the United States, to press Ankara for concessions when Turkish air bases were being used to supply humanitarian aid to the Iraqi Kurds.

As before, the Secretary-General took a more optimistic view of matters in his report to the Security Council [S/24830, 11/19/92], maintaining that a number of the outstanding differences could probably be resolved in forthcoming meetings. He pointed out, however, that "some of the positions voiced by the Turkish Cypriot side are, in a fundamental way, outside the framework of the set of ideas" and "needed to be reviewed" if talks were to succeed. And once again among the problem areas were the "concept of federation," displaced persons, and territorial adjustments. Citing the "deep crisis of confidence between the two sides," the Secretary-General recommended more thorough preparations for the next round of meetings and the adoption of several "confidence-building measures" by the parties.

One of the Turkish Cypriot positions that fell outside the "framework" was its insistence that two sovereign states currently exist on Cyprus and that both would remain sovereign in a future federation. The Secretary-General pointed out in his report that the Security Council had repeatedly reaffirmed the unity of Cyprus and the single sovereignty and citizenship of the new federal state. In response to the Turkish Cypriot side's reiteration of its reservations regarding the rights of Greek Cypriot displaced persons to return to or reclaim property and its strong preference for monetary compensation, the Secretary-General stated that he questioned the north's acceptance of these rights even in principle. After all, he noted, the reservations cited—especially those affecting the ability of Greek Cypriots to reclaim property that Turkish Cypriots now purportedly "owned" and held "legal title" to—"would in effect preclude the possibility that any Greek Cypriot displaced persons would be able to return." The Secretary-General also noted that the Turkish Cypriot side refused to accept the map of proposed territorial adjustments "even as a basis for discussion." In sum, he said, a "lack of political will . . . continue[d] to block an agreement that is otherwise within reach" [ibid.].

The Security Council, after pronouncing itself satisfied that all the issues contained in the Set of Ideas had been discussed and that areas of agreement existed, concurred with the Secretary-General that "certain positions adopted by the Turkish Cypriot side were fundamentally at variance with the Set of Ideas" and called upon that side to "adopt positions that are consistent" with those ideas. In this November resolution it also urged the implementation of the confidence-building measures recommended by the Secretary-General—among them, reductions in the number of "foreign troops" on the island and decreases in the defense expenditures of both sides; the "unmanning" of more military positions on both sides of the buffer zone; the lifting of restrictions on the movement of Cypriots and foreign visitors across the zone; the development of "bi-communal projects"; and cooperation with the United Nations on a "Cyprus-wide" census and on two "feasibility studies," one on the eventual resettlement of displaced persons, the other on a program of economic development for the area under Turkish Cypriot administration in the future federation [S/Res/789 (1992)].

Further Restructuring of UNFICYP?

Reporting on the status of UNFICYP on December 1, as another mandate period was coming to an end, the Secretary-General informed the Security Council that the force reductions and restructuring announced in September had commenced November 16 with the withdrawal of 63 Austrian personnel from the operation [S/24917]. By December 15—the proposed date for the full implementation of the restructuring plan—198 British and 322 Danish troops would also be withdrawn, with 61 Canadian personnel to follow at an unspecified time. The cuts, amounting to 28% of the original size of the Force, would reduce UNFICYP's strength from 2,078 to 1,488. A fifth troop contributor, Finland, had scheduled the withdrawal of its seven-man contingent by the end of 1993.

The Secretary-General recommended extending the operation's mandate through June and requested troop-contributing countries to refrain from withdrawing additional troops before that time. But in fact, he noted, several contributors were planning further reductions in 1993; and an unconfirmed press report two weeks later indicated that personnel would number fewer than 1,000 by September [*The New York Times*, 12/14/92]. The Secretary-General said he would endeavor to absorb the effects of future withdrawals through restructuring, but emphasized that the cuts to date—and the financial situation that caused them—had already placed UNFICYP's future in jeopardy. Without commenting publicly on these assertions, the Security Council granted a mandate extension through June 15, 1993, and welcomed the Secretary-General's "intention" to consult further with the troop contributors on the matter of restructuring [S/Res/796 (1992)].

A Third Round of Direct Talks

Interpreting Security Council Resolution 789's criticism of the Turkish Cypriot negotiating position as a U.N. endorsement of their own views, the Greek Cypriots were quick to announce their acceptance of the confidence-building measures contained in that November resolution (particularly those referring to the removal of foreign troops and the taking of an islandwide census) [A/47/736, 11/27/92], accused the other side of rejecting these measures, and reaffirmed their support for the complete demilitarization of the island—pending the withdrawal of all Turkish troops and settlers. They also agreed to U.N. monitoring of the disarmament process [A/47/759, 12/7/92] and reasserted their long-standing claim that the Turkish Cypriot side had deliberately and systematically attempted to alter the demographic structure of the population by encouraging massive emigration from Turkey, particularly in the 1975–77 period [A/47/536, A/47/856].

The Turkish Cypriots, for their part, offered no official response to Resolution 789. They had previously criticized the other side for supporting demilitarization while spending "a million dollars a day on rearmament" [A/47/618], maintaining that Turkish troops were indispensable and the real peacekeepers on Cyprus.

The narrow **defeat of Greek Cypriot President George Vassiliou by conservative rival Glafcos Clerides** on February 14, 1993, promises both continuity and change in the negotiations ahead. Vassiliou, who ran with the support of Communists and Socialists, was a strong supporter of U.N. mediation and worked closely with both Boutros-Ghali and his predecessor in drafting and revising the Set of Ideas [*The Economist*, 2/20/93]. Clerides, elected by a center-right coalition, has criticized the U.N. plan as providing too many concessions to the Turkish Cypriots and has promised to win better terms for Greek Cypriots, especially regarding the return of property and the payment of compensation to displaced persons [*Financial Times*, 2/16/93]. He also pledged to request a delay in the resumption of direct talks to allow for consultations with his political backers and demanded that alleged flaws in the Set of Ideas be corrected before negotiations reopen.

But the five decades' long personal relationship between Clerides and the **Turkish Cypriot leader and chief negotiator Rauf Denktash** could supply the trust and confidence that the peace process has sorely lacked [*The Washington Post*, 2/18/93]. Both men found enough common ground to meet with Boutros-Ghali at U.N. Headquarters on March 30 to discuss the conditions under which a third round of joint talks would be held. Reflecting the wishes of both the new President (he assumed office March 1) and Mr. Denktash, the Secretary-General said he would welcome private meetings between the leaders and consultations between their respective political parties in parallel with his own good offices mission. Boutros-Ghali likewise promised to "clarify and address the specific concerns" of each side regarding the Set of Ideas before the convening of direct talks. This preparatory process would also cover the confidence-building measures approved by the Security Council.

Joint talks resumed on May 24. By June 1 the Secretary-General's **Special Representative for Cyprus, Joe Clark**, announced that sufficient progress had been made to allow both sides to formally commit to the implementation of all the measures under consideration. Denktash, however, insisted on more time for consultations with his political advisors. In a statement to the press issued June 1, Clark stressed that the package of confidence-building measures was "eminently fair" and would require neither side to compromise on substantive political matters.

Assessed Funding and Confidence-Building Measures

As the June 15 deadline neared for the extension of the UNFICYP mandate, the Secretary-General warned that scheduled troop withdrawals would reduce the force to only 850 personnel and render the operation unviable [S/25492]. He again requested the immediate conversion of UNFICYP to assessed funding, arguing that the $47.1 million annual cost would constitute only 1.7% of a total U.N. peacekeeping bill, running some $2.8 billion for 1992. The government of Cyprus, for its part, reiterated its willingness to contribute $15.7 million to the maintenance of the operation, roughly a third of the total cost [S/25647, 4/21/93]. But a U.K.-

sponsored draft resolution mandating assessments and troop reductions to a minimum acceptable level was defeated by **a Russian veto on May 11—the first veto cast in the Security Council in two years** [U.N. press release SC/5629, 5/27/93].

On May 27 the Security Council adopted a compromise solution, deciding to assess on all member states only those costs for UNFICYP not covered by voluntary contributions [S/Res/831 (1993)]. In doing so, the Council called for maximum voluntary contributions in the future, and expressed its concern that the United Nations not enter into "open-ended peacekeeping commitments." The new funding arrangements were to take effect once the Security Council reconvened to formally extend UNFICYP's mandate, which it did on June 11 [S/Res/839]. The Council also approved the Secretary-General's recommendation that UNFICYP be further reduced to three infantry battalions of at least 350 troops each, the minimum number required to maintain effective control of the buffer zone. By November 1993 the Secretary-General is to submit a report assessing progress achieved in the implementation of all confidence-building measures and political negotiations, as well as "possible progressive steps" toward the conversion of UNFICYP to an observer mission—an option favored by most troop contributors. On the basis of that report, the Security Council would conduct a "comprehensive reassessment" of the operation in December.

II
Arms Control and Disarmament

By Ivo H. Daalder

During the past year the momentum that had characterized arms control and disarmament efforts in the preceding years began to slow. There was significant progress on some issues, including the signing of the START-II Treaty by Presidents Bush and Yeltsin in January 1993, the completion of the Chemical Weapons Convention (CWC), a de facto moratorium on all nuclear testing, and the resolution of outstanding differences surrounding Argentine, Brazilian, and Chilean ratification of the Treaty of Tlatelolco. But there were also notable reversals. Ukraine failed to ratify the START-I Treaty or sign the nuclear Non-Proliferation Treaty (NPT), as it had promised to do in May 1992. The NPT also came under attack by the decision of North Korea, announced in March 1993, that it was withdrawing from the treaty in response to repeated requests by the International Atomic Energy Agency (IAEA) to conduct a special inspection of two sites suspected of storing nuclear waste products. The same month, South Africa stunned the international community by announcing that it had manufactured six nuclear weapons in the 1980s, although these had since been destroyed. Finally, Iraq continued to defy U.N. Security Council resolutions mandating the destruction of its weapons of mass destruction and ballistic missiles with ranges over 150 kilometers.

These mixed results reflected the continuing transition of the arms control and disarmament agenda from Cold War issues to issues more pertinent in the post-Cold War era. A significant step in this direction was the report by Secretary-General Boutros Boutros-Ghali entitled "New directions of arms regulation and disarmament in the post-Cold War era" [A/C.1/47/7, 10/23/92]. The report suggested three new directions for arms control and disarmament: integration of arms regulation efforts into the broader structure of international peace and security, notably by incorporating appropriate measures in preventive diplomacy, peacemaking, peacekeeping, and post-conflict peacebuilding efforts; globalization of the arms control and disarmament process so that states move in practice to accept the limitations they have long supported in theory; and revitalization of arms control by building on past achievements, particularly in the elimination of weapons of mass destruction, the control of proliferation, greater transparency in armaments, and the negotiation of other confidence-building measures.

The Secretary-General's report elicited numerous comments from member state governments, the General Assembly, the Conference on Disarmament, and the First Committee—notably less on the substantive parts of the report than on its concluding comments concerning the U.N. disarmament machinery. The First Committee was reconvened in early March 1993 to reassess this machinery, and the General Assembly adopted its recommendations on how further to rationalize the U.N. disarmament machinery.

The challenge for the 48th Session of the General Assembly will be to act on the Secretary-General's report and the work of the First Committee, the U.N. Disarmament Commission, and the Conference on Disarmament to ensure that the arms control and disarmament agenda more clearly reflects the realities of the post-Cold War period. This will involve not only the rationalization of the U.N. disarmament machinery but also effective action in the three areas outlined in the Secretary-General's report. The member states will, of course, have to take the lead in this effort. Much will also depend on how some of the outstanding issues on the arms control and disarmament agenda—particularly in the areas of bilateral nuclear arms control, nuclear testing, nuclear proliferation, and chemical and biological weapons—will be resolved.

1. Nuclear Arms Control and Disarmament

The historic progress achieved in U.S.–Soviet arms control in the early 1990s was significantly extended when, on January 3, 1993, the **United States** and **Russia** signed the **START-II Treaty**, which, once implemented, will reduce U.S. and Russian strategic nuclear forces to 3,000–3,500 weapons on each side—a 70% reduction from current levels. At the same time, ratification and implementation of this historic arms control agreement must await the ratification of the **START-I Treaty**, which has been held up by the Ukrainian parliament's refusal to bring the matter to a vote. The future of the bilateral nuclear arms control agenda hinges on a successful resolution of Ukrainian political, economic, and security concerns that would accompany its ratification of START I and adherence to the nuclear **Non-Proliferation Treaty** as a non-nuclear weapons state.

The START-II Treaty builds on the START-I agreement signed by the United States and Soviet Union in July 1991. Reductions from current levels are to be achieved in phases. After the first phase, which must be completed within seven years after START I enters into force, actual warheads will be limited to 3,800–4,250, with multiwarhead or MIRVed land-based warheads limited to 1,200; submarine-launched ballistic missiles (SLBM) warheads to 2,160; and warheads on Russia's SS-18 missiles limited to 650. In the second phase, actual warheads must be reduced to 3,000–3,500; MIRVed ICBM warheads eliminated completely; and SLBM warheads limited to 1,700–1,750. Phase two of the agreement must be completed by 2003, or by the end of the year 2000 if the United States can help finance the elimination of Russian weapons.

To achieve these reductions, the treaty employs the agreed provisions of the START-I agreement, including provisions for off-loading excess warheads from missiles to achieve the reductions. In a few cases, these provisions were specifically modified. Four changes are especially significant. First, whereas the SS-18 missile silos to be reduced under START I have to be destroyed, under START II, 105 SS-18 silos may be converted for use of a smaller missile. In return, Russia has agreed to eliminate all SS-18 missiles, which it had not been required to do under START I. Second, although under START I no more than four warheads can be off-loaded from a missile to achieve the reductions, START II provides that Russia can remove five warheads from 90 SS-19 missiles to comply with the ban on MIRVed ICBM warheads. Third, under START II up to 100 strategic bombers that have never been equipped with air-launched cruise missiles can be oriented to conventional roles. These bombers will still count under START I, but not under START II unless they are again reoriented to nuclear roles. Fourth, whereas bomber weapons were deliberately undercounted in START I, START II will limit these weapons to the actual number for which bombers are equipped. This change not only results in a very substantial reduction in bomber weapons but also necessitates intrusive Russian inspections of the American B-2 bomber to determine how many weapons it can carry. A one-time inspection of the B-2 is therefore allowed, something Washington had successfully avoided in the START-I negotiations [*Arms Control Brief* 1, no. 3 (1/93)].

Full implementation of START II, however, must await ratification of the START-I Treaty by **Ukraine**, which, like **Kazakhstan** and **Belarus**, was made a party to START I under the **Lisbon Protocol of May 1992** because weapons covered by the agreement were stationed on its territory [see *A Global Agenda: Issues/47*, p. 120]. To date, all but Ukraine have ratified this agreement. Ukraine has insisted that before it moves to ratify START I and sign and ratify the NPT as a non-nuclear weapons state, a number of conditions must be met. As explained by **Ukraine's President, Leonid Kravchuk**, in a speech before the World Economic Forum in Davos in January 1993, these conditions include:

- the provision of "legally binding political instruments adopted at the highest level by the nuclear Powers, and first and foremost Russia and the United States of America, to the effect that those Powers will not use nuclear weapons against Ukraine, will not employ conventional weapons or the threat of force, will refrain from applying economic pressure in order to resolve any contentious issues, and will respect Ukraine's territorial integrity and the inviolability of its borders";
- financial and technical assistance to aid Ukraine in the destruction of the strategic offensive weapons on its territory; and
- a recognition that Ukraine, as the legal owner of "all the components of the nuclear warheads that are subject to dismantling and to destruction," can use these "to resolve problems of Ukraine's economic development and, in particular, of fuelling Ukraine's power stations" [CD/1181, 2/5/93].

Behind these conditions lurks the suspicion, substantiated in part by statements of Ukrainian parliamentarians during the ratification debate, that Ukraine is less interested in resolving this matter than it is in retaining at least part of the weapons as a future deterrent force. Indeed, there is some indication that the Ukrainian parliament may well ratify START I and move to destroy all but 46 10-warhead SS-24 missiles but renege on Kiev's pledge to accede to the NPT as a non-nuclear weapons state [*The New York Times*, 3/31/93].

The United States and Russia have tried actively to forestall such a development. In early January 1993, Washington sought to reassure Kiev on all three conditions by making clear that it was prepared to offer security assurances similar to the ones it had made previously in regard to the START-I Treaty. These assurances would include: a commitment, first made in 1968, to seek immediate action by the U.N. Security Council to assist a non-nuclear weapons state party to the NPT that is subject to actual or threatened aggression involving nuclear weapons; reaffirmation of the principles enshrined in the **1975 Helsinki Final Act** of the **Conference on Security and Cooperation in Europe (CSCE),** which recognizes existing borders and permits their change only by peaceful and consensual means; and reiteration of the 1978 U.S. commitment not to use nuclear weapons against non-nuclear weapons states party to the NPT unless they were engaged in an attack together with a nuclear weapons state against the United States or its allies.

A few weeks later, Russia made a similar commitment to security assurances in the event Ukraine ratified the START-I Treaty and signed and ratified the NPT. However, the absence of a commitment to forgo economic pressure would appear to have left Kiev unsatisfied by these statements [*Arms Control Today* 23, no. 1 (1/93), pp. 22, 28].

On the economic front, the Bush administration pledged $175 million to aid in the destruction of strategic weapons on Ukrainian territory, and the Clinton administration has since reiterated that this amount is a "starting point, not the final offer." At the same time, Ukraine has told Washington that it might need up to $2.8 billion for this task [*The Washington Post*, 12/10/92; RFE/RL Daily Report, no. 89, 5/11/93; *Arms Control Today* 23, no. 4 (5/93), p. 24]. Finally, the issue of compensation for fissile materials in Ukrainian warheads has proven even more difficult, primarily because of Kiev's claim to ownership of the nuclear weapons components, including the fissile materials. Recognition of Ukrainian ownership by the United States may imply tacit recognition of Ukraine as a nuclear power, which would be contrary to Washington's interests. So far, the United States has dealt with the issue indirectly, agreeing to purchase up to 500 tons of highly enriched uranium from Russia provided Moscow works out an agreement with Belarus, Kazakhstan, and Ukraine to share the proceeds equitably [*Arms Control Today* 23, no. 2 (3/93), pp. 22, 26].

Prospects for resolving the outstanding difficulties on this issue were significantly enhanced when U.S. Secretary of Defense Les Aspin traveled to Kiev in June 1993. In an attempt to skirt the ownership question, Aspin proposed that Ukraine agree to remove the nuclear warheads from all weapons on its territory and store them in sites to be monitored by U.S., Russian, and Ukrainian personnel [*The New York Times*, 6/8/93]. The proposal—which would reassure Ukraine that the weapons on its territory would not become part of the Russian inventory and reassure Russia and others that Ukraine would not gain positive control over these weapons—was received with much interest in Kiev, and might therefore prove to be a workable solution to the problem.

The 47th Session of the General Assembly recognized that the fundamental changes in the international environment had permitted agreements on deep reductions of nuclear armaments and welcomed further progress to this end. It also urged the parties to the START-I Treaty and the Lisbon Protocol "to take the steps necessary to bring this Treaty and the accompanying protocol into force at the earliest possible date" [A/Res/47/52K]. During its 48th Session the General Assembly is likely to reiterate this position, mindful that to date only Ukraine has refused to ratify the START-I agreement and that Kazakhstan and Ukraine have yet to accede to the NPT as non-nuclear weapons states. At the same time, the General Assembly, while welcoming the conclusion of START II, is also likely to urge further steps by Russia and the United States, as well as other nuclear weapons states, to reduce their nuclear arsenals.

2. Nuclear Testing

As in previous years, the 47th Session of the General Assembly passed two resolutions dealing with nuclear testing, one dealing with an amendment to the **Limited Test Ban Treaty (LTBT)**, which would ban testing underground as well as in the atmosphere, outer space, and under water, and another calling for the negotiation of a **Comprehensive Nuclear Test Ban Treaty (CTBT)**, which would be an essential step toward preventing the improvement of nuclear weapons and their further proliferation and would contribute to the eventual elimination of nuclear weapons [A/Res/47/46; A/Res/47/47]. The United States voted against both resolutions while Russia supported both. The United Kingdom voted against the first and abstained on the second resolution, while France and China (neither of which are parties to the LTBT) were absent during the vote on the LTBT amendment resolution and abstained on the resolution calling for a CTBT.

Although the 48th Session is sure to return to the issue of nuclear testing, it may do so more enthusiastically than in previous years as a result of a significant change of policy by the United States. In October 1992, in the middle of a heated presidential election, President Bush signed a bill that would place severe restrictions on the future ability of the United States to test nuclear weapons and, at the same time, compel efforts to negotiate a CTBT. Under the legislation, the United States could not conduct any tests prior to July 1, 1993. The president must report to Congress on the number and type of nuclear tests planned for each subsequent year. The total number of tests cannot exceed 15, of which no more than 5 can be conducted each year. All but one of these nuclear tests must be to check upgraded safety features of new nuclear warheads; one test annually can be conducted for reliability purposes. The United Kingdom, which has long tested at the U.S. site in Nevada, may be granted one test annually, but this would count against the annual and overall testing quota. Finally, the legislation states that "no underground test of nuclear weapons may be conducted by the United States after September 30, 1996, unless a foreign state conducts a nuclear test after this date," thus effectively instituting an **indefinite testing moratorium** [*Arms Control Today* 22, no. 8 (10/92), pp. 32, 40].

After the passage of the testing legislation, both **France and Russia** have declared that they would extend their own testing moratorium until July 1993. **Great Britain**, which initially opposed the legislation, was effectively barred from nuclear testing, given its reliance on the U.S. site, while **China** refused to announce a moratorium of its own, even though it conducted no tests after the U.S. halt went into effect.

The Bush administration had opposed the legislation and pledged to work for new legislation, but the Republican President's defeat in the November elections put a whole new light on the issue, particularly since the new President had long supported a comprehensive test ban achieved in phases. In April 1993 the Clinton White House announced that it would begin a consultative process within two months with Russia, U.S.

allies, and other states "aimed at commencing negotiations toward a multilateral nuclear test ban" [White House statement, 4/23/93]. The change in policy was also reflected in the **Conference on Disarmament**, which agreed to reestablish the **Ad Hoc Committee on Nuclear Testing**, something it had failed to do in years past.

Before negotiations on a CTBT could start, however, two issues had to be resolved. The first concerned the degree to which a multilateral test ban should be truly comprehensive. Within the Clinton administration some agencies favored a multilateral ban that would allow testing below one kiloton or 1,000 tons of TNT, which would be sufficient to check the reliability of the U.S. nuclear stockpile [*The Washington Post*, 4/30/93]. This proposal generated heated opposition in Congress, with the three principal authors of the nuclear testing law writing to the administration that such a proposal would be inconsistent with the law, which called for negotiation of a *comprehensive* test ban. As a result, the administraiton decided to drop the idea of trying to negotiate a less-than-comprehensive test ban [*The New York Times*, 5/15/93].

The second issue related to whether the United States should resume nuclear testing after the initial nine-month moratorium had lapsed. An interagency task force reportedly favored a resumption of testing in early 1994 for reliability and safety purposes. A total of six additional U.S. tests and three British tests were proposed [*The Washington Post*, 6/11/93]. Informal briefings on Capitol Hill of the proposed resumption resulted in large-scale opposition, with 36 Senators and over 100 Representatives urging the President to adopt a no-first-testing policy. In the end the administration opted to continue the moratorium, which would remain in effect until September 1994 unless another country tested first [ibid., 7/4/93].

The 48th Session of the General Assembly is likely to welcome the new atmosphere surrounding the nuclear-testing issue. A critical issue in the debate about testing will be the forum in which to negotiate a CTBT. There is significant support for convening another conference to amend the LTBT. According to Article II of the treaty, any amendment approved by a majority of all parties, including all original parties (the United States, Great Britain, and the Soviet Union—now Russia), shall be binding on all parties once the original parties have deposited their instruments of ratification. It is therefore possible to bind all LTBT signatories to a comprehensive test ban, even if the party concerned opposes the amendment. There are, however, two problems with this approach. First, neither China nor France is a party to the treaty, and unless they endeavor to do so, neither would be a party to a CTBT. Second, an amendment requires the approval of the United States, Britain, and Russia, and at least the former two are unlikely to endorse this path toward a CTBT. Thus, a CTBT will require new negotiations, most probably in the Conference on Disarmament. The General Assembly is sure to debate this issue in its coming session.

3. Nuclear Proliferation

Seven countries joined the NPT in the last year, bringing the total number of states parties to 158. But the biggest issue facing the future of the NPT was not its growing acceptance but the fact that on March 12, 1993, the **North Korean government** announced that it would withdraw from the treaty in order to protect its supreme national interests. Since the treaty states that any party must give three months' notice of its intention to withdraw, the withdrawal would take effect on June 12, 1993 [A/48/133, 4/12/93, Annex 7]. Similarly disturbing was the announcement by President de Klerk of South Africa on March 24, 1993, that South Africa had built six nuclear weapons, though these had since been destroyed.

It was only in 1992 that **North Korea**, which had ratified the NPT in 1985, signed the safeguards agreement with the IAEA that allowed the agency to inspect Pyongyang's civilian nuclear facilities in order to ensure North Korea's compliance with the NPT. Data presented by North Korea and subsequent inspections revealed that North Korea had produced a small amount of plutonium in what it termed a "radiochemical laboratory . . . designed for research on the separation of uranium and plutonium" [*The Washington Post*, 5/6/92]. Subsequent analysis of the plutonium samples raised doubts about the veracity of the North Korean declaration that the plutonium had been produced from a single batch of reprocessed fuel. Instead, analysis showed that nuclear waste had been reprocessed more than once [A/48/133, 4/12/93, p. 5].

In a series of meetings between IAEA and North Korean officials, the discrepancies went unresolved. Repeated requests to inspect two nuclear waste sites identified by U.S. satellites were denied by Pyongyang on the ground that the sites were military, though non-nuclear, and that the IAEA had lost its impartiality by relying on data from a third party. On February 9, 1993, the IAEA requested North Korea to provide access to the sites on the basis of Article 73(b) of the **safeguards agreement between North Korea and IAEA** [INFCIRC/403]. This was the first time in the IAEA's history that the agency had demanded a **special inspection** of a site without the affected government giving prior approval. Pyongyang repeatedly rejected an inspection and, a month later, stated that it intended to withdraw from the NPT. As a result, on April 1, 1993, the IAEA's Board of Governors adopted a resolution that, inter alia, found North Korea "in noncompliance with its obligations under its Safeguards Agreement with the Agency." The IAEA was "not able to verify that there has been no diversion of nuclear materials," it said, and consequently decided to report North Korea's noncompliance to the Security Council [ibid., p. 3].

Although reaction to the North Korean decision was swift and universal in its opposition, there was little agreement on what should be done. China firmly opposed referring the matter to the Security Council, let alone passing a resolution calling for economic sanctions—a course initially favored by the United States [*The New York Times*, 3/24/93; *The Washington Times*, 3/26/93]. South Korea urged a moderate approach, relying at least initially on emphasizing possible incentives, including allowing inspections of U.S. military bases in the South, a repeat of Washington's pledge not to launch a nuclear strike against Pyongyang, and holding out the prospect of economic aid [*The New York Times*, 3/30/93].

The United States agreed to try a cooperative solution to the North Korean nuclear issue by directly engaging Pyongyang in high-level bilateral talks. The objective of these discussions was to convince the North Koreans to remain a party to the NPT, cooperate fully with the IAEA, and implement the December 1991 North-South denuclearization declaration, which prohibits the acquisition of nuclear weapons, bans reprocessing and enrichment facilities, and calls for bilateral inspections [*The Washington Post*, 5/25/93; *The New York Times*, 5/27/93]. As an incentive, the United States reportedly was prepared to offer a guarantee that, as a party to the NPT, the North would not be threatened by or attacked with U.S. nuclear weapons. Washington was also willing to allow inspection of U.S. military bases in the South and to encourage the IAEA to inspect nuclear facilities in the North and South simultaneously. Finally, the United States offered the prospect of additional discussions on future political and economic relations and the termination of "Team Spirit," an annual U.S.-South Korean military exercise.

Initial discussion between the two countries were not encouraging, but after four days of talks the North did agree to "suspend" its withdrawal from the NPT, which would have gone into effect the next day. Pyongyang also pledged to continue to accept routine IAEA inspections, but it refused to allow special inspections of the two suspect sites. Although the United States offered general assurances of the North's security, it did not offer any of the incentives mentioned earlier. Finally, both sides agreed to continue their dialogue on the nuclear issue in an attempt to resolve the matter [*Joint Statement of the DPRK and the United States*, 6/11/93].

Although legally less troubling than North Korea's noncompliance with the IAEA safeguards agreement, an equally disturbing development for nuclear nonproliferation was the announcement by **South Africa** that it had built six nuclear weapons and started work on a seventh before it decided to destroy them in 1990 and accede to the NPT in 1991 [A/CN.10/179, 4/26/93]. The statement followed disclosures in the U.S. press that Washington suspected that South Africa had not provided a full accounting of all its weapons-grade material to the IAEA and may have hidden or, less plausibly, exported some material [*The Washington Post*, 3/18/93].

The public revelation of past South African nuclear weapons activities and the continuing doubts in Washington about the accuracy of Pretoria's accounting records are sure to be addressed by the 48th Session. Until the 46th Session, the General Assembly had repeatedly passed a resolution on "Nuclear Capability of South Africa," which condemned South Africa's failure to adhere to the NPT. A milder version of this resolution was passed during the 46th Session, and none was passed at the 47th. The 48th Session is, however, likely to take up the issue once again.

4. Nuclear Weapons-Free Zones

The problems in North Korea and the revelations concerning South Africa may have halted the momentum toward the negotiation of nuclear weapons-free zones (NWFZ) in these regions. This would be all the more discouraging, since progress in other regions, notably Latin America, has been considerable in recent years. At the same time, a successful resolution of the North Korean problem and complete satisfaction that South Africa has now revealed all, may stimulate efforts to negotiate a NWFZ in Africa and on the Korean Peninsula, providing a welcome example for other regions, notably the Middle East and South Asia.

The 47th Session of the General Assembly addressed the progress made toward the implementation of the **Declaration on the Denuclearization of Africa**, which had been considerable following South Africa's accession to the NPT in September 1991. In April 1992 a group of experts, set up jointly by the **Organization of African Unity (OAU)** and the United Nations, held its second meeting to consider how to implement the declaration. On the basis of this report, the General Assembly requested the Secretary-General, in consultation with the OAU, to convene the group of experts in 1993 "in order to draw up a draft treaty or convention on the denuclearization of Africa" [A/Res/47/76]. The group of experts' report should be ready in time for the 48th Session, at which time formal negotiations on the issue may be possible.

Significant progress on consolidating the NWFZ in Latin America was achieved during 1992, with many of the outstanding issues finally resolved. At an extraordinary meeting of the **Organization for the Prohibition of Nuclear Weapons in Latin America (OPANAL)**, Argentina, Brazil, and Chile jointly submitted four amendments to the **Treaty of Tlatelolco** that changed some verification and reporting requirements. The amendments were unanimously accepted by all parties to the treaty and, following ratification, the treaty will enter into force for these three outstanding countries. The sole nonparty in the region, Cuba, also stated that it would accede to the treaty once it had been ratified by the other parties, thereby completing the NWFZ for the entire region [*Arms Control Today* 23, no. 2 (3/93), p. 5]. The 48th Session is sure to welcome this development.

Prospects for the establishment of nuclear weapons-free zones in two other regions—**the Middle East and South Asia**—have not changed much in the past year. In the Middle East the long-standing and unresolved differences between Israel and its Arab neighbors continue to stymie progress on the issue. As in the past, however, the 48th Session is likely to take up the issue by passing resolutions on the establishment of a nuclear weapons-free zone in the region of the Middle East and on Israeli nuclear armaments [see, for example, A/Res/47/48; A/Res/47/55]. The 48th Session is also likely to reiterate its call for the establishment of a nuclear weapons-free zone in South Asia, as did the 47th Session [A/Res/47/49]. But since one of the key players in the region, India, has long opposed regional disarmament measures relating to weapons of mass destruction, including specific resolutions calling for a NWFZ in South Asia, little progress in this area is likely to be achieved.

5. Chemical and Biological Weapons

Perhaps the most significant arms control development of the past year was the conclusion of the **Convention on the Prohibition of the Development, Production, Stockpiling and Use of Chemical Weapons and on Their Destruction** (also known as the **Chemical Weapons Convention, or CWC**) after nearly a quarter-century of negotiation. This completes international negotiations on the elimination of chemical and biological weapons, the latter having been banned since 1975 under the **Biological and Toxin Weapons Convention (BWC)**. Some significant developments also occurred in the biological weapons area with the conclusion of an agreement among the United States, Britain, and Russia on reciprocal visits of civilian biological research centers in order to enhance confidence in Russian compliance with its obligations under the BWC. An experts group studying means to verify the provisions of the BWC also continued to meet throughout the year.

The 47th Session welcomed the conclusion of the CWC and called upon all states to sign, ratify, and implement the convention [A/Res/47/39]. The CWC is the most ambitious disarmament agreement ever negotiated, banning the possession, acquisition, production, stockpiling, transfer, and use of chemical weapons and mandating the destruction of any chemical weapons stocks and production facilities within ten years after the Convention's entry into force. The CWC's verification regime is also the most comprehensive to date, mandating routine and ad hoc inspections of civilian industries and military sites, and challenge inspections with guaranteed access to any suspect site, although the degree of access to be granted is subject to negotiation between the inspected state and the inspectors. The CWC will enter into force 180 days after the 65th signatory has ratified the convention or two years after it is opened for signature, whichever is later.

The success of the CWC will depend in part on who signs and ratifies the Convention. Reasons for optimism include the fact that on January 13, 1993, 130 countries gathered in Paris to sign it. By mid-May, the total number of signatories had risen to 144. It is noteworthy that of the 15 countries known or believed to possess chemical weapons (in addition to the United States and Russia), nine signed the Convention, including China, India, Iran, Israel, and Pakistan. Israel's accession is especially noteworthy. By signing the CWC, it will be subject to intrusive inspections, including possibly its nuclear facilities at Dimona—a historic first. In addition, Israel signed the Convention despite the decision of the 22 Arab League nations in early January to boycott the Paris signing ceremony as a means of pressing Israel into joining the NPT [*Arms Control Today* 23, no. 1 (1/93), p. 20].

Although 12 Arab and Middle Eastern countries have signed the Convention since the Paris signing ceremony (Algeria, Bahrain, Iran, Kuwait, Mauritania, Morocco, Oman, Qatar, Saudi Arabia, Tunisia, the United Arab Emirates, and Yemen), the absence from the list of such major states as Egypt, Iraq, Jordan, Libya, and Syria is especially disappointing, since all but Jordan are believed (or, in the case of Iraq, *known*) to possess chemical weapons. Convincing these states (as well as North Korea, the only other presumed chemical weapons proliferator not to sign) to join the Convention will be a difficult but very important task toward ensuring the complete and total abolition of chemical weapons.

There were also interesting developments in the biological weapons area, with Russia acknowledging that the Soviet Union had violated the BWC ever since its entry into force in 1975. In a joint U.S.-Russian-British statement on September 14, 1992, Moscow agreed to allow "visits to any non-military biological site at any time to remove ambiguities" [*Arms Control Reporter*, 10/92, p. 701.D.1]. U.S. and British inspectors would have unrestricted access to the facilities, and subsequent Russian visits to U.S. and British facilities would also be made. This agreement should go a long way toward resolving long-standing U.S. charges of Soviet noncompliance with the BWC and toward ensuring that any illegal activity will be halted.

The tripartite agreement also underscored that greater openness, through regular and reciprocal inspections, could strengthen the BWC, which lacks any verification provisions. In September 1991 the parties to the BWC agreed to set up an experts group to study whether adding a verification protocol to the BWC would be desirable. Although the Bush administration opposed the negotiation of a protocol, believing that effective verification was impossible, the U.S. State Department announced that through the visits allowed under the tripartite agreement "we expect to be able to demonstrate to the satisfaction of ourselves as well as to anybody else who's worried about this kind of thing that the Soviet program to develop offensive biological weapons is effectively ended" [ibid., p. 701.B.100]. This suggests that a combination of regular inspections, ad hoc visits, and data exchanges could provide greater confidence that parties to the BWC were complying with its provisions.

The 48th Session is likely to address chemical and biological disarmament efforts by welcoming the many signatures to the Chemical Weapons Convention. At the same time, the General Assembly will probably call upon those who have signed the Convention to ratify it promptly, while urging those who have not yet signed it to do so. Although the issue of biological weapons was not addressed during the 47th Session, the General Assembly may do so during its 48th Session in reference to the work currently under way by the experts group that is considering the means of verifying the Biological Weapons Convention.

6. Transparency in Armaments

After the Gulf War, the sale of conventional arms became a hot topic on the international arms control agenda. One of the more immediate results was the establishment of the **United Nations Registry of Conventional Arms** by the General Assembly in December 1991 [*A Global Agenda: Issues/47*, pp. 133–34]. The registry will contain data on arms imports and exports that are submitted annually by member states on a voluntary basis. The 47th Session of the General Assembly returned to the issue of transparency in armaments by endorsing the recommendations contained in a report by the Secretary-General on the technical procedures and adjustments to the data-reporting requirements. The resolution also called upon all member states to submit the requested data and information to the United Nations annually by April 30, beginning in 1993 [A/Res/47/52L].

The report endorsed by the General Assembly set out seven categories of armaments on which data should be reported: battle tanks, armored combat vehicles, artillery, combat aircraft, attack helicopters, warships, and missiles and missile launchers. The data should consist of all imports and exports of these armaments that were completed in the previous year. Although only the number of weapons in each category is to be reported, the form to be used for the reporting contains a column in which countries can provide additional information, including the type of system transferred, if they so wish. Countries are also requested to submit background information on their military holdings, procurement through national production, and relevant policies [A/47/342, 8/14/92].

To familiarize member states with the operation of the registry, the United Nations convened a number of workshops in early 1993 at which participants were instructed on how to fill out the forms. Participants were also shown how to fill out the optional parts of the forms in the hope that more information would then be provided [BASIC Reports, no. 27, 12/23/92, no. 29, 4/16/93].

The success of the arms registry in creating greater transparency will depend to a large extent on how many members submit the requested data. Critically important will be the receipt of data from those countries that transfer the bulk of all armaments covered by the registry—principally the five permanent members. Once these data are available, it is possible to cross-check imports and exports to get a comprehensive picture of arms transfers that occur annually. Greater transparency will also be gained once the registry is expanded to include national production and holdings. The 47th Session reaffirmed the decision adopted as part of the original resolution to convene a group of experts to examine the continuing operation of the registry and its further development in 1994. The 48th Session is sure to return to this issue.

7. U.N. Disarmament Machinery

Questions concerning the adequacy of the U.N. disarmament machinery were among the most important issues during the 47th Session of the General Assembly and are sure to receive much attention during the 48th. The issue arose as a result of three short paragraphs appended to the Secretary-General's report on "New directions of arms regulation and disarmament in the post-Cold War era," in which the Secretary-General urged that the U.N. machinery "be reassessed in order to meet the new realities and priorities of our time." Specifically, he suggested that the Security Council become more involved in disarmament matters, "in particular the enforcement of non-proliferation." The report noted that under the U.N. Charter, the **Military Staff Committee** "is to provide assistance to the Security Council on all questions relating, inter alia, to the regulation of armaments and possible disarmament." In addition, the Secretary-General seemed to propose a change in the mandate of the **Conference on Disarmament (C.D.)** when he suggested that its efforts "might be focused on well-defined and urgent issues." The C.D. "could also be considered as a permanent review and supervisory body for some existing multilateral arms regulations and disarmament agreements" [A/C.1/47/7, 10/23/92, p. 12].

The suggestions were the subject of much debate in the General Assembly's **First Committee** in late 1992 and were commented upon in statements sent to the Secretary-General [A/47/884/Add.1–4]. First, the report omitted any reference to the role of the General Assembly in furthering arms control and disarmament, despite the fact that the First Committee and the **Disarmament Commission** had particular authority in this area. Second, the suggestion that the Security Council and the Military Staff Committee adopt a higher profile in this area was received with skepticism. The Japanese delegate to the First Committee stated, for instance: "I wish to point out that the delegations to the Conference on Disarmament include many competent military staff members whose advice has always been useful. My feeling is that the Security Council could in turn benefit from the advice of the CD" [*Arms Control Reporter*, 4/93, p. 801.B.33]. Finally, the omission in the report of any mention of the C.D.'s role as the sole multilateral negotiating body on disarmament also received much notice. The Japanese delegate noted that Japan would "not support any effort or proposal that might undermine such an important character of the CD" [ibid.].

As a result of the Secretary-General's report, the General Assembly decided to reconvene the First Committee in March 1993 to reassess the U.N. arms control and disarmament machinery, including the roles of the First Committee, Disarmament Commission, the Conference on Disarmament, and the **Office for Disarmament Affairs** [A/Res/47/422]. At its meeting, the First Committee drafted a consensus resolution for the General Assembly that basically reaffirmed the competence and roles of these bodies. Specifically, the resolution decided that the First Committee would continue to deal with disarmament and related international security issues; reaffirmed the role of the U.N. Disarmament Commission as a specialized deliberative body within the disarmament machinery; welcomed the fact that the C.D. was undertaking a review of its composition, agenda, and methods of work; and urged that the Secretary-General take concrete steps to strengthen the Office of Disarmament Affairs [A/47/693/Add.1, 3/18/93]. The resolution was adopted by the General Assembly on April 8, 1993.

During the First Committee debate on the rationalization of the U.N. disarmament machinery, the 12 **European Community** members introduced a paper suggesting a more coherent agenda for the First Committee that would better express the integrated approach proposed by the Secretary-General in his report. The proposed agenda would cover nine clusters, including nuclear weapons, other weapons of mass destruction, conventional weapons, transparency in armaments, regional disarmament and security, outer space, disarmament machinery, international security, and related matters of disarmament and international security [A/C.1/47/15, 3/9/93]. One of the issues to be discussed during the 48th Session is likely to be that of restructuring the First Committee agenda, be it along the lines proposed by the E.C. countries or some other proposal.

Just as the General Assembly was moved to address its disarmament machinery, so the Conference on Disarmament decided to review its membership and agenda. Following informal consultations by the President of the C.D. on these issues, two Special Coordinators were appointed to conduct consultations on the issues of membership and the agenda. On the question of membership, there appeared to be widespread agreement among the C.D. members (and even more strongly among nonmembers) that an expansion was warranted [CD/1184, 2/18/93]. Such a move has also been urged by the General Assembly. While there is not yet agreement on the degree of expansion, by April 1993 a consensus seemed to have emerged in favor of adding about 20 new members to reach a total of 60 [*Arms Control Reporter*, 4/93, p. 805.B.50].

On the issue of the agenda, there was much agreement among the C.D. members that it should be changed but little on how to do so. According to the President of the C.D., members regarded the following issues as important: (in order of preference) nuclear test ban and transparency in armaments, negative security assurances, outer space, a new item on nonproliferation of weapons of mass destruction, global and regional confidence-building measures, and radiological weapons. But there was no agreement on what to do about the other agenda items, including the cessation of the nuclear arms race and the prevention of nuclear war, with some members favoring keeping both, others supporting their elimination, and yet others urging that the items be combined [CD/1184, 2/18/93, Annex].

The 48th Session is likely to continue to address the question of how the U.N. disarmament machinery can best be restructured to reflect the new priorities of the international arms control and disarmament environment. Given current sentiments, it is unlikely that any drastic changes will be agreed upon concerning the nature, number, or competence of the existing U.N. forums. On the other hand, there appears to be a growing realization that the past agenda, which still dominated the 47th Session, is no longer responsive to present political and security realities. It is therefore probable that the 48th Session will examine in detail how that agenda can be restructured.

III
Economics and Development

By George H. Mitchell, Jr.

1. Overview: "A Place Called Hope"

"I still believe in a place called Hope," declared Bill Clinton, then governor of Arkansas and Democratic party candidate for the office of president of the United States, in concluding his acceptance speech at his party's July 1992 nominating convention [*The New York Times*, 7/17/92]. Clinton, who went on to defeat incumbent President George Bush in November and to become the 42nd U.S. president, was speaking both literally (about his hometown—Hope, Arkansas) and metaphorically (about the economic and social future of the United States). He might also have been referring to the global economy, which influences significantly, even as it is significantly influenced by, U.S. economic performance. For although Clinton defeated Bush mainly because of Bush's apparent failure to manage the U.S. economy effectively (a sign in Clinton's campaign headquarters intended to help the candidate and his advisors stay focused, read: "It's the economy, stupid"), by mid-1993, six months into Clinton's four-year term, the future course of both the U.S. and the world economies remained uncertain indeed.

Why Hope Was Needed

Actually, in early 1993 the U.S. economy was performing well relative to most of the other advanced industrial economies. But that relative success was in reality a mixed blessing: Because the United States was growing faster than its major economic partners, U.S. imports were outpacing U.S. exports, widening the U.S. trade deficit and making the external sector a drag on the already tenuous U.S. economic recovery. Thus, there was good reason for U.S. policy-makers to hope that recoveries would get solidly under way in Europe, especially in Germany and in Japan. For the same reason, there was also good cause for European and Japanese policy-makers to hope that the U.S. recovery would prove to be solid and sustained. As spring turned into summer, however, indications of U.S. economic weakness, such as an unemployment rate that refused to fall and consumer confidence that declined steadily during the second quarter, began to outnumber or outweigh indications of economic strength.

What to do? The United States, as usual, urged the Germans and Japanese to stimulate their economies by lowering interest rates, increasing government spending, or both. The Europeans, the Japanese, and the Organization for Economic Cooperation and Development (OECD), as usual, urged the United States to reduce its federal budget deficit by raising taxes, reducing government spending, or both. Others, including especially the General Agreement on Tariffs and Trade (GATT), strongly urged the United States and European Community to resolve their differences over agricultural subsidies and trade so that the Uruguay Round of multilateral trade negotiations might be successfully completed. It was widely believed that a global agreement to liberalize trade and investment would provide a major stimulus to the world economy. However, except for an occasional hint of compromise, the news from the Uruguay Round of negotiations was not good. Moreover, both the outgoing Bush administration and the incoming Clinton administration felt it necessary to engage the European Community and Japan in major bilateral trade rows, which did nothing to improve the atmosphere surrounding the multilateral talks.

Separately, the European Community and Japan were facing major home-grown economic and political problems. The E.C. appeared by mid-1993 to have implemented more-or-less successfully and effectively "Europe 1992"—the plan for a Single European Market in which goods, services, money, and people would be permitted to move freely across national frontiers. In other areas, however, the picture was much less reassuring. For example, the proposal for economic and monetary (and political) union (EMU), adopted at Maastricht, the Netherlands, in December 1991, threatened to unravel after Danish voters rejected it in mid-1992. It was only in May 1993, following a second Danish referendum, in which the EMU proposal passed by a comfortable margin after modifications had been made in it, and a worrisome but ultimately supportive vote by the House of Commons in Great Britain, that EMU's prospects brightened [see, for example, "Maastricht Sails On," *The Economist*, 5/22/93].

The Exchange Rate Mechanism (ERM) of the European Monetary System (EMS) also ran into severe difficulty. Between September 1992 and May 1993, the ERM and EMS experienced severe upheavals, sparked by German interest rate hikes, which resulted in the withdrawal from the ERM, first, of the British pound sterling and the Italian lira and, later, the Spanish peseta and Portuguese escudo. Moreover, some former European Free Trade Area (EFTA) nations that were anticipating (and continue to anticipate) joining the E.C. (specifically Finland and Sweden), found themselves forced to abandon an E.C.-recommended policy of acting as if their currencies were already part of the ERM/EMS. The full implications of these developments remain to be seen.

Hope was also needed because of troubling developments in Central and Southern Europe. In Central Europe, the reconstruction of eastern Germany and its integration with western Germany proved much more difficult, expensive, and time-consuming than German policy-makers had expected. More ominous, however, was the deteriorating economic and political situation in the Russian Federation, the largest of the former Soviet republics and the legal successor-state to the Soviet Union. There, the economy was in a virtual free-fall, despite (and perhaps to some degree because of certain aspects of) the reform program of Russia's President, Boris Yeltsin. In addition, Yeltsin's authority was being openly challenged by the Russian parliament, the membership of which was set before the dissolution of the Soviet Union in December 1991. As Russia teetered between chaos and a return to totalitarianism, Western governments figuratively held their breaths and wondered whether Russia would end up launching hordes of refugees or hordes of tanks and missiles. Another source of anxiety was the former Yugoslavia, where unspeakable acts were being committed in a context of ethnic and religious civil war. Apart from the fact that the former Yugoslav economy was being destroyed either by fighting or by international sanctions intended to slow or stop the conflict, European and American policy-makers worried about the possibility of a broader war that would draw in such nations as Greece and Turkey and, ultimately, the United States, members of the E.C., or even Russia, with major implications for the world economy, if not for international security.

Why Hope May Have Been Justified

The need for hope being clear, it may be asked whether any genuine basis for hope existed. Several developments suggest that the answer may well be yes.

First, both the German and Japanese governments recognized, implicitly or explicitly, that a continuation of recessionary conditions in Europe and Japan was undesirable and, therefore, that certain proactive measures were indeed in order.

Second, the government of the United States began to behave as if it understood the economic importance of the Uruguay Round negotiations. And, perhaps by chance, a new conservative French government took office in April 1993 [*The New York Times*, 4/2/93] promising to pursue "trade peace," especially with the United States [*The New York Times*, 4/8/93].

Third, the Group of Seven advanced industrial states displayed a new spirit of cooperation, coordination, and even collaboration as they grappled with various problems, including Russia's political economy [*The New York Times*, 3/1/93, 5/2/93].

Fourth, in a spring 1993 referendum, Russia's President Yeltsin won a vote of confidence in both himself and his economic reform program. In response, the Group of Seven undertook to be more supportive.

Fifth, in the Central European economies of Poland, Hungary, and the former Czechoslovakia, the worst appeared to be over and the path to market-based economic growth seemed clearer.

Sixth, it became clear that, at least for Western banks and for several countries in Latin America, the developing-country debt crisis had ended satisfactorily. Disaster had been averted.

Seventh, the new, welcoming attitude toward foreign direct investment that had emerged during the 1980s and continued into the 1990s was expanded to include energy—a very sensitive sector in most developing countries.

Eighth, and finally, a consensus was forming that, all things being equal, strong economic growth would continue in Asia, especially in China, through the 1990s and into the next century, which could well become the "Asian century" [*The Wall Street Journal*, 5/17/93]. Separately, the International Monetary Fund (IMF) unveiled a new ranking of the world's economies based on the concept of purchasing power parity instead of simple conversion of local currency Gross Domestic Product (GDP) statistics into U.S. dollars. By this measure, China's may be the third largest economy in the world [*The New York Times*, 5/20/93], and the gap between rich and poor nations may be less than commonly believed [*The Economist*, 5/15/93]. All this could constitute good news both for development theory and for market-hungry developed nations.

2. The World Economy: Retrospect and Prospect

A Mostly Disappointing Performance in 1992

To understand why the 0.4% rate of world economic growth recorded in 1992 should be characterized as disappointing—given that it followed a year (actually, the first such year in the post-World War II period) in which the rate of growth was negative (−0.6%)—one need only refer to some of the economic forecasts made in late 1991. The IMF's *World Economic Outlook* (WEO) of October 1991, for example, projected worldwide economic growth of 2.8% in 1992, a rate comparable to the 2.9% annual average recorded during the relatively prosperous period of 1981–89 [ECOSOC, "The World Economy at the End of 1992," E/1993/INF/1, 2/1/93]. In short, in late 1991 the IMF thought that 1992 would be a year of "moderate" global economic growth. The IMF based its projections on the following anticipated developments, among others: recovery from recession in North America, the United Kingdom, and some other industrial countries (generating a growth rate of 2.8%), a decline in oil prices, the end of uncertainties associated with the Persian Gulf War of early 1991, 4.8% growth in the developing countries other than the then-Soviet Union, and modest increases in output in Eastern Europe (not including the Soviet Union, where output was expected to continue to fall).

By May 1992, however, the IMF had revised its global forecast downward, from 2.8 to 1.4%. According to the *World Economic Outlook* of May 1992, the less optimistic prediction was occasioned by the following developments: economic weakness in the United States and Canada, continued recession in the United Kingdom, a slowdown in Japan and continental Europe (the latter closely related to Germany's tight-money stance adopted to contain inflationary pressures generated by both monetary and fiscal problems connected with the unification of West Germany (FRG) and the former East Germany (GDR), the inability of the former Soviet Union to maintain supplies of energy and raw materials to its former partners in the Council for Mutual Economic Assistance (CMEA, or COMECON), and Eastern Europe's large terms-of-trade loss vis-à-vis the former Soviet Union.

In the event, the global economy hardly grew at all in 1992—only 0.4% or nearly 2.5 percentage points less than the IMF had anticipated in late 1991. That result can surely be described as disappointing. What happened? According to data prepared by the U.N. Secretariat's Department of Economic and Social Development (DESD), "the sluggishness of world output in 1992 was largely the reflection of two major phenomena: the slowdown of growth in some large, developed market economies, which offset a weak recovery in certain others, and the sharp decline in output in the transition economies [of Eastern Europe and the former Soviet republics]" [ibid.]. These developments are discussed in greater detail below.

Modest Expectations for 1993

After having been forced by events to lower their estimates of 1992 growth repeatedly, the major producers of international economic forecasts appear to have adopted a cautious approach and conservative posture with respect to 1993. The U.N.'s "World Economy at the End of 1992," for example, predicts global growth of only 2% but qualifies its estimate with the statement that "it must be recognized that growth after a protracted slow period might be significantly higher than forecast." The rather modest 2% figure is based mainly on expected continued sluggish-

Table III-1
World Output, 1990–93

	1990	*1991*	*1992**	*1993‡*
Output (percentage of annual change)				
World	1.7	−0.6	0.4	2.0
Developed market economies	2.4	0.7	1.5	2.0
United States	0.8	−1.2	1.8	2.6
European Community	2.8	0.6	1.3	1.2
Germany	5.0	n/a	2.1	0.8
Japan	5.2	4.5	1.8	2.3
Canada	−0.5	−1.7	1.3	2.5
Economies in transition	−5.0	−16.0	−18.4	−3.5
Russia	n/a	n/a	−22.0	−7.0
Poland	−12.0	−9.3	0.0	2.0
Hungary	−4.0	−10.2	−3.0	1.5
Czechoslovakia	−4.7	−15.1	−5.3	2.0
Developing countries	3.4	3.4	4.5	5.0
Latin America	0.1	2.9	2.0	2.5
Mexico	4.4	3.6	2.7	n/a
Africa	2.9	2.1	2.3	3.0
South and East Asia	6.3	5.6	5.5	6.0
China	5.2	7.0	10.0	10.0

Source: ECOSOC, "The World Economy at the End of 1992," E/1993/INF/1, 2/1/93.

*Estimate
‡Forecast

ness among the developed market economies. The United States (2.6%) and Japan (2.3%) might well be the leaders of the developed-country group in 1993, although neither's growth is expected to be strong. Europe is expected to lag, with average growth forecast at only 1% by the U.N. document and at nearly zero growth by the IMF. The latter, in its May 1993 *World Economic Outlook*, forecast global growth of 2.2% for 1993—"a big downward revision from [its] prediction of a healthy 3.6 per cent, made in October [1992]," noted *The New York Times* [4/27/93].

The true global leaders, at least in terms of economic growth, will likely be the developing countries of Asia (6.7% growth, according to the IMF), including especially China (perhaps more than 10%) and the countries of South and East Asia (about 6%). Improvement is expected among the transitioning economies of Eastern Europe, although the former Soviet republics will most likely experience continued economic decline, albeit at a slower rate (i.e., −11.8%, according to the IMF) than in recent years (e.g., −18.5% in 1992, per the IMF). Some fast-growing Latin American developing countries, including especially Argentina, Chile, and Venezuela, may slow to more moderate rates of growth. In 1993 the countries of Africa may well record a slight improvement, on average, in their pace of output (about 3%) over 1992 (2.3%).

The Group of Seven: Not Yet Out of the Woods

As discussed in *A Global Agenda: Issues/47* and *The World Economy in Transition* [UNA-USA Global Policy Project Briefing Book, 1993], the economic summits of the Group of Seven (G-7) countries (United States, Germany, Japan, United Kingdom, France, Canada, and Italy) constitute the most prominent forum for high-level international discussion of issues relating to the world economy. More important, perhaps, the G-7 account for about two-thirds of the world's production. Therefore, their economic performance is of vital importance to the performance of the global economy.

As it happens, most of the G-7 countries have been struggling economically in the last one-to-three years, with the unsurprising results that (a) global growth has slowed noticeably and (b) the principal concern of most economists and economic policy-makers around the world is whether and when this group of countries will resume robust economic expansion. The situation in each of the G-7 countries is discussed below.

United States

It is generally agreed that the United States is experiencing one of the most unusual (in its weakness) and confusing (in its erratic course) economic recoveries since the Great Depression of the 1930s. While some observers may have expected the defeat of former President Bush (who took a laissez-faire approach to economic management) and the election of President Clinton (who prides himself on his readiness to devise innovative governmental economic strategies) to clarify and perhaps even "correct" the situation, by late spring 1993 the current status and future performance of the U.S. economy seemed as puzzling and unpredictable as at any point in 1992. One heard with increasing frequency that "This is no ordinary recession; it is a fundamental restructuring of the American economy." Whether that statement is true will probably be known only in retrospect.

The more immediate problem for policy-makers and other interested parties was what, if anything, could be done to set the U.S. economy on a path of steady, if not necessarily rapid, expansion. Analysts noted that the usual fiscal policy instruments were either unavailable or working in the opposite direction (e.g., toward reductions in defense spending) because of the large federal budget deficit, and that monetary policy was as relaxed as it had ever been in 30 years [OECD, *Economic Outlook*, 12/92]. To be sure, there were some structural problems, such as business and consumer debt loads and banks' balance sheets, that needed time to resolve themselves; but the "real" problem seemed to be consumer confidence, a largely psychological phenomenon, though one that is often related to objective economic conditions or, if not, then at least to economic expectations that are not entirely unreasonable. Consumer confidence rose sharply in the fourth quarter of 1992, apparently in connection with the presidential election; but it fell again in the second quarter of 1993 [*The New York Times*, 5/22/93] as optimism about Clinton's ability to manage the economy more successfully than his predecessor began to decline. (The Republican opposition in the U.S. Senate later drove home that point by forcing Clinton to abandon his already-modest fiscal-stimulus proposal.) Similarly, economic growth was recorded at an impressive 4.7% in the fourth quarter of 1992 (contributing to an annual growth rate of 1.3%, compared with 0.6% in 1991), then dropped to 1.9% in the first quarter of 1993.

U.S. growth in 1993 was forecast by the IMF at 3.2% and by the U.N.'s "World Economy at the End of 1992" at 2.6%. The IMF said that deeper reductions in the U.S. federal deficit than those sought by President Clinton would have been desirable. However, a Clinton administration official argued that deeper deficit reduction would have endangered the already-fragile economic recovery [*The New York Times*, 4/27/93].

Japan

Somewhat like the United States, Japan is grappling with an unfamiliar economic situation. Specifically, Japan is experiencing its slowest economic growth since the mid-1970s ["The World Economy at the End of 1992"]. The slowdown is generally attributed to the inevitable ending of a speculative boom, or "bubble," that sharply inflated the prices of real estate and stocks during the late 1980s and early 1990s. As both banks and corporations struggled with equity losses, reduced asset values, and problem loans, the usually smooth-running Japanese economy began to flounder. Cautious lending behavior by balance sheet-conscious Japanese banks tended to negate the efforts of the Bank of Japan to ease credit. A series of fiscal policy measures, especially in the form of substantial public investment expenditures, was announced beginning in late 1992 and culminated in a "major stimulus package" announced just before Prime Minister Kiichi Miyazawa's visit to Washington, D.C., where President Clinton and his advisors had expressed deep concern about relatively low Japanese demand for imported goods [*The Wall Street Journal*, 4/13/93; see also Section 5, "Trade and the Trading System," below]. There was widespread suspicion, however, that the Japanese fiscal measures "might not be sufficient to boost private demand [and that] a further monetary easing as well as additional fiscal stimulus, including tax cuts, may be needed over the coming year"

["The World Economy at the End of 1992"; see also *The Wall Street Journal*, 4/14/93]. Japanese GDP was expected to fall in the 1.3–2.3% range in 1993, as it did in 1992.

Germany

Germany, too, finds itself on unfamiliar terrain. The German economy (and German politics, for that matter) has been greatly complicated by the unification of West and East Germany, a unique development that took place officially on October 3, 1990. Unification, as implemented by the government of Chancellor Helmut Kohl, has resulted in both monetary and fiscal stress in Germany. On the one hand, the conversion of East German marks to West German marks at a 1:1 ratio greatly increased the supply of (West) German marks, as a result of which inflationary pressures accelerated. On the other hand, the economic, political, and social integration of East Germany into the former West Germany has proven to be very expensive in budgetary terms for the government of the new Germany. Massive public expenditures related to unification have added to unification-related inflationary pressures. In response, both fiscal and monetary policies in Germany have been tightened. Initially, however, monetary policy carried the larger portion of the anti-inflation burden. This translated into relatively high German interest rates, which dampened growth prospects not only in Germany but elsewhere in Europe through the operation of the Exchange Rate Mechanism (ERM), which effectively requires most members of the European Community to follow Germany's interest rate leadership.

German growth slowed for a second consecutive year in 1992, to 1.4% from 3.7% in 1991 [OECD, *Economic Outlook*, 12/92]. Moreover, the IMF projected "miserable" German economic performance in 1993 (−1.3% growth in Gross Domestic Product) [*The New York Times*, 4/27/93]. (In May, six German economic institutes projected −2.0% growth in 1993 [*The New York Times*, 5/4/93].)

The OECD, however, argued more optimistically (though, admittedly, this was back in December 1992) that, as Germany's underlying fiscal position shifted toward consolidation, German monetary policy would ease, and that "by the end of 1994, German GDP could be growing at close to its potential rate of about 3 per cent" [*Economic Outlook*, 12/92]. Such optimism seems likely to prove unfounded, however, given that it was premised largely on (a) an expected slowing of wage and price increases and (b) a strengthening of world economic activity, both of which were questionable by late spring 1993, and considering that (c) workers in eastern Germany went on strike for the first time in 60 years [*The New York Times*, 5/15/93] and (d), as reported above, international economic activity is projected to be much slower than anticipated only a half-year earlier.

Other G-7 Economies

The **United Kingdom** of Great Britain and Northern Ireland had been mired in recession for about three years when, in the first quarter of 1993, clear signs of recovery began to appear [*The Wall Street Journal*, 4/26/93; *The New York Times*, 4/27/93]. The recession may be traced on the one hand to anti-inflation policies adopted as early as 1988 (but effective only since 1990) and, on the other hand, to the U.K.'s October 1990 decision to join the Exchange Rate Mechanism, a move that also entailed anti-inflation measures. The nascent recovery seems connected to Her Majesty's Government's decision of September 16, 1992, to suspend participation in the ERM, which permitted an easing of the high interest rates that had been sustained for many months. Perhaps not surprisingly, inflation has been projected, at least by the OECD, to rise in the near term. However, the OECD also anticipates that inflation will recede again given the large amount of slack in the U.K.'s economy (e.g., the unemployment rate was between 10 and 11% during 1992–93) [OECD, *Economic Outlook*, 12/92].

The **French economy** was declared to be in recession at the end of the first quarter of 1993 [*The Wall Street Journal*, 5/14/93]: Despite "good results on the external account, low inflation and somewhat better growth prospects than most European countries," that economy had worsened during 1992–93. There appear to be two villains, both of which are increasingly familiar to Western observers. One is the Exchange Rate Mechanism, which is dominated by the German Bundesbank and the deutschmark. When Germany raised its interest rates to dampen unification-related inflationary pressures, France was compelled to do the same to protect the franc's exchange value. (In the event, the Germans joined forces with the French to defeat speculation against the franc.) The second villain is low consumer confidence, which has bedeviled U.S. as well as French policy-makers. As in the United States, many workers and families in France are concerned about poor job prospects amidst uncertainty about financial market and foreign demand developments [OECD, *Economic Outlook*, 12/92].

Along with other factors, the economic malaise apparently cost French President Mitterrand and his Socialist party dearly: They lost control of the National Assembly and the prime ministership to a conservative coalition in late March 1993 [*The New York Times*, 3/29/93]. Shortly afterward, the Socialists' former Prime Minister, Pierre Bérégovoy, committed suicide, apparently because of a pending criminal investigation, as well as despair over the Socialists' defeat and perhaps the state of the French economy [ibid., 5/2/93, 5/7/93]. Mitterrand has himself come under intense pressure to resign as president before his term ends, but he has refused even to consider stepping down.

Canada, like its neighbor, the United States, has been experiencing an agonizingly slow recovery from a recession that occurred mainly in 1990 and 1991. According to the OECD, "the sluggishness of the current recovery [in Canada] is without precedent in the post-war era" [OECD, *Economic Outlook*, 12/92]. After contracting by −0.5% in 1990 and −1.7% in 1991, Canadian GNP grew in 1992 at about 1.3%, the rate forecast by the OECD [ibid., and "The World Economy at the End of 1992"]. As in the United States, the Canadian recovery has been hampered by lower-than-normal consumer spending (in light of newly eased monetary policy), which appears to be a result of job insecurity related to fundamental economic restructuring. Canada's unemployment rate rose for a second consecutive year in 1992 to 11.2% (from 10.3% in 1991) and is projected to peak at 11.3% in 1993 before declining moderately in 1994 [OECD, *Economic Outlook*, 12/92]. Noteworthy is the fact that, notwithstanding intense opposition among some Canadians to free trade with the United States (and perhaps soon with Mexico under the North American Free Trade Agreement (NAFTA), Canadian growth in 1992 was "substantially boosted by a swing in net exports;" and industrial restructuring, together with a lower exchange rate for the Canadian dollar, has left the Canadian economy "well positioned to compete internationally." Canadian output overall is forecast to reach a respectable 3.2% in 1993 [ibid.].

As the Italian government has been struggling to bring the national budget into better balance, while grappling with its most serious political corruption crisis since World War II, the **Italian economy's** growth has been slowing down. After peaking at 4.1% in 1988, the overall rate of growth has declined annually. Output growth in 1992 was recorded at 1.2% and was expected to decline again in 1993 to between 0.5 and 0.8% before turning upward again in 1994 [ibid.; and "The World Economy at the End of 1992"]. Apart from the political corruption crisis, which involved important sectors, industries, and firms, perhaps the most noteworthy economic development in Italy was the government's decision in mid-September 1992 to withdraw the lira from the Exchange Rate Mechanism of the European Monetary System. In the face of continuing heavy losses of foreign exchange reserves, despite sharply increased Italian interest rates in response to sharply increased German interest rates, the government of Italy at first accepted a realignment of the lira within the ERM. Ultimately, however, it concluded that the price of trying to maintain even the new exchange rate was too high. By mid-November 1992, the lira was trading at about 11% below its previous floor against the deutschmark [OECD, *Economic Outlook*, 12/92].

Newly Industrializing and Other Developing Economies: The Dream Is Alive

The average rate of growth in the more than 100 countries of the developing world, or "South," was a vibrant 4.5% in 1992, which contrasts noticeably with the sluggish 1992 experience of the several large economies of the "North," whose collective growth rate was only about 1.5%. However, the developing countries' average masks widely diverse performances. For example, there was, according to U.N. findings, "a marked acceleration of growth in China, strong growth in South and East Asia, a modest recovery in West Asia, a repetition of slow growth in Africa and a slow-down in Latin America and the Caribbean" ["The World Economy at the End of 1992"].

Though it is not the only exciting economic story of the early 1990s, **China**'s is genuinely remarkable. Between 1983 and 1988, China's rate of growth averaged 11%. Growth slowed in 1989 and 1990, partly because of the bloody clash between the government and the prodemocracy movement, but in the "post-Tiananmen" period, or since 1991, China's rapid economic expansion has resumed. Growth was recorded at 7% in 1991 and 10% in 1992 and is forecast to reach 10% again in 1993 [ibid.]. China's continuing economic development appears to be closely connected to its government's firm embrace of "broader and bolder" economic reforms, a strategy reaffirmed in late 1992.

Relatively rapid growth was also recorded in **South, East, and West Asia.** "The Republic of Korea, Malaysia, Thailand and Viet Nam will have ended [1992] with 7 per cent growth or more," predicted the U.N.'s "The World Economy at the End of 1992," and "Indonesia, Hong Kong and Taiwan . . . will have had over 6 per cent." In West Asia, growth averaged 5%, the highest rate since the early 1980s. Unfortunately, much of the growth was attributable to reconstruction activity in countries damaged by the Persian Gulf War of 1991. Moreover, "some consequences of the war persist. . . . Trade, transfers from migrant labourers and soft loans . . . have not returned to their former scale" [ibid.].

In **Latin America and the Caribbean,** growth slowed to an average 2% in 1992 from about 3% in 1991. The decrease was attributable mainly to recession in Brazil, which accounts for about 40% of regional Gross Domestic Product and where inflation has more than doubled to over 1,200%. Highly respectable growth of about 6% was recorded by Argentina, Chile, and Venezuela. Mexican growth, however, slowed to less than 3% as imports outpaced exports in the context of generally rapid expansion. Latin American growth is expected to average 2.5% in 1993 [ibid.].

African economic growth continued to lag behind expectations, as well as behind the rate of population expansion. In sub-Saharan Africa, excluding Nigeria, growth averaged less than 1% in 1992. Among the more important negative influences were drought in eastern and southern Africa, as well as in the Horn of Africa and Morocco, and civil strife in such countries as Sudan, Somalia, and Zaire [ibid.].

The Transitioning Economies of Eastern Europe and the Former Soviet Republics: Maybe, Just Maybe, the Worst Is Over

Despite expectations among some observers that 1992 would bring a turnaround for the severely contracting transitioning economies of Eastern Europe and the **former Soviet republics,** those economies generally continued to contract at a fairly high rate. The most dramatic events, both politically and economically, unfolded in the Russian Federation, where, in early 1993, President Boris Yeltsin and his proreform advisors ultimately prevailed in an intense political struggle with antireform leaders of the Russian parliament. Afterward, there was hope both inside Russia and among foreign supporters of Russian economic and political reform that the resolution of central political issues might bring greater stability to the Russian economy. While it remains to be seen whether such will be the case, even after the energetic, positive response of the Group of Seven, 1992 left no doubt about the urgent need for stability. "[Russia's gross domestic product] appears to have fallen [22% or] more than a fifth in 1992, which, after three years of decline, puts it at about two-thirds of its 1989 level," states the U.N. report. Ukraine's economy also shrank significantly, by 24% in 1992, but, as is not the case with Russia, the forecast calls for a return to positive growth (3%) in 1993. Output also fell sharply in the **Baltic states of Latvia, Lithuania, and Estonia** ["The World Economy at the End of 1992"].

It was in the so-called **Northern Tier countries—Hungary, Poland, and Czechoslovakia** (as of January 1993, the Czech Republic and the Slovak Republic)—that the worst seemed genuinely to be over, even though 1992's results were mixed. Despite early international optimism, Hungary's return to growth has been much slower than expected. The Hungarian economy shrank by nearly 5% in 1992 [*The Wall Street Journal,* 3/24/93], a year in which positive growth had been anticipated. It now appears that Hungary will finally return to positive growth in 1993, and current forecasts place that growth at about 1.5%. Poland, which unlike Hungary adopted a "shock therapy" approach to economic reform, emerged from 1992 as perhaps the most promising of the former command economies. Although Polish output did not grow in 1992, neither did it contract; and Poland appears poised for a respectable 2% rate of growth in 1993. Poland's commitment to liberal economic reform was reaffirmed in late April/early May 1993, when the Polish parliament voted to support the country's privatization program [*The New York Times,* 5/1/93].

In 1992, the economy of Czechoslovakia contracted by 5.3%, following a 15% contraction in 1991. The forecast for the two newly separated states was a modest but positive growth of about 2% in 1993. However, it is generally believed that the Czech Republic will fare significantly better economically than will the Slovak Republic, at least in the near-to-medium term. At the time of the separation, unemployment in Slovakia was 11%—four times higher than in the Czech Republic. There was also a suspicion, especially in the West, that the Slovak Republic would abandon the reform program that had been pursued by Czechoslovakia [*The New York Times*, 1/1/93].

3. External Debt: The Crisis Is Over for Some, But Not All

To the question, "Is the Debt Crisis Over?" the World Bank provided the following answer:

> For the commercial banks and some of their middle-income developing-country borrowers, the debt crisis . . . is largely over. Developing-country debt no longer poses a systemic threat to the international banking system, and for some of the previously debt-distressed middle-income countries, renewed portfolio flows are part of a wider (albeit still fragile) return to market access. The crisis is certainly far from over, however, for many other developing countries. External viability remains elusive for many low- and lower-middle-income countries (especially in Sub-Saharan Africa), who are indebted largely to official bilateral creditors and whose debt burdens are, in some cases, unsustainably high. Furthermore, for some smaller middle-income countries, resolution of commercial debt problems has still to be achieved through Brady-type [debt-reduction] agreements [*World Debt Tables, 1992–93*].

Regarding the external debt of developing (and former Communist) countries, there was good, mixed, and bad news. The good news came mainly from Latin America, where several countries enjoyed a marked improvement in their access to international finance and, consequently, witnessed a "remarkable turnaround" in private capital inflows, which amounted to $36 billion in 1992. The mixed news came from the former Soviet Union, where despite a sharp increase in the stock of debt since 1985 (from $29 billion to about $70 billion), various measures by the IMF and members of the Group of Seven have provided temporary liquidity relief and facilitated restructuring of the debt. The bad news came mainly from sub-Saharan Africa, where the majority of severely indebted low-income countries (SILICs) remained far from external viability, despite continued significant external official support.

Ten years into the debt crisis, the World Bank looked back and listed some "Lessons of the Crisis," offering the following observations on "Preventing a Crisis":

- Prudent lending and borrowing policies should take into account the vulnerability to adverse external shocks;

Table III-2
Selected External Debt Indicators

	1985	*1990*	*1991*	*1992‡*
Total external debt, all developing countries (U.S.$ billions)	1,123	1,531	1,608	1,703

Country	*Debt Outstanding 1991, U.S.$ billions*	*Debt Service 1991, U.S.$ billions*	*Ratio of 1991 Debt Service to Exports of Goods and Services*
Brazil	116.5	10.7	30.8
Mexico	101.7	14.0	30.9
Indonesia	73.6	10.8	33.0
India	71.5	7.4	30.6
Argentina	63.7	7.1	48.1

Share of 1991 total debt by region (%)	
Latin America and the Caribbean	29
Europe and Central Asia	19
East Asia and Pacific	19
Middle East and North Africa	12
Sub-Saharan Africa	12
South Asia	8

Source: World Bank, *World Debt Tables, 1992–93*, Tables 1.1, 1.4, and Country Tables.

‡ Projected

- Building risk-sharing contingencies into financial contracts makes crises less likely and less costly if they occur; and
- External finance for investment in low-income countries must come largely from official concessional sources.

On "Dealing with a Crisis," the Bank came to the following conclusions:

- In a solvency crisis, early recognition of insolvency as a root cause and [of] the need for a final settlement are important for minimizing the damage;
- A final settlement of a solvency crisis requires debt and debt-service reduction;
- Good domestic policy is the basis for capital market access; and
- The official sector has an important role to play in implementing a final settlement and solving the crisis.

4. Economic Development: Its Uncertain Meaning and Future in a Changed Global Context

What is development? That was the theme of the Spring 1992 issue of *Praxis*, a journal of development studies. Although the question may seem an elementary one and answered long ago, the journal left no doubt that, as the editors wrote in their introduction,

> Development is [in fact] an increasingly ambiguous concept. The social, political, economic and legal changes of the new decade challenge previous theories, strategies and practices. . . . Clearly, scholars and practitioners must reconsider the definitions and strategies of development from the 1960s, the 1970s, and the 1980s.

The editors distilled from the issue's articles "three elements common to evolving conceptualizations and reconceptualizations of development":

> The first is a redefinition of [development to include] the ecological environment [and] women (in all their roles) and their activities. . . . The second commonality is . . . [an acknowledgment of] the tension between society and its social institutions. . . . The third common element . . . is the process of [human] actualization [or] realizing the inner potentials of individuals and communities, and [then building] economic, social, political or legal change [upon those individuals and communities].

Economic, social, political, and legal change both defines development and influences it decisively. The rapid, and in some instances revolutionary, occurrence of such change during the last few years has confronted the international development community with serious philosophical and practical challenges. Some of those challenges are discussed below, as are the responses of the development community.

Development Challenges

Current development reports suggest that at present the international development community has four major areas of concern: the distribution of overseas development assistance; the supply of overseas development assistance; environmental protection and the related issue of population growth; and concern for the least-developed countries, especially those in Africa.

The Distribution of Overseas Development Assistance

Both developed and developing countries are keenly aware that the end of the Cold War, together with the dissolution of the Soviet Union, has resulted in new claims on already-scarce overseas development-assistance funding, not the least because, as the **Development Assistance Committee (DAC) of the OECD** noted, "Some of the countries of the former Soviet Union . . . have the same characteristics as developing countries" [OECD, *Development Co-operation, 1992 Report*]. In addition, developed-country governments generally have felt obligated (if not compelled by self-interest) to transfer a substantial amount of their resources to help insure stability, relatively free markets, and relatively democratic governments in countries of the former Soviet bloc. Ideally, of course, the developed countries would have come up with new funding to meet these objectives. In the event, however, as discussed below, the diversion or reallocation of existing development assistance was the more common policy. This was not lost on the developing countries, which strongly supported a request to the Secretary-General of the United Nations for a report on the impact of the evolution of East-West relations on global growth and development. This was duly prepared [A/47/403].

During the 47th Session the General adopted without a vote a resolution urging the developed countries and the multilateral financial institutions to "ensure that the resources allocated to the economies in transition do not reduce or divert official development assistance allocated to the developing countries," and it called on the international community "to consider assisting the developing countries whose economies have been most affected by the changes in their economic relations with the economies in transition, in order to adapt to those changes" [A/Res/47/175].

The Supply of Overseas Development Assistance

Closely related to the question of the future distribution or allocation of development assistance is the question of just how much development assistance will be available. The issue of the supply of development assistance is best understood, perhaps, in relation to the issue of expected demand for such assistance. According to the OECD's DAC, a consensus is emerging that demand, especially to meet Africa's needs, will require real growth of about 5% in development assistance. However, concessional resource flows have continued to grow in the 1990s only at about the same rate as in the 1980s, i.e., between 2 and 2.5% annually. The DAC explained that, at present, prospects for significantly increased levels of overseas development assistance are not very bright:

> The donor community continues to face great difficulties in generating increased flows of concessional assistance. The impediments are many—lagging economies at home; concerns about the effectiveness of development aid; the exploding competition for resources, owing to rapidly changing world conditions; and growing uncertainty as to the context and rationale for development assistance in the post-Cold War world. The search for this new rationale is most notable in countries like the United States, but to a considerable degree a reexamination is under way in most DAC countries [OECD, *Development Co-operation, 1992 Report*].

Environmental Protection, Population Growth, and Development

As the DAC noted, the 1992 **United Nations Conference on Environment and Development (UNCED)** "reinforced the emerging global partnerships based on the undeniable link between environment and development. UNCED underlined the interrelationship and interdependence of all the world's nations, and especially the integral nature of the world's development and environment agendas" [ibid.].

"UNCED follow-up" has become not only a familiar phrase to members of the international development community but also a reminder that the Conference's significant achievements and lofty goals should not be allowed to fade from international view. The DAC, for its part, pledged to, among other things: (1) review the adequacy of resource flows to implement Agenda 21, UNCED's strategic plan; (2) assess donor responses to Agenda 21; and (3) help ensure that DAC members have followed through on "the population dimension" by giving even greater attention to helping the developing world "achieve a demographic transition."

The 47th General Assembly also adopted a resolution concerning population and development. Declaring the General Assembly's support for a 1994 International Conference on Population and Development to be hosted by Egypt, this resolution went on to emphasize the need for comprehensive national population policies based on national priorities and compatible with sustained economic growth and sustainable development, and it spoke of the need to raise the priority given to population issues on the international development agenda [see A/Res/47/176].

The Least Developed Countries

During the 47th Session the "Group of 77" developing countries introduced, and the General Assembly adopted, by consensus, a resolution concerning the least developed countries. The resolution noted that six countries had been added to the list and recommended, in light of such expansion, that the Programme of Action for the Least Developed Countries for the 1990s be implemented, that commitments and levels of overseas development assistance be adjusted, that the least developed countries implement national policies in line with the Programme of Action mentioned above, and that the aggregate level of external support be increased substantially [A/Res/47/173]. In a second resolution related to the first by virtue of the fact that the great majority of the least developed countries are located in Africa, the Assembly urged that the countries of Africa, the institutions and agencies of the U.N. system, the international financial institutions, and all bilateral and multilateral funding institutions give their full support to the **Second Industrial Development Decade for Africa, 1993–2002** [A/Res/47/177]. Separately, the DAC noted that Africa's resource-flow profile and future prospects are greatly at odds with the fundamental objective of foreign assistance, which is to help developing countries build self-sustaining economies in which import requirements are fully met by their own foreign exchange earnings and normal capital inflows. Sub-Saharan Africa continues to be primarily dependent on official development finance to meet such requirements. For example, in 1990, sub-Saharan Africa enjoyed only $1.1 billion in new direct investment, and that sum was offset by net foreign borrowing of −$1.1 billion [OECD, *Development Co-operation, 1992 Report*].

Development Assistance

Members of the DAC provided $57 billion in official development assistance in 1991, compared with $53 billion in 1990. This translated into a 3.3% real increase when adjustments are made for prices and exchange rates [ibid.]. The DAC noted that the 1991 increase was especially critical, given a continuing decline in overseas development assistance from Eastern Europe and the former Soviet Union. Japan and the United States remained the largest donors, while the Scandinavian countries remained the leaders in terms of aid as a percentage of gross national product (GNP).

The DAC also reported that 42% of the $131 billion of overall resource flows to developing countries in 1991 came from private, not of-

Table III-3
Selected Overseas Development Assistance Indicators

Sources of Overseas Development Assistance, 1991

Country	*U.S.$ Amount (billions)*	*Percent of GNP*
United States	11.2	0.20
Japan	10.9	0.32
France	7.5	0.62
Germany	6.9	0.41
Italy	3.4	0.30
United Kingdom	3.2	0.32
Canada	2.6	0.45
Netherlands	2.5	0.88
Sweden	2.1	0.92
Norway	1.2	1.14

Geographical Distribution of Overseas Development Assistance, 1990–91, percentage of total

	Sub-Saharan Africa	*South Asia*	*Other Asia*	*Middle East*	*Latin America & Caribbean*
Bilateral	31.3	10.0	18.9	26.6	13.0
Multilateral	9.0	7.4	15.8	66.2	1.6
Total	31.6	11.6	17.2	27.9	11.4

Source: OECD, Development Assistance Committee (DAC), *Development Co-operation, 1992*, Tables 1 and 9.

ficial, sources. These flows included foreign direct investment ($28.4 billion) and grants from nongovernmental organizations, or NGOs ($5 billion). Concerning foreign investment, both developed and developing countries have become strongly interested in the role of "privatization" in economic development. According to the DAC, "[There was] a major shift in development thinking [during] the decade of the 1980s—a shift that emphasized greater reliance on markets and the resulting adjustment of the balance between the public and private sectors. The lesson that . . . led to this shift [was] the fact that public enterprises largely have failed to live up to developmental expectations." A February 1992 DAC meeting regarding privatization concluded that:

- Thinking on privatization cannot be disassociated from thinking about the proper role of the state;
- Macroeconomic stability and deregulation are prerequisites for success;
- Private ownership leads to a new incentive structure;
- Methods of sale may vary;
- Public sector reform is a substitute, but not a very good one, for the privatization or even the liquidation of inherently uneconomic state-owned enterprises [ibid.].

The General Assembly too expressed, by consensus, strong support for privatization as a means for mobilizing resources and promoting economic growth and sustainable development [A/Res/47/171].

5. Trade and the Trading System

International Trade 1992

The volume of world trade increased by about 4.5% in 1992, more than ten times the rate of growth of world output and three times the rate of growth of developed-country output. (World output grew by only about 0.4% in 1992; developed-country output increased by 1.5%.) According to the U.N.'s "World Economy at the End of 1992," it was the ninth consecutive year in which world trade grew more rapidly than world output [see also *The New York Times*, 3/29/93]. **Exports** from developing countries rose an impressive 10.6%, led by countries in South and East Asia, including especially Hong Kong, Republic of Korea, Singapore, and Taiwan, whose exports increased by nearly 16%. (China's exports rose an impressive 9.4%.) Exports from developed countries rose by only about 3%, led by the North Americans, whose exports increased by more than

5%. Developing countries also imported at a higher rate (i.e., a bit less than 10%) than did developed countries (3.7%). China, with an increase of about 15% over 1991, was a leader in import growth, followed by the South and East Asian region (11.5%) and the Latin American region (11.1%).

The International Trading System

Multilateral Relations

To the frustration of much of the international economic community, the dispute between the United States and the E.C. regarding agricultural policies and practices continues to impede completion of the **Uruguay Round of multilateral trade negotiations.** During and after the U.S. presidential campaign, U.S. President George Bush made a determined effort to secure a multilateral trade agreement and was partially successful, although complete agreement eluded him. His successor, President Bill Clinton, proceeded to raise questions about the U.S.–E.C. deal reached by Bush, and then entered into several new disputes with the E.C. By late spring 1993, however, the Clinton administration appeared to favor early completion of the Round. To facilitate that process, it requested from Congress an extension of its "fast-track" negotiating authority beyond the March 1 expiration of the existing authority [*The New*

Table III-4
World Trade, 1988–92

	1988	*1989*	*1990*	*1991*	*1992‡*
(Annual percentage change in volume)					
Exports					
World	8.4	7.5	4.8	3.7	4.5
Developed market economies	8.6	6.7	5.7	3.0	3.1
Developing countries	9.6	9.7	6.1	10.4	10.6
Economies in transition	4.3	−0.9	−10.7	−20.8	0.0
Imports					
World	9.5	7.9	4.4	4.0	4.7
Developed market economies	8.7	7.5	4.6	2.9	3.7
Developing countries	14.2	10.0	6.0	12.8	9.6
Economies in transition	3.5	5.0	−5.2	−31.4	0.0

Source: ECOSOC, "The World Economy at the End of 1992," E/1993/INF/1, 2/1/93, Table A.8.
‡Estimate

York Times, 4/10/93], declaring a desire to complete the round by mid-July 1993.

"Plurilateral" and Regional Relations

In mid-August 1992, not long before the E.C. would begin implementing its plan for a Single Market, the United States, Canada, and Mexico reached preliminary agreement on a **North American Free Trade Agreement (NAFTA).** Once elected, President Clinton vowed to strengthen environmental enforcement and workers' rights provisions of the NAFTA in supplemental agreements. The process of negotiating the supplemental agreements continued into late spring/early summer 1993, making it unlikely that the U.S. Congress could vote to ratify (or reject) the entire agreement before October 1993. In Canada, Prime Minister Brian Mulroney appeared determined to secure Canadian ratification before leaving office in June 1993. It was also expected that Mexico would go along if the supplemental agreements were negotiated in a manner satisfactory to the Mexican government.

Elsewhere, "plurilateral" and regional trading arrangements were proliferating, or at least expanding. As noted earlier, the E.C. is negotiating with Sweden, Finland, Austria, and Norway, all of which are interested, to varying degrees, in becoming members. Currently, these four and the other former European Free Trade Area (EFTA) countries have combined with the E.C. to create a **European Economic Area,** or EEA. The E.C. has also opened discussions with Poland, Hungary, and the Czech and Slovak republics about the possibility of membership in the Community at a future time. In the former Soviet Union, almost all of the former republics (excluding the Baltic republics) agreed in early 1993 to establish an economic association, building on the **Commonwealth of Independent States** framework. Meanwhile, four Latin American states—Argentina, Brazil, Paraguay, and Uruguay—are strengthening their economic relations under the **Mercosur** framework. And an ASEAN (Association of South East Asian Nations) Free Trade Association came into existence on January 1, 1993.

Bilateral Relations

Bilateral trading relations have featured most prominently disputes involving the United States and the E.C., the United States and Japan, the E.C. and Japan, and the United States and China. Each of these situations highlights the need for an effective multilateral dispute settlement mechanism, such as those embodied in the U.S.–Canada Free Trade Agreement of 1988 and the pending NAFTA.

Unilateral Liberalization

Even as the Uruguay Round remains stalemated and the regional bloc phenomenon spreads, a number of developing countries are acting unilaterally to lower their barriers to trade. Mexico is a prominent example in Latin America, India in Asia, and Zimbabwe in Africa ["The World Economy at the End of 1992"].

6. Transnational Corporations and the Global Economy

The United Nations Centre on Transnational Corporations was abolished in an early-1992 reorganization of the U.N. Secretariat, but its functions and duties were to be continued in a new organizational framework known as the Transnational Corporations and Management Division (TCMD) located in the newly created Department of Economic and Social Development. Also retained was the U.N. Commission on Transnational Corporations, which held its 19th session in April 1993. A selection of topics on the Commission's agenda provides a useful guide to current developments concerning international investment and multinational corporations.

Transnational Corporations in the World Economy

In its July 1992 publication, *World Investment Report 1992: Transnational Corporations as Engines of Growth*, the TCMD departed sharply from much of the international rhetoric of the 1970s by maintaining that transnational corporations serve as an engine of growth in developing countries by providing investment capital, technology, and human resource development, expanded trade opportunities, and support for long-term growth. To be sure, some negative aspects of transnationals were also listed, including the possibility of adverse environmental impacts, dualistic economic structures, transfer pricing, and abuse of market power. Nevertheless, the report said, developing countries should be sensitive to the potential positive contributions of transnationals to the development programs of developing countries [see also "Everybody's Favourite Monsters: A Survey of Multinationals," *The Economist*, 3/27/93].

Trends in Foreign Direct Investment in Developing Countries

The TCMD reported to the Commission on Transnational Corporations in April 1993 that one of the most significant features of foreign direct investment flows to developing countries in 1991 was that such investment increased in both absolute and relative terms. Moreover, all regions of the developing world—Latin America, Asia, and Africa—benefited from the increase. And, perhaps even more remarkable, this development occurred in the context of an unusual overall decline in foreign direct investment (the first such decline since 1982), and in an era in which North-North investment (that is, among and between members of the developed-country "Triad" of Europe, North America, and Japan) was expected to dominate all other international investment patterns, including especially the North-South pattern. Recessionary conditions in a number of the Triad countries were said to have contributed both to the overall decline and to the shift in direction of direct foreign investment [see, for example, "Trends in Foreign Direct Investment, Report of the Secretary-General," E/C.10/1993/2, 3/3/93; and "Foreign Direct Investment in the U.S. Turns Negative, Reversing Long Trend," *The Wall Street Journal*, 3/18/93].

The Role of Transnational Corporations in Central and Eastern Europe

Foreign direct investment is, of course, a relatively recent phenomenon in the former command economies of Central and Eastern Europe. However, the nations of those regions, many of them newly independent, fervently want and desperately need as much foreign investment as they can attract, despite the recognized risks. Today, the principal foreign investment problem for the newly opened economies of Central and Eastern Europe is that the amounts actually invested, as well as the size of the average investment, remain small by international standards. The TCMD

Table III-5
Inflows and Outflows of Foreign Direct Investment, 1990–91

	1990	*1991‡*	*1991‡*	*1991‡*
Countries	*(Billions of U.S. $)*		*Share in Total Percentage*	*Growth Rate (percentage)*
Developed countries				
Inflows	172	108	74	−37
Outflows	226	174	97	−23
Developing countries				
Inflows	30	36	25	21
Outflows	5	2	3	−35
All countries				
Inflows	202	147	100	−27
Outflows	234	180	100	−23

Source: "Trends in Foreign Investment," Report of the Secretary-General, E/C.10/1993/2, 3/3/93, Table 1.
‡Estimate

maintained that to attract more foreign direct investment (FDI) governments in the regions would need to "enhance domestic policy coordination, abolish the remaining restrictions on FDI, strengthen management capacity for the efficient implementation of policies governing FDI, implement programs of macroeconomic stabilization and economic transformation, and maintain social stability" [see "Foreign Direct Investment in the Newly Opened Economies of Central and Eastern Europe, Report of the Secretary-General," E/C/.10/1993/5, 3/15/93].

International, Regional, and Bilateral Arrangements and Agreements Relating to Transnational Corporations

At its 18th session, the Commission on Transnational Corporations had noted that the legal and institutional approaches to international law- and policy-making with respect to international investment and multinational corporations had become quite diverse—that is to say, global, regional, interregional, and bilateral. The Commission had asked the TCMD to review recent trends and developments in this regard and to suggest present and future needs for further action regarding international cooperation on issues relating to transnational corporations.

During the 19th session, the TCMD reported that, at the global level, legally binding commitments had been made on some aspects of foreign direct investment, including especially environmental protection, and that other multilateral efforts were continuing in the context of the Uruguay Round of trade negotiations. The TCMD noted that only one universal set of guidelines had been established, namely, the World Bank Guidelines for the Treatment of Foreign Direct Investment. A separate effort, under ECOSOC's aegis, had failed to generate a consensus after about 15 years of negotiation. Without denying the merits of a global agreement, the TCMD noted that in recent years it has been at the regional and interregional levels that international activity is most intense, and most fruitful. In the European Community and in North America, among other places, states have made legally binding commitments regarding foreign direct investment as a part of (ostensibly free trade) packages that cover a number of interrelated issues. The TCMD also noted that the network of bilateral treaties for the promotion and protection of foreign investments has continued to expand, as have other types of bilateral treaties that address issues of concern to foreign investors, such as the one on double taxation. The TCMD anticipated that the elaboration of the international framework relating to transnational corporations will continue to evolve along these multiple paths [see "International Framework for Transnational Corporations, Report of the Secretary-General," E/C.10/1993/8, 3/24/93].

IV
Global Resource Management

1. Environment and Sustainable Development

By Jennifer Metzger

With the U.N. Conference on Environment and Development (UNCED), held in Rio de Janeiro on June 3–14, 1992, "sustainable development" was elevated from a somewhat esoteric concept to something of a maxim. "We have to find a balance between the exploitation of [the] environment, which is vital to people's survival, and the conservation of [the] environment, which is vital to *its* survival," declared British Prime Minister John Major in the presence of over 100 heads of state and government, 8,000 journalists, 1,500 accredited nongovernmental observers, and other official delegates from 170 nations [*Report of the United Nations Conference on Environment and Development* (hereafter, *UNCED Report*), A/CONF.15/26/Rev.1 (Vol. III)]. Another 30,000 private citizens turned out for parallel nongovernmental events, making it the largest international political gathering of its kind.

The Rio conference marked the 20th anniversary of the **1972 U.N. Conference on the Human Environment**, which was held in Stockholm and which gave birth to the **U.N. Environment Programme (UNEP)**. While significant progress has been made in addressing such problems as marine pollution and depletion of the Earth's ozone layer, the health of the planet has continued to deteriorate as a consequence of population pressures, grinding poverty in the South, high rates of consumption in the North, and the failure of economic policies in both hemispheres to take the environment into account. In the years since Stockholm, farmers have lost almost 500 billion tons of topsoil through erosion and, at the same time, have been called upon to feed 1.6 billion additional people [*State of the World 1993*, Worldwatch Institute]. The annual pace of tropical deforestation increased from 11.4 million hectares in 1980 to 15.5 million hectares in 1990 as growing numbers of poor people in the developing world cleared land for agriculture [U.N. press releases FAO/3560, 3/9/93]. In other parts of the world, the burning of fossil fuels by industry and consumers helped to raise atmospheric concentrations of carbon dioxide—the principal greenhouse gas—by 9% over the past two decades [*State of the World 1993*].

The most ambitious undertaking in the field of the environment, UNCED attempted to tackle these and virtually all other environment and development issues facing the world community. UNCED's mandate, as set out by the 44th General Assembly, was to produce global strategies that would foster economic growth and development without jeopardizing the planet's capacity to sustain future generations. After two-and-a-half years of painstaking negotiations that often divided not only North and South but also the members of each group, governments reached consensus on three nonbinding agreements: the **Rio Declaration on Environment and Development**, containing 27 principles intended to guide nations along the path of sustainable development; **Agenda 21**, a 500-page plan detailing over 2,500 national and international actions in areas ranging from poverty alleviation to the management of radioactive wastes; and a **Non-Legally Binding Authoritative Statement of Principles for a Global Consensus on the Management, Conservation, and Sustainable Development of All Types of Forests** [for background on the negotiating process, see *A Global Agenda: Issues/47*, pp. 171–91]. The conference also saw over 150 nations sign conventions on biological diversity and climate change, which were negotiated in separate forums parallel to UNCED negotiations.

The agreements adopted in Rio—rife with fragile compromises among nations and often reflecting the lowest common denominator—point to a difficult road ahead as governments attempt to reconcile their economic and environmental priorities. Among the obstacles are the successful efforts of the United States and Arab oil-producing nations to block Agenda 21 proposals designed to reduce fossil fuel use; and the equally fruitful efforts of a group of developing countries, whose economies depend heavily on their timber industry, to water down any proposals in the forest agreement that could be interpreted as limiting their right to exploit their resources. The forest agreement issues a meek call to nations to manage their forests "on the basis of environmentally sound guidelines" as well as on the basis of "national development policies and priorities" [*UNCED Report* (Vol. I)].

Though less rigorous than some might have hoped, the agreements have laid the groundwork for global efforts to address environment and development issues in an integrated manner. "Rio started a process, and the results of the Conference provide a good basis for decisive action based on a new global partnership," Torben Mailan-Christensen, a representative of Denmark, told the 47th Session of the General Assembly [A/47/PV.58, 11/18/93]. The Rio Declaration contains a number of principles that provide new standards for behavior on national and global levels—among these, that "environmental protection shall constitute an integral part of the development process and cannot be considered in isolation from it" [*UNCED Report*]. The Declaration sets in stone the "precautionary principle," which would deny nations the opportunity to cite scientific uncertainty as the reason for continuing a practice considered harmful to the environment. (Such a justification was used by the United States during negotiations on the climate change convention to block agreement on targets for the reduction of carbon emissions.) Nations are also called upon to cooperate "in an expeditious and timely manner" in developing international law regarding liability and compensation for transboundary damage to the environment.

New Institutions, New Players, New Mandates

One of the most important achievements of UNCED was an agreement to create a high-level **U.N. Commission on Sustainable Development (CSD)** to monitor progress in implementing the goals set in Rio and to promote integrated policy-making on environment and development issues. After weeks of closed-door negotiations during the 47th Session, the General Assembly authorized the U.N. Economic and Social Council (ECOSOC) to establish such a body, and elaborated its mandate and composition. With no enforcement power other than peer pressure, the intergovernmental commission is to monitor the efforts of nations and international organizations in carrying out Agenda 21; to assess the adequacy of financial and technical assistance to developing countries in helping them meet their UNCED commitments; and to make policy recommendations to the General Assembly, through ECOSOC.

Many have questioned whether the Commission will be an effective monitor of national progress, since governments will not be required to report on their efforts. (The full membership of the European Community has already pledged to submit to the CSD regular progress reports on the implementation of Agenda 21.) Governments, however, will not be the only source of information for the CSD: The Rio action plan calls on the Commission "to receive and analyze relevant input from competent nongovernmental organizations, including the scientific and the private sector, in the context of the overall implementation of Agenda 21" [ibid.].

The role played by nongovernmental organizations (NGOs) in the UNCED process itself was without precedent. Not only did they provide governments and the conference secretariat with a great deal of the information and expertise necessary for negotiations but also maintained the necessary political pressure for agreement. In all, some 1,800 NGOs from developed and developing countries were accredited to participate as observers and were able to make written submissions and to address the negotiating committee at the chairman's discretion. Tens of thousands more participated outside the official process by lobbying governments, forming networks and alliances of NGOs, holding public hearings and conferences, and raising awareness through the media.

Agenda 21 recognizes these groups as "important partners" with governments in the pursuit of sustainable development, and calls on the U.N. system to ensure their effective participation. Still, there was heated debate during the 47th Session over the process by which NGOs would be granted consultative status at the CSD. Initially, the United States and the Group of 77 developing countries argued in favor of extending to the Commission the traditional ECOSOC procedures, which tend to limit participation to well-established international NGOs. (Since the 1960s, ECOSOC has granted consultative status to three sets of NGOs, each with its own criteria and rights: Category I, Category II, and the Roster—the last bestowing the most limited rights of participation.) The issue was put off until ECOSOC's organizational session in mid-February 1993, when it formally established the CSD and elected its membership of 53 states. Owing much to the vigorous lobbying efforts of the NGOs, ECOSOC decided to grant Roster status to all groups accredited to UNCED, many of which had no previous U.N. affiliation. All three categories are to participate in the Commission on a roughly equal footing [*The InterDependent* 19, no. 1, Spring 1993].

From February 24 to 26, the new Commission met in New York to elect its bureau of officers and to adopt the provisional agenda for its first substantive session, scheduled for June 14–25 in New York. Members also made minor revisions in the Secretary-General's proposed work plan for the CSD. The plan divides Agenda 21's myriad program areas into manageable clusters of issues so that the CSD, if it keeps to its schedule, will be able to complete a full review of the action plan by 1997—the target date for a special session of the General Assembly devoted to appraising the legacy of UNCED. The June 1993 meeting finalized the CSD's work plan, then discussed efforts to implement Agenda 21 and reviewed the status of financial and technical resources available to developing countries for sustainable development efforts. All CSD sessions conclude with a ministerial-level meeting to consider emerging policy issues and to provide the necessary political impetus for action.

U.N. Secretary-General Boutros Boutros-Ghali gave sustainable development high priority as he sought to overhaul the structure of the Secretariat. As other departments were being dissolved and consolidated, he established a new **Department for Policy Coordination and Sustainable Development** to provide support for ECOSOC and its subsidiary bodies, including the CSD. Heading up the new department is Nitin Desai of India, who served as deputy to UNCED Secretary-General Maurice Strong, a Canadian.

The Secretary-General will also soon surround himself with the pundits of sustainable development: Upon the recommendation of

UNCED's Agenda 21, Boutros-Ghali will create a **high-level advisory board** consisting of 15–25 "eminent personalities broadly representative of all regions of the world," with "recognized expertise" in sustainable development issues [Report of the Secretary-General, E/1993/15, 2/1/93]. The functions of the board, as spelled out in the report to ECOSOC, are to advise the Secretary-General on issues to be addressed by the CSD, to bring to his attention emerging problems relating to sustainable development as well as recommendations for resolving them, and to help build partnerships among the United Nations and the scientific, business, and academic communities and nongovernmental groups. During ECOSOC's annual session at the end of April 1993, the Group of 77 voiced opposition to Boutros-Ghali's suggestion that the advisory board communicate directly with the CSD rather than "through" the Secretary-General [U.N. press release ECOSOC/5426, 4/29/93]. As of this writing, the Secretary-General has yet to appoint the board's members.

Boutros-Ghali also plans to establish a "roster of rosters" that would draw largely, though not exclusively, from existing rosters of experts thoughout the U.N. system. This open-ended roster will be maintained by the new Department for Policy Coordination and Sustainable Development to widen the pool of expertise available on sustainable development issues.

Elsewhere in the U.N. system, agencies and departments have begun to organize their work around the sustainable development objectives set out in Rio. The U.N. Development Programme (UNDP), which coordinates and administers much of the U.N.'s technical assistance programs, is initiating a **Capacity 21 program** "to assist developing countries in formulating development goals, plans, and programs that lead to sustainable development," and to enhance their capacity to implement them effectively. According to a UNDP study of 80 developing countries, the lack of endogenous capacities poses a formidable constraint to sustainable development efforts ["Capacity 21," UNDP background paper]. The new program will focus on developing the skills and expertise of national governments and local communities, with projects ranging from training farmers in alternative and sustainable agricultural methods to assisting governments in developing economic instruments—such as user's fees and taxes—to deter environmentally destructive practices. Ten governments submitted project proposals in anticipation of the June 1993 meeting of UNDP's Governing Council, which was expected to launch the pilot phase of Capacity 21. By the end of May, donor nations had contributed a total of $25 million to the program's trust fund—$75 million short of what UNDP has estimated as necessary for the pilot phase of Capacity 21.

The environment is expected to figure even more prominently in the work of UNDP with the appointment of **James Gustave Speth**, President of the Washington, D.C.-based World Resources Institute, as **UNDP's new Administrator.** Speth, a former head of the U.S. administration's Council on Environmental Quality, was nominated by President Bill Clinton to replace William Draper III, a Reagan nominee, who stepped down on July 15. (By something of a tradition, the post of UNDP Administrator goes to an American.) The Secretary-General, after endorsing Speth, presented his name to the General Assembly for approval [*The New York Times*, 5/11/93].

Another new U.N. chief with strong "green" credentials is **Elizabeth Dowdeswell of Canada,** who succeeded Mostafa Tolba of Egypt as **Executive Director of UNEP** in December 1992. Dowdeswell, Canada's former Assistant Deputy Minister of Environment, co-chaired negotiations for the Framework Convention on Climate Change signed in Rio. Not long after her appointment, she submitted to governments a report on the "Future Course of UNEP," which seeks to align the Programme's priorities with the demands of Agenda 21. "I want to cause constructive damage to the status quo," she announced in her first appearance before UNEP's Governing Council. The 58-member Council, which held its biennial meeting in Nairobi, May 10–21, gave her the backing she needed. Its government members decided to reorient the activities of the Programme, endorsing many of the proposals outlined in the Executive Director's statement. These include a shift in priorities from monitoring the state of the environment to enhancing capacity-building, in cooperation with UNDP, and promoting the spread of environmentally sound technologies throughout the developing world. UNEP will continue its critical work in environmental sensing—i.e., gathering data on environmental problems and presenting them to governments in "usable form"—but it will also give high priority to environmental economics, including the development and promotion of such tools as natural resource accounting and environmental impact assessments [U.N. press release HE/815, 5/24/93, International Documents Review 4, no. 17, 5/10–14/93].

The Global Environment Facility

Over the course of 1993 the Global Environment Facility (GEF) is expected to evolve from a less-than-perfect pilot project to the primary international funding mechanism for Agenda 21 and the biological diversity and climate conventions. The GEF was launched by the World Bank, UNDP, and UNEP in 1990 as an experimental three-year program to help developing countries cope with the costs of environmental management in a limited number of areas of global concern. Of its so-called "core fund" of $860 million, GEF had earmarked 47% for biodiversity projects, 36% for global warming, and 17% for international waters [GEF report, *The Pilot Phase and Beyond*, Working Paper Series no. 1, 5/92]. A separate fund of

$200 million was set up to assist developing countries in phasing out ozone-depleting substances in accordance with the **1989 Montreal Protocol on Substances that Deplete the Ozone Layer.**

Virtually since its inception, the GEF has been widely criticized by NGOs and developing countries, which view it as lacking in transparency, accountability, and southern participation in decision-making. A source of concern to developing countries (and a source of comfort to the governments of industrialized countries) is the fact that despite the facility's three organizational sponsors, the actual manager is the World Bank, whose governing structure is dominated by its largest donors. Many have complained about the lack of publicly available, complete, and timely information on GEF projects, and the lack of participation by NGOs and affected communities in all phases of the project cycle ["Restructuring the Global Environment Facility," *Policy Focus*, 1993, no. 1].

In the Rio and climate negotiations, developing countries agreed to rely on the GEF rather than create new funding mechanisms on the condition that the facility be thoroughly overhauled by the conclusion of the pilot phase in 1993. Soon afterward, GEF participants (which have been rather loosely defined as the 30–40 developed and developing country governments that attend meetings) began negotiations on restructuring and, at a meeting in Beijing May 26–28, adopted a plan.

Picking Up Where UNCED Left Off

Owing to a lack of consensus in Rio on how to manage fish stocks that straddle two different jurisdictions—an **Exclusive Economic Zone (EEZ)** and the high seas—the 47th Session of the General Assembly has called for a **United Nations Conference on Straddling and Highly Migratory Fish Stocks,** to be held in New York from July 12 to 30. Although the 1982 U.N. Convention on the Law of the Sea obligates states parties to take measures aimed at preventing overexploitation on the high seas, monitoring and enforcement have often been lax. At UNCED, some coastal states wanted to extend their EEZs to help manage depleting stocks, while those states with high-seas fishing fleets opposed the measure on the grounds that high-seas fishing resources are held in common. The U.N. conference will seek to resolve the matter and formulate recommendations for effective conservation and management of these resources.

In another Rio follow-up action, the General Assembly called for a **Global Conference on the Sustainable Development of Small Island States,** to be convened in Barbados in April 1994. The decision is as much a result of the successful lobbying efforts of the Alliance of Small Island States (AOSIS)—a transregional group of 41 members that spoke as one voice at UNCED—as it is of the now widespread recognition of their unique plight. According to Agenda 21,

> Their small size, limited resources, geographic dispersion and isolation from markets, place them at a disadvantage economically and prevent economies of scale. . . . They are considered extremely vulnerable to global warming and sea-level rise, with certain small low-lying islands facing the increasing threat of the loss of their entire national territories. Most tropical islands are also now experiencing the more immediate impacts of increasing frequency of cyclones, storms, and hurricanes associated with climate change. These are causing major setbacks to their socioeconomic development.

The objectives of the conference are to develop sustainable development plans and programs tailored to the specific needs of these states, and to adopt measures to cope "effectively, creatively, and sustainably with environmental changes and to mitigate impacts and reduce the threats posed to marine and coastal resources" [A/Res/47/189].

At the conference Preparatory Committee's organizational session in April, debate split along North-South lines over the subject of financial assistance for sustainable development in small island states—revisiting an issue that had mired negotiations leading up to UNCED. (Developing countries sought a commitment from the North for "new and additional" funds to assist them in meeting the costs of implementing Agenda 21, but several industrialized countries, particularly the United States, argued that existing resources allotted to development aid should cover the bill. Northern countries eventually conceded that current levels of assistance would not be enough, but the actual aid commitments made in Rio fell far short of the what UNCED Secretary-General Maurice Strong and most NGOs believed were necessary [for further background, see *A Global Agenda: Issues/46*]. Here, at the April meeting, members of the European Community opposed including the issue on the provisional agenda of the first negotiating session, arguing that the level of provision of aid to developing countries would be a perennial CSD agenda item and would duplicate that body's work. AOSIS and the Group of 77 insisted that it be retained, since access to financial resources is a "core" issue in efforts to address the problems faced by these states. Though developing countries won out in the end, G-77 Spokesman Juanita Castaño voiced their concern that "the political will to help developing countries exhibited at UNCED seemed to have been reversed," and expressed their hope that a "more positive approach" would be adopted at the August 2–13 negotiating session in New York.

Combating Desertification

Desertification affects about 70% of all drylands, amounting to a quarter of the total land area on Earth and home to a sixth of the world's population [*UNCED Report*]. The most severely affected region is Africa, where drought, overpopulation, and the overworking of marginal lands have turned rangeland to desert, jeopardizing the livelihoods of millions.

Yet the issue did not receive serious consideration until the final weeks of the Rio negotiations, when the lobbying effort of African countries succeeded in winning agreement from every industrialized country but the United States for negotiation of an **International Convention to Combat Desertification.** (Unable to win support for its position, the U.S. delegation withdrew its objections in the 11th hour.) Upon the recommendation of UNCED, the 47th General Assembly established an Intergovernmental Negotiating Committee (INC) open to all member states, and set June 1994 as the target date for "finalizing" the convention [A/Res/47/188]. At a January organizational meeting, the INC scheduled the first of five negotiating sessions for May 24–June 3, in Nairobi.

Honing the Ozone Treaty

Spurred by scientific evidence that the Earth's ozone layer is being depleted far more rapidly than previously thought, delegates of close to 90 governments that are signatories to the 1989 Montreal Protocol met in Copenhagen in late September 1992 to speed up production bans on the offending chemicals. Damage to the ozone layer permits higher concentrations of ultraviolet radiation to reach the Earth, endangering humans and other living organisms. The new agreements move up the deadline for ending production of chlorofluorocarbons (CFCs, which are primarily used as refrigerants, cleaning agents, and solvents) from the year 2000 to January 1, 1996, and halons (used in fire extinguishers) to January 1, 1994. Hydro-chlorofluorocarbons, a CFC substitute that depletes the ozone layer at a slower rate, will be phased out in stages between 2004 and 2030. Signatories failed to agree to a production ban on methyl bromine, a pesticide that scientists predict will account for 15% of ozone depletion by the end of the century [*The New York Times*, 9/26/92]. Then-UNEP Executive Director Mostafa Tolba was among many who stated that the new measures did not go far enough. So that developing countries will be able to meet the costs of substituting more ozone-friendly chemicals under the new, stricter deadlines, parties to the treaty agreed to establish a Multilateral Fund for financing the transfer of technology. For 1993 the budget is expected to total $113 million [*The Independent Sectors' Network*, no. 22, 1/93].

Toxic Dumping

In September 1992, UNEP Executive Director Mostafa Tolba accused Swiss and Italian companies of taking advantage of Somalia's anarchy to dispose of their toxic wastes [*The Boston Globe*, 9/11/92]. In a war-torn country with no central government at all, a man claiming to be Health Minister reportedly granted these firms an $80 million, 20-year contract [ibid.]. The episode helped to reinforce a long-standing claim of developing countries and NGOs: Nothing short of a ban on the transboundary movement of hazardous wastes will prevent the "toxic dumping" that is taking a toll on the environment and human health in the Third World. Though many developing countries have adopted legislation banning or severely restricting waste imports—the bulk of which comes from the United States—these laws have proven difficult to enforce. During UNCED negotiations, developing countries sought endorsement of an international ban by Agenda 21, winning instead a rather porous commitment "to adopt a ban on or prohibit, as appropriate, the export of hazardous wastes to countries that do not have the capacity to deal with those wastes in an environmentally sound way or that have banned the import of such wastes" [*UNCED Report*].

A call for a complete ban was again made at the conclusion of a two-day ministerial-level conference of 56 countries, held in Piriapolis, Uruguay, in early December 1992. The conference assembled for the first time most of the 36 countries that have ratified the **1989 Basel Convention on the control of transboundary movements of hazardous wastes**, which was negotiated under the auspices of UNEP and which entered into force in May 1992. The convention seeks to reduce the risk of sending dangerous wastes to countries where it would not be treated properly, but its provision permitting the export of such wastes to the Third World for "recycling" is considered by the convention's critics to be a major loophole. At the December meeting, developing countries pointed out that many do not have the capacity to recycle wastes, and that the recycling label is often used to camouflage unrecyclable wastes for the purpose of dumping [U.N. press release HE/801, 12/16/92]. The conference asked industrialized countries to report on what they have done about the requested ban at the next meeting of the parties to the treaty in early 1994. Basel treaty parties also decided to establish a technical working group to produce guidelines and offer advice on evaluating and safely handling wastes labeled "recyclable," and to create a working group to draft a protocol on liability and compensation in accidents involving hazardous waste.

In the spring of 1993 the members of the European Community began debate on Denmark's suggestion that the E.C. propose a blanket ban through amendment to the Basel convention. According to Reuters, some E.C. diplomats expressed concern that such a move would scare major waste exporters like Japan, which have yet to ratify the treaty [3/8/93]. The Community agreed to a deadline of February 6, 1994, for its own ratification of the treaty.

Timber vs. Forests: Revamping the ITTA

The NGOs and northern governments that failed at UNCED to get a convention on forests—or even an inspired statement of principles—are looking for a window of opportunity in negotiations for a successor to the **1983 International Tropical Timber Agreement (ITTA).** The Agreement, which was negotiated under the auspices of the U.N. Conference on Trade and Development, expires on March 31, 1994. As the name implies (it is a "timber," not a "forest," agreement), the ITTA is tilted more toward economic than ecological concerns. Of its eight objectives, the majority focus on strengthening cooperation among producer and consumer countries in expanding and diversifying international trade in tropical timber and in improving the marketing, distribution, and processing capacities of producer nations. Only two objectives specifically address conservation and sustainable management of these resources.

Over time, however, the **International Tropical Timber Organization (ITTO)**—which was established by the Agreement and which executes the policies and projects approved by the Council of ITTA member states—has focused increasingly on the long-term viability of tropical forests. In 1990 the Council launched an ITTO Action Plan aimed at "bringing all productive forest estates as soon as possible under sustainable management, so that, by the year 2000, the total exports of tropical timber products should come from sustainably managed resources" [Report of the U.N. Conference on Trade and Development, TD/TIMBER.2/3, 2/26/93].. By the end of 1992 over half of the 179 projects approved by the Council were in the field of reforestation and forest management [ibid.]

Any successor agreement that emerges from negotiations currently under way will have a major impact on the course of forest conservation and management in the years ahead. Unlike the forests principles adopted in Rio, the ITTA is a legally binding agreement. The parties to the agreement include 23 (developing) producer countries (accounting for 89% of the world's tropical forests) and 27 (primarily industrialized) consumer countries (accounting for 80% of net imports of tropical timber) [ibid.].

The first negotiating session, held in Geneva, April 13–16, 1993, was devoted to a preliminary reading of proposals submitted by the groups of consumer and producer countries. While both groups advocate making sustainable development the preeminent objective of the new agreement, the proposals have little else in common. The producer countries hope to change the focus of the entire agreement by extending it to all internationally traded timber—a position that environmental NGOs support. These countries have viewed the efforts of the North to promote forest conservation in tropical countries as a double standard and as unfair trade, since timber industries in temperate countries like the United States could continue to produce as they pleased. Indeed, if the ITTA was extended, the countries most affected would change significantly: The United States, which is the largest ITTA consuming member, would replace Malaysia as the largest ITTA producing member. The producer group is also calling for a new mechanism within the ITTA framework to provide financial and technical assistance to developing producer countries for promoting sustainable policies and practices.

As for the consumer group, these countries hope to make trade in sustainably produced tropical timber by the year 2000 the central goal of the new ITTA, and they further propose to endow the ITTO Council with a policy-making function. Under the current agreement, the main functions of the Council are to review projects for sponsorship and to provide a forum for an exchange of views on issues related to the tropical timber economy.

Neither group has offered any proposals that commit governments to take specific measures aimed at preventing unsustainable management practices, but an ITTO Council with a policy-making mandate could perform this function—if member states agree to it. Formal negotiations were expected to get under way at the negotiating session scheduled for June 21–25.

The United States on Sustainable Development: From Reactionary to Global Leader?

As a nation that generates a quarter of the world economic product and consumes a disproportionate share of the world's resources, the United States is generally regarded as a pivotal player in most questions of environment and sustainable development. Such was the case in negotiations on the framework convention on climate, when the United States used its leverage as the largest emitter of greenhouse gases to scrap language that committed nations to targets and timetables for stabilizing those emissions. In UNCED negotiations, NGOs as well as official delegates commonly expressed frustration with U.S. intransigence on issues ranging from desertification to technology assistance for developing countries. Once the world's leader in matters environmental, the nation gained a reputation in Rio for blocking global efforts in this area.

The election of **Bill Clinton** as President the following November raised prospects of **renewed U.S. leadership** on the global environment. He not only pledged during the campaign to reverse the policies of his predecessor but also chose as his running mate Tennessee Senator Al Gore, a champion of the environmental cause in Congress. In his first major environmental policy address, on the eve of Earth Day (April 22), President Clinton declared:

> For too long we have been told that we have to choose between the economy and the environment . . . between our obligations to our own

> people and our responsibilities to the future and to the rest of the world; between public action and private economy. I am here today in the hope that we can together take a different course of action, to offer a new set of challenges to our people [USUN press release, 4/21/93].

He then committed the United States to stabilizing carbon emissions at 1990 levels in accordance with the voluntary target set by the climate convention, and announced his intention to sign the Biodiversity Treaty that the Bush administration had refused to sign in Rio. Like his predecessor, however, he expressed concern that certain provisions of the Biodiversity Treaty would weaken patent protections on biotechnology. The administration plans to attach an "interpretative statement" to the U.S. signature aimed, among other things, at protecting the interests of the U.S. biotechnology industry.

In a move intended at least as much for its symbolic value as for its ecological value, Clinton also announced that he would sign **five Executive Orders** to help clean up the government's act. These ranged from requiring the federal government to buy thousands more vehicles that run on fuels that pollute less (e.g., natural gas, ethanol, or electric power) to committing the government and its agencies to buy energy-efficient computers.

Whether or not the Clinton administration has both the commitment and the clout to direct the nation down a more sustainable path remains to be seen. On the domestic front, many felt that he fared poorly in an early test of this commitment when he bowed to pressures from a group of western senators and dropped his proposal to end long-standing federal support programs that encourage logging, mining, and ranching on public lands—subsidies that often have the effect of promoting unsustainable land-use practices. Since they do so at the taxpayer's expense, environmental groups thought the subsidies a natural for spending cuts at a time of heightened concern about the deficit. "I've never seen a white flag run up so fast," said Michael Francis, Director of the Wilderness Society's national forest program [*Greenpeace News*, 4/93].

Statements by Vice President Al Gore and other U.S. officials at the CSD's first meeting in June were welcomed as signs that the United States *will* be taking a leadership role in global environmental affairs.

2. Food and Agriculture

By Martin M. McLaughlin

There are two main problems in composing the annual report in this sector. The first is that the topic is rarely addressed directly by the General Assembly. It is true that the terrible situation in Bosnia or Somalia includes the prevalence of widespread hunger and that the vivid images on our TV screens feature, inter alia, hungry people, especially children. The focus of both reporting and policy, however, is mainly on peacemaking and peacekeeping rather than on hunger itself.

The other problem is that progress, such as it is, is so glacially slow in the food system that observations and descriptions of the prevalence of chronic hunger do not vary greatly from one year to the next. The pessimistic prose of 1992 regrettably remains valid for 1993.

Thus when the **World Food Council**, the U.N.'s highest political body dealing with the food issue, reported to the General Assembly on the work of its 18th annual meeting, in Nairobi, Kenya, June 23–26, 1992 [Suppl., #19: A/47/19], the language was reminiscent of earlier accounts:

"As we approach the third millennium, the challenges posed by hunger, poverty, population growth and environmental decline are greater than ever." Regional situations don't change much, either: "The largest increases in the numbers of hungry people have been in Africa. . . . We are particularly alarmed by the fact that the total number of the world's malnourished children has increased in the 1980s, especially in Asia and sub-Saharan Africa" [ibid., part 1, paras. 3–5, passim].

The Council acknowledged the progress that has been made, crediting the **U.N. Conference on Environment and Development** (UNCED) with "creating a new spirit of partnership and cooperation among the nations of an increasingly interdependent world" [ibid., para. 3]. Indeed, the massive report of that Conference (Agenda 21) includes two major segments dealing specifically with food and agriculture.

The Council also focused on some of the more visible, because less chronic, features of the food and agriculture situation: "Food emergencies threatening the lives of millions of people continue in the Horn of Africa and parts of central and west Africa" [ibid., para. 11]. "Immediate humanitarian assistance to southern Africa and other emergency-affected countries is vital," the Council's report added [para. 14]. Moreover, the Council warned that "future support to the Eastern European region must remain additional to official development assistance (ODA) flows to the developing countries" [para. 21].

The general debate in the Council remained pessimistic:

> At a time when the number of the chronically hungry in the developing world was estimated at more than 550 million and was expected to grow in most regions, global food supply was coming under pressure. . . . A number of delegates . . . pointed out that ensuring adequate aggregate supplies of food staples, although desirable and necessary, needed to be accompanied by measures aimed at improving the poor's access to food. Long-term food security could not be achieved if the purchasing power of the poor and vulnerable could not be increased and sustained. . . . Delegates agreed that the long-term

> solution to the problems of hunger and malnutrition was more political than technical. . . . Specific national experiences amply showed that when political will was mobilized and concerted efforts were made, hunger and malnutrition could be alleviated [ibid., part 2, paras. 32–35, passim].

In other words, it was clear that what is most needed is development—improvement of the quality of life of the poor. Many delegates talked of a Green Revolution for Africa that might increase food production where the hungry people are, rather than feeding them perpetually from the surplus-producing industrialized countries. Others expressed concern about the impact of structural adjustment programs on poor people in some developing countries, or worried about the deflection of donor interest toward the "new democracies" in Eastern Europe and the former Soviet Union—a concern shared by the Under-Secretary-General for Economic and Social Development's *World Economic Survey 1992* [E/1992/40 ST/ESA/231].

The only General Assembly resolution on this subject [A/Res/47/150], noting the Council's annual report, decided explicitly to "address these issues in the context of the discussions on restructuring and revitalization of the United Nations in the economic, social and related fields . . . [ibid., para. 3].

Thus the Council has been caught up in the general overhaul of the United Nations by its new Secretary-General. With this in mind, the Secretary-General has decided to **move the Council's venue from Rome to New York**, thus separating its policy role from the activities of the **three operating agencies** the **Food and Agriculture Organization (FAO) of the United Nations,** the **World Food Programme (WFP)**, and the **International Fund for Agricultural Development (IFAD)**, which remain in Rome and, together, constitute the U.N.'s operational approach to world hunger. This move may have some impact on the character of the Council, all of whose official participants have been ministers of agriculture and have therefore tended to emphasize the supply side of the food equation rather than the demand side, where the more intransigent problems are found. The Council member countries represent about 70% of the world's people and 75% of its income.

Although there appear to be no plans for a 20th anniversary conference on food in 1994 (to match other 20th anniversaries), the FAO and the World Health Organization (WHO) did convene an **International Conference on Nutrition** in Rome in December 1992, which published an assessment of the nutritional status of people worldwide [International Conference on Nutrition: *Nutrition and Development: A Global Assessment* (revised edition), FAO and WHO, 1992] and adopted a **World Declaration on Nutrition** [*World Declaration and Plan of Action for Nutrition*, FAO and WHO, 1992].

The Assessment found that the number of chronically undernourished people declined from 36 to 20% of the population of food-deficit countries (from 941 million in 1971 to 786 million in 1990) and therefore concluded that "The objective of eradicating hunger and malnutrition and the consequent human suffering is within the reach of humanity" [p. vii]. The Declaration, representing 159 states, nevertheless deplores the lack of access by so large a number of people to their nutritional needs and asserts that "Hunger and malnutrition are unacceptable in a world that has both the knowledge and the resources to end this human catastrophe" [para. 1]. Member governments and U.N. bodies are called upon, as always, to "establish focal points," "provide capital and/or technical assistance," "prepare and disseminate information," etc.

The concluding language of the Assessment returns once again to the theme of development:

> The task of meeting the nutrition challenge is formidable, but it is attainable provided there is a global commitment and concerted actions on the part of governments, local communities, NGOs, the private sector and the international community, including international organizations. A fundamental need in many cases is simply to focus the attention of planners and policy-makers on the need to make improvements in human welfare the primary objective of the development process. This is not to suggest that economic development is not important, it is. It is now generally accepted that the essence of development should be to provide people, especially the poor and disadvantaged, with the social and economic environments necessary for them to lead healthy lives [p. 120].

Even before the Nutrition Conference, in November 1992, IFAD, the U.N. agency most attuned to demand-side considerations and to authentic development, published a slim but significant report, *The State of World Rural Poverty* [see also A/C.2/47/SR.32, para. 51 ff.], which draws some conclusions from its 14 years of experience in supporting small agriculture and rural development projects in food-deficit countries. IFAD was established as a result of the 1974 U.N. World Food Conference in Rome, which initiated the present broad concern about world hunger.

The report decries both "the simple assumption that the poor would benefit from general economic growth" (trickle-down) and the basic-needs and social-safety-net approach that succeeded it, because they stress the "need for some sort of transfer of resources to them from the more productive and dynamic sectors of accumulation. In short, the poor have been portrayed as a net burden on the growth process" [*The State of World Rural Poverty* p. 3] rather than as contributors to it.

IFAD's report is remarkable for its cogent and explicit critique of conventional development theory:

> While substantial progress has been made by several developing countries in reducing the percentage of the rural population below na-

tionally defined poverty lines, the absolute number of the rural poor has increased. . . .

Thus the pursuit of growth in the industrialized world and even in some "enclaves" in the South demonstrably has not solved the development problem. Trickle-down has not worked or it has not worked enough. The massive persistence of poverty, particularly in rural areas, represents a problem for the popular acceptance of continued economic adjustment; and it represents a problem for growth itself. The problem lies not only in the unintended consequences of the prevailing development paradigm but also in the viability of the paradigm itself [ibid., p. 4].

IFAD's message is straightforward:

> The perspective is not that growth achieved by the better-off will pull the poor out of poverty, but that the mobilization and enhancement of the resources and activities of the poor themselves can uphold their dignity and free them from the shackles of misery, while at the same time making a vital contribution to overall sustainable growth. . . . Most of the forces creating poverty are essentially social. They reflect systems of resource allocation that are made by societies. . . . Pricing policies, credit systems, and social and productive services which neglect the poor . . . are not natural, universal and inevitable facts—and neither is the poverty they give rise to [ibid., p. 14].

IFAD has also been ahead of the curve in two other areas. The *first* is the **central importance of rural women**, who produce more than half the food in the developing world. IFAD's analysis of that situation in 114 nations showed that the number of poor rural women has increased 47% in the past two decades, that 16 million landless women care for 80 million other family members, that women make the key decisions on nutrition, education, and consumption, that their economic contribution has been consistently underestimated, and that they suffer from many forms of discrimination.

"Notwithstanding the increasing female responsibility for agricultural production and income generation in rural areas, women have the least access to means of production, receive the lowest wages, and are the least educated" [ibid., p. 22]. IFAD's conclusion (their emphasis): **"The poverty question has thus become inseparable from the gender question"** [ibid.].

IFAD has also pioneered in a *second* area: **environmentally sustainable agriculture.** Several years ago sustainable resource management was adopted as a key requirement for new projects, because "Many of the rural poor . . . live in areas of extreme environmental fragility, a circumstance often prompted by a high level of control by the better-off over more stable and productive resource areas. Here the poor are extraordinarily exposed to the dangers of erosion, whittling away at an already meager productive base."

Typically, IFAD gets to the heart of the matter: "The threat is not entirely due to nature. Rather, poverty accelerates erosion. . . . Access to conservation technology is important; but more so are security of land tenure and resources to invest. Combating poverty means not only increasing the production of the poor, but also preserving and enhancing the long-term value of the resources they control" [ibid., p. 20].

In order to understand the persistence of hunger in a world that produces enough food each year to feed everyone, it may be useful to repeat some of the context in which this issue presents itself to the international community.

This year's food production feeds well over a billion more people than at the time of the 1974 U.N. World Food Conference, but the number of hungry people has grown as steadily as the general population. And every year more than half a billion people, mainly women and children, still face starvation daily.

The most widespread form of hunger is chronic undernutrition, which is especially hard on women of childbearing age, female children, and the elderly. More than half the world's hungry people live in East and South Asia, a little more than a quarter in Africa, and about a tenth in Latin America. The vast majority are in rural areas, where they are generally unable to produce enough food to feed themselves or to earn enough money to purchase it. In the vocabulary of the international food community, they suffer from **food insecurity.**

The right to food is thus still denied to hundreds of millions of people, and their numbers increase every day. Famine and displacement by war or other conflict threaten millions of lives, and hundreds of thousands of deaths result from specific nutritional deficiencies each year. UNICEF estimates that a quarter of a million children die every week from malnutrition and the diseases to which it renders them vulnerable.

Production of cereal grains, which everyone eats directly or indirectly, is forecast to increase by about 2% in 1992–93 [FAO, *Food Outlook*, 3/93], which should lighten the food burden for the time being. But supply expectations for the following year are somewhat less optimistic—especially given the shortfall in output in the former Soviet Union. Most production increases will take place in the usual exporting countries, mainly in the industrialized world. Export prices are down for the current year because of increased production, but the income to purchase the food is still not well distributed.

The FAO believes that the regional food situation in sub-Saharan Africa will remain perilous, and food aid shipments are expected to decline nearly 7%, to about 11.1 million tons. Fortunately, the drought that threatened Africa last year has eased somewhat; and good harvests in some parts of the continent have slightly reduced the need for food aid [FAO, *Foodcrops and Shortages: special report*, 3/93].

Of the annual 2 billion-ton cereal output total, the industrialized world produces more than two-fifths (800 million tons); nearly half of the rest is rice, which is grown and eaten mainly by people in the developing world. A little more than 10% of the cereal total (200 million tons) is traded or donated internationally. Even in countries where food production decreased last year, aggregate consumption levels were maintained through imports from the surplus countries.

The development community—including its agricultural segment—appears to be moving away from its almost exclusive concentration on production and growth toward a greater anxiety about the **increasing deterioration of the natural resource base.** Although international conferences are more important for their educational than for their policy outcomes, UNCED seems to have been mainly responsible for the deepening concern about the environmental aspects of agriculture. The World Bank's *World Development Report 1992* [p. 134 and passim] also underscores the importance of careful management of agricultural resources in order to feed increasing populations and reduce environmental damage.

As the foregoing summary and even the most cursory attention to the news media readily confirm, the main arena of direct action on food policy is more likely to be the GATT and other international trade negotiations and arrangements and/or the boardrooms of international banks and transnational enterprises dealing with debt and investment than it is to be the U.N. General Assembly. In this connection, significant changes in several important countries during the past year can be expected to alter the overall situation. Nevertheless, action on food and agriculture will continue to be driven by considerations of economic profit rather than nutritional need.

Agriculture continues to be one of the most controversial and contentious economic sectors; indeed, more than ever the success or failure of the **Uruguay Round of trade negotiations** appears to rest with the outcome of negotiations in that sector. Although trade in food products (75% of agricultural trade) has declined steadily since World War II, it still amounts to about $300 billion and remains vital for many countries, accounting for between one-sixth and one-third of GDP in developing countries [*UNCTAD Trade and Development Report*, 1991, Part III, Chapter II, passim].

Yet the developing countries' share in these agricultural exports on which they depend so heavily has declined steadily during the last 20 years; and they have little weight in the GATT negotiations, which mainly pit the United States against the European Community. The developing countries also face the dilemma of whether elimination of industrialized countries' agricultural export subsidies, which have largely closed industrialized country markets to them, would outweigh the threat to their agriculture from penetration of their markets by the highly capitalized exports of the traditional surplus producers. Mexico, for example, faces this prospect with respect to maize production under the proposed North American Free Trade Agreement (NAFTA).

At UNCED, the watershed event for the United Nations in 1992, there was significant attention to agriculture. Two substantive chapters of the 800-page report of that meeting, Agenda 21, are devoted specifically to agriculture. Chapter 14, "Promoting Sustainable Agriculture and Rural Development" [A21C14.W51], deals with the problem; and Chapter 32, "Strengthening the Role of Farmers" [A21C32.W51], states the central thesis of UNCED's solution.

The first of these segments questions the capacity of the food system to satisfy the requirements of a growing population and notes that "Major adjustments are needed in agricultural, environmental and macroeconomic policy, at both national and international levels, in developed as well as developing countries, to create the conditions for sustainable agriculture and rural development (SARD)" [para. 14.2]. "The main tools of SARD," it says, "are policy and agrarian reform, participation, income diversification, land conservation and improved management of inputs" [ibid., para. 14.3]. The chapter then deals with 12 program areas ranging from policy review to integrated pest management.

The second of these segments notes, as its basis for action, that "Agriculture occupies one-third of the land surface of the Earth, and is the central activity for much of the world's population. Rural activities take place in close contact with nature, adding value to it by producing renewable resources. . . . The rural household, indigenous people and their communities, and the family farmer, a substantial number of whom are women, have been the stewards of much of the Earth's resources" [ibid. paras. 32.2 and 32.3]. It concludes that "The key to successful implementation of these programmes lies in the motivation and attitudes of individual farmers and government policies that would provide incentives to farmers to manage their natural resources efficiently and in a sustainable way" [ibid., para 32.5].

Indeed, there are few human activities more directly ecological than the food and agricultural system, which is rooted in natural forces. But the UNCED delegates did not propose to solve food problems through the kind of capital-intensive agriculture we have developed in the industrialized food-exporting countries. That system is demonstrably damaging to the resource base: intensive irrigation depletes water tables; land, lakes, and streams are inundated with toxic chemicals; land-depleting, soil-compacting heavy equipment is employed to plant, cultivate, and harvest crops; and then those crops are converted into new, attractive, minimally nutritious products heavily advertised and sold to consumers at high prices.

There is little question that UNCED has already had a positive educational value; what remains uncertain—because it is in the realm of policy—is whether the event will have an impact on the objectives and goals of the actors in the food system and whether it will, by moving toward relief of chronic hunger, help improve the quality of life of poor people.

At the end of this survey, we come back again to the theme of development. Hunger, after all, is a symptom of underdevelopment; and the food and agriculture system is an integral part of every economy. In underdeveloped economies, it is central; development means, first of all, agricultural development. But in recent years it has not been high on the priority list of development agencies or of developing countries. It is possible that some complacency about the world food problem has displaced the concern that gave rise to the U.N. World Food Conference two decades ago. But those who heard the Director-General of the International Food Policy Research Institute (IFPRI), one of the components of the Consultative Group on International Agricultural Research (CGIAR), describe "The future Food situation in the Third World" to a packed congressional hearing room on May 3, 1993, were reminded that the problem remains critical.

"During the 1980s," the Director-General said, "food production failed to keep pace with population growth in two-thirds of the developing countries and in more than 80% of African countries. . . . As a consequence, the number of Africans who do not have access to enough food rose from 130 million to 170 million (30%) during the decade: 40 million more Africans were food insecure in 1990 than in 1980." The number of malnourished children in the region also increased by 40%.

South Asia is also at risk as populations continue to grow and the production increases of the Green Revolution begin to level off or even decline.

Over all, the picture of food and agriculture, although perhaps encouraging in the aggregate, is not bright for the majority of the world's poor people, who continue to be both poor *and* hungry. Food production continues to keep pace, statistically, with population growth, but its distribution has not improved. And the 1974 World Food Conference's recommendation that food production be increased in the food-deficit countries where most of the hungry people live has not been implemented. Most of the production increase has been in the capital-intensive, resource-depleting agriculture of the industrialized world.

One of the more hopeful indications of increased U.N. attention to the problems of food and agriculture in the future has been the establishment, in accordance with the recommendations of UNCED, of the **U.N. Commission on Sustainable Development.** The Commission, essentially, is to be the follow-up organization for UNCED, to monitor the implementation of Agenda 21, and to encourage the participation of all U.N. agencies, as well as NGOs, in the urgent matter of sustainable development for the foreseeable future. Once the political problems of membership, staff, and venue have been resolved, it should be able, within the bureaucratic vocabulary of the international organization world, to raise for us collectively and personally the question of how we escape mortgaging the future of generations to reap the short-term gains the global market offers.

3. Population

By Craig Lasher

As the world community prepares for the **International Conference on Population and Development** in Cairo next year, a continuing stream of data reinforces the fact that global population is growing faster than at any point in human history. Virtually all of this growth occurs in the less-developed countries, which have the least capacity to respond to the challenges such growth poses to the success of their sustainable development efforts.

World population will reach 5.5 billion by mid-1993 [Population Reference Bureau, *1993 World Population Data Sheet*]. Ninety-seven percent of population growth over the next decade will occur in Africa, Asia, and Latin America [U.N. Population Fund (UNFPA), *State of World Population 1992*, p. 2]. The global growth leader is Africa, where women bear on average 6 children, compared with 1.6 in Europe and 2 in the United States. Among wealthy nations, the United States is the population growth pace-setter. The U.S. Census Bureau projects that the U.S. population will increase by 128 million people by 2050, from 255 million to 383 million people [*The Washington Post*, 12/4/92].

Although the rate of population growth has declined, the number of people added annually to the world's population is now at record levels. In 1993, world population will grow by about 90 million people. The acceleration in the absolute number of people added to the world's population is illustrated by the number of years it took to add each additional billion people since 1960. It took 15 years for world population to increase from 3 billion to its 4 billion total in 1975, 12 years to increase to 5 billion in 1987, and it is projected to reach 6 billion by 1997—a span of only 10 years.

According to U.N. projections, global population will increase to 6.25 billion by the year 2000, 8.5 billion in 2025, and 10 billion in 2050, assuming birth rates continue to fall. Significant growth will probably continue until about 2150, and population will eventually stabilize at a level of about 11.6 under the most likely scenario [U.N. Population Division, *World Population Prospects 1990*]. The ultimate size of world population would have been even larger had it not been for the **drop in the fertility rate** (average number of children per woman) in developing countries, from 6.1 between 1965 and 1970 to 3.9 in 1990. The reduction in the birth rate corresponds to the rise in contraceptive use in developing countries (defined as the percentage of couples of reproductive age using any form of contraception) from 9 to 50% during the same time period [UNFPA, *State of World Population 1990*, p. 3].

About 400 million married couples use family planning today. Roughly 350 million couples, and a substantial but uncounted number of sexually active unmarried women and men, are not using any method of family planning [Thomas W. Merrick, "Meeting the Challenge of Unmet Need for Family Planning," prepared for IPPF Family Planning Congress, 3/92]. Demographers estimate that there are between 90 and 160 million married women of reproductive age who did not want their last pregnancy, would like to delay their next pregnancy, or already have all the children they want, and yet are not practicing family planning [John Bongaarts et al., "The Demographic Impact of Family Planning Programs," *Studies in Family Planning* 21, p. 305]. Taking the middle of the range at about 125 million couples, it would cost an additional $2 billion to meet the expressed need for good-quality family planning services [Sharon L. Camp, "Population: The Critical Decade," *Foreign Policy* 90, p. 139], or a relatively small increase in the $57 billion of official development assistance provided by bilateral foreign aid donors [OECD, *Development Co-operation*, 1992, p. A-72]. Population and family planning expenditures in developing countries currently total about $4.6 billion from all sources, but donor nations provide only about $1 billion [*The Wall Street Journal*, 5/17/93].

As part of the celebration of the 20th anniversary of the **Special Programme of Research Development and Research Training in Human Reproduction**, the World Health Organization (WHO) issued a fascinating report on reproductive health and sexual behavior around the world. The report estimated that over 100 million acts of sexual intercourse occur every day. As a result, 910,000 conceptions and 356,000 sexually transmitted infections take place. About 150,000 unwanted pregnancies end in abortion every day. A third of these abortions are classified as unsafe, resulting in 500 deaths. Maternal deaths, caused by the complications of pregnancy and childbirth, number 1,370 daily, and many more women suffer significant injuries. Nearly 40,000 infants and children under five years of age die each day. As the report states, "family planning not only prevents birth, it also saves the lives of women and children" [WHO, *Reproductive Health: A Key to a Brighter Future*, 1992, p. 5].

The outcome of the deliberations of two major international conferences will have an important impact on the U.N.'s response to global population problems in the future and on the question of whether the international community will be mobilized to find the political will and financial resources to stabilize world population. The first of these gatherings, the **U.N. Conference on Environment and Development (UNCED)**, was held in June 1992 and established principles (an Earth

Charter) and action plans (Agenda 21) that give greater recognition of the interrelationship of widespread poverty and environmental degradation. Although the 44th General Assembly's resolution establishing the conference did not include any reference to population matters, the next Assembly emphasized the importance of "addressing the relationship between demographic pressures and unsustainable consumption patterns and environmental degradation" at UNCED [A/Res/45/216]. Nonetheless, governments disagreed throughout the preparatory process on the importance of the population issue at UNCED. Many of the developing nations believed, for example, that too little weight was given to the development side of the UNCED agenda and that the effect of focusing attention on population problems would be to shift the blame for environmental degradation unfairly, away from consumption patterns in the North. Developing countries also saw such a shift as adding to their difficulty in making a case for debt relief, technology transfer, and increased aid flows from the industrialized nations to help underwrite the cost of sustainable development. A number of developing countries maintained that the international population conference, scheduled for 1994, was a more appropriate forum for discussing population issues [*E Magazine* 5, 6/92].

By the final UNCED Preparatory Committee meeting in New York in March 1992, population had received attention throughout Agenda 21, which now included a separate chapter on "Demographic Dynamics and Sustainability." However, when the U.S. delegation moved to delete references to overconsumption by the developed countries, the Group of 77, representing the political interests of the developing world, deleted most references to population as an important factor in environmental degradation [*The Washington Post*, 4/12/92]. The final version of Agenda 21 adopted by the Earth Summit in June 1992 also made no specific mention of "family planning" or "contraception"—the result of vigorous lobbying by the Vatican with the support of Argentina, the Philippines, and a few other governments [*Dallas Morning News*, 6/5/92]. Nor does the document offer any concrete recommendations for programs to stabilize global population or for providing the necessary financial resources to accomplish the goal.

Preparations for the decennial **International Conference on Population and Development (ICPD)**, which will be held in Cairo, September 5–13, 1994, have gathered momentum. The major theme of the conference is population and sustainable development. The overall aim is to increase awareness of population issues, encourage governments to adopt effective and updated population policies, and secure the commitments and resources needed for both international and national efforts to address global population and related development problems. The U.N. Secretary-General appointed **Dr. Nafis Sadik**, Executive Director of UNFPA, as Secretary-General of the conference, and **Dr. Shunichi In-**

oue, Director of the Population Division of the U.N. Secretariat, as her deputy [UNFPA, "Current Status of Preparatory Activities for the ICPD, 1994—End of 1992 Update"].

The 1994 meeting will be the fifth in a series of population conference convened by the United Nations at ten-year intervals. The first two were purely technical meetings, while the two subsequent meetings—in 1974 at Bucharest and 1984 at Mexico City—set goals and made recommendations for governments on population issues. The 1994 conference will review progress on the World Population Plan of Action revised in 1984 and prepare a new plan of action for the coming decade.

The preparatory process for the 1994 conference has included expert group meetings convened around the world by the United Nations and focused on six topics: population policies and programs; population and women; population and environment; family planning, health, and family well-being; demographic structure; and international migration. Also held were five regional conferences for Asia and the Pacific, the Arab states, Latin America and the Caribbean, Africa, and Europe and North America, organized by the United Nations jointly with various regional institutions [ibid.]. Reports indicate that the preparatory meetings have been well organized and have had a broad representation of policy-makers, program managers, academics, and multilateral and nongovernmental organizations. Among the recommendations, the need for improvements in the status of women and the quality of family planning services have been prominent and are themes that are likely to be emphasized at the conference itself. The inclusion of women's status as a priority theme reflects the growing consensus that improving the status of women is central to achieving a broad range of social goals as well as to achieving sustainable economic development. It also suggests that the organizers are anxious to avoid the polarization between population supporters and feminist groups that took place at the Earth Summit [Marguerite Holloway, "Population Pressure—The Road from Rio is Paved With Factions," *Scientific American*, 9/92].

The recommendations prepared by the expert group and regional meetings will provide the basis for the final action plan to be presented in Cairo. Each national delegation will also prepare a report on its own country's situation. Although governments are the primary participants at the conference, the United Nations is encouraging NGO involvement and is considering whether to host a separate NGO meeting.

The second Preparatory Committee meeting (PrepCom II) for ICPD was held in New York during May 1993. There, country delegations began the process of formulating actionable recommendations to be agreed to at the ICPD, focusing on the theme of "Choices and Responsibilities." Official delegations from more than 100 countries participated, and were joined by more than 420 NGOs—an unprecedented number for a population meeting.

One highlight of PrepCom II was the announcement of the **dramatic changes in U.S. population assistance policy**, which received a wildly enthusiastic reception from the other official delegations and from the gallery filled with NGO observers. The official head of the U.S. delegation, State Department Counselor Tim Wirth, stated that "President Clinton is deeply committed to moving population to the forefront of America's international priorities." In a reversal of recent policy, he announced that the U.S. position is "to support reproductive choice, including access to safe abortion," and noted that the "abortion issue should be addressed directly with tolerance and compassion, rather than officially ignored while women, especially poor women, and their families suffer" [*The New York Times*, 5/12/93].

The Clinton administration has indicated it will take a broader approach to reproductive health and will strive to advance women's rights and educational and economic empowerment as part of its population strategy. The U.S. position at PrepCom II reflected the efforts of feminist groups, who have been actively seeking to redirect U.S. population-assistance policy. However, the statement also noted that the United States would work to develop international consensus around "priority, long-term and quantitative goals for stabilizing world population." The ideological tensions apparent within U.S. government policy could foreshadow debates at the critical third preparatory committee meeting, scheduled for April 11–22, 1994, in New York and for the 1994 ICPD in Cairo.

A major subject of controversy at PrepCom II was the extent to which the conceptual framework for the conference action agenda should be modified to address broad development and health issues. Some Southern and feminist NGOs lobbied to shift the emphasis away from demographic realities to the negative impact of structural adjustment and gender inequality. Alternative language circulated by some NGOs actually sought to eliminate references to population stabilization and family planning. These efforts to dilute the focus on concrete actions necessary for the achievement of population stabilization led to objections from several official delegations and family planning activists, including representatives from India, Bangladesh, and Indonesia.

The **issue of abortion** is also expected to be controversial with some country delegations, particularly those nations in which the procedure remains illegal, and with official observers, most notably the Holy See. Nevertheless, several speakers, including the leader of the Indian delegation, made powerful official statements at the PrepCom on the importance of access to safe abortion services. The Vatican, supported by delegates from at least two countries, argued that the desired outcome of the Cairo conference should be to turn the clock back to the agreement reached by the international community at the first population conference in 1974 at Bucharest, which declared that "development is the best contraceptive." In response to the Vatican's intervention by Archbishop Renato Martino condemning abortion and artificial contraception, the **Chairman of the PrepCom, Dr. Fred T. Sai of Ghana**, thanked the Archbishop for introducing the moral and ethical dimensions of the issues but questioned his call for sharing the benefits of modern medicine while declaring certain contraceptive methods illicit [*Earth Times*, 5/18/93].

Other topics that could be controversial at the 1994 conference but were not the subject of extensive debate at the PrepCom include contraceptive services for adolescents, international migration policy, the demographic impact of AIDS, and the willingness of developed and developing countries to make a real commitment to providing the financial resources necessary for worldwide family planning efforts.

U.S. Policy and the New Administration

After a 12-year absence of U.S. leadership on international family planning, the inauguration of Bill Clinton signals a dramatic improvement in the political climate for international population assistance in Washington and sets the stage for the reversal of Reagan–Bush policies [Sharon L. Camp, "Population: The Critical Decade," *Foreign Policy* 90, p. 135]. On January 22, President Clinton used the occasion of the 20th anniversary of the *Roe v. Wade* decision legalizing abortion to sign five presidential memoranda overturning anti-choice policies, including: reversing the "gag rule" in the Title X domestic family planning program; repealing the "Mexico City policy," which prohibited U.S. funding of foreign nongovernmental organizations that provide abortion services; ending the moratorium on federal funding of fetal tissue research; reexamining the Food and Drug Administration ban on the importation of the contraceptive RU-486 for personal use; and allowing abortions in overseas military hospitals. Population-assistance advocates worked closely with domestic family planning groups like Planned Parenthood to ensure that the Mexico City policy was included in the package. Named for the site of the 1984 U.N. population conference at which the policy was announced, the Mexico City restrictions were implemented through clauses attached to Agency for International Development (AID) grant agreements, so that no legislation was required to scrap them. Dr. Nafis Sadik was invited to the signing ceremony, along with U.S. family planning leaders, signaling the administration's interest in re-funding UNFPA [*The New York Times*, 4/1/93].

The repeal of the Mexico City restrictions will allow AID to resume financial support of the International Planned Parenthood Federation (IPPF) and Planned Parenthood Federation of America's Family Planning International Assistance—the two most important organizations to be defunded for refusal to comply with the policy. AID plans to provide sizable funds for IPPF in FY 1993. A small financial contribution to the WHO's Human Reproduction Programme (WHO/HRP), the major multilateral organization for contraceptive and abortion research, is also expected.

As announced by the U.S. delegation at the second PrepCom in May, the Clinton administration is expected to restore U.S. support to UNFPA, although the timing and level of funding is still under discussion because of recent congressional action in response to reports of a new family planning crackdown in China. Since 1985, AID has withheld the U.S. contribution to UNFPA, normally budgeted at $25 to $30 million, because of the presence of a **UNFPA program in China**. AID claimed that UNFPA was co-managing China's population program and that the Chinese program relied on coercive abortion and involuntary sterilization to implement its "one child per couple" policy.

As the basis for its decisions to withhold funds during the Reagan and Bush administrations, AID cited the so-called **Kemp-Kasten amendment**—part of a 1985 supplemental foreign aid appropriations bill—prohibiting U.S. funding of any organization that "supports or participates in the management of a program of coercive abortion or involuntary sterilization." Political appointees at AID maintained that the activities of neither the Chinese government nor UNFPA changed sufficiently to warrant renewed U.S. support. UNFPA has repeatedly pointed out that it does not currently support abortion in China or anywhere else in the world and denies the charge that it "manages" China's program.

The size of UNFPA's contribution relative to the Chinese government's expenditures and the number of UNFPA staff in Beijing compared with the number of employees of the State Family Planning Commission suggest that allegations that UNFPA "manages" the Chinese program are not credible. Of the funds that have been allocated by UNFPA for projects under the five-year program that began in 1990, only 1% has gone directly to the government of China, with the remainder channeled through "executing" agencies, such as WHO, UNICEF, the Food and Agriculture Organization (FAO), and several NGOs [UNFPA, "Facts About UNFPA and China," 10/90]. Critics of Washington's policy have long maintained that the U.S. government has never been able to produce evidence of UNFPA complicity. Such critics argue that, rather than conditioning the restoration of a contribution to UNFPA on its withdrawal from China, the United States should take more appropriate steps to end family planning abuses in the Chinese program. One of the steps would be to place these concerns on the Sino-American bilateral agenda, along with other important human rights issues, and link them to trade and other negotiations, such as those leading to the renewal of most-favored-nation trading status.

With respect to UNFPA's program in China, the U.S. government could, and probably will, use the occasion of the UNFPA Governing Council meeting in June 1993 to ask for a full report on the organization's activities in China and its success in promoting a more humane population program. In concert with the major donors, the United States could base a decision to encourage the withdrawal of UNFPA, UNICEF, WHO, and other international agencies from family planning activities in China (now or at the end of the current 1990–94 funding cycle) on an objective assessment of whether these agencies are effectively promoting voluntarism.

Defenders of UNFPA believe that the Fund plays a positive role by strengthening voluntarism in the Chinese population program. The Fund's program in China, undertaken in collaboration with other U.N. agencies, includes support for production of high-quality, modern contraceptives, especially IUDs; training for family planning workers in better interpersonal and counseling skills; and public education programs to raise awareness of China's population problems and the benefits of family planning. All of these elements were designed to enhance client satisfaction and to reduce reliance on abortion or compulsion. The program was designed to accommodate the critics of UNFPA's presence in China by eliminating the types of activities in the previous five-year program that prompted the objections.

Counselor Wirth's speech at PrepCom II partially allayed concern that news reports of a new tightening of official Chinese birth control policy had stalled administration efforts to refund UNFPA [*The New York Times*, 5/15/93]. Population-assistance supporters have been concerned since late April, when the Chinese government released data from a sample survey suggesting a dramatic decline in fertility, accompanied by anecdotal reports of human rights abuse by overzealous local officials [ibid., 4/25/93]. The incidence of sterilization and IUD insertions are also believed to have risen dramatically in 1991. A number of foreign experts, however, believe that methodological flaws in the survey may have overestimated the amount of fertility decline.

In his statement, Wirth indicated that the U.S. government regarded the birth control policies of China as coercive and would not allow U.S. funds to be used by UNFPA in China. The administration subsequently announced that it will prohibit the use of any of the U.S. contribution in China [*The Washington Times*, 5/13/93]. Using the accounting system maintained by UNFPA that designates each project by funding source, U.S. funds could be placed in segregated accounts easily monitored by independent auditors to ensure that they are used exclusively to finance non-China projects. In testimony before the House Foreign Affairs Committee on May 18, Secretary of State Warren Christopher indicated that the United States would favor UNFPA's withdrawal from China in order to "simplify" U.S. re-funding. As politically expedient as this course of action might seem, UNFPA has never withdrawn from a recipient country, and such a step would require the approval of its Governing Council. Since few, if any, of the other members of the UNFPA Governing Council are believed to favor withdrawal, and because decisions of the Governing Council are made by consensus, withdrawal from China does not appear to be a viable solution. In addition, the Chinese government has given no indication that it would unilaterally request the termination of UNFPA assistance.

Christopher's remarks, however, have been taken by some members of Congress as an invitation to condition the restoration of U.S. support to UNFPA on its withdrawal from China. Withdrawal from China is likely to be added to the list of restrictions on UNFPA's use of U.S. funds that population supporters in Congress have crafted over the last several years as a compromise with critics of human rights abuses in China. Amendments attached by Rep. Howard Berman (D-Calif.) to the State Department authorization bill and by Rep. David Obey (D-Wis.) to the foreign aid appropriations bill would withhold the amount of funds UNFPA spends in China unless the agency withdraws support from the Chinese population program. The two amendments restrict the release of funds in fiscal year 1994. The passage of the amendments at a very early stage in the legislative process has raised questions about whether AID can release the funds set aside for UNFPA for the current fiscal year. Under existing law, the President has the authority under the Kemp-Kasten amendment to make a determination that UNFPA is eligible to receive U.S. funds without any congressional action. But from a political standpoint, a UNFPA contribution for fiscal year 1993 remains in doubt.

U.N. Population Awards

The winners of the U.N. Population Award for 1993 are Dr. Fred T. Sai, a leader of the worldwide family planning movement, and the Mainichi Shimbun Population Problems Research Council of Japan [U.N. press release POP/452, 1/29/92]. Dr. Sai was recognized for his contribution to research on nutrition, community welfare, and family planning. In addition to chairing PrepCom II, he has served as the Chairman of the Main Committee of the 1984 International Conference on Population, senior population advisor at the World Bank, and President of IPPF since 1989.

Mainichi Shimbun Population Problems Research Council was cited for its success in creating awareness of population issues through *Mainichi Shimbun*, the Japanese newspaper that created the council in 1949, and for generating support in Japan for international population assistance.

4. Law of the Sea

By Lee A. Kimball

In 1992 the General Assembly's annual discussion of the Law of the Sea coincided almost to the day with the tenth anniversary of the ceremonial signing of the **U.N. Convention on the Law of the Sea.** Arvid Pardo, the former U.N. Representative of Malta whose speech to the General Assembly in 1967 triggered the 15-year negotiation, was invited to mark the occasion.

The tenth anniversary may in fact mark a turning point for the Convention itself, since five important events have taken place during the anniversary year:

1. The number of countries ratifying the Convention reached 55, and another has ratified it since—only **four short of the number required for the treaty to enter into force.**

2. The Preparatory Commission (PrepCom) for the International Seabed Authority (ISA) and the International Tribunal on the Law of the Sea (ITLOS) was effectively suspended on April 2, 1993, having resolved a number of technical questions about implementation and helped to sharply define the "hard-core problems" that have now been passed to the Secretary-General's consultations (see below). PrepCom was convened in 1983 by resolution of the Third U.N. Conference on the Law of the Sea to lay the groundwork for the Convention's entry into force.

3. The Clinton administration has indicated its interest in **reactivating U.S. involvement** in the Convention if outstanding problems related to the regime for mining the deep seabed beyond national jurisdiction can be resolved to U.S. satisfaction.

4. U.N. Secretary-General Boutros Boutros-Ghali resumed the consultations launched by his predecessor in July 1990 to resolve such controversial mining issues and to promote universal support for the treaty [see *A Global Agenda: Issues/46* and *Issues/47*, pp. 159–60, and 206, respectively].

5. As noted in UNCED's Agenda 21, numerous international developments have reaffirmed that the Convention's provisions serve as the international legal basis for sustainable use of oceans and their resources.

In reports to the General Assembly in 1992, the Secretary-General indicated the extent to which the provisions of the Law of the Sea (LOS) Convention provide the basis for state practice, the work of international organizations, and decisions by international tribunals on the use and development of the oceans [A/47/512, A/47/623]. Those same reports, however, take note of **national legislation** and actions—for example, regarding the breadth of territorial sea claims or the penalties for foreign vessels that violate a coastal state's fishing rules—that deviate from the Convention. They also document different views among states on the question of whether prior notification or permission is required for **innocent passage by warships** in the territorial sea, and whether restrictions on entry into waters within state jurisdiction by vessels carrying hazardous wastes are compatible with the LOS Convention regime. The Secretary-General's reports go on to note with concern the increasing incidence of **illegal actions at sea**. These include piracy, armed robbery, and trafficking in drugs. There is concern that such actions will grow in number the longer it takes the treaty to enter into force, and that failure to secure the support of the major industrialized nations will serve to undermine the Convention's ability to deter violations.

As the number of treaty ratifications nears 60, efforts to "fix" the treaty's **mining provisions** have taken on new urgency. Most countries would prefer to find solutions in the near term and bypass a variety of complications—legislative and practical—that may occur once the Convention enters into force. The Secretary-General has stressed that the aim of his consultations is not to renegotiate the treaty but, rather, to take into account the political and economic changes that have taken place in the past ten years—notably, that "the great majority of the industrialized states are opposed to the provisions governing the international regime for the seabed"; that "economic and technological conditions for seabed mineral development do not yet exist"; and that "it would be wise to make arrangements for an institutional framework adaptable to change, representing the interests of the international community in its entirety" [SG/SM/4917, SEA/1346, 1/29/93]. Following two desultory consultations in 1992, the Clinton administration expressed its intention "to take a more active role in the search for a solution" [statement by U.S. Permanent Representative Madeleine K. Albright, 3/27/93]. The United States has, nonetheless, warned that "finding solutions to the Part XI [deep-seabed mining] issues may be no less difficult now" than it was in 1973 or 1982 [statement by Assistant Secretary of State Curtis E. Bohlen at the Council on Ocean Law Forum, Washington, D.C., 2/18/93], and it "continues to believe that there are serious problems with those provisions" [Albright]. For the second year in a row the United States chose to abstain from voting (it has traditionally voted "against") on the annual General Assembly LOS resolution, which in 1992 was adopted by a vote of 135-1, with 9 abstentions [Council on Ocean Law, *Oceans Policy News* X, no. 1, 12/92–1/93].

The pace of **the Secretary-General's informal consultations** picked up in 1993, with meetings January 28–29 and April 27–28 and a one-week session scheduled for August 2–6. Since these discussions began in 1992, about 75 states have attended, approximately the number of states that have attended recent PrepCom sessions. These consultations have been based on notes prepared by the Secretary-General and papers presented by delegations. Of the nine substantive issues originally considered [see *Issues/47*, p. 206], one—having to do with environmental matters—was dropped from the list when found to be not controversial at all. The remaining topics divide into those addressed by more specific texts, which spell out the "findings" accepted to date, and those addressed by general "principles," to be revisited once commercial production becomes feasible ["Information Notes" by the Secretary-General, 12/10/92 and 4/8/93]. The former involve institutional issues, including composition, decision-making, and cost considerations. They specify interim arrangements for the ISA and **the Enterprise** (the public entity that could actually undertake deep-seabed mining operations) before commercial mining becomes feasible; procedures for determining when that moment has arrived and agreeing on a definitive regime; and certain aspects of the definitive institutional arrangements, including transfer of technology for the Enterprise. They also address decision-making in the seabed mining regime review conference for which the Convention makes provision. The general "principles" for later consideration deal with the limitation of production, a compensation fund, and the financial terms of contracts contemplated in the treaty.

The procedural and decision-making mechanisms to be used in determining the definitive deep-seabed mining regime, what pre-agreed conditions will shape it, and how Convention provisions and decisions made by PrepCom are factored into the regime—all these are crucial to finding a solution that can win broad support for the LOS Convention. Another significant procedural issue involves the form that any agreements resulting from the Secretary-General's consultations will take, in the interests of confirming that they will be binding under international law. This **"form" issue** is a concern both for the countries that have already ratified the treaty and for those whose decision to ratify may depend on the agreements reached during the consultations. At the 1992 General Assembly, the Ambassador of Brazil urged member states to resolve these issues by the 1993 Session [A/47/PV.83], and whether this is in the realm of the possible remains to be seen.

Many countries supported the **termination of PrepCom** in the belief that it had accomplished all it could until some fundamental obstacles to universal participation in the Convention had been overcome. At the 11th PrepCom session, held in Jamaica from March 22 to April 2, 1993, it was decided to provide for a two-week annual meeting until the Convention enters into force but that PrepCom Chairman, José Luis Jesus of Cape Verde, would consult each year about the need for one. Meanwhile, PrepCom's executive organ, the General Committee, will get together for two to three days each year to monitor the implementation of arrangements for the six **pioneer investors** registered by PrepCom (and their certifying states) and to consider new registrations. The six (and the corporate entities that will undertake the mining) are: France, on behalf of IFREMER/AFERNOD; Japan, on behalf of DORD; the Russian Federation, on behalf of Yuzhmorgeologiya; India; China, on behalf of

COMRA; and the IOM consortium, sponsored by Bulgaria, Cuba, Czechoslovakia, Poland, and Russia. These states are given different responsibilities for training developing-country personnel and exploring mine sites for the Enterprise [see SEA/1372, 4/5/93; *Issues/46*, p. 161; and *Issues/47*, p. 206]. The spring meeting also "took note" of the provisional final reports of the informal plenary of PrepCom and its four special commissions, first considered in August 1992. These reports summarize PrepCom deliberations, the current status of agreement, and pending issues. They also contain the detailed working documents of PrepCom, including the rules, regulations, and other texts it has refined to date. These will be issued as a consolidated, provisional final report "at the appropriate time" [LOS/PCN/L.113].

The **U.N. Conference on Environment and Development (UNCED)** underscored the importance of the LOS Convention as the global "framework agreement" for sustainable use of the marine environment and its resources. The Convention, with its carefully crafted balance between the rights and obligations of coastal states in offshore zones and the rights and obligations of those enjoying high seas navigational freedoms, provides the basis for continued standard-setting and enforcement actions by states individually and collectively, and establishes principles for supplementary international agreements. Moreover, during the 1992 U.N. General Assembly debates, many speakers emphasized that working by consensus during Convention negotiations, while inevitably prolonging discussions, nevertheless allowed due account to be taken "of the legitimate concerns and interests of different States." As a consequence, noted one speaker, "governments were more willing to incorporate in their national legislation the rules set forth in the Convention, accepting the burden as well as the benefit of the balanced provisions" [A/47/512, para. 9].

This legacy affects a broad range of interstate relations concerning ocean use. One issue—that of access to and from the sea by landlocked countries through "transit" states and related transport systems—has grown in importance with the emergence of six new landlocked states following the breakup of the Soviet Union. The Convention also establishes the principles and procedures for determining boundaries between states in extended zones of offshore jurisdiction and between national and international ocean zones, and for resolving such conflicts as may arise. Provisions of the LOS Convention form the basis for regional and bilateral agreements that have begun to refine the procedures for enforcing regulations against drug trafficking, piracy, and illegal fishing and for strengthening the international rules governing vessel safety and pollution control. And building on discussions at UNCED, the international community has begun to recognize the need to provide resources to assist developing nations in implementing this complex of ocean-use obligations [A/47/623, para. 53] as well as in combating piracy and avoiding accidents at sea [statement by Datuk Abdullah bin Haji Ahmad Badawi, Foreign Minister of Malaysia, A/47/PV.9, pp. 89–90].

This evolutionary process will continue to take place within many regional bodies and U.N. agencies with active marine programs—notably, the International Maritime Organization, the Food and Agriculture Organization (its fisheries programs in particular), and UNESCO's Intergovernmental Oceanographic Commission (IOC)—and UNCED called for several specific follow-up actions as well. The U.N. Environment Programme (UNEP) will be arranging a 1995 intergovernmental meeting to address land-based sources of marine pollution. Already scheduled for July 1993 is a U.N. conference on international fisheries, and for April 1994 a conference on small island developing states. And the new Global Environment Facility (cosponsored by the World Bank, UNEP, and the U.N. Development Programme) and the Development Assistance Committee of the Organization for Economic Cooperation and Development are both considering new guidelines for funding related to international waters (including oceans) and marine pollution control.

Another result of UNCED and of new international institutional arrangements mandated by it is that the 1993 session of ECOSOC will reconsider the **coordination arrangements among U.N. oceans organizations.** Moreover, the new **U.N. Commission on Sustainable Development** is to inventory regional arrangements and proposals for UNCED follow-up by 1994. It has been suggested that the Commission also review the status and functions of a growing array of regional and subregional arrangements for oceans-related legal, political, economic, scientific, technological, and financial matters to promote coordination and exchange of information [A/47/623, para. 4].

In early 1992, Under-Secretary-General for Legal Affairs Carl-August Fleischhauer assumed responsibility for the **Division of Ocean Affairs and the Law of the Sea.** States increasingly turn to this office for assistance in drafting national legislation, for advice on managerial, scientific, and technical aspects of implementing the LOS Convention, and for assistance in resolving interstate disputes over ocean use. It serves as the focal point for monitoring progress on the many facets of Convention implementation, and it synthesizes national, regional, and global developments for the Secretary-General's annual report on the LOS to the General Assembly. Demand is growing for additional publications and handbooks on state practice to help other states implement this comprehensive oceans regime, and there are calls for workshops and seminars in collaboration with the relevant specialized agencies of the U.N. and still other organizations. Scheduled for publication in 1993 is a book that will assess the **impact of the LOS Convention** to date, drawing on information presented at a meeting of experts in 1992. A further experts meeting is in the planning. It will consider criteria and approaches for applying the Convention's complex formula for defining the outer limits of coastal-state jurisdiction over the seabed.

5. Antarctica

By Christopher C. Joyner

The tenth year of debate in the General Assembly on the question of Antarctica ended in deadlock over a single, consolidated resolution. Although the resolution was approved by majority vote, no parties to the **Antarctic Treaty** participated in the vote. This resolution differed from previous General Assembly resolutions on Antarctica in that it emerged in whole form, rather than in two or three subsections, to be voted upon. Consequently, six treaty parties (India, China, Brazil, Cuba, Ecuador, and Colombia) opted not to participate in the vote, despite their previous support of "sub-resolutions" that had favored the exclusion of the "*apartheid* regime" of South Africa from **Antarctic Treaty Consultative Party Meetings (ATCMs).** Germany, speaking on behalf of the parties to the Antarctic Treaty, urged that consideration of the question of Antarctica proceed on the basis of consensus.

A number of developing countries focused debate on the significance of Antarctica as "our last continental wilderness." As a global monitor and laboratory for the earth's environment, they argued that Antarctica must be appreciated for its role in affecting global climate change, ozone depletion, biological diversity, marine pollution, and natural use and development of marine living resources. "Protection of the environment of Antarctica and its unique position as a storehouse of mineral, marine and other resources is seen as a crucial part of protection of the global ecosystem" [statement by Kushairi Redzuan, Permanent Representative of Malaysia to the U.N., A/C.1/47/PV.38]. In their view, "[t]he future of Antarctica as a common heritage of all mankind can best be preserved through the United Nations" [statement by Lionel Hurst, Permanent Representative of Antigua and Barbuda to the U.N., A/C.1/47/PV.38]. Most participants viewed the signing in Madrid of the 1991 Protocol on Environmental Protection by the Antarctic Treaty parties as a "positive step," especially given the significance of the U.N. Conference on the Environment and Development (UNCED) in Rio de Janeiro in June 1992. Speakers noted, however, that serious problems persist concerning the protocol's enforcement, liability, tourism, and conservation of marine living resources. The slow pace of the protocol's ratification by **Antarctic Treaty Consultative Parties (ATCPs)** was also a concern. A recurring theme was that the Antarctic Treaty system should have more universal participation in making decisions, and its workings should be more transparent and accountable to the international community.

The 1992 resolution expresses regret that the ATCPs have not heeded previous resolutions calling for the Secretary-General or his representative to be invited to their meetings, and encouraged them to provide more information on "all aspects of Antarctica" to the Secretary-General. While welcoming the commitment made under UNCED's Agenda 21 to ensure the availability of Antarctic scientific data to the international community and U.N. agencies, the resolution urges the ATCPs to "explore the possibility of organizing" an annual symposium to analyze Antarctic environmental issues. It also urges them to set up monitoring and implementation mechanisms to ensure compliance with the 1991 Environmental Protocol. The resolution reiterates a call for the ban on prospecting and mining in and around Antarctica to be made permanent and for full international participation should a convention be negotiated to establish Antarctica as a nature reserve or world park. It also encourages the ATCPs to reduce the number of scientific stations in Antarctica [A/Res/47/57].

The most polemical facet of the resolution is the annual call upon the ATCPs "to prevent **South Africa** from participating fully in their meetings pending the attainment of a non-racial democratic government in that country." Unlike the past, however, no Antarctic Treaty parties opted to support this point, since it was integrated into the whole resolution. In the First Committee, the resolution was adopted by a vote of 71 to 0, with 6 abstentions and 45 nonparticipating [A/47/696].

Though no extraordinary studies were requested for next year, the resolution does request that the Secretary-General explore the possibilities of publishing "extracts of data" submitted by various organizations as official U.N. documents in preparing his future annual reports on Antarctica.

The **Secretary-General submitted three reports** as a follow-up to the debate in the 46th General Assembly. A brief report concerning apartheid contains Germany's response on behalf of the treaty parties, which reiterates their call on the General Assembly to seek compromise and consensus when dealing with the question of Antarctica [A/47/542, 10/20/92]. A second report deals with the evaluation of the United Nations as a repository for all information concerning Antarctica. The document consists mainly of a summary of the final report of the 16th Antarctic Treaty Consultative Party Meeting that was furnished by the ATCPs to the Secretary-General. This summary details that meeting's agenda, various scientific research activities by ATCP states during 1991, and other official meetings by Antarctic Treaty committees [A/47/541, 10/20/92].

The third and most substantive report concerns environmental issues affecting Antarctica. The report discusses Antarctica's role in the global environmental system, particularly as the ice-covered continent serves as the earth's "refrigerator" to affect weather patterns, atmospheric conditions, and ocean circulation. Concern over Antarctic ozone depletion is also mentioned. Regarding environmental protection in the Antarctic, the Secretary-General's report draws from a report by the **Scientific Committee on Antarctic Research (SCAR)** that calls attention to the growing need for comprehensive environmental monitoring of human activities in the region. The inaccessibility of Antarctica and the high cost of conducting scientific research there make international cooperation necessary for protecting the Antarctic ecosystem. The Secretary-General's environmental report cites the relevant part of the UNCED Agenda 21 document as it calls upon states with scientific activities in Antarctica to ensure that research data are made freely available to the international community and that access to such data by the international scientific community should be enhanced, in part by convening seminars and symposia. Replying for the ATCPs, Germany underscored the 1991 Madrid Environmental Protection Protocol as establishing a "comprehensive, legally binding regime to ensure that activities undertaken by Parties in Antarctica are consistent with the protection of the Antarctic environment and its dependent and associated ecosystems" [A/47/624, Annex].

Among the additional documents referenced before the 47th General Assembly were those adopted by the Tenth Conference of Heads of State or Government of Non-Aligned Countries (September 1–6, 1992) [A/47/675-S/24816, Annex], by the second meeting of States of the Zone of Peace and Cooperation of the South Atlantic (June 25–29, 1990) [A/45/474, Annex], by the 20th Islamic Conference of Foreign Ministers (August 4–8, 1991) [A/45/421-S/21797, Annex IV, Res. 17/19-E], and by the meeting of the Commonwealth Heads of Government in Harare (October 16–22, 1991) [A/46/708, Annex, para. 44].

During the past year the Antarctic Treaty membership grew as Ukraine acceded to the treaty as a Non-Consultative Party (NCP). This brought the total of NCPs to 15, while the number of Consultative Parties remained at 26. The Russian Federation holds the ATCP seat formerly occupied by the Soviet Union.

International attention focused on the agreed-upon comprehensive environmental protection regime for Antarctica. On October 4, 1991, the Protocol on Environmental Protection to the Antarctic Treaty [Ant. Doc. XI ATSM/2] was formally adopted by the ATCPs and opened for signature. Negotiated over three years, this protocol, augmented by annexes, stands as the most comprehensive multilateral instrument ever adopted on protection of the environment. Ratification of the protocol by all the ATCPs remains an immediate priority, albeit so far only Ecuador, France, Peru, and Spain have deposited ratifications.

The protocol represents a significant shift by the ATCPs away from the possible exploitation of minerals in the region toward the preservation of Antarctica as an international conservation zone. Four years after the adoption of the Convention on the Regulation of Antarctic Mineral Resource Activities (CRAMRA), Antarctica has been designated a "natural reserve, devoted to peace and science." The protocol establishes fundamental environmental principles for the planning and conduct of all activities and creates a **Committee on Environmental Protection.** Though lacking decision-making authority, the Committee is responsible for advising ATCMs and formulating recommendations for them with regard to the protocol's implementation.

Article VII of the protocol prohibits all **commercial mining activities,** but subsequent amendment and modification procedures indicate that the ban may not be unconditional. The protocol may be modified at any time, provided all ATCPs agree; and after 50 years, an amendment proposed at a Review Conference requires the agreement of only three-quarters of the original ATCPs for adoption and three-quarters of all ATCPs for ratification. The prohibition on mining, however, cannot be lifted until a legally binding regime has been established to regulate mineral resources.

No mineral deposits of commercial interest have yet been discovered in Antarctica, although there is circumstantial evidence of offshore oil. Even if major discoveries were made, the exorbitant costs of extraction in and transportation from this remote, forbidding region means that it could take decades for any venture to become economically viable.

The protocol includes five integral annexes that reinforce measures previously adopted by the ATCPs as Antarctic Treaty "recommendations," including those pertaining to conservation of Antarctic fauna and flora, prior assessment of environmental impacts, marine pollution control, waste management and disposal, and the system for protected areas. The protocol's provisions on environmental impact assessments and emergency response, and its prohibition of mineral activities are subject to compulsory, binding dispute settlement procedures, as are provisions in the annexes. A draft annex relating to tourism was considered (but not adopted) at the regular consultative meeting in Venice, and an annex on liability is likely to be considered this year in Rome.

The protocol emphasizes Antarctica's **intrinsic wilderness values** and its role in the conduct of global scientific research. Its provisions reassert the Antarctic Treaty's call for cooperative scientific investigation—in the location and sharing of facilities, the preparation of environmental impact assessments, the avoidance of pollution and environmental hazards, and the minimizing of the environmental effects of accidents.

The Antarctic Treaty parties held their XVII regular Consultative Party Meeting November 11–21, 1992, in Venice. An informal working group on tourism and nongovernmental activities, attended by all Treaty parties, SCAR, interested nongovernmental observer groups, and several tourist organizations, convened in Venice on the eve of that meeting. There a proposed annex to regulate tourism in the Antarctic was introduced by France, with the support of Germany, Italy, Spain, and Chile. Its adoption fell short, however, as other ATCPs thought such restrictions would impose overly onerous rules on tourism and nongovernmental activities.

The main success of the Venice ATCM meeting was seen in Argentina's move away from its opposition to a **treaty secretariat.** Consensus emerged out of the discussions on the need for and importance of a secretariat, and the meeting set out the terms for such an institution. A small secretariat was agreed to in principle, to be funded by the ATCPs paying equal shares, at least during the early years. Agreement was elusive, however, on its location. Both the United States and Argentina offered their capitals as sites, but the United Kingdom found Buenos Aires unacceptable. The site question dominates ATCP diplomatic exchanges on Antarctica but should be resolved during 1993.

Progress was made on other issues at XVII ATCM. Draft rules of procedure for the protocol's Committee on Environmental Protection were agreed to; alternative means for negotiation of an annex on liability was debated, with varying degrees of enthusiasm; an annex proposed for the regulation of tourism was defeated; the need for environmental monitoring of impacts associated with Antarctic research stations was briefly considered; and revised management plans for specially protected areas were discussed, in light of having to redesignate the ecosystem classification system under the Environmental Protection Protocol.

Four recommendations were adopted at the ATCP meeting. Recommendation XVII-1 concerns environmental monitoring and data management; Recommendation XVII-2 revises descriptions for specially protected areas; Recommendation XVII-3 adds the rock cairn at Penguin Bay to the list of historic monuments; and Recommendation XVII-4 welcomes the SCAR Group of Specialists on Global Change and the Antarctic, and gives high priority to implementing a regional program of global change research in the Antarctic. The next regular ATCM will be held in the spring of 1994 in Japan. An important meeting on liability, to be held in Rome in the fall of 1993, could produce a new annex for the protocol.

At the 11th annual meeting of the 21-member **Commission of the Convention for Conservation of Antarctic Marine Living Resources (CCAMLR),** held at its headquarters in Hobart, Tasmania, Australia, October 26–November 6, 1992, 19 conservation measures and one resolution were adopted, while two conservation measures were amended, most of which concerned prohibitions on direct fishing of designated species around South Georgia Island. The most significant accomplishment, however, was consensus agreement on a scheme of scientific observation.

Under this system, members agree to take observers on board both scientific and harvesting vessels. To implement the scheme, the state wanting observers on board must make bilateral arrangements with the fishing state on how, when, and where "observation tasks" will occur. Krill catches fell from previous years. Consequently, the precautionary approach adopted in 1991 by the Commission in Conservation Measure 32/X, which placed a catch limitation of 1.5 million tons of krill in any fishing season around South Georgia, was not necessary [Report of the Eleventh Meeting of the Commission]. In order of reported catches, countries fishing for krill during the 1991–92 season included Russia, Japan, Ukraine, Poland, Korea, and Chile. Krill fishing activities were not expected to expand during the 1992–93 season.

Fishing nations, especially Russia and Japan, attempted to gain consensus for finfish catch levels that were economically beneficial, regardless of the fishery's condition. That strategy met with little success. Ukraine, Bulgaria, Chile, and the United States reported that they were starting new and "exploratory" Antarctic fisheries in 1993. France proposed at the June 1992 meeting of the **International Whaling Commission (IWC)** that the whole Southern Ocean south of 40 degrees South latitude be declared a **"whale sanctuary,"** in which all commercial whaling would be prohibited. Although no decision was made at the 1992 IWC meeting, the issue was placed on the CCAMLR agenda and taken up by its Scientific Committee. Opponents of the sanctuary proposal—mainly Japan and Norway—managed to neutralize the issue in that committee and temper the language in the CCAMLR Report. Nonetheless, the Antarctic whale sanctuary is scheduled for decision in May 1993 at the next IWC meeting in Japan.

Several important international meetings concerning Antarctica convened in 1993. The Group of Specialists on the Environment and Antarctic Conservation held its fourth meeting April 22–25 at Paimpont, France; the Antarctic Treaty Group of Experts Meeting on Environmental Monitoring convened in Buenos Aires in June; SCAR and the International Council of Scientific Unions (ICSU) convened a joint workshop on protected areas in Cambridge, England, June 29–July 2; and SCAR held its 22nd meeting in Bariloche, Argentina, June 8–19. All these meetings took on new meaning after the successful negotiation of the Environmental Protection Protocol in late 1991.

V
Human Rights and Social Issues

1. Human Rights
By Charles H. Norchi

In June 1993 the United Nations convened a **World Conference on Human Rights** in Vienna, only the second global human rights meeting in the history of the Organization. Despite an inability to forge agreement on a "Declaration of Vienna" during four Preparatory Meetings held in Geneva, the World Conference has emerged as a critical event in the international human rights constellation. The human rights debate of Vienna, and the decisions reached in the Conference, will shape human rights issues before the 48th General Assembly and beyond. This chapter examines those debates and issues.

The World Conference on Human Rights was authorized by General Assembly Resolution 45/155, setting forth six objectives:

1. to review and assess the progress that has been made in the field of human rights since the adoption of the Universal Declaration of Human Rights, and to identify obstacles and ways in which they can be overcome to further progress in this area;
2. to examine the relation between development and the enjoyment of economic, social, and cultural rights as well as civil and political rights, recognizing the importance of creating the conditions whereby everyone may enjoy these rights as set out in the **International Covenants on Human Rights**;
3. to examine ways and means to improve implementation of existing human rights standards and instruments;
4. to evaluate the effectiveness of the methods and mechanisms used by the United Nations in the field of human rights;
5. to formulate concrete recommendations for improving the effectiveness of U.N. activities and mechanisms in the field of human rights through programs aimed at promoting, encouraging, and monitoring respect for human rights and fundamental freedoms; and

6. to make recommendations for ensuring the necessary financial and other resources for U.N. activities in the promotion and protection of human rights and fundamental freedoms.

The Vienna Declaration

The culmination of the two-week U.N. World Conference on Human Rights was a document entitled the Vienna Declaration and Programme of Action, the product of often torturous intergovernmental negotiations but one that also records some important achievements. The Vienna Conference sought to resolve a broad array of issues, as an examination of the Declaration reveals. A few of the more salient are reviewed below. (In each case, reference is made to the final draft Vienna Declaration and Programme of Action, released at the conclusion of the Conference; the official version of the Declaration was not available at the time of writing).

The Universality of Human Rights

There had been concern that the "universality" of the human rights system would be under attack at the Vienna Conference, since in preparatory meetings certain states continued to assert that human rights can mean different things in different ethnic, cultural, or religious traditions. Such a "relative" approach to the interpretation of human rights standards could well affect the way nations enforce these standards at home. U.S. Secretary of State Warren Christopher warned the Conference that "cultural relativism could not become the last refuge of repression."

The 1948 Universal Declaration of Human Rights represents a broader consensus on human dignity than does any single culture or tradition. The Vienna Conference recognized this in the Declaration's preambular paragraph 3, which affirms a commitment "to the purposes and principles contained in the Charter of the United Nations and the Universal Declaration of Human Rights," as well as in preambular paragraph 6, which emphasizes that the Universal Declaration of Human Rights "constitutes a common standard of achievement for all peoples and all nations."

Strong language in Part II, paragraph 1, asserts that the "universal nature" of human "rights and freedoms is beyond question." Paragraph 3 asserts that "All human rights are universal, indivisible and inter-dependent and inter-related." A later sentence in the same paragraph of Part II appears to leave the universality door slightly ajar: "While the significance of national and regional particularities and various historical, cultural and religious backgrounds must be borne in mind, it is the duty of states, regardless of their political, economic and cultural systems, to promote and protect all human rights and fundamental freedoms." "Cultural and religious backgrounds must be borne in mind" is language of potential concern.

Although the Vienna Declaration strengthens the cause of "universality," the issue remains unsettled and will continue to permeate the human rights debate. An accompanying call for universal ratification of the core human rights treaties by a fixed date could strengthen the cause of human rights even further. Questions of interpretation and universality aside, a government must back up its commitment to respect such rights by accepting the obligations of the international human rights treaties and the accountability mechanisms they establish.

The "Right to Development"

Some states feared that at Vienna, as in other human rights forums, the right to development would be claimed as a precondition to implementing other basic rights. In Part II, paragraph 5, however, the Declaration makes the link between **development and democracy** explicit, stating that "Democracy, development and respect for human rights and fundamental freedoms are interdependent and mutually reinforcing."

In Part II, paragraph 6, the Vienna Declaration "reaffirms the right to development, as established in the Declaration on the Right to Development, as a universal and inalienable right and an integral part of fundamental human rights." And the paragraph goes on to call for international cooperation in promoting this right and eliminating obstacles to development. At the same time, the paragraph [6.3] asserts that "While development facilitates the enjoyment of all human rights, the lack of development may not be invoked to justify the abridgement of internationally recognized human rights." Addressing a related matter, this paragraph affirms that "The right to development should be fulfilled so as to meet equitably the **developmental and environmental needs** of present and future generations." It goes on to express concern about environmental abuses generally, and toxic dumping in particular, both having an effect on development.

Although the Vienna Declaration makes no explicit link between development *assistance* and human rights, it "calls upon the international community to help alleviate the external debt burden of developing countries, in order to supplement the efforts of the governments of such countries to attain the full realization of the economic, social and cultural rights of their people" [Part II, para. 6].

Indigenous People

The Vienna Declaration's preamble welcomes the "International Year of the World's Indigenous People in 1993 as a reaffirmation of the commitment of the international community to ensure their enjoyment of all human rights and fundamental freedoms and to respect the value and diversity of their cultures and identities" [Part I, para. 10]. Part II, paragraph 11 asserts that states "should ensure the full and free participation of indigenous people in all aspects of society, in particular in matters of concern to them." Further, "States should take concerted positive steps to ensure respect for all human rights and fundamental freedoms of indigenous people, on the basis of equality and non-discrimination and recognize the value and diversity of their distinct identities, cultures and social organization."

Part III of the Vienna Declaration also takes up the subject of indigenous people. Calling upon the **Working Group on Indigenous Populations** of the U.N.'s Subcommission on Prevention of Discrimination and Protection of Minorities "to complete the drafting of a declaration on the rights of indigenous people, at its eleventh session," the Conference recommended that the Commission on Human Rights "consider the renewal and updating of the mandate of the Working Group." Further recommendations call for the establishment of advisory services and technical assistance programs for indigenous people and call on the General Assembly to proclaim an International Decade of the World's Indigenous People, to commence in January 1994, when the International Year of the World's Indigenous People has come to its close. In this connection the Declaration suggests the establishment of both a Voluntary Trust Fund for "action-oriented programs" and "a permanent forum for indigenous people in the United Nations."

The Human Rights of Women

The human rights of women are an integral component of universal human rights, yet only in recent years has the United Nations begun to acknowledge the importance of addressing women's specific concerns. The Vienna Conference made significant progress here. Part II, paragraph 9 of the Declaration asserts that one of the international community's highest priorities is "the full and equal participation of women in the political, civil, economic, social and cultural life, at the national, regional, and international levels, and the eradication of all forms of discrimination on grounds of sex." The international community, it maintained, must work to eliminate gender-based violence, sexual harassment, and exploitation of women through legal measures, national action, and international cooperation in such fields as economic and social development, education, and safe maternity and health care.

Part III, Section IIC, of the Vienna Declaration, "**The Equal Status and Human Rights of Women,**" called upon governments and the United Nations to give priority to the full and equal enjoyment by women of all human rights. It highlights the importance of the integration and full participation of women as both agents and beneficiaries of the development process—and the importance of integrating these goals into the programs and projects of the entire U.N. system, requiring greater coordination and cooperation between the various commissions, committees and agencies.

The World Conference called upon the General Assembly to adopt the **draft Declaration on Violence Against Women** and urged states to combat violence against women, as provided in that document. The Vienna Declaration emphasizes the need to work toward eliminating violence against women in public and in private, all forms of sexual harassment, exploitation and trafficking in women, gender bias in the administration of justice, and any conflict that might arise between the rights of women and certain traditional practices or cultural and religious prejudices. The Declaration urges all states not party to the Convention on the Elimination of All Forms of Discrimination against Women to ratify the document before decade's end, and urges all parties to the Convention to withdraw reservations that are contrary to the object and purpose of the Convention. The decision of the Commission on Human Rights to consider the appointment of a Special Rapporteur on Violence against Women at its 50th session was also welcomed by the World Conference.

Similar attention was given to a woman's right to accessible and adequate health care, to the widest range of family planning services, and to equal access to education at all levels. The Vienna Declaration urges governments and regional and international organizations to facilitate the access of women to decision-making posts and a larger role in the decision-making process. Continuing, it encouraged further steps by the U.N. Secretariat to appoint and to promote women staff members, in accordance with the United Nations Charter, and to also encourage other U.N.-related organs to guarantee the participation of women under conditions of equality. The Vienna Declaration welcomed the **World Conference on Women,** to be held in Beijing in 1995, and urged that the human rights of women play an important part in the Beijing conferences' deliberations on its themes of equality, development, and peace.

A U.N. High Commissioner for Human Rights

Part III of the Vienna Declaration "recommends to the General Assembly that, when examining the report of the Conference at its forty-eighth session, it begin as a matter of priority consideration of the question of the establishment of a High Commissioner for Human Rights for the promotion and protection of all human rights." There have been numerous proposals for a High Commissioner for Human Rights, with general responsibility for coordinating the work of all U.N. agencies in the field of human rights, including the activities of the **U.N. Human Rights Centre**, located in Geneva.

A strong argument has been made for situating the Commissioner at U.N. Headquarters in New York, proximate to the General Assembly, the Security Council, and the Secretary-General. The Commissioner would oversee country-specific and thematic mechanisms and work at integrating human rights concerns into U.N. peacekeeping and humanitarian operations. It also has been proposed that the U.N. High Commissioner for Human Rights be empowered to call emergency sessions of the Commission on Human Rights and to raise human rights concerns directly with the Security Council. The establishment of a High Commissioner's office is expected to top the human rights agenda at the 48th General Assembly.

Other Issues

The Vienna Declaration takes up a variety of other issues, and those interested in the evolving human rights agenda should undertake a review of that document. Importantly, it calls for strengthening human rights resources, particularly the U.N. Human Rights Centre at Geneva. It also recognizes the rights of children and deems it imperative to implement thoroughly the Convention on the Rights of the Child. Freedom from torture is recognized as "a right which must be protected under all circumstances, including in times of internal or international disturbance or armed conflicts" [Part III.D], and the rights of the disabled are recognized as well. The Declaration calls upon governments to repeal impunity laws and ensure the prosecution of human rights violators. Part IV underscores the need for human rights education.

However, there are some clear problems with the document. Particularly glaring is paragraph 26 of Part I, which "encourages the increased involvement of the media, for whom freedom and protection should be guaranteed *within the framework of national law*" [emphasis added] and could thus encourage state restrictions on the media.

The Vienna Declaration and Programme of Action is not a legal instrument in the prescriptive sense, but it is an important document of promotion and appraisal, reflecting emergent issues on the international human rights agenda. Vague and ambiguous in many areas, it leaves much to be sorted out in other international forums.

The General Assembly and International Human Rights

The General Assembly supervises the U.N.'s human rights programs and is the final arbiter of standards adopted, issues addressed, and the proportion and nature of administrative and budgetary resources devoted to U.N. human rights machinery. This is apparent in the six objectives of the World Conference on Human Rights and in many decisions adopted during the Conference.

The General Assembly approves decisions taken in subsidiary human rights bodies, but it also instructs those bodies in addressing new problems or resolving highly controversial issues—structural, political, or substantive. Because it meets only six weeks before the Commission on Human Rights, the General Assembly is where political negotiations occur on the critical aspects of country resolutions.

The institutional capacity of the General Assembly to explore linkages between human rights and other issues, such as development or women's rights, combined with its coordinating role in New York at the center of U.N. activities, is often overlooked. For example, conflicting perspectives of the World Conference on Human Rights, the monitoring of free elections, the priority attached to violations-focused mechanisms, and the activity of nongovernmental organizations in U.N. human rights work and the right to development are a few of the critical issues directly tackled by the General Assembly in recent years.

Two important new standards were adopted by the General Assembly during its 47th Session.

Declaration on the Rights of Persons Belonging to National or Ethnic, Religious, and Linguistic Minorities

With Ukraine, East European countries, and the Russian Federation as its champions, the Declaration on the Rights of Minorities was adopted by the General Assembly at its 47th Session, having survived 14 years in the drafting stage. Much time was initially spent addressing the definition of a minority (an effort ultimately abandoned) and refuting numerous attacks from countries fearful that the declaration would increase demands for autonomy or independence, that it constituted interference in internal affairs of states, and that its special protective measures designed to ensure equality would lead to reverse discrimination. Previous U.N. human rights instruments have concerned themselves with ensuring the equality of treatment of all citizens; this was the first universal instrument to focus on protecting of the rights of minorities.

The declaration, which was described by the Russian delegation as "a minimum," calls on states to "protect the existence and . . . identity of minorities," and gives *persons* belonging to minorities the explicit "right to participate effectively in decisions on the national and . . . regional level" that concern them. The Secretary-General was requested to report to the 48th General Assembly on the implementation of the declaration.

Declaration on the Protection of All Persons from Enforced or Involuntary Disappearances

This declaration worked its way through the U.N. process rather quickly as a result of the outrage—expressed by NGOs and Latin American groups representing the families of the disappeared—at various amnesty laws and at the impunity of perpetrators of disappearances. The declaration, adopted December 18, 1992, is the first instrument to define a "disappearance" as a human rights violation, and aims at ensuring legal safeguards against disappearances in domestic law. Article 14 establishes a duty to prosecute perpetrators of disappearances criminally, and Article 17 establishes that disappearances are "a continuing offence as long as the perpetrators continue to conceal the fate and the whereabouts of persons who have disappeared and these facts remain unclarified." In 1992 the Commission on Human Rights extended the mandate of the Working Group on Arbitrary or Involuntary Disappearances for three years. The question of enforced disappearance will be considered again by the General Assembly during its 48th Session.

The U.N. Human Rights Machinery

The 53-member Commission on Human Rights, composed of government representatives, has established a variety of implementational mechanisms. "Working groups" that engage in drafting standards have worked to draft declarations on disappearances, the rights of members of minority groups and of human rights defenders, and gross violations examined under the so-called "1503" confidential procedure. The 47th General Assembly adopted two of these: the Declaration on the Protection of All Persons from Enforced or Involuntary Disappearances and the Declaration on the Rights of Persons Belonging to National or Ethnic, Religious, and Linguistic Minorities.

Central to the work of the Commission are the "special procedures"—thematic and country mechanisms termed "working groups" and "special rapporteurs"—established for a year and renewed beyond to investigate and take effective action both on global human rights problems and on situations in particular countries. As of mid-1993, special mechanisms examined and took emergency action on individual cases falling into their mandated "thematic issue": (a) enforced or involuntary disappearances; (b) religious intolerance; (c) arbitrary detention; (d) summary or arbitrary executions; and (e) torture. Two other "thematic rapporteurs" address the problems of mercenaries and the sale of children but do not intercede on individual cases as the other five do. The 49th Commission created two new posts: one to document contemporary forms of racism and the other to document violations of freedom of opinion and expression.

Meanwhile, special rapporteurs (or "representatives" or "experts") have been appointed to report to the Commission on human rights situations—and violations—in **Afghanistan, Cuba, El Salvador, Iran, Iraq, Myanmar (Burma), Haiti**, and **Equatorial Guinea**. Also, a working group established in 1967 continues to report on the situation in **South Africa**. An important distinction imposed by the Commission is that those serving on "special procedures" are appointed in their individual capacity as experts, not as government representatives.

Other working groups and rapporteurs add to the U.N.'s human rights work, but they are the creations of the **Subcommission on Prevention of Discrimination and Protection of Minorities** ("the Subcommission"). At the end of its 1991 session the Subcommission had working groups on communications concerning consistent patterns of gross violations of human rights (where the screening of the "1503" confidential communications on human rights violations begins), on contemporary forms of slavery, on indigenous populations, on detention, and on the methods of work of the Subcommission. It also had 20 special studies or reports in progress, conducted by its members or former members, who are often called "special rapporteurs," although their role is rather different from that of their namesakes at the Commission. Five of these reports address discrimination or minorities: Two studies and a drafting initiative focus on indigenous people, one focuses on peaceful solutions of minority problems, and another on discrimination against persons infected with the HIV virus. The other topics reveal the breadth of subjects covered at the Subcommission: annual reports on banks doing business with South Africa and on countries that have proclaimed states of emergency; studies on impunity of perpetrators of violations of human rights and on the rights of victims to restitution; and examinations of freedom of expression, the right to fair trial, independence of the judiciary, detention of U.N. staff members, human rights and youth, detained juveniles, traditional health practices harmful to women, the realization of economic and social rights, the right to adequate housing, human rights and the environment, and the rights of the internally displaced.

In addition to the political bodies cited above, each of the U.N.'s six principal human rights treaties now establishes an independent supervisory committee composed of expert members who monitor compliance. The treaty bodies include:

- Human Rights Committee [International Covenant on Civil and Political Rights], 18 members;
- Committee on Economic, Social, and Cultural Rights [International Covenant on Economic, Social, and Cultural Rights], 18 members;
- Committee on Elimination of All Forms of Racial Discrimination

(CERD) [International Convention on the Elimination of All Forms of Racial Discrimination], 18 members;
- Committee against Torture (CAT) [Convention against Torture and Other Cruel, Inhuman, or Degrading Treatment or Punishment], 10 members;
- Committee on the Rights of the Child (CRC) [Convention on the Rights of the Child], 10 members;
- Committee on the Elimination of All Forms of Discrimination against Women (CEDAW) [Convention on the Elimination of All Forms of Discrimination Against Women], 23 members.

These committees examine reports officially submitted by the countries that become party to the treaties, and may make general comments or recommendations about the treaty. They report annually to the General Assembly, although all but the Economic and Social Rights Committee are technically independent bodies set up by the treaties, independently of the U.N. Charter. But because the treaties are dependent on the United Nations for logistical support and personnel, they are generally regarded as bodies functioning within the general framework of the U.N. system. The Economic and Social Rights Committee is a subsidiary body of ECOSOC.

The work of the thematic and country mechanisms during 1992–93 is discussed below.

Disappearances

Since 1984 the Working Group on Disappearances has insisted that an international instrument be drawn up on enforced or involuntary disappearances, and in 1992 the General Assembly gave its approval to a **Declaration on the Protection of All Persons from Enforced or Involuntary Disappearances**. Set up in 1980 by the Commission on Human Rights, the Working Group was the first of the U.N.'s specialized "theme mechanisms" and the first to begin to intervene with governments for information on behalf of individual victims and their families.

Disappearances occur when individuals are seized—often by persons in plainclothes and either in government service or protected by government agencies—and never seen or heard from again. The government denies any knowledge of the individual or any responsibility for his or her whereabouts. The practice eliminates victims, terrorizes family and friends, and leaves the government unaccountable. In 1992 the General Assembly expressed its continuing concern about the practice of forced or involuntary disappearances [A/Res/47/132 and 133], and it will address these issues again at its 49th Session when it considers the current Report of the Commission's Working Group on Disappearances [E/CN.4/1993/25].

In its past few sessions the Working Group has been particularly disturbed by reports of intimidation of relatives of the disappeared who contact the Working Group. Likewise troubling, governments have persisted in preventing witnesses from having access to representatives of U.N. human rights bodies during country visits.

Pursuing a strictly "non-accusatory approach" focused on finding out what happened to the victim rather than on assigning blame, whether to governments or specific officials, the Working Group has examined disappearances throughout the world. In its 13 years it has asked some 45 governments to explain more than 35,000 cases of disappearances. In 1992 the Group reported processing 8,651 cases. The Special Rapporteur noted that this number was twice as high as the number for 1991. Of these cases, 6,000 are attributable to the former Yugoslavia. Last year Sri Lanka claimed the dubious distinction of being the state with the largest number of disappearances considered by the Working Group.

In 1991 three members of the Group went to Sri Lanka to undertake consultations and investigations regarding disappearances. In their report [E/CN.4/1992/18/Add.1] they provide details on the conflicts in the country that have led to the deterioration in human rights and the increase in disappearances; on the legal and judicial systems, including problems with habeas corpus; and on meetings they had with government officials as well as with representatives of nongovernmental organizations and relatives of victims. They noted that the government policy not to ask questions of or prosecute armed forces fighting the insurgency has encouraged a climate of impunity.

A follow-up visit took place October 5–15, 1992. An addendum to the Working Group's report [E/CN.4/1993/Add.1] detailing the mission found that the human rights situation had improved since the last visit, but still remained an issue of concern. The Group commented that the government had made serious efforts to eliminate disappearances but was finding it difficult to prevent them altogether. The government of Sri Lanka was urged to consider seriously undertaking a general overhaul of its emergency legislation relating to arrest and detention with a view to ensuring that Sri Lanka's internal obligations on the matter were proportionate to the exigencies of the situation.

The Working Group has previously explained that while only 7–8% of all disappearance cases it has adopted have been formally clarified; the rate rises to 25% of cases submitted promptly and taken up within three months of the actual "disappearance." Yet it reports that, like its new "prompt intervention" procedure, its regular "urgent action" procedure is not being used enough at present.

Of the 1992 caseload, the countries with the largest number of new reported disappearances were:

Iraq: 5,573 cases, of which 0 were reported to have occurred in 1992;
Sri Lanka: 1,802 cases, of which 62 occurred in 1992;
Peru: 339 cases, of which 151 occurred in 1992 (compared with 154 cases a year ago, of which 117 occurred in 1991);
Indonesia: 214 cases, of which 4 reportedly occurred in 1992.

It is interesting to note the sharp decline in reported cases of disappearances in several other countries visited by the group that previously had widespread disappearances:

Morocco: 2 new cases, of which 0 occurred in 1992 (compared with 115/101 in 1991);
Iran: 9 new cases, of which 1 occurred in 1992 (compared with 40/2 in 1991);
Guatemala: 10 new cases, all of which occurred in 1992 (compared with 33/30 in 1991);
El Salvador: 17 new cases, of which 0 occurred in 1992 (compared with 46/30 in 1991).

Despite these statistics, the Group has made vigorous efforts to draw attention to the shortage of resources devoted to its work and the work of the entire "special procedures" section, which coordinates activities for all of the thematic and country-specific rapporteurs and working groups. It has highlighted the thousands of cases it could not act upon due to staff-resource limitations. The Working Group's report concluded that enforced disappearances could be reduced significantly by the independent and efficient administration of justice, incorporating such methods as the habeas corpus procedure. In its consideration of impunity, the Working Group stated that the investigation of disappearances and the publication of investigation results were perhaps the most important means of establishing accountability of the government concerned.

Religious Intolerance

The 47th General Assembly adopted a resolution by consensus calling for advisory services in the area of human rights to accord a higher priority to the promotion and protection of the right to freedom of thought, conscience, and religion. Measures to end religious intolerance will be considered again during the Assembly's next Session. The **Special Rapporteur on Religious Intolerance** was established in 1985 by the Commission on Human Rights. Angelo Vidal d'Almeida Ribeiro of Portugal currently holds this position; his mandate was extended by the Commission at its 48th session.

The Commission also adopted by consensus Resolution 1992/17 entitled the "Implementation of the Declaration on the Elimination of All Forms of Intolerance and of Discrimination based on Religion or Beliefs." This resolution urged states to take all appropriate measures to eliminate religious intolerance and requested that the Secretary-General continue to encourage dissemination of the text of the Declaration and to provide all necessary assistance to the Special Rapporteur to facilitate further reports to the Commission.

In his latest report [E/CN.4/1993/62] Ribeiro provides information on his correspondence with 24 governments in 1992 regarding allegations of religious discrimination or intolerance "inconsistent with the provisions of the Declaration." Thirteen governments replied to 1992 inquiries and four to earlier ones, making his response rate especially good. Where it is relevant, the Rapporteur presents the government's reply verbatim and without comment.

Among the countries (and religious minorities) cited in the Rapporteur's 1993 report are:

- **China**, for persecution of Tibetan monks and nuns as well as for arrests of Muslim clergy, Uyger religious personalities, Jesuit and other Catholic clergy.
- **Egypt**, for actions against Coptic Christians, including forced conversion to the Islamic faith and measures against their churches and associations.
- **Indonesia**, for persecution against members of the Baha'i faith.
- **Iraq**, for actions against the Shi'a religious community, including persecution and killing of religious leaders and scholars, arrests of 1,300 members of the Shi'a faith, systematic destruction of religious educational institutions, destruction or damage to numerous holy shrines and mosques, etc.
- **Myanmar**, for persecution of Muslims, including killings, abduction for forced porter duty by the military, gang-rape, eviction, land confiscation, systematic destruction of towns and mosques, etc.
- **Pakistan**, for persecution of Ahmadis, including killings, destruction of villages, closing of newspapers, and an amendment to Pakistan's Penal Code making the death penalty mandatory for statements deemed insulting to the prophets.
- **Saudi Arabia**, for discrimination against Shi'a Muslims.
- **Vietnam**, for reports that increasing numbers of clergy and religious activists have been arrested, persecuted, and tortured in labor camps, and that the practice of religion in general is subjected to severe restrictions.

In the past the Rapporteur has noted that infringement of religious freedoms usually results in infringements of other human rights. This year the Rapporteur noted that curtailment of religious freedom continues, taking place under different forms of government, carried out by individuals as well as by extragovernmental groups.

Like the other thematic rapporteurs, Mr. Ribeiro does not comment on the replies, nor offer country-specific recommendations for alleviating infringements of religious freedoms. Still, he has previously characterized his inquiries as situations "which seemed to involve a departure from the provisions of the Declaration." In comments addressed to the Commission on Human Rights, Mr. Ribeiro lamented that the optimism generated last year by the improved situation in Eastern Europe and in the territory of the former Soviet Union was being dampened by setbacks in other regions. The Rapporteur was referring specifically to Iran's increase in the reward for the murder of author Salman Rushdie and Pakistan's institution of the death penalty for blaspheming the Prophet Mohammed. In closing, the Rapporteur informed the Commission that he would not be returning due to ill health and that the Commission should identify a new Rapporteur.

Arbitrary Detention

In 1991 the Commission on Human Rights created a regionally balanced Working Group of five experts with a three-year mandate to investigate, study, and take action in cases of arbitrary detention [Res/1991/42]. With the establishment of this new mechanism, the Commission was able to monitor and report on all areas of major human rights violations covered by its "thematic mechanisms."

The Working Group presented its second report to the Commission at its 49th session [E/CN.4/1993/24], addressing 34 communications regarding reported cases of alleged arbitrary detention. The countries approached were Burundi (1 case), Chile (3), Côte d'Ivoire (1), Cuba (61), Iran (9), Israel (2), Laos (1), Libya (9), Malawi (3), Mexico (2), Myanmar (2), Peru (1), Sudan (6), Syria (60), Tanzania (1), Tunisia (2), and Uganda (1).

The Working Group expressed concern that the list of countries approached appeared selective, considering that the Group must rely on information provided only by sources allowed contact with the Group and is forbidden to investigate governments on its own initiative. However, the Group hopes that in the future sources, particularly nongovernmental organizations, will provide information on a greater number of countries.

In compliance with the requirement of objectivity imposed by the Commission on Human Rights, the Working Group adopted an adversarial rather than accusatory procedure to communicate with the various governments. This adversarial approach, along with an updated questionnaire, has improved the accuracy of the Group's reports by enhancing communications with governments and facilitating the collection of additional information.

Unlike the Group's first report to the Commission, the second report contained general conclusions and recommendations regarding submitted cases. The recommendations included a call for more comprehensive and timely information submitted by the sources involved, as well as a demand that the information cover both legislative aspects (constitutional and legal provisions, regulations, and jurisprudence) and the actual deeds that allegedly warrant the detention of the person(s) concerned. The report also stressed the necessity of identifying with accuracy the authority ordering the detention, along with the court—if any—trying the case. It was further suggested that governments make serious efforts to bring their laws into accordance with the principles of the international human rights instruments as well as to strengthen the use of the writ of habeas corpus.

Summary and Arbitrary Executions

In 1992, Mr. S. Amos Wako of Kenya, the U.N. Special Rapporteur on Summary and Arbitrary executions for ten years, resigned. His successor, Bacre Waly Ndiaye, presented his first report to the Commission on Human Rights this year—the tenth such report since this "thematic mechanism" was established by the Commission in 1982. Mr. Ndiaye will continue to address ways to combat summary and arbitrary executions and to detail numerous cases raised with governments.

The report by Mr. Ndiaye demonstrated concern about massive killings conducted by governments and by death squads that operate outside the law. Use of the death penalty against political opponents was reported in thousands of cases in which governments ignored national laws guaranteeing the accused's due process rights to a lawyer or to an appeal.

Since 1982 the Commission, the General Assembly, and Mr. Wako (now Mr. Ndiaye) have expanded the scope of the Rapporteur's concern. The Rapporteur's mandate has grown from a scholarly focus on *actual* deaths to an activist effort to do something about *imminent* deaths. He inquires about death penalty cases without legal safeguards and about suspicious deaths at the hands of governments or their agents. In Mr. Wako's last report to the Commission [E/CN.4/1992/30 and Add. 1] he presented an account of the first decade of activities of the Rapporteur. He discussed his mandate and its growth, citing the responses of governments, and noted that over those ten years he had addressed letters or appeals to over 100 different states. He recalled that he had identified the following practices as falling within his mandate: death threats, deaths in custody, executions following inadequate trial or judicial procedures, and extralegal executions in situations of armed conflict. Mr. Wako and Mr. Ndiaye both have identified as primary areas of concern: deaths as a result of torture; abuse of force by police, military, or other government institutions; assault by individuals or paramilitary groups acting with official collusion or connivance, as well as by similar bodies that oppose the government or are outside its control.

In earlier reports Mr. Wako stated that he found summary and arbitrary executions to occur in all world regions and to have one common factor: the "opposition, or perceived opposition, of the victims to those who wielded political or economic power." He also mentioned the increased occurrence of summary and arbitrary executions in internal conflicts. He noted that the violation of human rights is often a warning signal that summary or arbitrary executions might occur if the problems were not remedied [E/CN.4/1992/SR. 33].

Most of Mr. Ndiaye's 1993 report consists of specific documentation, including names and dates, about cases he has raised with governments and the replies, if any. Over the years the Special Rapporteur has found the number of cases reported growing dramatically. Mr. Wako had speculated that this is due to the mandate becoming better known worldwide. In fact, only a fraction of these incoming cases end in cables or letters from the Rapporteur, but that fraction has increased in recent years. It has been noted that "most of the allegations concerning summary or arbitrary executions and death threats . . . are presented by nongovernmental organizations" but that "some governments" get into the fray, presenting allegations of executions attributed to opposing forces.

During the first six months of Mr. Ndiaye's mandate, he contacted a total of 52 governments about more than 3,500 allegations concerning extrajudicial, summary, or arbitrary executions. In 189 of the cases the victims were alleged to be under 18 years of age. In these instances the Special Rapporteur reminded the governments of the Convention of the Rights of the Child and "other pertinent international instruments." The Rapporteur also drew attention to governments that failed to reply to the Special Rapporteur's 1992 allegations, listing the following: Afghanistan, Angola, Azerbaijan, Burundi, Cambodia, Chile, Dominican Republic, Equatorial Guinea, Haiti, Honduras, Iran, Iraq, Israel, Lesotho, Malaysia, Mali, Nepal, Pakistan (since 1989), Paraguay, Rwanda, South Africa, Sudan, Togo, Ukraine, the United States, Yemen, and Zaire. He has begun including a list of questions and conditions that should help clarify the allegations being advanced and readily permit a case to be considered "clarified."

Among the situations cited in the 1993 report were:

- **Afghanistan**, concerning death sentences and executions carried out by or at the command of a newly set up Islamic court for the crimes of looting, robbery, and murder.

- **Bangladesh**, concerning extrajudicial, summary, or arbitrary executions carried out by military personnel, members of the Village Defense party, and "Ansar" guards.
- **Brazil**, concerning death threats and summary or arbitrary executions.
- **China**, concerning acts of violence leading to the death of Tibetans and members of the Roman Catholic Church, as well as applications of the death penalty contrary to internationally recognized fair trial standards.
- **Colombia**, concerning killings of citizens for political reasons or in "social-cleansing" activities—i.e., beggars, street children, mentally handicapped people—carried out by security forces, paramilitary groups, civilian "death squads," and guerrillas.
- **Cuba**, concerning deaths in custody or at the hands of police officers as well as death threats against human rights activists.
- **Haiti**, concerning killings by security forces acting with total impunity.
- **India**, concerning killings by security forces acting with impunity in the states of Assam, Jammu, Kashmir, and Punjab.
- **Iran**, concerning executions of demonstrators against the government's economic and social policies.
- **Peru**, concerning death threats, summary executions, and human rights abuses leveled against peasants by the army, security forces, and the Communist party (Shining Path).
- **Sudan**, concerning summary trials and legal proceedings as well as killings of civilians in connection with internal conflict.
- **Turkey**, concerning killing of civilians in the Kurdish population by Turkish Security Forces.

The Special Rapporteur also noted that various republics of the former Soviet Union and such countries as Liberia and Somalia face serious right-to-life problems. However, without proper identification of authorities that might be addressed, he can do little, but he has offered to cooperate in any way he can with other U.N. mechanisms already in place in those areas.

The 49th General Assembly will be discussing the report of Mr. Ndiaye, having decided to consider the topic biennially, in even years. In the past the General Assembly has adopted resolutions that strongly condemn the practice of extrajudicial, summary, and arbitrary executions; appealed urgently for effective action to combat them; and asked the Rapporteur to respond effectively to information that is presented to him.

To improve the effectiveness of the Rapporteur's work, some NGOs have drawn attention to the need for country-specific recommendations and follow-up. More sustained interaction with the governments in question, and regular and more routine follow-up could help. To date, governments have failed to respond to the Rapporteur's request for support in establishing sanctions against governments that repeatedly fail to respond to his requests. Commission and General Assembly encouragement of "cooperation" by governments has had only a limited impact.

Torture

The U.N.'s efforts to prevent human rights violations have focused on eradicating torture. As part of the rationalized plan for the agenda of the Third Committee, the 47th General Assembly received a report from the Committee against Torture (CAT), a treaty body that monitors compliance with the Convention against Torture [see below]. In a resolution on CAT's report, the Assembly expressed serious concern "about the alarming number of reported cases of torture," requested a report from the Secretary-General on the status of the Convention against Torture by the 49th General Assembly, and decided to consider the reports of the Secretary-General and of CAT at that 1994 Assembly session, under the sub-item "Implementation of human rights instruments." The Assembly also adopted a pro forma resolution on the low-key **Voluntary Fund for Victims of Torture**, in which it urged governments, organizations, and individuals not only to continue but also to increase their donations to the Fund.

The **Special Rapporteur on Torture**, established by the Commission on Human Rights, examines emergency reports of torture cases worldwide and intervenes in an attempt to prevent torture when possible; asks governments to clarify detailed allegations of torture; and appraises the situation and the measures taken to prevent torture in various countries, visiting some "upon their request." Since 1984 the Special Rapporteur, Prof. Peter Kooijmans of the Netherlands, has recommended an array of international and national measures designed to curtail the practice of torture.

In October 1992, in accordance with a Commission resolution [E/CN.4/1992/S-1/1], the Special Rapporteur on Torture joined the Commission's Special Rapporteur on the situation in the former Yugoslavia, Tadeusz Mazowiecki, in his second mission to the former Yugoslavia, where he visited Bosnia-Herzegovina, Croatia, and Serbia [A/47/666]. A report from this mission observed that "the seeds of torture are sown whenever a society tolerates a situation where respect for the inherent dignity of fellow citizens is taken lightly."

The bulk of Special Rapporteur Kooijmans's annual report to the Commission on Human Rights offers details on specific cases, the Rapporteur's correspondence with governments, follow-up measures to past visits, and conclusions and recommendations. In his 1992 report, the Special Rapporteur noted that he had sent 44 urgent communications, addressing a total of 700 cases of alleged torture, to 43 governments. Seventy-nine urgent appeals were sent to 31 governments, dealing with cases involving roughly 300 individuals as well as several groups. Among the countries contacted were China, Cuba, Egypt, Greece, the Philippines, Turkey, the then Yugoslavia, and Zaire.

The 1992 report also notes the 55 countries (down from 65 in 1991) with whom the Rapporteur conducted correspondence about individual cases and situations involving torture. The Rapporteur encouraged countries to invite him to examine reported cases of torture in person, reiterating that his visits are consultative and preventive, not accusatory or investigative. Although he had approached some governments when the situation in the country appeared to make a visit imperative, the Special Rapporteur did not receive a single invitation to visit a country in 1992. On-site investigations by the Rapporteur are critical: Few governments undertake independent inquiries into allegations of torture, and fewer still provide details of any investigations that might have been made.

In his **recommendations on eliminating torture**, the Rapporteur stressed the need for the judiciary to "play an active role" in guaranteeing the rights of detainees, the need to ensure prompt access to a lawyer, and the individual's right to initiate proceedings on the lawfulness of his detention. Professor Kooijmans also called for: interrogations only at official interrogation centers; the establishment of independent national ombudsmen/human rights commissions with the power to investigate complaints of torture; the enactment of measures to outlaw incommunicado detention; and "strict measures" against medical professionals who collaborate in torture. Wherever complaints of torture are justified, Kooijmans stated, "the perpetrators should be severely punished, especially the official in charge of the place of detention where the torture took place."

At the conclusion of his report, the Rapporteur reminded the Commission on Human Rights that torture is "the most intimate of human rights violations," normally taking place in isolation and with the torturer deliberately anonymous; the victim is often hooded or blindfolded. In its own resolution, the Commission reiterated the Rapporteur's recommendations on ending torture, emphasized the importance of training programs for law enforcement officials, and emphasized too the need to utilize U.N. advisory services programs to educate and improve behavior by police and by law enforcement and other authorities. The Rapporteur's mandate was extended for three years [Commission resolution 1992/32, 2/28/92].

Convention Against Torture

A binding treaty adopted in 1984, the Convention against Torture formally criminalizes torture. As of July 1993 the Convention had been ratified by 75 states, up from 71 in December 1992. Monitoring compliance with this treaty is the **Committee against Torture (CAT)**, which meets twice annually to review states parties' reports in public session. The Committee, the Convention's only implementational mechanism, is similar to those established under other U.N. human rights treaties, although many observers believe CAT may develop stricter enforcement procedures than those of other treaty supervisory bodies, because it contains strong optional procedures. The Committee's next report will be reviewed by the General Assembly at its 49th Session (1994); thereafter, the General Assembly will consider Committee reports on a biennial basis in even years.

The Convention against Torture has the onerous requirement that states parties must themselves pay for all expenses of the Committee, including its meetings, documents, and staff. The 47th General Assembly stressed the importance of strict adherence by states parties to the obligations under the Convention regarding financing, thus enabling it to carry out in an effective and efficient manner all the functions entrusted to it under the Convention; states parties that had not yet paid their assessed contributions were urged to fulfill their obligations forthwith.

Country Situations

During its 49th session the Commission on Human Rights made several new appointments: Special Rapporteurs were named to report on the human rights situation in Israeli-occupied territories, Sudan, and Equatorial Guinea; new posts were created to document contemporary forms of racism and violations of freedom of opinion and expression; and a 15-member Working Group was asked to study the problems of economic development and human rights. The Commission called for the appointment of an Independent Expert to assist the Secretary-General's Special Representative in Somalia. During the Commission's next session it will be considering the appointment of its own **Sepcial Rapporteur on violence against women.**

The 49th Commission adopted public resolutions pertaining to 20 countries: the former Yugoslavia, Myanmar, Iraq, East Timor/Indonesia, Sudan, Iran, Haiti, Equatorial Guinea, Cuba, Papua New Guinea, Afghanistan, Zaire, Southern Lebanon, Romania, El Salvador, Togo, Albania, Georgia, Cambodia, and South Africa. It considered seven countries under the "1503" confidential procedure: Bahrain, Kenya, Rwanda, Somalia, Sudan, Chad, and Zaire. Sudan, as the new appointment of a Special Rapporteur on Sudan indicates, will now come under public scrutiny; Zaire has since been removed from the list too but will be the subject of a report by the Secretary-General; and Bahrain and Kenya have been removed from scrutiny entirely, at least for the moment.

Iraq

In Special Rapporteur Max van der Stoel's report [E/CN.4/1993/45] to the 49th session of the Commission on Human Rights, he continued his disclosure and documentation of what he called "human rights violations of the gravest nature and on a massive scale." In addition to the Special Rapporteur's conviction that abuses have taken place and continue to occur, he held out little hope that the present government would institute any reforms that would lead Iraq to fulfill its international human rights obligations.

The Special Rapporteur holds responsible for the numerous human rights violations the ruling elite of the Iraqi government. It is the policy of the complex and well-entrenched dictatorial infrastructure that grants security forces license to injure and kill with impunity anyone suspected of infringing on "security and order" [para. 181]. Additionally, the years-long domination of the media—and, indeed, of the entire society—by the Arab Baath Socialist party, led by Saddam Hussein, has resulted in widespread terror and subjugation. Ethnic chauvinism and intolerance of any kind of opposition, be it real or imagined, are at the core of this repression.

The Special Rapporteur details an enormous list of violations by Iraqi security forces against the population in general: summary or arbitrary execution; torture and other cruel, inhuman, or degrading treatment; arbitrary arrest and detention; and other varieties of oppression and deprivation. Disappearances continue on a very large scale.

Response by the government of Iraq to the above allegations has consisted basically of denial and counteraccusations of forgery and conspiracy, van der Stoel reports. Given that the government of Saddam Hussein keeps extensive records on members of the population, Baghdad's failure to produce conclusive evidence for its defense suggests that the allegations themselves are true, van der Stoel asserts [para. 182].

The chief targets of Iraq's discriminatory racial policy are the **Shi'a community, the Kurds**, and **the Ma'dan population**. Crimes perpetrated against the Shi'a community, which constitutes a majority in Iraq, include continued desecration of mosques and personal violations against members of the Shi'a clergy. The government has continued to interfere with Shi'a institutions and has outlawed various religious practices.

The Kurds living in northern Iraq have established a democratic local government out of the vacuum created by the Gulf War. Despite the Kurds' agreement on a unified Iraq, the people of this region are subjected to ongoing terror, including military attacks, forced displacement, mines, and most recently a car-bombing in the city of Arbil on January 22, 1993, that killed 11 and injured 128 civilians.

The Ma'dan people who inhabit the southern marshlands of the country are victims of mass bombings, an economic embargo, and a disastrous drainage project, which has created an ecological wasteland.

Following his conclusions, the Special Rapporteur proposed again to send human rights monitors so that information could be more easily transmitted and verified. The Commission adopted the recommendation [Res/1993/74] and requested that the Secretary-General "take the necessary measures in order to send human rights monitors to such locations." The Commission also urged the government of Iraq to permit the Special Rapporteur to visit the country, and extended his mandate for one year. The Special Rapporteur was asked to submit an interim report to the 48th General Assembly and a report to the Commission at its 50th session.

Cuba

In March 1992 the Commission on Human Rights resolved to replace the position of Special Representative to Cuba with a Special Rapporteur. Later that month the Special Representative, Rafael Rivas Posada, informed the Centre for Human Rights in Geneva that he declined to fill the new position. Mr. Rivas Posada's resignation sparked a conflict over the monitoring of the human rights situation in Cuba between the Commission and the government of Cuba. The Chairman of the Commission invited the Secretary-General to appoint another Special Representative, who would then carry out the duties of Special Rapporteur. The government of Cuba responded by declaring the Chairman's action illegal, saying that neither the Chairman nor the Secretary-General has the right to extend the mandate of anyone other than Mr. Rivas Posada.

As a result, the Cuban government did not allow the newly appointed Special Rapporteur, Carl-Johan Groth of Sweden, to visit the country; and the Special Rapporteur was limited to gathering testimony outside the country from those in exile, representatives of various nongovernmental organizations, and Cuban human rights groups. From these sources Special Rapporteur Groth compiled a report [E/CN.4/1993/39] that included documentation of cases of infringement on the right to freedom of opinion, assembly, and association (directed against human rights advocates); the right to leave and enter the country; and the rights of prisoners. The Special Rapporteur detailed information he had received on conditions in certain Cuban prisons, including accounts of brutality, food of poor quality and insufficient supply, inadequate medical attention (resulting sometimes in death), and other forms of maltreatment.

Special Rapporteur Groth expressed disappointment at the continued refusal of the Cuban government to cooperate with him in accordance with his mandate, and voiced hope that he might soon be permitted to visit the country unimpeded. He furthermore defended the Commission's resolutions against the government's claims that the United

Nations is targeting Cuba for political reasons and that violations in Cuba do not occur on a scale comparable to the mass violations of other targeted countries [paras. 82–83]. Affirming his duties as Special Rapporteur, Groth outlined specific recommendations intended to improve the human rights situation in accordance with international instruments. In what is Mr. Groth's most important point, related to the worsening economic situation in Cuba, he calls for an end to the international economic sanctions against the country. This forced isolation, he states, only makes less likely any improvement in human rights, since the government will be more inclined to use repression to enforce stability [paras. 89–91].

The Commission's resolution of March 10, 1993 [1993/63], extended the mandate of the Special Rapporteur, and Mr. Groth was asked to submit reports to the next Commission session and to the 48th General Assembly.

Iran

In 1992 the Special Representative on Iran, Reynaldo Galindo Pohl of El Salvador, was not permitted to visit the country, although the government of the Islamic Republic of Iran did respond in part to the Special Representative's request for information regarding the current human rights situation there. Upon analysis of the material he was able to collect, the Special Representative concluded that no significant progress had been made toward compliance with international requirements.

As in his previous report, Representative Galindo Pohl expressed concern at the continuing violations occurring within Iran, most notably the rising rate of executions; the cases of torture and other cruel, inhuman, or degrading treatment or punishment; the lack of guarantees of due process of law; discriminatory treatment of religious minorities (especially the Baha'ists); restrictions on the freedoms of expression, thought, opinion, and the press; and the lack of recognition of women's rights. The Special Representative details cases of executions by the Iranian government, some of which were attributed to drug crimes and some of which were without explanation. He also expresses concern over the report of 500 cases of missing persons transmitted by the Working Group on Enforced or Involuntary Disappearances of the Commission on Human Rights to the government of Iran [para. 98]. The government responded by dismissing the Group's claims as "baseless." Iran has defended itself against most accusations of transgressions of human rights, emphasizing the difficult internal problems it faces as a result of drug traffic destined for European markets.

Among the Special Representative's recommendations was that the **International Committee of the Red Cross** be allowed to resume its agreement of November 1991 concerning visits to prisons and prisoners without distinctions between ordinary offenses and political offenses [para. 327].

The Commission on Human Rights passed resolutions extending the mandate of the Special Representative and repeating the Special Representative's request to be permitted to visit Iran. Given the lack of improvement documented by Mr. Galindo Pohl, the Commission decided to continue its consideration of human rights in Iran at its next session.

Myanmar (Burma)

In accordance with Resolution 1992/58 adopted by the Commission on Human Rights at its 48th session, Prof. Yozo Yokota of Japan was appointed Special Rapporteur on the human rights situation in Myanmar. The first reports by the Special Rapporteur were submitted to the 47th General Assembly and to the 49th Commission.

Professor Yokota's report [E/CN.4/1993/37] detailed his meetings with several government authorities, including the Minister for Foreign Affairs and the Secretary of the State Law and Order Preservation Council. Both emphasized that the government's highest priority was the maintenance of political stability, leading to more economic and social rights for the people of Myanmar. Each official denied all allegations of human rights abuses (including torture, ill-treatment of prisoners, and unfair refugee repatriation procedures) and asserted the right of Myanmar as a sovereign nation to conduct its internal affairs without outside interference.

The Special Rapporteur was invited by the government, and his visit was facilitated by officials within the country. However, "full and unreserved cooperation" was not offered. Additionally, information received by Yokota indicated that serious human rights violations continue to occur in Myanmar. He stated that many individuals and private groups were prevented from making contact with him because of threats and intimidation by military intelligence. Political prisoners, whom government officials deny even exist, were likewise not allowed to meet with Professor Yokota. Daw Aung San Suu Kyi, Nobel Peace Prize laureate and the nation's best-known political prisoner, is in her fourth year of detention without trial.

Yokota's report details the allegations of summary or arbitrary executions in the conflict zones of the Kayin, Kachin, and Karenni states, despite official suspension of offensive operations by the military. Villagers suspected of insurgency or of supporting the insurgency have been killed while attempting escape. Those villagers who refuse to relocate upon orders or who attempt to avoid relocation are often executed by the military.

In addition to executions during the forced relocation of villages in this area, the military allegedly has also been responsible for the rape and often subsequent death of Muslim women from the Rakhine state and other conflict areas. The report also documented testimony received about deaths of forced porters, other laborers, those participating in political activities, persons in custody, and HIV-positive female prostitutes. Forced porters, often young boys and Muslims taken from Kalor and Palong, are subjected to the danger of crossfire, minefields, and brutality. The railroad construction site of which government officials are so proud is also the site of abuses—namely, deaths of workers from constant beatings, unsanitary conditions, and lack of food and medical treatment.

The Special Rapporteur raises his concerns about punishment of those wishing to exercise their right to political participation, expression, and assembly. Political leaders, elected representatives, students, and monks who are detained in Myanmar prisons suffer dismal conditions, including poor sanitation, insufficient and spoiled food, and inadequate shelter. Torture has resulted in the death of many prisoners. Many detainees were initially among the "disappeared" and were held incommunicado for long periods of time.

The report also contains information regarding the treatment of ethnic minorities in the state of Myanmar. These minorities are singled out as victims of physical integrity violations. There are 265,000 Rakhine Muslim refugees in Bangladesh, most of whom fled Myanmar in 1991. Since then there have been efforts to repatriate them, but human rights organizations fear that the conditions under which these efforts have been conducted are not voluntary, dignified, or safe. The Myanmar government does not allow monitoring of this situation.

Yokota recommended that the government fulfill its obligations to obey international human rights regulations. He called for an extension of the mandate of the Special Rapporteur due to continued abuses. The 49th session of the Commission on Human Rights adopted without a vote resolutions urging the government of Myanmar to conform to human rights standards and to take steps toward establishment of a democratic government. Again the Commission called for the release of Daw Aung San Suu Kyi and other political prisoners, and it extended the mandate of the Special Rapporteur by one year. The 47th General Assembly and the Commission agreed to continue consideration of the Myanmar question at the next session.

East Timor/Indonesia

Despite a history of prior gross violations of human rights on East Timor—the former Portuguese colony occupied since 1975 by Indonesian forces—the Commission on Human Rights first cited Indonesia/East Timor only at its 48th session. Indonesia was addressed in consensus "chairman's statements." The citation was prompted by the Dili massacre in 1991, when security troops in East Timor opened fire on pro-independence demonstrators as they marched to a cemetery to protest human rights abuses. Officially, casualties were placed at 23, but unofficial estimates placed the casualties at 50–60 persons dead and 112 persons unaccounted for.

The European Community issued a "Chairman's Statement" in 1992, expressing "serious concern" over the human rights situation in East Timor, "strongly deplored" the Dili incident, and welcomed Indonesia's decision to set up a commission of inquiry to investigate the deaths and to clarify the fate of those unaccounted for. It also encouraged the Secretary-General to continue to use his "good offices" to achieve "a just, comprehensive, and internationally accepted settlement of the question of East Timor."

The U.N. does not recognize the annexation of the island by Indonesia, and the Secretary-General has continued to seek an internationally accepted settlement of the issue. The most recent round of talks between the Secretary-General and the foreign ministers of Indonesia and Portugal took place in Rome on April 21, 1993. Portugal, at odds with Indonesia, has stressed the need for East Timor to exercise its right to self-determination. The foreign ministers have agreed to continue meeting to solve the question, and further talks are scheduled in New York on September 17, 1993.

Also on the question of East Timor, on April 2, 1992, the Secretary-General sent S. Amos Wako, Attorney-General of Kenya and an international authority on human rights, to Indonesia and East Timor as his special envoy. The three-day tour was a follow-up to a visit in February 1992 to determine if Mr. Wako's earlier recommendations were being implemented. The tour also served to gather information on human rights conditions on the island. The Special Envoy has sent conclusions and recommendations to the Secretary-General; the results have not yet been made public, but a summary of the report was provided to Indonesia's Foreign Minister.

The Human Rights Commission at its 49th session invited the Secretary-General to transmit to them the full reports of Mr. Wako's missions to Indonesia. The Commission again expressed grave concern about the human rights violations occurring in East Timor, specifically regarding the reports of the Special Rapporteur on the question of torture [E/CN.4/1993/26]; of the Special Rapporteur on extrajudicial, summary, or arbitrary executions [E/CN.4/1993/46]; and of the Working Group on Enforced or Involuntary Disappearances [E/CN.4/1993/25]. The Commission "urged" the government of Indonesia to invite the Special Rapporteur to East Timor and to facilitate the discharge of his mandate.

A resolution on the invitation was adopted by a vote of 22 in favor and 12 against, with 15 abstentions. The Indonesian representative criticized the resolution as too harsh in light of the recent progress Indonesia had made on human rights. In fact, the Commission did commend the Indonesian government for the greater access recently granted to human rights organizations. At the same time, it recognized the gravity of the violations occurring on the island and called on Indonesia to increase even further the access granted to human rights organizations. The Commission will further consider the situation of East Timor at its 50th session.

Human Rights After the Vienna Conference

With the Vienna Declaration, however flawed, governments have confirmed that human rights are the legitimate concern of the international community. Indeed, the very fact that the Vienna Conference was convened, and that a Declaration emerged, demonstrates the importance of human rights to states, to individuals, and to **nongovernmental organizations (NGOs).**

Most of the proposals considered by governments at Vienna were initially forwarded by NGOs. Despite an early attempt to sideline these organizations, they were important participants in the process, and governments recognized this.

Present at Vienna were 3,000 NGO delegates representing 1,500 organizations. Most of these were new voices—grass-roots entities demanding the fulfillment of their human rights. Most groups did not hold U.N. consultative status and could not participate in the official Conference, but they made themselves heard, often in new and colorful ways.

Part II, paragraph 25, of the Vienna Declaration "recognizes the important role of non-governmental organizations in the promotion of all human rights and in humanitarian activities at national, regional and international levels" and concludes: "Non-governmental organizations should be free to carry out their human rights activities, without interference, within the framework of national law and the Universal Declaration of Human Rights." Although this language is generally supportive of the work of NGOs, the phrase "within the framework of national laws" is open to interpretation by states, some of which may wish to curtail NGO activities.

The legacy of the World Conference on Human Rights is sure to be more significant than the Conference itself. If little new ground was broken, the pot was certainly stirred. The Vienna document is not binding international law, but it contributes to the development of that law. Now the development process continues in other arenas—beginning with the U.N. General Assembly.

2. Refugees
By Kathryn C. Lawler

The end of the Cold War has brought new opportunities for international cooperation in addressing the problems that cause people to seek refuge outside their countries. This new international political climate has already led to the settlement of many regional conflicts, opening the way for the repatriation of over a million-and-a-half refugees in 1992 alone. At the same time, however, ethnic violence, the breakup of states, internal conflicts, human rights violations, and still other factors have led over 3 million other people to flee their homelands, raising the total world refugee population to 18 million [statement by Sadako Ogata, U.N. High Commissioner for Refugees, to the Third Committee of the General Assembly, 11/10/92].

These developments place enormous pressure on the Office of the **U.N. High Commissioner for Refugees (UNHCR)**, the agency created in late 1950 to extend international protection to refugees and to seek permanent solutions to their problems. Addressing the General Assembly in late 1992, U.N. High Commissioner for Refugees Sadako Ogata stated that UNHCR's work has "never . . . been so intensely relevant and so extensively tested" [ibid.]. In **the former Yugoslavia**, UNHCR is currently assisting over 3 million people affected by the conflict [UNHCR Briefing Notes on the former Yugoslavia, 3/23/93]. In the **Horn of Africa**, the agency is struggling to meet the needs of approximately 1.2 million refugees and returnees in Ethiopia, 400,000 refugees in Kenya, 730,000 refugees in Sudan, and 20,000 refugees in Djibouti [UNHCR World Refugee Statistics, 9/92]. The increasing demand on UNHCR's expertise has been accompanied by enormous growth in its budget, which in 1992 exceeded $1 billion dollars [Ogata statement of 11/10/92].

Asylum

The **1951 Convention Relating to the Status of Refugees and its 1967 Protocol** are the bedrock of international refugee protection, enshrining such principles as the right of refugees to seek asylum and the right of refugees not to be forcibly returned to their country of origin. These principles, however, are currently under threat. Although 117 governments have ratified the 1951 Convention and/or its 1967 Protocol (as of March 1, 1993), 65 U.N. member states are not yet parties to either of these instruments. Among the nonparties are some of the very countries in which large numbers of people have sought refuge—for example, Thailand, Mexico, and Pakistan. Refugee protection is particularly precarious in such countries because the international obligations of states not parties to the Convention or Protocol are unclear, and the UNHCR cannot exert much leverage on national policies regarding refugees.

A second threat to international refugee protection is the fact that even the states parties to international instruments do not always fulfill their obligations under them. While these instruments establish the right of a refugee to seek asylum, this right cannot be exercised unless the country of asylum gives asylum seekers access to a legal system through which they can make their claims to refugee status. Governments often exploit the ambiguity between political refugees and economic migrants as a way of turning asylum seekers away without hearing their cases.

The right to asylum is also under pressure from such forces as nationalism, xenophobia, and economic hardship. For example, the arrival of over 450,000 asylum seekers in Germany during 1992 sparked a wave of rightist violence against foreigners [*The New York Times*, 2/7/93]. The U.N. General Assembly's 47th Session acknowledged the rise in "persistent problems in some countries or regions seriously jeopardizing the security or well-being of refugees, including incidents of refoulement, expulsion, physical attack and detention under unacceptable conditions," and it called upon member states "to take all measures necessary to ensure respect for the principles of refugee protection" [A/Res/47/105].

UNHCR plays an important role in countering these threats to asylum. It continues to promote the accession of states to the 1951 Convention and its Protocol, and of late it has become increasingly critical of government policies that threaten the ability of people to flee from danger. On February 2, 1992, for example, the U.N. High Commissioner for Refugees issued a statement expressing regret that the U.S. government had decided to return **Haitian asylum seekers** and noting that "the High Commissioner had sought assurances from the U.S. government at a very high level that those seeking safety abroad would not be forced to return until the situation in Haiti has evolved positively and has stabilized" [UNHCR Information Service, 2/2/92].

Defining a "Refugee"

The Convention Relating to the Status of Refugees applied to refugees affected by events in Europe prior to 1951. Drafters of the 1967 Protocol Relating to the Status of Refugees removed these geographic and time limitations but retained the Convention's definition of a refugee as someone with a well-founded fear of persecution on the basis of one of the following: race, religion, nationality, membership in a particular social group, or political opinion. This definition was shaped during the Cold War, when the causes and characteristics of population displacement were different from what they are today, and problems arise when it is applied in contemporary refugee situations. First, the majority of **refugee situations today involve large numbers of people rather than one or a few individuals**, and in most cases it is logistically impossible to determine the refugee status of each person by conducting a personal interview. Second, most refugees today are not fleeing persecution directed at themselves as individuals but, rather, are **fleeing life-threatening conditions of general violence and repression.**

Some progress has been made on the regional level in developing refugee protection standards that comport more closely with contemporary refugee situations. An African and a Latin American regional instrument, for example, have broadened the 1951 Convention's definition of refugees to include **additional categories** of people, such as those fleeing foreign aggression and internal strife [Organization of African Unity (OAU) Convention Regarding the Specific Aspects of Refugee Problems in Africa of 1967 and the Cartagena Declaration of 1984].

Nor does the 1951 Convention's definition address **gender-based persecution**—specifically (as UNHCR's 1991 "Guidelines on the Protection of Refugee Women" puts it), "the claim of refugee status by women fearing harsh or inhumane treatment because of having transgressed their society's laws or customs regarding the role of women." Recognizing the "difficulties" such a claim presents under the Convention, UNHCR's "Guidelines" recommend that states "consider women so persecuted as a 'social group.'" The most notable progress toward implementing this recommendation has been made in Canada, where in March 1993 the head of the country's Immigration and Refugee Board issued guidelines encouraging those who adjudicate asylum claims to consider gender-related persecution as one ground for granting refugee status ["Guidelines Issued by the Chairperson Pursuant to Section 65(3) of the *Immigration Act*—Women Refugee Claimants Fearing Gender-Related Persecution," Ottawa, 3/9/93].

Internally Displaced Persons

There are approximately 24 million internally displaced persons in the world today ["Comprehensive Study of the Secretary-General's Representative on Internally Displaced Persons," E/CN.4/1993/35]. These people have fled their homes for many of the reasons that people flee across borders, but, because no international border has been crossed, they are not protected by the international refugee system. Located as they are within their own country's borders, internally displaced persons are apt to face many of the same dangers that forced them to flee their homes in the first place; and it is their own governments—often the very source of their problems—that must be relied on to provide help or to permit outside assistance into the country.

Although internally displaced persons do not fall within UNHCR's purview, the agency is often called upon to put its expertise to use in assisting them. In Afghanistan, northern Iraq, Ethiopia, and Central America, UNHCR repatriation programs have included in their target population the internally displaced persons who now live in the areas to which refugees are returning. In other cases—the former Yugoslavia and Sri Lanka among them—the U.N. Secretary-General has explicitly requested UNHCR to address the needs of this population.

At the request of the U.N. Commission on Human Rights at its 1992 session, the Secretary-General designated a representative to conduct a study of the **human rights dimension of internal displacement** [1992/73]. The study was submitted to the Commission in January 1993 [E/CN.4/1993/35], and in March the Commission requested that the Secretary-General's representative continue his work for two years, "with a view to identify . . . ways and means for improved protection for and assistance to internally displaced persons" [1993/95], and governments are called upon to extend invitations for country visits by the representative "where appropriate." These visits will provide the Secretary-General, the General Assembly, and the Commission on Human Rights with a direct channel of information about the human rights situation of internally displaced persons.

Repatriation

The cessation of conflict on many Cold War battlefields has allowed the UNHCR to implement massive voluntary repatriation programs in various parts of the world. During 1992 approximately 1.8 million Afghans returned home from Pakistan and Iran; 249,000 Cambodians returned from Thailand; and 100,000 Somalis returned from Ethiopia/Eritrea. These people returned voluntarily either through formal programs administered by UNHCR or spontaneously, outside of any formal repatriation channels [U.S. Committee for Refugees, World Refugee Survey 1993].

UNHCR's experience with repatriating over a million-and-a-half refugees during 1992 indicates the difficulty of deciding **when refugees may safely return home**. In the case of such heavily mined countries as Cambodia and Afghanistan, there is obviously considerable risk at any stage. In the case of 2,480 exiles who returned to Guatemala from Mexico in January 1993 [U.N. press release REF/1010, 1/20/93], there is the reality of continuing conflict and only scant possibility of obtaining land to live on. At present, UNHCR is preparing a voluntary repatriation operation that will bring 1.1 million Mozambican refugees home from Malawi, Zimbabwe, Swaziland, Zambia, and Tanzania over the next three years—a home where homelessness is already endemic, where 2 million landmines dot the landscape, and where there is no infrastructure to speak of [REF/1024, 5/4/93].

In **Central America**, repatriation has received increased attention in recent years as peace negotiations in the region advance. UNHCR regional offices report that, since 1989, some 119,000 refugees have returned to their homes, primarily in Nicaragua and El Salvador. These returns have been facilitated by a regional process known as **CIREFCA** after the International Conference on Central American Refugees that launched the process in 1989. In follow-up meetings at the regional and national levels, governments of the region, international agencies, non-governmental organizations, and donor countries have discussed durable solutions for refugees, returnees, and internally displaced persons. The CIREFCA process has been successful in the political sphere by promoting dialogue among divergent sectors, and in the economic sphere by attracting funding for specific projects. In July 1993, as CIREFCA moves into its final year, the coordination of this process will be transferred from UNHCR to the U.N. Development Programme (UNDP), giving greater emphasis to the reintegration of returnees, reconstruction of war-torn societies, and the transition from relief to development.

At a time when the sheer volume of refugees adds to UNHCR's challenge in carrying out its primary role—that of protecting the right of refugees to seek asylum and the refugees' right not to be forcefully returned to their countries of origin—the High Commissioner's Office is increasingly involved in efforts to identify and address the root causes of refugee flows. Said the High Commissioner recently: "The magnitude of the challenges clearly exceeds the capacity of UNHCR alone" [statement of Ms. Ogata to the Executive Committee of the High Commissioner's Program (EXCOM), 10/5/92]. In recognition of the need for a comprehensive approach to refugee problems, EXCOM called upon the High Commissioner "to continue to seek expanded cooperation with [international] bodies, such as UNDP, UNICEF, WFP [World Food Programme], FAO [Food and Agriculture Organization of the United Nations], UNEP [U.N. Environment Programme], the Centre for Human Rights, the Commission on Human Rights, IOM [International Organization of Migration] and ICRC [International Committee of the Red Cross], and thereby, *inter alia*, to promote broadened awareness of the link between refugees and human rights, as well as development and environmental issues" [A.AC.96/804].

3. Health

By Haseena J. Enu

The World Health Organization (WHO) continues to make progress toward its goal—"the attainment by all peoples of the highest possible level of health"—but recent political and economic developments have changed "the road and the road conditions," said WHO Director-General Hiroshi Nakajima in January. That road, he warned the WHO Executive Board, is even rougher than before [press release WHO/3, 1/18/93]. **WHO,** a U.N. specialized agency, is the coordinating body for international efforts to protect and promote human health. Among those efforts are the prevention and eradication of infectious diseases, the development of national health care systems, and the dispatch of humanitarian relief in emergency situations.

At its January 1993 meeting, the Executive Board gave considerable attention to the preliminary report of the year-old "Working Group on the WHO Response to Global Changes." That report, analyzing various aspects of the agency's mission and structure, concludes that both WHO and its member states have not worked effectively enough at achieving the goal of "**Health for All by the Year 2000**," established as a WHO priority in 1977.

New realities and new perceptions have given rise to WHO's "**New Health Paradigm**"—a flexible and "multidisciplinary" framework for public health action that recognizes the difficulty of upholding the fundamental right to health in the absence of a certain level of economic and social development. According to this paradigm, individuals, families, and communities are ultimately responsible for their own health needs, but governments must recognize that their policies have a significant effect on the quality of life for their citizens and on the quality of health care they receive. WHO's primary role will be to provide direct support to member states, particularly those in greatest need, as they begin implementing national health-for-all strategies. Addressing the May 1993 meeting of WHO's governing World Health Assembly, Dr. Nakajima called for an international health partnership—between WHO and its member states, among member states, and between North and South—in the recognition that no single entity, working alone, can achieve major improvements in health care [Xinhua General News Service, 5/4/93].

WHO member states opened that May 1993 Assembly in Geneva by voting overwhelmingly to **bar the Federal Republic of Yugoslavia (Serbia and Montenegro) from all work of the organization** [UPI, 5/3/93]. The resolution, sponsored by the European Community, was based in part on an earlier decision of the U.N. General Assembly to prevent the rump Yugoslav Republic from continuing automatically the membership of the splintered former Socialist Federal Republic of Yugoslavia. The Health Assembly stressed that the resolution was without prejudice to the continuation of WHO's humanitarian assistance to affected populations in all parts of the former Yugoslavia [ibid.].

Among its administrative decisions at Geneva, the 1993 World Health Assembly voted to confirm Dr. Nakajima for a second five-year term as WHO's Director-General, despite active opposition from the Western nations and an external audit's findings of irregularities in the awarding of contracts to Executive Board members. The size of the negative vote—the final tally was 93–58—indicates that an even wider group of member states joined in criticizing Dr. Nakajima's leadership [*The New York Times*, 3/3/93 and 5/6/93].

Disease Control

The Assembly also discussed WHO's continuing efforts, in concert with UNICEF, to achieve universal immunization of children under five years of age against six childhood killer diseases. The **Children's Vaccine Initiative (CVI)**, an arm of the Expanded Programme on Immunization, involves the mobilization of U.N. agencies, public and private foundations, private industry, and bilateral aid programs to attain one of the major goals articulated at the World Summit for Children in 1990: a one-third reduction in the mortality of infants and children under five by the year 2000. At the annual meeting of the Consultative Group of the CVI held in November 1992, two CVI task forces reported that a comprehensive data base of global vaccine production and quality-control capacities is being compiled and that preliminary analysis is already providing guidance for investment strategies to assure that affordable vaccines are available for all children and on a financially sustainable basis. It is estimated that the deaths of some 8–9 million children could be averted each year with the further development, improvement, and application of appropriate vaccines [WHO Features 170, 11/92].

Having wiped out smallpox in 1977 through such an immunization campaign, WHO is now seeking a triumph over **polio**. Exactly 13,201 cases were reported to WHO in 1991—a 60% decrease since 1988. A recent Executive Board resolution reaffirms that the goal of eradication by the year 2000 is achievable, and it called on U.N. and government agencies to lend support to countries committed to eradication. An outbreak of polio in the Netherlands earlier this year, however, underscores the dangers of incomplete immunization. Most of those affected were members of a religious group that rejects immunization on principle [*The InterDependent*, Spring 1993]. "As long as even small pockets of unvaccinated persons exist, even the richest countries will be at risk of sudden outbreaks of polio," said Dr. R.H. Henderson, Assistant Director-General of WHO [press release WHO/16, 2/26/93].

Continuing its fight against the spread of communicable diseases, WHO declared **tuberculosis** a global emergency this year, warning that this curable disease will claim 30 million lives in the next decade unless immediate steps are taken to curb its spread [U.N. press release H/2795, 4/26/93]. Every year, 8 million people develop TB, and among the factors in the spread of the disease is the modern transport that carries business travelers and migrants to far-off destinations in hours. What is more, there is now clear evidence that HIV infection permits the activation of tuberculosis in those with previously inactive cases by weakening their natural defenses, and there is evidence too that tuberculosis may speed the progression to AIDS in the HIV patient. WHO experts say that public policy neglect, demographic factors, and poorly organized national control programs are responsible for the resurgence of the disease itself [ibid.].

Health and Environment

Environment-related infectious diseases remain the most serious health threat in the developing world—and water-borne diseases in particular. Each year more than a million people die from malaria, perhaps the deadliest of all tropical diseases, and 100 million more are infected [WHO Features 169, 10/92]. Although WHO declared in 1955 that the disease would soon be eradicated, today the number of cases is on the rise, and most notably in Southeast Asia and Africa, where malarial areas are being opened to human habitation and various strains have developed resistance to once-curative drugs. In Cambodia, for example, a serious, drug-resistant form of malaria threatens the 16,000 members of the U.N. peacekeeping force as well as the hundreds of thousands of returning refugees [U.N. press release H/2777, 3/17/92]. At an October 1992 ministerial conference on malaria in Amsterdam, WHO administrators described a new strategy based on controlling the disease rather than on eliminating the malaria-carrying mosquito [WHO Features 169, 10/92].

In response to these continuing threats to health, and with the June 1992 Earth Summit serving as catalyst, WHO developed a **Global Strategy for Health and the Environment**. This attempt to "provide a new orientation for multi-disciplinary and multi-sectoral efforts to ensure that health considerations are fully incorporated and are placed at the core of all development and environmental activities, from policy planning to project implementation, monitoring, and evaluation" [press release WHO/2, 1/15/93] engages every health issue—from primary health care to pollution, from disease prevention and control to chemical safety. The first national action plans will take the form of pilot projects in a small number of countries yet to be identified [ibid.].

The environmental and medical fallout from the 1987 **Chernobyl nuclear power plant accident** is still being calculated. A recent report of the International Programme on the Health Effects of the Chernobyl Accident (IPHECA), established in 1991 to assist health authorities in Russia, Belarus, and Ukraine, notes that children who were exposed to radiation from the Chernobyl plant are developing thyroid cancer sooner and in larger numbers than expected (the radioactive iodine said to be causing this is mostly ingested through cow's milk). The study also reports nutritional problems that are a result not of eating local produce but of avoiding it—out of fear that it has been contaminated [*The New York Times*, 9/3/92].

AIDS Pandemic

Perhaps the greatest challenge to the world health partnership, however, is the continuing spread of HIV/AIDS. WHO's **Global Programme on AIDS**—the body that is directing and coordinating the global response to the AIDS crisis—estimates that 2.5 million people have developed the disease and that another 13 million (a million of them children) are infected with the AIDS virus [press release WHO/8, 1/29/93]. Nor is the challenge primarily medical, since socio-economic factors are involved in preventing the transmission of HIV and in dealing with the effects on vulnerable populations—notably women and children. And statistics show that AIDS is spreading in Asia at the same rate it spread in Africa a decade ago. For now, Africa remains the region that is the hardest hit; in some of its cities as many as a third of adults are infected with HIV [*Global Child Health News and Review* 1, no. 1, 1993, p. 3].

The May 1993 World Health Assembly gave unanimous approval to a resolution calling for a study of the benefits of a proposed joint **U.N. Programme on AIDS** [*The New York Times*, 5/15/93]. The study will identify and explore the uses of existing financial and human resources, consider how to develop new ones, and examine what is known about HIV/AIDS, using that information to improve the U.N. system's efforts at combatting the disease. As directed by the resolution, four areas will be singled out for attention: the anticipated growth and consequences of the AIDS pandemic over the next two decades; the likely level of resources available to combat it during the next single decade; the practical arrangements for establishing a U.N. AIDS program, including management systems and structures; and the need for global leadership to coordinate a response to the pandemic [press release WHA/15, 5/14/93]. The results of the study will be presented to the WHO Executive Board in January 1994.

Although some 15 experimental vaccines are now undergoing safety tests, WHO considers it unlikely that a vaccine capable of preventing the disease will be available before the end of the decade [ibid.]. WHO itself has initiated a series of mass field trials of three groups of AIDS vaccines in order to isolate, collect, and identify locally dominant strains of the virus. Samples will be supplied to vaccine manufacturers to assist them in developing appropriate products [*The InterDependent*, Fall 1992]. The recent discovery of an AIDS-like illness in which there is no detectable evidence of HIV is likely to complicate the search for a cure. Reported cases of this "new" illness are rare, but there is no underestimating the threat an undetectable virus would pose to national blood supplies. WHO has urged public health researchers to share their data so that more can be learned about the disease [*The New York Times*, 7/22/92].

WHO has chosen "Time to Act" as the theme for **World AIDS Day** 1993, traditionally observed on December 1. "If we want to alter the course of this dreadful pandemic, the time to act is now," said Dr. Michael Merson, head of WHO's Global Programme on AIDS [U.N. press release H/2796, 4/27/93].

Malnutrition

The recently published findings of a WHO study on **malnutrition and diet-related illnesses** indicate that death rates from the so-called "life-style diseases"—heart conditions, cancer, and diabetes—are also on the rise, and not only in lands of ease and plenty but in the developing world as well. A **Conference on Nutrition** in Rome last December, co-sponsored by WHO and the Food and Agriculture Organization (FAO) of the United Nations and attended by many ministers of health and agriculture, adopted a **World Declaration expressing determination to eliminate hunger and many of the causes of malnutrition**. The conferees called on the United Nations to consider declaring an International Decade of Food and Nutrition, noting the urgency of achieving the Declaration's objectives [press release ICN/5, 12/11/92].

On another nutrition front—the feeding of infants—WHO has announced considerable success. By the end of 1992, over 120 developing countries had discontinued the practice of distributing free or low-cost supplies of **infant formula** to maternity wards and hospitals—a marketing practice demonstrated to contribute to a cycle of infection and malnutrition among the newborn. WHO experts also report that a considerable number of both developing and industrialized countries have initiated a process of evaluating and certifying hospitals as "baby friendly." Under the **Baby Friendly Hospital Initiative**, authorities train staff and modify hospital procedures to remove barriers to breast-feeding; WHO estimates that effective breast-feeding could prevent some 1.5 million infant deaths every year [press release WHO/10, 2/2/92].

Other Health Issues

Turning to **traditional practices that affect the health of women and children**, the 1993 World Health Assembly adopted a resolution calling for the elimination of such practices as child marriage, dietary limitations during pregnancy, and female genital mutilation [press release WHA/15, 5/14/93].

WHO's **Action Programme on Essential Drugs**, established a decade ago, has prepared a Model List of Essential Drugs containing nearly 270 drugs covering most health needs. Meeting at WHO headquarters in Geneva in February 1993, the Management Advisory Committee of this WHO program reaffirmed the agency's commitment to assuring the availability of such drugs throughout the world. WHO estimates that half of the world's inhabitants have no access to the most basic drugs, and that "75% of the world's population consumes less than 20% of the drugs on a market recently valued at around 170 thousand million US dollars" [press release WHO/15, 2/25/93]. Many of the products on the "Model List" are no longer under patent, it is pointed out, and can now be produced by different manufacturers.

In March 1993, WHO published its first comprehensive report on "**Drug Use and Sport**," based on information from a variety of national programs, evaluation studies, and interviews. The overriding conclusion is that the use of drugs in sport is on the increase and that more should be done to counter this trend [press release WHO/19, 3/19/93].

Devoting **World Health Day 1993** to the prevention of accidents and injuries, WHO drew attention to the fact that at least 3.5 million people die each year from such occurrences, many of them avoidable. The slogan of the day was "Handle Life with Care: Prevent Violence and Negligence."

WHO is increasingly called upon to respond to health **emergencies** throughout the world, coordinating its efforts with a wide variety of U.N. bodies. A WHO mission to war-torn Somalia in winter 1992–93, for example, sought to prevent death or blindness related to Vitamin A deficiency. In the course of this mission WHO nutrition experts delivered Vitamin A supplements to children in refugee camps and WHO doctors trained Somalian health workers to assess and monitor associated problems [press release WHO/5, 1/22/93].

4. Drug Abuse, Production, and Trafficking

By Rebecca M. Rosenblum

With no end to the international battle against drug abuse and trafficking in sight, the United Nations has focused its attention on achieving a "critical mass" of involvement in combatting a problem that transcends national boundaries and leaves almost no society untouched. At the U.N.'s **International Day against Drug Abuse and Illicit Trafficking** in 1992, the Secretary-General emphasized that international drug control mechanisms are not enough. "Every effort must be made to tap the energy and determination which exists at the local level among families, teachers, religious leaders, social and health-care workers to combat the scourge of drug abuse," he counseled [nar/inf.lett./1992/3].

Echoing much the same theme, Executive Director Giorgio Giacomelli of the **United Nations International Drug Control Programme (UNDCP)**—the umbrella agency established in 1991 to coordinate U.N. drug control activities—highlighted the need for the international community "to work together in a new partnership with society as a whole" to address the corrosive effects of drug abuse and illicit trafficking upon an ever-increasing number of nations [ibid.]. And Giacomelli emphasized his agency's continued reliance upon cooperation and coordination not only at the international, regional, and subregional levels but also among the U.N. agencies—the World Health Organization and the U.N. Development Programme (UNDP) are prominent examples—with the resources and experience for tackling the broader social, economic, and political problems that helped to create the drug epidemic and are now exacerbated by it ["World Chronicle," Program No. 489, recorded 11/5/92].

Such appeals for a more vigorous and broad-based effort in combatting drug abuse and trafficking were accompanied by discomforting news of regional trends from the **International Narcotics Control Board (INCB)**—the body of experts that monitors the legal production of drugs and their movement from source to consumer, tracing illegal diversions of substances covered in the 1988 Convention against Illicit Traffic in Narcotic Drugs and Psychotropic Substances. Indeed, the 1992 annual report of the INCB provides an almost unremittingly grim rundown of the worldwide drug situation.

In **Africa**, the report notes, a worsening abuse and trafficking situation—cocaine use, intravenous heroin abuse, and the traffic in *khat* are all on the increase—has added to a climate of political and economic instability. **East and Southeast Asia**, despite increasing cooperation between neighboring countries to control trafficking, remains a major supplier of illicit heroin, with China facing growing addiction and trafficking problems and signs that Vietnam may be next. Along the Indo-Pakistan border of **South Asia**, smuggling of heroin bound for Europe continues unabated; and in the **Near and Middle East**, the illicit cultivation and production of cannabis and opium, the clandestine manufacture of morphine and heroin, an explosion of heroin addiction among Afghan refugees, and a sharp rise in drug abusers in Pakistan are only a few of the problems cited [U.N. press release SOC/NAR/628, 2/10/93].

The INCB report also notes that while drug abuse in the **former Soviet Union**, the **former Yugoslavia**, and the countries of **Eastern Europe** has not yet reached the level in Western Europe, only a concerted effort to integrate these regions into the international drug control system will prevent international drug traffickers from taking advantage of chaotic conditions to make greater inroads into a vulnerable region. The former Soviet-bloc countries do, in fact, have a daunting task ahead of them. Political liberalization and the easing of social controls have led to increased use of psychoactive substances. And, as pointed out in a recent piece in *Foreign Policy*, "Uncertain economic conditions, weak law enforcement, permissive drug laws, unprotected frontiers and porous financial systems further bolster the rapid rise of a new narcotics industry" [Rensselaer W. Lee III and Scott B. MacDonald, "Drugs in the East," Spring 1993].

On a slightly more positive note, the INCB report indicates that major law enforcement efforts undertaken in **South and Central America and the Caribbean** have resulted in a considerable reduction of drug cultivation and trafficking in the region, and that an increased level of cooperation among regional governments has had the effect of reducing money-laundering schemes and of helping to locate viable economic substitutes for traditional drug crops. The strengthening of control mechanisms has had a discouraging flip side, though: Trafficking organizations no longer concentrate on any one country but have been spreading throughout the region. The result has been a continued growth of drug abuse in that region [U.N. press release SOC/NAR/628, 2/10/93].

The INCB continues to reject unequivocably any proposal favoring full or partial **legalization of drugs** used for nonmedical purposes. In its view, "legalization advocates have not yet presented a sufficiently comprehensive, coherent or viable alternative to the present system of international drug abuse control." Furthermore, said INCB, "permitting the recreational use of drugs would have a substantial and irreversible adverse impact on public health, social well-being and the international drug control system" [E/INCB/1992/1].

During the 47th Session of the General Assembly, the Third (Social, Humanitarian, and Cultural) Committee was briefed by UNDCP Executive Director Giacomelli on the efforts of his agency over the past year. Essential short-term priorities have included encouraging member states to ratify the U.N. drug control conventions as speedily as possible, helping governments to update and harmonize national legislation relating to drug control issues, promoting international cooperation on the persistent problem of money laundering, and establishing a more effective system of control over the so-called "**chemical precursors**" that are used in the illicit manufacture of narcotic drugs or psychotropic substances.

The UNDCP also turned its attention to developing a coherent approach to **subregional initiatives**, including two programs to be carried out by the governments of China, Myanmar, and Thailand—to reduce opium cultivation and heroin trafficking along common border areas, and to lower drug abuse and associated HIV/AIDS infection among hill tribes [A/C.3/47/SR.27]. These types of efforts reflect a decided shift in the UNDCP's operational focus to subregional activities, as was discussed and agreed upon at a technical consultation on drug issues among a wide range of donor and recipient countries in Southwest Asia, September 21–31, 1992 [nar/inf.lett./1992/4].

Based upon the recommendations of the Third Committee, the General Assembly adopted six resolutions on narcotic drugs. Among the most noteworthy of these was its "Examination of the Status of International Cooperation against the Illicit Production, Sale, Demand, Traffic and Distribution of Narcotics and Psychotropic Substances" [A/Res/47/99], which calls for four high-level plenary meetings to be held during the 48th Session. These meetings are intended to provide an opportunity for evaluating the implementation of the **Global Programme of Action** [A/Res/S-17/2] adopted by the General Assembly during its **Special Session on Drugs in 1990**. Among the subjects considered will be measures to enhance international cooperation in programs of alternative rural development and the eradication of the growing and dangerous links between terrorist groups, drug traffickers, and their paramilitary gangs [nar/inf.lett./1992/5].

The other five resolutions adopted by the 47th General Assembly stressed still other drug control and trafficking-related issues. All states that have not yet done so were urged to ratify the **1988 Convention against Illicit Traffic in Narcotic Drugs and Psychotropic Substances** (the number that had completed the process stood at 77 in May 1993), and to provide political and financial support to UNDCP for expanding and strengthening its operational activities and technical cooperation with developing countries [ibid.].

The **Commission on Narcotic Drugs**—the main policy-making organ for international drug control, reporting to ECOSOC—was thus confronted with a formidable agenda when it convened its 36th session in Vienna from March 29 to April 7, 1993. These ten days of intensive meetings—during which the Commission reviewed reports by the U.N. Secretary-General, the Director of the UNDCP, and the INCB—yielded a wide range of resolutions that addressed many of the concerns articulated by the international community over the past year.

On the subject of coordinated activities against **money laundering**, the Commission requested the UNDCP to continue studying ways of "controlling the proceeds from illicit traffic in narcotic drugs and psychotropic substances" and to pinpoint the various activities of criminal organizations involved in drug trafficking. On the subject of the ecological damage caused by illicit cultivation, the Commission urged the UNDCP to design and implement **crop survey systems** in vulnerable areas. On the volatile issue of **arms trafficking**, member states were requested to consider establishing or improving appropriate controls on arms transfers and explosives, based on the acknowledged link between the illicit traffic in arms and the drug-trafficking industry [U.N. press release SOC/NAR/646].

The Commission also endorsed the INCB's opposition to legalizing all uses of narcotic drugs and urged governments to continue to limit the use of such drugs to medical and scientific purposes, as permitted by the relevant conventions. A lone voice of dissent was that of the Representative of the Netherlands, who indicated that his government's legalization of "soft drugs" had "reached a generally acceptable level of containment of drug abuse-associated social and individual problems, if not succeeding in the eradication of drug abuse" [SOC/NAR/640].

Finally, in accordance with prevailing sentiment in the international community, governments were urged to develop a balanced and comprehensive approach to **demand reduction**, giving priority to prevention, treatment, research, social integration, and the training of professional staff [SOC/NAR/646].

Further evaluation of the prospects for international cooperation in the global drug battle awaits the high-level plenary meetings scheduled to take place during the General Assembly's 48th Session.

5. The Status of Women

By Donna C. Dayton

On the agenda of ECOSOC's **Commission on the Status of Women (CSW)** when the CSW met in Vienna in March 1993 for its 37th annual session was **violence against women**—a topic to be considered at the **World Conference on Human Rights** three months later. The definition of such abuse, prepared by a working group of the Commission that has been drafting an international instrument on the subject, includes not only physical, sexual, and psychological violence within the family but also sexual harassment at work and violence condoned or perpetrated by the state.

Overshadowing the issue of domestic violence at CSW's Vienna meeting this spring was "the use of **systematic rape as a 'weapon of war'** " in former Yugoslavia [U.N. press release WOM 696, 3/25/93]. A CSW resolution condemned such "abhorrent practices" in that region [ibid.]. The governmental representatives at the human rights conference in June will be voting on a document that calls, among other things, for the punishment of the perpetrators [HR/3813, 5/10/93; for a discussion of the human rights conference's Vienna Declaration see Section 1 of this chapter]. At the same time, a Commission of Experts formed by the Security Council [S/Res/780 (1992)] is investigating breaches of the Geneva Convention on the treatment of civilians in time of war. The CSW, for its part, expressed the hope that the Security Council would establish a **tribunal** to try those accused of such breaches—and that the tribunal would "reflect gender balance" in its composition [U.N. press release WOM 696, 3/25/93]. Security Council Resolution 827 of May 25, 1993, formally established a tribunal for trying serious violations of international humanitarian law, and U.S. Representative Madeleine Albright told members of the Council that the Clinton administration was determined to ensure that women prosecutors and jurists have a prominent role in the proceedings [U.N. press release SC/5624, 5/25/93].

The 45-member CSW—founded in 1946 to monitor the status of women around the world and point to areas for immediate attention—considered the issue of violence under the heading of "equality," one of three interrelated "priority themes" (the others are development and peace) of the **Forward-Looking Strategies for the Advancement of Women to the Year 2000**. These Strategies, contained in the declaration of the world conference in Nairobi that capped the **U.N. Decade for Women (1975–85)**, shortly became the official U.N. guide for national and international action on behalf of women [A/Res/40/108].

Other issues of political violence considered under the "equality" theme involved women and children in the Occupied Territories [U.N. press release WOM 699, 3/29/93]; migrant women [ibid.], such as those whose abuse at the hands of employers in some host countries has made recent headlines; and women and children under apartheid [WOM/698, 3/25/93]. Equality was also the heading under which the session considered the need for women's awareness of their legal rights. Integration of women in development planning was considered under the "development" theme and women's role in the military and in decision-making was considered under "peace." The General Assembly's comprehensive annual resolution on the Forward-Looking Strategies tied these themes together [A/Res/47/95]. A separate resolution on the subject of violence against migrant women asks the Secretary-General to give an oral report to the 48th Session about the steps being taken to assure the migrants' well-being [A/Res/47/96].

According to the provisional agenda the CSW drafted for its next annual session—number 38—it will be looking at the issue of equal pay for equal work; at some problems faced by rural women; at population issues; and at such health matters as the impact of drug abuse and AIDS on women [WOM 699, 3/29/93].

Looking ahead too, the CSW examined the proposed systemwide **medium-term plan for the advancement of women for the period 1996–2001** prepared by the Secretary-General at ECOSOC's request. (The first review of the plan that covers the period 1990–95 had called "insufficient" the "pace of implementation" of the Strategies [E/1993/43].) The newest plan (which sees continuing obstacles to women's full participation in society, despite "significant advances in reducing legal and attitudinal bases of discrimination" against them [E/1993/43]) will be examined by the Fourth World Conference on Women in 1995.

CSW is the primary preparatory body for this next **Conference on Women** (subtitle: "Action for Equality, Development, and Peace"), to be held in Beijing on the tenth anniversary of the Nairobi meeting. (The first Asian country to host one of these conferences on the status of women, China was ranked 101st in gender equality on the latest "Human Development Index" [UNDP, 1993]. Japan was No. 1.) The General Assembly and the CSW had asked the Secretary-General to appoint a woman to head the 1995 Conference by the end of 1992, and this he did, naming Gertrude Mongella of Tanzania. Ms. Mongella, then Tanzania's High Commissioner to India, has held high-level posts in several government ministries, including that of Minister of State responsible for women's affairs [U.N. press release SG/A/519, 12/4/92].

There will be several regional preparatory meetings in 1994 to set the stage for the Conference's evaluation of national progress in implementing the Forward-Looking Strategies and to draft a "Platform for Action" to reflect changing economic, social, and political conditions [*WEDO News & Views*, 4/93]. A newsletter, *Conference 95*, will be issued biannually, in six languages, beginning in June 1993.

Scheduled for distribution at the 1995 Conference on Women is the third "World Survey on the Role of Women in Development" (previous surveys bear the dates 1985 and 1989), which the Secretary-General is preparing at the General Assembly's request [A/Res/44/77] and a preliminary version of which will be submitted to the 48th Assembly through the CSW and ECOSOC. The final version, available in 1994, is intended as one of the Conference's principal documents [E.1993/16, A/48/70]. An "updated edition" of *The World's Women, 1970–1990*, first published in 1991, will also be available to Conference participants [A/Res/47/95].

The Conference organizer is the **Division for the Advancement of Women**, which serves as the secretariat of CSW as well as the secretariat of the **Committee on the Elimination of Discrimination against Women (CEDAW)**—the 23-member expert body that monitors implementation of the **1979 Convention on the Elimination of Discrimination against Women.** The Convention, often described as a Bill of Rights for women, had been ratified by 123 countries (the United States not yet among them) by May 1993.

Sitting for its 11th annual session, in 1992, CEDAW had addressed the issue of violence against women from its perspective as treaty monitor, noting that "not all the reports of States parties adequately reflected the close connection between the discrimination against women, gender-based violence, and violations of human rights and fundamental freedoms" [A/47/38]. Among its recommendations were better fact-finding and reporting of the incidence of violence, effective national measures to overcome attitudes and practices that breed such violence, and measures to protect the victims and punish the perpetrators [ibid.]. The General Assembly "supported" these CEDAW recommendations; requested that the Secretary-General "ensure adequate support to CEDAW from within the existing budget"; and "supported" too the Committee's desire to extend to three weeks, up from two, its 12th and 13th sessions [A/Res/47/94]. At the Assembly's request, the Secretary-General will report to the General Assembly's 49th Session and the CSW's 39th on developments in these areas.

At its 12th session, held between January 18 and February 5, 1993, CEDAW spent a major portion of its time reviewing the reports of 11 states parties on four continents. Requesting the Secretariat to prepare an annual report on "ways and means of improving the work of the Committee" (based, among other things, on "developments elsewhere in the human rights regime"), it asked that two more of its annual sessions—numbers 14 and 15—be extended to three weeks to draw down the pile of reports [CEDAW/C/1993/L.1/Add.13].

Two *autonomous* U.N. agencies concerned with raising women's social and economic status—the U.N. International Research and Training Institute for the Advancement of Women (INSTRAW) and the U.N. Development Fund for Women (UNIFEM)—were active participants in the preparations for June 1992's **U.N. Conference on Environment and Development (UNCED)** and helped to ensure the integration of women's concerns in UNCED's two principal documents: the Rio Declaration and Agenda 21. Ireland's Prime Minister, Albert Reynolds, spoke about women's role in sustainable development when he stood up to address the government leaders gathered in Rio. "Agenda 21 rightly underscores the special role of women in caring for the environment," he said, adding: "Guardianship of the environment by women is an important and positive force, and one which we must harness in our various environment action programmes" [A/Conf.151/26/Rev.1, Vol. III].

It was **UNIFEM** that contributed a Special Advisor on Women, Environment and Development to the UNCED process, naming Senior Program Advisor Dr. Filomina Chioma Steady of Sierra Leone. **INSTRAW**, for its part, had a ready supply of information on women's role in, e.g., water supply and sanitation. **Agenda 21's Chapter 24**—"Global Action for Women towards Sustainable and Equitable Development"—makes explicit women's role in sustainable development, highlights the fact that environmental degradation has an extreme effect upon the lives of poor women, and encourages an increase in the proportion of women as "decision-makers, planners, technical advisors, managers, and extension workers in environment and development fields" [ibid., Vol. I]. The General Assembly "welcome[d]" the recommendations contained in Chapter 24 and "urge[d] governments to consider nominating women as representatives to the Commission on Sustainable Development"—the new body that will monitor implementation of Agenda 21 and promote coordination among the U.N.'s economic and development bodies [A/Res/47/95]. In a subsequent resolution the Assembly "recogniz[ed] the critical role of rural women as food producers and architects of household food security" [A/Res/47/174].

A 300-page report on one aspect of the working lives of women in the industrialized world—*Combating Sexual Harassment at Work*—was issued in winter 1992 by the International Labour Organisation [ILO, *Con-*

ditions at Work Digest 11, no. 1, 1992]. This first international survey on the subject states that as many as 1 in 12 women in the First World are forced out of their jobs by such practices [*The Boston Globe*, 12/1/92]. The United States, cited as the first nation to denounce and prosecute **sexual harassment**, is also cited as lagging behind when it comes to taking a preventive approach to the problem [ibid.].

On March 8, the traditional **International Women's Day**, representatives of the **Group on Equal Rights for Women in the U.N.** met with the Secretary-General to discuss the treatment of women in the Secretariat. Boutros Boutros-Ghali "affirmed his commitment to achieving a 50:50 ratio of men to women" in senior-level positions by the United Nations's 50th Anniversary in 1995 [*Secretariat News*, 3/93]. (A discussion of the status of women in the Secretariat may be found in Chapter VII of this volume, "Finance and Administration.")

6. Other Social Issues

Children and Youth

By Natalie Blaslov

The youngest and most vulnerable of the U.N.'s constituents—from the moment of conception to teenagehood—are the concern of UNICEF, the U.N. Children's Fund, headquartered in New York. The interests of their older brothers and sisters—youths in the 15-to-24 age bracket—have been looked after traditionally by the **Centre for Social Development and Humanitarian Affairs (CSDHA),** located in the U.N. Office at Vienna (UNOV) and reporting to the Economic and Social Council. On May 30, 1993, following a new round of U.N. Secretariat restructuring, youth programs (as well as the aging and the disability-related programs that are discussed below) came to rest in ECOSOC's newly designated **Department of Policy Coordination and Sustainable Development.**

For those attempting to respond to the needs of children of all ages, 1992 brought a considerable, budget-draining series of "loud" emergencies, as UNICEF Executive Director James P. Grant described the year's headline-making wars and wars-cum-famine in such parts of the world as Eastern Europe and the Horn of Africa. The number of children under five who died during the year as a result of such emergencies was approximately 500,000. Even this figure, Grant points out, is only a small proportion of the 13 million children who die every year, many of them needlessly. These deaths from what UNICEF calls "silent" emergencies—malnutrition, disease, and poverty—claim some 35,000 young lives every day [UNICEF Annual Report 1993].

As of May 1993, 136 states had ratified the U.N.'s 1989 **Convention on the Rights of the Child**—up from 114 the year before. The committee established by the convention to monitor the implementation of its provisions has begun to meet, and at its second (October 1992) session it considered ways to make the monitoring process more efficient [U.N. press release HR/3675, 9/23/93]. In December the General Assembly approved the states parties' recommendation, relayed by the Committee on the Rights of the Child, to hold two committee sessions per year, each of up to three weeks' duration, and to establish a presessional working group [A/Res/47/112]. At the Committee's subsequent session, in January 1993, it began to examine the very first of the reports that the Convention requires of those who ratify it.

The year brought some signs that government leaders were preparing to implement the commitments they had made at the 1990 World Summit for Children: As of February 1993, 137 countries had signed the **World Summit Declaration on the Survival, Protection and Development of Children** and the accompanying **Plan of Action**. Some 75 had already submitted final reports on their plans for a national program of action (NPA) to carry out the Declaration's child-welfare goals, another 30 reports were available in draft form, and at least 32 more were in preparation. The Latin America and Caribbean region and sub-Saharan Africa accounted for the greatest number of completed reports [E/ICEF/1993/12].

The goals—to be reached by the year 2000—include a halving of child malnutrition and maternal mortality rates, a one-third reduction in the death rate of children under five, a safe water supply for all communities, universal availability of family planning services, and a basic education for all children [UNICEF, *State of the World's Children 1993*].

UNICEF estimates that it would cost some $25 billion a year to meet the needs of the world's children in the areas of nutrition, clean water, basic health care, and primary education by the end of this decade. This, notes *State of the World's Children 1993*, is about the same amount "as the support package that the Group of Seven [industrialized countries] agreed on in 1992 for Russia alone," is "significantly less than Europeans will spend this year on wine or Americans on beer," and could save the lives of more than 4 million children in the course of a single year.

Criticized in recent years for not being active enough in **family planning**, UNICEF has devised a medium-term plan of assistance to countries that want to provide information, education, and communication about birth-spacing and "responsible parenthood." This is seen as a complement to UNICEF's "safe-motherhood initiative": prenatal care, sanitary delivery of postnatal services, improved nutrition, and reducing the incidence of sexually transmitted diseases, to name a few [E/ICEF/1993/L.5].

UNICEF, along with the World Health Organization, wrote to all governments to seek their "personal support" for **breastfeeding** and for the "baby-friendly hospital initiative" launched in 1991. By the end of 1992, 122 developing countries had begun to end low-cost or free supplies of breastmilk substitutes. A target date of mid-1994 has been set for completely halting the distribution of such supplies [UNICEF Annual Report 1993].

An increase in the number of humanitarian emergencies, both man-made and natural, is straining UNICEF's budget as well as its Emergency Reserve Fund (renamed the **Emergency Programme Fund** in 1992). In this past year, emergency expenditures increased more than 35% over the previous year and 300% over 1990, reaching $167 million [E/ICEF/1993/2, Part (II)]. Among the regions requiring emergency assistance for the first time was the former Yugoslavia, where aid took the form of blankets, clothing, food, and medical supplies for more than a million children as winter set in. Emergency aid to Africa retained its priority status. For war-ravaged Somalia, UNICEF undertook a 100-day Action Program of accelerated humanitarian assistance in October 1992. It then turned to drought-and-war-ridden Sudan, restarting the relief flights halted a few months before [E/ICEF/1993/11].

The bright side of the picture in Africa, said Executive Director Grant, is that apartheid is being overcome and some wars of long duration—in Angola, Ethiopia, and Mozambique—are ending. "By comparison, many of the challenges that remain—in terms of debt and the situation of children—should be far simpler to solve" [Global Child Health Society (Vancouver), *Global Child Health News & Review* 1, no. 1 (1993)].

In November 1992, 48 African countries and 18 donor countries met to address those challenges at an International Conference on Assistance to African Children, held in Dakar under the auspices of the Organization of African Unity. In the "Consensus of Dakar," African governments pledged to make their NPAs as cost-specific as possible and to restructure the budget of NPAs with an eye to including the needs of women and children. They also spelled out six intermediate goals for child development to be reached by 1995, with the aim of saving perhaps a million lives [UNICEF, *First Call for Children*, 1–3/92]. There were high-level conferences on children on other continents as well [E/ICEF/1993/12].

Youth were on the agenda of the Commission for Social Development's (CSD) 33rd session in February 1993—specifically, the upcoming **tenth anniversary of International Youth Year 1985 (IYY)** and a **World Programme of Action** for young people that will look to the year 2000 and beyond. The Secretary-General had submitted his draft of such an action program to the CSD, which recommended that ECOSOC request the Secretary-General to continue working on his draft, that member states and concerned nongovernmental organizations be urged to prepare national programs of action in anticipation of the anniversary, and that a working group be formed for the purpose of refining the draft Programme [U.N. press release SOC/4245, 2/18/93]. The General Assembly will consider revised drafts at its 49th Session in 1994; the CSD will review the effort at its session in early 1995; and the General Assembly is expected to adopt a final draft at the 50th Session in that anniversary year [E/CN.5/1993/10].

The Secretary-General's second submission to the February CSD session was a draft calendar of activities for the IYY celebration. That calendar has a "preparatory phase" for the period ending 1994 (featuring activities that will raise awareness and stimulate interest) and an "observance phase" that begins in 1995. Whether this latter phase actually "provide[s] an opportunity to initiate substantive measures in favour of youth," it is noted, will depend on the success of the preparatory period [ibid.].

ECOSOC has suggested that those preparing for the IYY anniversary consider a linkup with, among other events, the **International Year of the Family 1994 (IYF)** [ibid.], and the then CSDHA began preparing a program of action for the observance of the year, whose theme is "Family: Resources and Responsibilities in a Changing World." A forum for international nongovernmental organizations concerned with family-related issues, hosted by Malta in late November 1993, will conclude the preparations for the IYF, which will be formally launched by the General Assembly in early December [U.N. press release SOC/4249, 4/12/93].

The **United Nations Educational, Scientific and Cultural Organization (UNESCO)** also sponsors a wide variety of programs aimed at training and empowering young people. Among those currently receiving funds from this U.N. specialized agency are the Baltic Sea Project (with seminars and problem-solving exercises to teach students about taking responsibility for environmental protection) and a series of "Under Twenty" clubs throughout the Caribbean (with family-planning seminars, youth rallies, and cultural activities to combat teen pregnancy and AIDS). A UNESCO-sponsored annual Collective Consultation—the 19th of these is scheduled for Paris in November 1993—seeks to strengthen the partnership among youth, youth organizations, and its own organization [*UNESCO Sources*, 4/93].

Aging

By Natalie Blaslov

Nineteen ninety-two marked the **tenth anniversary of the International Plan of Action on Aging.** Adopted at the **1982 World Assembly on Aging**, the Plan aims not only at meeting the needs of the "elderly" but also at empowering "older persons" to participate fully in society and contribute to it. In the course of the anniversary year there were forums on topical issues, a special U.N. stamp, and an exhibit at U.N. Headquarters. And on October 1, communities around the world celebrated the second annual International Day for the Elderly.

As the celebration was under way, however, the U.N. Secretary-General told the General Assembly that "the broad and ideal goals of the Plan of Action have not been reached over the first decade" [A/47/339]. He stressed the need for a "must-do" attitude toward the Plan by multilateral and governmental agencies, as well as the need for a **positive outlook on aging**—by society as a whole and by older persons themselves [U.N. press release GA/3379, 10/15/92].

The 47th General Assembly observed the anniversary in October with four plenary meetings that took the form of an international conference on aging. This was the first time the Assembly had addressed in plenary session the subject of an **aging world population**. According to recent calculations, the number of elderly (defined as those 60 years of age or older) will have increased sixfold between 1950 and 2025, reaching 1.2 billion in the latter year; and by the end of the present millennium, one person in every ten will be elderly—a situation without historical precedent [CSDHA/UNOV, *The World Ageing Situation 1991*, 1991; U.N. press release AG/64, 10/2/92].

On October 16 the Assembly adopted a **Proclamation on Aging** [A/Res/47/5] in which it urged the international community to promote the implementation of the Plan of Action and to disseminate the **U.N. Principles for Older Persons** adopted in 1991 [see *A Global Agenda: Issues/47]*, and it encouraged national initiatives to "include older persons in their development programs." The same resolution proclaimed **1999** as the **International Year of Older Persons**, "in recognition of humanity's demographic coming of age and the promise it holds for maturing attitudes and capabilities in social, cultural, and spiritual undertakings, not least for global peace and development in the next century."

Responding to the 46th Assembly Session's call for a practical strategy to begin meeting the needs of the elderly over the next decade, the Secretary-General drafted a set of eight "**Global Targets on Ageing for the Year 2001**" and 38 national targets [A/47/339]. The eight are intended to supply help to governments that are setting national targets, generate support for integrating aging into national and international development programs, promote community-based programs for and with the elderly, improve cross-national research on aging, include an item on aging in international events, and facilitate cooperation among nongovernmental as well as intergovernmental organizations, with the suggestion that a global network of senior volunteers be established to aid in social and economic development. The targets were adopted by the General Assembly, which requested the Secretary-General to report to the 48th Session on the progress made in reaching them [A/Res/47/86].

Every year since the adoption of the Plan of Action, the Centre for Social Development and Humanitarian Affairs (CSDHA) of the U.N. Office of Vienna (UNOV)—the U.N. focal point on aging until the Ageing Unit was placed under the Department of Policy Coordination and Sustainable Development this past spring—has monitored its implementation and reported to the Assembly on the progress being made. The more detailed **review and appraisal of the action plan** is a quadrennial exercise, mandated by the Assembly, that begins with a global survey prepared by CSDHA for ECOSOC's Commission for Social Development.

The first two of these every-four-year appraisals—based on replies to a questionnaire submitted to member states, agencies in the U.N. system, and selected international nongovernmental organizations—concluded that policies and programs to meet the needs of older persons were "severely limited." The third review, issued in February 1993, states that some progress has been made but that meeting the objectives of the Plan of Action remains "difficult," particularly in developing countries. This latest survey generated an increased number of replies—77 as opposed to the previous 59—but more than a third of the countries reported that they have yet to establish a national coordinating body for aging [E/CN.5/1993/7].

Commenting on the rate of progress over the decade, Sylvie Bryant, Chief of the New York office of UNOV, noted that "Aging is not perceived as a priority for international action," because "older people do not tend to threaten society" [interview with *A Global Agenda*, 4/14/93]. The Chair of the NGO Committee on Aging in New York seconded that analysis. An issue like peacekeeping tends to take precedence over social issues, Susanne Paul stated, adding: "The tremendous energies and creative resources of older people should be used to bring peace and justice in the world" [interview, 4/14/93].

Additional evidence of the low priority given to such social programs is supplied by the size of the former CSDHA's **regular program budget**—$2,735,700 for 1992–93. Of this, 37% was allocated for aging, and the rest was shared by the programs for youth and for disabled persons. "There is just not any money there," said the Dominican Republic's Alternate Permanent Ambassador, Julia Tavares de Alvarez, who had had a hand in introducing the draft Proclamation on Aging [interview, 4/15/93]. The 47th General Assembly called on the Secretary-General to give all possible support to the Ageing Unit so that it could fulfill its mandate as lead agency for the program on aging in 1992 and beyond [A/Res/47/86]. The same resolution invited contributions to the voluntary **U.N. Trust**

Fund for Aging and the new Banyan Fund, which is "under the patronage" of the U.N.

With one of the new Global Targets in mind, the organizers of the **International Day for the Elderly** have tied the day's themes to major U.N. events—in this case the U.N. World Conference on Human Rights in June (the human rights of older persons) and the International Year for the World's Indigenous People 1993 (the indigenous knowledge and skills of older persons) [A/47/369]. The U.N. International Conference on Population and Development in Cairo and the International Year of the Family are among the events that could set the themes of the October 1 observance in 1994. "Because aging is not a burning problem now does not mean that it will not be," says Bryant of UNOV's New York office, noting that "Demographic growth and age structure" is given a prominent place on the agenda of the Cairo population conference [interview with *A Global Agenda*].

Disabled Persons
By Tamara Babiuk

Marking the conclusion of the U.N. **Decade of the Disabled Persons (1983–92)**, the 47th General Assembly held a total of four plenary meetings on two consecutive days to assess the achievements of the Decade and generate enthusiasm for further efforts on behalf of a ten-year-old **World Programme of Action Concerning Disabled Persons**. The Decade itself had been seen as a means of inaugurating the program—"Towards a Society for All—From Awareness to Action"—which was aimed at preventing disabilities, at rehabilitating those with disabling conditions, and at equalizing opportunity for disabled persons. At the October 12 and 13 plenary meetings, the United Nations Headquarters staff made temporary provisions for wheelchair-bound and/or hearing or visually impaired visitors, constructing access ramps and offering two varieties of sign language interpretation—an Assembly first, noted the event's coordinator [*Secretariat News*, 10/92].

The member state delegates agreed that the Decade was successful in increasing awareness of the needs—and the capacities—of disabled people [A/Res/47/88]; and the Secretary-General affirmed that the philosophy of disability policy had moved "away from charity [and] toward an integrated social development approach," that misconceptions about disability had been clarified, and that the number of organizations run by disabled persons had grown, increasing their influence in the national policy-making process [A/47/415]. At the same time, both the delegates and the Secretary-General agreed, in some regions even the awareness part of the plan had made little headway during the Decade, inhibiting action in the future.

Nor was the problem a lack of will in many cases. U.N. administrators, nongovernmental organizations, and the national delegates themselves stated time and again that the global recession prevented the implementation of even **the most basic projects**—notably those that, by preventing disease and malnutrition, would help to lower the number of people who develop disabilities and later require complex and costly treatment. According to statistics cited at the first plenary session, some 500 million people around the world are affected by one or more forms of disability; 80% of this number live in developing countries; only 1% of those in the latter group have access to basic health, education, and sanitation; and two-thirds of the total are women and children [A/47/PV.34]. (The statistics did not distinguish between those who developed disabling conditions and those who were born with them.)

The ten-year-old **Voluntary Fund for the U.N. Decade for the Disabled** supplied some $3 million in "co-financing grants" for 176 projects aimed at institutional development and improving national capabilities to address disability-related issues [A/47/415]. In July 1992, the U.N. Economic and Social Council approved the Secretary-General's suggestion that the Voluntary Fund continue beyond the decade with a new name, the **U.N. Voluntary Fund on Disability** [1992/276]. The hope is that the private sector, as well as governments, will be moved to contribute generously [ibid.].

In the same report, the Secretary-General recommended devoting more resources to revising the **International Classification of Impairment, Disability and Handicap** so that governments can "harmonize terminologies and definitions" at the national level in carrying out the World Programme of Action. The Secretary-General had been asked by the 46th General Assembly to "finalize the review" of the very words used to express the notions of "impairment," "disability," and "handicap" in each of the U.N.'s six official languages, but by the 47th session the "review" had not been completed. Those associated with the project are aware of the need to remain sensitive to the wishes of disabled persons themselves, notes Bill Hass, Project Manager of Disability-Related Programmes of the U.N. Department of Public Information [interview with *A Global Agenda: Issues/48*, 4/7/93].

The focal point within the U.N. system for disability-related issues and programs was, until May 1993, the **Centre for Social Development and Humanitarian Affairs (CSDHA)** of the U.N. Office at Vienna, and during the Decade of the Disabled Persons, it established a network of communication between and among U.N. agencies, member states, and nongovernmental organizations to aid in planning conferences, in training the administrators of community-based therapy and prevention programs, and in disseminating information and statistics on disability. The 47th General Assembly acknowledged CSDHA's work in this latter area.

Continuing this effort, the Centre announced the first **worldwide data base on disabled persons** (officially, the Clearing-house Database on Disability-related Information, or CLEAR) [U.N. press release DIS/51, 12/4/92]. Statistical data on disability, which in 1960 was available in only 15 countries, is now available in over 55 [U.N. press release DPI/1265, 8/92].

Among the other bodies involved in the effort of translating "awareness" of disability-related problems into "actions" to address those problems include the World Health Organization (WHO) and UNICEF, with strategies and immunization programs to prevent disability; and the International Labour Organisation, with cooperative community-based projects that help disabled persons strengthen their vocational skills and that open up new channels of employment. CSDHA, together with WHO, UNICEF, and the U.N. Development Programme, established an International Initiative against Avoidable Disablement in 1982, which worked throughout the Decade to promote low-cost disability prevention, the training of midwives, the maintenance of health equipment, nutrition, and an adequate supply of such supplements as iodine [A/47/415].

Responding to a call by ECOSOC and the General Assembly, a group of experts met in Vancouver in April 1992 to devise a "**long-term strategy**" to advance the prospects for the Action Programme. A report of their meeting was submitted to the Commission for Social Development in February 1993, which recommended to ECOSOC the development of a draft action plan for implementing the long-term strategy, to be approved by the 48th General Assembly. At the same time, an ad hoc, open-ended working group of the Commission has been elaborating "**Standard Rules on the Equalization of Opportunities for Disabled Persons**" to provide the actual framework for national policies in this area [A/47/PV.33]. This too will be submitted to the 48th General Assembly.

The 32 member states represented on the Commission for Social Development advised in February that the problems of persons with disabilities should not be considered in isolation but, rather, viewed within the context of sustainable development, human rights, and other social and economic issues—and given a place on the agenda of, e.g., the forthcoming Population Conference and the World Conference on Human Rights [E/CN.5/1993/4]. In this way, the Commission pointed out, the needs of disabled persons have a better chance of remaining visible.

Shelter and the Homeless

By Tamara Babiuk

The long-term objective of U.N.'s shelter programs and its **Global Strategy for Shelter (GSS) to the Year 2000** [A/Res/43/180] is to improve the *living environment* of all people—an effort linking human settlements with such concerns as environmental protection and sustainable development. The U.N. Conference on Environment and Development (UNCED), held in June 1992, made that relationship even clearer. **Agenda 21**, UNCED's action plan, contains specific proposals for improving the social, economic, and environmental quality of human settlements, both urban and rural. Land-use planning and management, energy-efficient technology, and the anticipation of natural disasters were among the headings of the chapter devoted to the subject of shelter.

"Shelter for Sustainable Development" was an obvious choice of theme for **World Habitat Day** 1992, observed annually on the first Monday of October. Heralding the celebration, the U.N. Secretary-General had noted that "there can be no sustainable development while there are over 1 million homeless people in the world" [U.N. press release SG/SM/4830/Rev. 1, 10/5/92]. Following up on Agenda 21's call for increased cooperation among international bodies, governments, and nongovernmental organizations in ensuring "shelter for all," representatives of the three groups met in The Hague in November to explore strategies and mechanisms [*Habitat News*, 12/92]. World Habitat Day 1993 will call attention to the role of women—as income earners, homemakers, and heads of household—in the solution of human-settlements problems, picking up an important theme of the Global Strategy [U.N. press release CHS/93/03, 2/11/93].

In 1976 the United Nations sponsored a Conference on Human Settlements in Vancouver, and two years later established the **U.N. Centre for Human Settlements (UNCHS, or Habitat)**, based in Nairobi, as its "focal point for facilitating human settlements solutions" ["UNCHS (Habitat) Profile," n.d.]. Habitat conducts research, organizes regional seminars, disseminates information, and provides technical assistance to some 280 shelter-related programs in over 100 countries—programs that range from the development of an institutional capacity for carrying out the GSS to the implementation of specific shelter projects.

A **second U.N. Conference on Human Settlements (Habitat II),** to be held in Turkey in June 1996 [A/Res/47/180]—the 20th anniversary of the Vancouver meeting—will evaluate ongoing trends in economic and social development that affect national and international planning and management of human settlements, assess the progress of the GSS, and adopt a strategy that looks beyond the millennium [A/Conf.165/PC/2]. A preparatory committee, composed of all member states and the various U.N. agencies that deal with settlements-related issues, began work on the agenda in March 1993. Robert Lloyd Wenman of Canada, elected Chairman, called on the international community "to hear the voices of the homeless of the world, the refugees and displaced persons as well as 'people who live in the streets of our own cities' " [U.N. press release HAB/70, 3/3/93]. The preparatory group is scheduled to meet once in 1994 and again in

1995, and the U.N. Secretary-General will report on its progress to the 49th and 50th General Assemblies.

The **U.N. Commission for Human Settlements**, the intergovernmental body charged with coordinating and monitoring the Global Strategy, met for its 14th biannual session from April 26 to May 7, 1993. On *its* agenda, among other items, were guidelines for the Habitat II Preparatory Committee, the elaboration of a work program for the 1994–95 biennium, and reports on two special themes: improvement of municipal management and "appropriate, intermediate, cost-effective building materials, technologies and transfer mechanisms for housing delivery" [HS/C/14/1/Add.1].

The International Year of the World's Indigenous People

By Brienne Cliadakis

On December 18, 1990, the General Assembly voted to proclaim 1993 the "International Year for the World's Indigenous People." The aim of the Year is "strengthening co-operation for the solution of problems faced by indigenous communities in such areas as human rights, the environment, development, education, health and so on" [A/Res/45/164].

Indigenous people are, by definition, the descendants of the original inhabitants of a given region. Today there are approximately 300 million such people spread throughout 70 countries [DPI/1296], usually with their own distinct languages and cultures, and many consider themselves to be self-governing nations [E/CN.4/Sub.2/1986/Add.4, p. 5]. Among these native groups, and to name only a few, are the Apache, the Micmac, the Bribri, the Zapotec, and the Quechua Indians of North, South, and Central America; the Ainu, Gadabas, and Chin peoples of Asia; the Kawahla and Somali peoples of Africa; and the Aboriginals and Rapa Nui peoples of Australia [DPI press kit/1316]. Indigenous people make up 4,000–5,000 of the world's 6,000 cultures, as defined by spoken language [Worldwatch Institute, *State of the World 1993* (New York: W. W. Norton, 1993), p. 81]. Despite these vast numbers, quite a few native tribes are in danger of extinction [DPI press kit/1296]. In the Amazon, for example, 90 tribes have ceased to exist in the past 100 years [UNDP, *Choices*, p. 5].

The initial coordinator for the Year was Antoine Blanca, Under-Secretary-General for Human Rights at the U.N. Centre for Human Rights in Geneva, but due to U.N. restructuring the role has gone to Ibrahima Fall, Assistant Secretary-General for Human Rights [A/Res/46/128]. The goodwill ambassador and spokesperson for the year is Rigoberta Menchu, winner of the 1992 Nobel Peace Prize [U.N. press release GA/8447]. In her book *I, Rigoberta Menchu: An Indian Woman in Guatemala*, Ms. Menchu examines how the Quiche live, as well as some of the issues that are confronted by this indigenous Indian people of Guatemala [New York: Verso, 1984]. Ms. Menchu will be traveling on behalf of the U.N. to South America and Asia. She will also be conducting an independent meeting in Guatemala to plan a strategy for indigenous people.

The **four main goals** for this Year are (1) developing partnerships and relationships between indigenous people and their states and the international community, as called for by the Year's theme, "Indigenous People—a new partnership"; (2) planning projects to benefit indigenous people in consultation with them; (3) reviewing and creating standards for the rights of indigenous people, and completing the **Universal Declaration on the Rights of Indigenous Peoples**; and (4) informing and educating the public about indigenous people and the issues they face [DPI press kit/1249]. In 1992 the United Nations also established a **Voluntary Fund** for the Year to assist indigenous people in funding projects that they propose to the United Nations [DPI press kit/1313]. The goal was to raise $500,000, but as of May 1993, reported the U.N. Department of Public Information, a total of $195,368 had been received in contributions and pledges from five countries and one nongovernmental organization (NGO): Australia, Denmark, France, New Zealand, Norway, and the Shimin Gaikou Center.

In March the **U.N. Center for Human Rights** selected six projects out of 102 proposals and set aside $53,076 to fund them. The indigenous community of the Garifuna People of Georgetown Village in Belize, for example, will use their funds to build a cultural center, while the Mujeres Aymaras del Kollasuyo in Bolivia will use theirs to teach Andean indigenous women about the concepts of democracy and human rights through seminars and radio programs. Helping to improve family nutrition will be the focus of a project run by Mapuche women in Chile, who hope to establish a small farm to raise chickens and rabbits. The question of nutrition also will be addressed by the Women's Organization of Huycotungo in Ecuador, which plans to construct a community bakery. A reforestation project was selected in Guatemala, and in the Philippines the Cordillera Peoples Alliance will use its funds to launch a campaign to educate indigenous people about their rights and about the U.N. system. A second review to select additional projects is expected to take place before the end of 1993.

When the Year was established, there was some debate about how to phrase the title and what date to select. The choice of the word "people" instead of "peoples" was a subject of conflict, just as it has been in the draft of the Declaration on the Rights of Indigenous Peoples. Many government representatives had argued that the use of the term "peoples" could lead to conflict with international law over the questions of land rights and territorial sovereignty [E/CN.2/Sub.2/1992/33]. Among those who disagree with the final choice is Oren Lyons, a chief of the Onondaga nation in New York. Chief Lyons stresses the importance of recognizing the independence and would-be sovereignty of indigenous *peoples* [interview with *A Global Agenda*, 2/11/93]. Some indigenous representatives argue further that the U.N. Charter speaks of "peoples," and that "people" does not carry with it any notion of the group, with attendant rights.

In the first resolution passed by the General Assembly, the title of the Year was "The International Year *for* the World's Indigenous People." According to Julian Burger, Secretary of the Working Group on Indigenous Populations, some people objected to the use of "for" because it could be interpreted as implying a paternalistic attitude toward indigenous people [interview with *A Global Agenda*, 4/26/93]. The draft resolution [A/47/L.33] of December 8, 1992, issued just before the ceremonies to launch the Year and adopted without changes, refers to the international year "of" indigenous people. That draft resolution effectively renames the Year, and any new documents reflect that change.

Some indigenous groups in the Americas wanted to mark the Year during 1992, to coincide with the 500th anniversary of Columbus' first voyage to the Americas—from which they date the invasion of their lands and their own struggle against domination and discrimination. Spain was among the member states opposed to this, fearing that the publicity given to indigenous people's issues would compromise their celebration of the Columbus anniversary. A number of indigenous people also objected to 1992 because it was not a meaningful date for all groups [Burger interview, 4/26/93]. Finally, all parties were able to agree on 1993.

As is often the case with international years, the Year of the World's Indigenous People has little money at its disposal and must rely for its success on the voluntary efforts of governments, individuals, and NGOs. According to Julian Burger, "the idea of a year is to create a space, an opportunity for other people [besides the United Nations] to step into and use the focus on a given issue." The U.N. Centre for Human Rights, with its small staff, is disseminating information about the Year and assisting indigenous people, U.N. agencies, member states, and NGOs in whatever other ways it can. The concept of indigenous people is not as immediately comprehensible as is the concept of, say, space (1992's subject) or family (the topic of the international year in 1994). The United Nations—with help from other organizations—must make the concept clear to the public before the Year can address the indigenous people's own concerns. Elsa Stamatopoulou, Chief of the U.N. Centre for Human Rights office in New York, also emphasized the goal of raising public awareness as a main priority for the Year: "If the average person in the street comes to understand who indigenous people are and what their needs are, then I think the year will be a success" [interview with *A Global Agenda*, 2/19/93].

The idea of a commemorative year of indigenous people was the outgrowth of a study—begun in 1971 and completed in 1986—by Special Rapporteur José R. Martinez Cobo, who suggested "a decade of action to encourage observance and protection of the human rights and fundamental freedoms of indigenous populations" [E/CN.4/Sub.2/1986/7/Add.4, para. 334]. This study was the first major effort to look seriously at the situation of indigenous people and examine discrimination, disadvantages, and various human rights abuses that many have faced.

How to **reconcile the conflict between states and indigenous peoples over self-determination and land rights** is what makes the theme of the Year, "Indigenous people—a new partnership," so important [A/47/PV.82]. As the original inhabitants of the land, indigenous people often feel that self-determination includes the right to political autonomy and the control of the natural resources of their territory. At the opening ceremonies for the International Year, held in the General Assembly on Human Rights Day, December 10, 1992, the Secretary-General observed that "For centuries indigenous people have lived at the margins of national and international life. . . . The examples of the marginalization and then the disappearance of cultures have indicated that when a community is kept outside international life it is very difficult to maintain among its members even the most elementary human rights" [A/47/PV.82]. The new relationships that the United Nations hopes to encourage would assist indigenous people in developing ways to be included in dialogues that concern their futures and in which they have hitherto been "marginalized."

Almost every indigenous speaker at the opening day ceremonies mentioned the issue of self-determination and called for the establishment of some sort of permanent body to represent indigenous people at the United Nations. At the moment there are **two forms of representation** available to indigenous people: the Working Group on Indigenous Populations, established in 1982, which is charged with reviewing the situation of the rights of indigenous people and creating standards for those rights [E/CN.4/Sub.2/1992.33]; and NGO consultative status with ECOSOC, which enables indigenous organizations to attend ECOSOC meetings and circulate documents. Eleven indigenous organizations have NGO status, and indigenous people have begun to use forums like the Ottawa Seminar at the University of Ottawa in Canada to discuss how to use the recognition they have gained during the Year to obtain more effective representation at the United Nations [Ottawa Seminar, "Indigenous Peoples and the U.N.: The Next Steps," 3/93].

Some concrete benefits of the Year can already be seen. The opening day ceremonies in December marked the very first time indigenous people have addressed the General Assembly. In addition, two indigenous representatives were asked to serve as Vice Chairs at the Reconvened Technical Meeting, which focused on planning the Year, marking the first time indigenous representatives were included in a "U.N. governmental meeting" [Four Directions Council, "Strategy for the Year"]. The Centre for Human Rights in Geneva has indigenous staff members working on the Year—members who are part of the secretariat for the Year and who include a representative of the Inuit tribe in Greenland, an Aboriginal representative from Australia, and a member of the Sami tribe in Norway. The draft of the Declaration of Indigenous Rights is near completion; and the Department of Public Information and the Centre for Human Rights have distributed many fact sheets, documentary radio and video programs that include sections on indigenous people, a calendar of events, handbooks, posters, a newsletter, etc. The International Labour Organisation is promoting the ratification of its Indigenous and Tribal Peoples Convention 1989 (No. 169); the U.N. High Commissioner for Refugees plans to include information on indigenous people in its guidelines for field officers [DPI/Calendar Highlights, 2/93]; and a review of the International Year and, by extension, of the situation of indigenous people was on the agenda of the World Conference on Human Rights, in Vienna in June.

VI
Legal Issues

By José E. Alvarez

A number of actions taken by the Security Council and the 47th General Assembly over the past year may have begun altering some fundamental concepts of international law, including basic principles of the U.N. Charter, and even the meaning of "sovereignty." One major impetus for these developments has been the variety and quantity of peace and security issues brought to the U.N.'s door in this post-Cold War era, and another is the Secretary-General's thought-provoking "An Agenda for Peace" with its recommendations for strengthening U.N. collective security mechanisms. Indeed, now under way are serious efforts to create not one but two international criminal courts for (among other things) trying those accused of war crimes; to alter the structure of the Security Council, entailing revision of the Charter; to modernize the concept of "peacekeeping" to bring it into line with institutional practice; and to enhance the effectiveness of Chapter VIII of the Charter dealing with cooperation between the United Nations and regional organizations. These developments, along with the less controversial proceedings of such bodies as UNCITRAL, the Committee on Peaceful Uses of Outer Space, and an increasingly active World Court, not only have significant legal consequences but also fuel the hope that the rule of law will be able to provide continuity during a time of profound change.

1. The International Law Commission

The International Law Commission (ILC), established to assist the General Assembly in the codification and progressive development of international law, met in Geneva for its 44th session from May 4 to July 24, 1992. That session, the first for the 34 commission members elected to a five-year term in 1991, devoted more time than usual to planning the work of the next quinquennium. It also considered three matters still on the Commission's agenda: creation of an international criminal court (in hand was the tenth report of its Special Rapporteur, addressing the possibility of establishing an international criminal court [A/CN.4/442; A/47/10, pp. 11–33]), "state responsibility," and international liability for injurious consequences arising out of acts not prohibited by international law.

The ILC has considered the possibility of an **international criminal court** since the 1950s; and in 1990 and 1991, the General Assembly asked the ILC for guidance prior to deciding whether to ask it to begin drafting a statute for such a court [*A Global Agenda: Issues/47,* pp. 293–94]. The Rapporteur's report proposes some tentative provisions to deal with many of the difficult issues raised in prior ILC discussions, including those spurred by the Rapporteur's previous report [see, e.g., *Issues/47,* pp. 293–94; and *Issues/46,* pp. 239–41]. Discussion of the Rapporteur's latest report revealed continuing differences among ILC members with respect to the feasibility and desirability of such a court. Some members advocate a standing court with compulsory and exclusive jurisdiction on the model of Nuremberg; some others argue that the post-World War II tribunals at Nuremburg and Tokyo responded to unique circumstances; and still others support flexible arrangements in lieu of a court, such as ad hoc procedures permitting the prosecution of individuals but subject to the agreement of concerned states [A/47/10, pp. 11–17; see also Robert Rosenstock, "The Forty-Fourth Session of the International Law Commission," 87 *American Journal of International Law* 138 (1993), pp. 138–39]. These divergent views, as well as fundamental questions relating to the subject matter jurisdiction of any proposed court and its relationship to the ILC's Draft Code of Crimes against the Peace and Security of Mankind [see *Issues/47,* pp. 290–93], led the ILC to establish a Working Group to, among other things, draft "concrete recommendations" to bridge the differences. The ILC reported the Group's findings to the Sixth (Legal) Committee at the 47th General Assembly.

The Working Group offered a history of U.N. deliberations on the subject of an international criminal jurisdiction and, concluding that the establishment of an international criminal court is "possible," identified the following elements of a "workable system":

1. The court would be established by statute in the form of a multilateral treaty.
2. It would exercise jurisdiction over individuals, not states.
3. Court jurisdiction would extend to crimes already defined in international treaties (for example, aircraft hijacking, hostage-taking, genocide, and grave breaches of the Geneva Conventions on the protection of victims of armed conflict) as well as to the other crimes identified in the Draft Code of Crimes.
4. The court would not have compulsory or exclusive jurisdiction but would be available to the states that are parties to its statute, with each free to accept the jurisdiction of the court on some but not all of the listed offenses.

5. It would not be a standing permanent body but an ad hoc mechanism called into operation as needed.

6. Court procedures would be marked by due process, independence, and impartiality [A/47/10, Annex].

The report identifies situations in which an international process, as opposed to adjudication before national courts, would be useful—for example, where an international forum is the only process on which the parties can agree, where domestic judicial systems are under threat by terrorists or cannot cope with the magnitude of a particular offense, or where the alleged offenders were members of a prior government and the present government is unwilling or unable to try them or believes an international trial will lend greater legitimacy to the verdict [ibid., p. 156]. Although the report acknowledges the difficulty of establishing an international criminal court, it argues that the effort should be made, since "the task of constructing an international order, an order in which the values which underlie the relevant rules of international law are respected and are made effective, must begin somewhere" [ibid., p. 160].

The Working Group's report makes recommendations on additional details that must be resolved before any such court gets down to work, advising, among other things, that the judges selected have experience in fact-finding as well as knowledge of international criminal law; that the court's jurisdiction extend only to the most serious offenses with an international dimension (and not, for example, to "illicit trafficking of certain quantities of drugs at the very end of the chain of distribution"); that the personal jurisdiction of the court be distinguished from existing treaty mechanisms to extradite suspects; and that the court, though established independently and by treaty, maintain an affiliation with the United Nations, as in the case of the Human Rights Committee established under the International Covenant on Civil and Political Rights.

With respect to due process, the ILC Working Group's report stresses the need to abide by the standards of the latter covenant, including the principle *nullum crimen sine lege* (no punishment for crimes unless the act is defined as criminal at the time committed). Furthermore, says the report, fairness dictates that none of the accused be tried in absentia and that possible penalties be clearly indicated [ibid., pp. 183–84].

The ILC Working Group noted that the period for preliminary consideration and analysis was now over and that it was time for "the General Assembly and for Member States to resolve whether the Commission should proceed to the detailed work that will be required in drawing up a Statute and associated rules of procedure" [ibid., p. 146],

While most delegates to the General Assembly's Sixth Committee approved of giving the ILC a mandate to draft a statute for a proposed international criminal court along the lines of the Working Group's recommendations (see, e.g., comments by the United Kingdom, speaking on behalf of the European Community, and Norway, on behalf of the Nordic countries), some states (including the United States) indicated that further study was appropriate, while others (such as China and Cuba) continued to question the feasibility of establishing a court and expressed concerns about its impact on national sovereignty [A/C.6/47/SR.20–30]. Many questioned particular aspects of the Working Group's recommendations, while others, such as the United Kingdom, noted that some aspects of the issue requiring close study had failed to receive attention thus far, among them the rules regarding the preservation, admissibility, and relevance of evidence; the burden of proof; the treatment of expert witnesses; the defendant's right to remain silent and to confront witnesses; and the nature and extent of prosecutors' ethical duties [A/C.6/47/SR.24].

Despite these caveats, the Sixth Committee proposed a draft resolution, ultimately adopted by the General Assembly, authorizing the ILC to elaborate a draft statute for an international criminal court "as a matter of priority" and requesting a progress report for the 48th Session of the Assembly [A/C.6/47/SR.35, A/Res/47/33]. The matter is thus expected to consume much of the ILC's time at its spring-summer 1993 session. (Several states [e.g., Cuba, Israel] indicated during the Sixth Committee debate that, had the draft resolution been put to a formal vote, they would have abstained from voting or opposed giving the ILC this mandate—suggesting that political obstacles still stand in the way of establishing an international criminal court.) The proposal for such a court remains on a separate track from the creation of an ad hoc tribunal to try alleged war criminals in the former Yugoslavia [see Section 2, "Peace and Security," below].

For the first time in years, the ILC devoted substantial time to the topic of **state responsibility** (addressing the extent to which states can make claims or bear responsibility). The general organization plan for the topic, adopted in 1975 when the subject was first introduced, had anticipated articles on (1) the origin of international responsibility; (2) the content, forms, and degrees of international responsibility; and (3) the settlement of disputes and implementation. As of 1986, the Commission had provisionally adopted five articles for part two and had referred to the drafting committee 15 other articles for parts two and three. While five additional articles for part two (on legal consequences deriving from an international delict) were considered in 1989 and 1990, the ILC's 43rd session heard the latest report of the Special Rapporteur but did not discuss the topic [*Issues/45*, pp. 195–96; *Issues/46*, pp. 241–42; *Issues/47*, p. 297].

Discussion at the ILC's 44th session focused on the Special Rapporteur's third and fourth reports, dealing with what he considers one of the most difficult issues of part two: rules governing countermeasures or reprisals—the otherwise illegal actions taken against a state that has committed an internationally wrongful act. (Countermeasures are therefore distinguishable from "retortions," which are legal responses to illegal action by one state.) The reports stated that much of the difficulty in handling the topic results from the absence of relevant domestic analogies as well as from the absence of institutionalized remedies when states commit wrongful acts. The Rapporteur opted to propose restrictions on the use of countermeasures by, for example, establishing as a precondition the "exhaustion of all the amicable settlement procedures available under general international law, the United Nations Charter or any other dispute settlement instrument to which [the injured state] is a party" [quoted in Rosenstock, *supra*, p. 141].

As might be expected, the subject of countermeasures, including the question of whether to include the subject within the draft on state responsibility at all, proved a contentious one both within the ILC and in the Sixth Committee. While most states agreed in the end that the topic was worth addressing, albeit with the utmost caution, and while they agreed too that the countermeasures under discussion would not involve the use of armed force, many took strong issue with the Rapporteur's general approach and the proposed draft articles. Several Third World and small states suggested that countermeasures were not only in the nature of a political response, which should not be legitimized by legal codification or progressive development, but were also incompatible with Articles 2(3), 2(4), and 33 of the Charter [see, e.g., A/47/10, p. 41]. China and Iran [A/C.6/47/SR.25] and Cuba [SR.29] were among those contending that such measures should not be encouraged and were apt to be used by the powerful against the weak. China argued further that it was impossible to reconcile practicality with "power politics," noting that "[a] bad law was often more undesirable than no law at all" [SR.25].

Some small states, however, drew the opposite conclusion, arguing that only by codifying the rules could restrictions be placed on the possibility that powerful states would resort to countermeasures [see, e.g., comments by Denmark, ibid.].

The United States and France also expressed qualms about the ILC taking on the subject of countermeasures, but on different grounds—that so sensitive a matter could derail efforts to complete a draft on state responsibility—and went on to state their disagreement with some of the Rapporteur's specific proposals. France, for its part, maintained that countermeasures should not be wholly precluded once the Security Council had adopted sanctions against the offending state under Chapter VII of the U.N. Charter [A/C.6/47/SR.26]. The United States representative indicated that "excessive burdens" on permissible countermeasures by an injured state would only strengthen wrongdoers and that requiring the prior exhaustion of dispute settlement "misperceived the important role of countermeasures in inducing agreements for the settlement of disputes" [SR.27]. Other states, such as Austria and Poland, while agreeing with the general approach taken by the Rapporteur, disagreed with such details as the purported distinction between "interim measures of protection" and "countermeasures." The Austrian representative suggested that these two types of actions were indistinguishable from each other and, therefore, that the first need not be exempted from the requirement of exhaustion of alternative forms of dispute settlement [SR.26, SR.28]. The ILC's 45th session is expected to continue this dialogue. The express goal is to complete the first reading of a full set of articles on state responsibility by 1996.

International Liability for Injurious Consequences Arising Out of Acts Not Prohibited by International Law, on the ILC's agenda since 1978, was given yet another mixed reception by the Commission and the Sixth Committee in 1992. Still essentially unresolved are the most basic issues: what to include in the topic, whether the ILC is engaged in codification or in progressive development of the law, what relationship exists between this topic and the ILC's efforts on state responsibility, and the nature of any prospective instrument [compare *Issues/47*, pp. 295–96].

When the ILC met for its 44th session during 1992, it considered the Special Rapporteur's eighth report on the topic, which reviewed the status and the purpose of proposed articles and indicated that a majority of states favor a separate recommendary instrument on the "procedural" obligations (notification, information, and consultation) to prevent transboundary harm, and that they also favor relegating to an annex the provisions on substantive "unilateral measures of prevention" (administrative or judicial actions requiring private parties to adopt the best preventive technology). After considering the recommendations of a Working Group established to examine general aspects of the topic, the ILC declined to make any final decision about the scope of the topic or about the exact nature of any possible instrument, but it did agree on priorities: The ILC would first consider preventive measures in respect of activities carrying a substantial risk of transboundary harm and only then take up the issue of remedial measures once harm had occurred [A/47/10, pp. 127–28]. The Rapporteur was instructed to propose to the 45th ILC a revised set of draft articles relating to the issues of prevention.

The representatives to the Sixth Committee were generally disappointed with the lack of progress on this topic—one that, many states noted, had grown in importance with the growth of concern for the environment—and some criticized the ILC's priorities, suggesting that the issues of reparation and compensation for injury were more important than the issue of prevention [see, e.g., comments by Australia, Canada, and Sweden on behalf of the Nordic countries, A/C.6/47/SR.27–28]. Still other states suggested that the issues of prevention and remedial measures are so intertwined as to make the distinction artificial [see, e.g., comments by Poland, SR.28].

There was, however, support for the Rapporteur's three principles to guide discussion of the topic of international liability, namely, that (1) any draft articles must ensure each state as much freedom of choice within its territory as is compatible with the rights and interests of other states; (2) the protection of such rights and interests will require measures of prevention and, where injury results, reparation; and (3) insofar as is consistent with the first two principles, the innocent victim should not be left without a remedy for loss or injury [see e.g., comments by Canada, SR.28]. The Chinese representative warned, however, that if a legal regime governing international liability were to treat all nations on equal terms, developing countries would be at a disadvantage because they lack the scientific, technical, and financial resources to take adequate preventive measures [U.N. press release GA/L/2761, 11/4/92]. Although the United States generally supported the ILC's decision to focus on prevention, it noted that the Commission had not yet clearly defined the scope of the topic or decided whether it aspired to a binding multilateral convention or merely to hortatory guidelines. Washington also indicated that the ILC should focus on regulating, through guidelines, "ultra-hazardous" activities to avoid including activities that are already prohibited by international law under the doctrine of state responsibility as well as activities that do not entail a risk of significant harm [A/C.6/47/SR.29].

In deference to the 1991 General Assembly's decision that the Commission consider establishment of an international criminal court [A/Res/46/54], the 44th ILC did not schedule a further discussion of its **Draft Code of Crimes against the Peace and Security of Mankind,** which had been completed during its 43rd session and subsequently released to governments for comment [see *Issues/47*, pp. 290–93]. The Commission resolved to complete a second reading of that Draft Code by 1996 [A/47/10, p. 133]. It similarly resolved to complete, by 1994, a second reading of its draft articles on the **Law of the Non-navigational Uses of International Watercourses.** The ILC completed a first reading of these articles during its 43rd session, and these had been submitted to governments for comment [*Issues/47*, pp. 294–95]. At the same time, the Commission resolved to drop from its agenda the topic **Relations between States and International Organizations.** Although the first part of this topic had led to the 1975 Convention on the Representation of States in Their Relations with International Organizations of a Universal Character, many of the governments that are host to international organizations have indicated their opposition to the Convention, and they and others have been slow to ratify it. The ILC's annual report to the Assembly indicates that doubts have arisen concerning the viability of part two of this topic and that Commission members believe that it should be dropped in the interest of more pressing needs [A/47/10, pp. 132–33], and the Sixth Committee concurred [A/C.6/47/SR. 20–30]. The Assembly approved this decision and also approved the ILC's current program of work [A/47/33]. It is generally assumed that, given its mandate to draft the statute for an international criminal court, the ILC will not be taking on any new topics in the near future.

The ILC's draft articles on **Jurisdictional Immunities of States and Their Property,** adopted during its 43rd session in late spring 1991, are still being examined by a Working Group established for this purpose pursuant to a request of the 46th Assembly [see *Issues/47*, p. 294; A/Res/46/55]. The goal remains that of deciding whether there is sufficient agreement on the articles to convene an international conference in 1994 (or thereafter) for the purpose of concluding a convention on the subject. Among the issues still awaiting resolution are the definition of the term "state," the scope and definition of "commercial transaction," the concept of segregated state property, and the handling of measures of constraint and mixed funds [see, e.g., comments by the United Kingdom, A/C.6/47/SR.32].

The Chairman of the Working Group presented many compromise proposals to resolve these issues, and the Group met from September to November 1992 to discuss them [A/C.6/47/L.10]. Regarding the question of the treatment of constituent units of a federal state, the Chairman proposed that jurisdictional immunities extend to such units when they are "entitled" to perform sovereign acts *and* when "actually performing" these acts [ibid., pp. 2–3]. To reconcile the views of those who disagree about whether the commercial character of a transaction should be determined by the "nature" or the "purpose" of the transaction, the Chairman proposed to have the "nature" test govern, subject to a state's ability to specify, in the contract or as part of the transaction, that it was reserving the right to have the "purpose" test apply [ibid., pp. 3–4]. On the issue of what type of state property would be subject to interim, prejudgment, or postjudgment measures of constraint, the Chairman struck a balance between competing views by distinguishing between interim and prejudgment measures on the one hand and postjudgment measures on the other. He proposed that postjudgment measures be available even with respect to commercial state property having no link with the underlying claim or with the agency or instrumentality concerned but that such a link be required for interim and prejudgment measures [ibid., pp. 4–5]. On the crucial question of which entities would be considered "state enterprises" and therefore potentially entitled to immunity, the Chairman proposed the following provision:

> Jurisdiction shall not be exercised over a State and its property by the courts of another State in a proceeding, not related to acts performed in the exercise of sovereign authority, involving a State enterprise or other entity established by the State which: (a) has independent legal personality; (b) is capable of suing or being sued; and (c) is capable of owning, controlling, and disposing of property [A/C.6/47/L.10, pp. 6–7].

The brief discussions of these and other compromise formulations in the Sixth Committee did not lead to a decision to ask the Assembly to authorize the convening of an international conference [see A/C.6/47/SR.32]. Instead, it was decided that the Working Group would continue its deliberations and give the draft articles some concentrated attention during the first two weeks of the 48th Session of the General Assembly in 1993 [A/Dec/47/414].

Neither informal consultations within the ILC nor discussion in the Sixth Committee led to a resolution of the continuing stalemate over the ILC's **Draft Articles and Draft Optional Protocols One and Two on the Status of the Diplomatic Courier and Diplomatic Bag Not Accompanied by Diplomatic Courier** [see *Issues/45*, pp. 192–93; *Issues/46*, p. 246]. States continue to disagree especially over the inviolability of the diplomatic bag in circumstances where a receiving state has serious reason to believe that the bag is being used for improper purposes, such as for drug trafficking. Some states believe that in exceptional circumstances a diplomatic bag might be subject to examination by electronic or other technical devices routinely used at airports and that such an examination might warrant a request for the opening of the bag. Others argue that the diplomatic bag is inviolable and cannot be subject to any intrusion, including an electronic one [see, e.g., comments by Argentina, A/C.6/47/SR.31]. Due to the lack of agreement, the Sixth Committee and the Assembly opted for postponement of further consideration, with the topic now included on the agenda of the 50th Session of the General Assembly [A/Dec/47/415].

2. Peace and Security

In June 1992, pursuant to an invitation issued at the end of the historic Security Council "Summit" of the previous January [see *Issues/47*, p. 309], the Secretary-General issued **"An Agenda for Peace"** [A/47/277], many of whose recommendations for strengthening the capacity of the Organization to maintain and restore international peace and security have considerable legal implications. Indeed, the Secretary-General's vision of preventive diplomacy, peacemaking, peacekeeping, and post-conflict peacebuilding, with responsibility to be shared among the General Assembly, the Security Council, other U.N. organs, and regional actors, takes off from institutional practice—activities developed over the years—rather than from any specific warrant in the text of the Charter. The ideas contained in and the reactions to "An Agenda for Peace" have cast a huge shadow on U.N. deliberations about peace and security issues [see, e.g., U.N. press release GA/8378, 10/14/92, summarizing comments before the 47th Session of the Assembly].

In the course of this report the Secretary-General provides definitions of "preventive diplomacy," "peacemaking," "peacekeeping," and "peacebuilding" and outlines specific measures within each category.

Along the way he affirms or proposes principles to guide such activities. Among these are:

1. Preventive deployment for the purposes of humanitarian assistance, provided with the consent of, or at the request of, the affected sovereign does not violate the U.N. Charter's Article 2 (7) [ibid., para. 30].

2. Preventive deployment should be permitted in instances where one nation, fearing a cross-border attack, requests a U.N. presence and the Security Council concludes that such a presence on one side of the border would deter conflict [para. 32].

3. The United Nations should be authorized to establish demilitarized zones by agreement of two parties on both sides of a border as a form of preventive deployment and not merely at the conclusion of a conflict [para. 33].

4. The General Assembly and the Secretary-General should exercise larger peacemaking roles (for example, by designating individuals for mediation and negotiation in consultation with the Security Council) [para. 37].

5. The Secretary-General should be authorized to request advisory opinions of the World Court pursuant to Article 96 (2) of the Charter [para. 38].

6. All members should be encouraged to accept the general jurisdiction of the World Court by the year 2000, or, alternatively, agree bilaterally or multilaterally on a "comprehensive list of matters" they are willing to submit to the Court [para. 39].

7. A mechanism should be established to permit U.N. organs to mobilize resources throughout the U.N. system to head off conflicts (such as by facilitating assistance to displaced persons) [para. 40].

8. Measures should be adopted, pursuant to Article 50 of the Charter, to protect states whose economies are adversely affected by Chapter VII sanctions [para. 41].

9. Article 43 special agreements should be negotiated to make armed forces, assistance, and facilities available to the Organization on a permanent basis, lending credibility to the U.N.'s claim to serve as guarantor of international security [para. 43].

10. "Peace-enforcement" units should be established, available on call and consisting of volunteer troops, to be used in "clearly defined circumstances" as a "provisional measure" authorized under Article 40 of the Charter [para. 44].

11. States should recognize the range of activities that now come under the heading of peacekeeping, including a variety of nonmilitary tasks requiring many subspecialties (electoral officials, human rights monitors, police, to name a few), and should supply the resources to support these efforts [paras. 50–52].

12. The Organization should engage in "comprehensive efforts" to

consolidate peace once achieved, and this "post-conflict peace-building" should extend to a full range of normally "sovereign" activities, from economic measures to arms control to consolidation of "democratic practices" [paras. 55–59].

13. Regional arrangements and agencies should be utilized, in consultation and cooperation with the Security Council, in preventive diplomacy, peacekeeping, peacemaking, and post-conflict peacebuilding, as envisioned by Chapter VIII of the Charter [paras. 60–65].

14. A variety of measures, including charging interest on arrears of assessed contributions and creating a "Peace Endowment Fund," should be implemented to ensure that the Organization has the financial resources for these activities [paras. 69–74].

The Secretary-General's "An Agenda for Peace" concludes with a general plea for consistency in the way the United Nations applies Charter principles, noting that selective application of the Charter only undermines "the moral authority which is the greatest and most unique [*sic*] quality of that instrument" [para. 82]. The 47th Assembly endorsed the bulk of the Secretary-General's proposals [A/Res/47/120].

Much of what the Secretary-General envisions in "An Agenda for Peace" either reflects or anticipates **recent deliberations in the Security Council,** where Cold War tensions have given way to a new spirit of cooperation in matters of peace and security. Among the decisions taken with regard to the crisis in the **former Yugoslavia,** many of them pathbreaking, are the condemnation of forcible expulsions, attempts at "ethnic cleansing," the systematic detention and rape of women, and violations of the territorial integrity of Bosnia and Herzegonia [see, e.g., S/Res/752, 757, and 798]; the adoption of Chapter VII sanctions with respect to Serbia and Montenegro, including bans on imports, exports, financial transactions, and airline traffic; the reduction of the level of staff at diplomatic missions and consular posts; prevention of participation in sporting events; suspension of scientific and technical cooperation and cultural exchanges; and prohibitions on the transshipment of a variety of products, including oil, through Serbia and Montenegro [S/Res/757 and 787]; the authorization of humanitarian assistance, backed by the possibility of force, including establishment of a security zone encompassing Sarajevo and its airport, under the auspices of the United Nations Protection Force (UNPROFOR) [see, e.g., S/Res/758, 761, 764, 770, and 776]; the establishment of cooperative arrangements with the European Economic Community (EEC) and the Conference on Security and Cooperation in Europe (CSCE) to seek a political settlement and for the purposes of fact-finding [S/Res/762, 764, 795, and 798]; the determination that the Federal Republic of Yugoslavia (Serbia and Montenegro) cannot "continue automatically" as a U.N. member, with a request that the General Assembly decide that it "shall apply for membership" and "not participate in the work of the General

Assembly" [S/Res/777]; the ban on military flights in the airspace of Bosnia and Herzegonia [S/Res/781 and 786] and authorization, under Chapter VII, to member states to take "all necessary measures . . . proportionate to the specific circumstances and the nature of the flights" to ensure compliance with this ban [S/Res/816; for detail concerning how UNPROFOR expected to monitor compliance with this ban, see S/24767]; the approval of the first preventive deployment of U.N. peacekeepers in history by dint of its having authorized the Secretary-General to establish an UNPROFOR presence in Macedonia [S/Res/795]; and the authorization to states, acting alone or through regional arrangements, to "use such measures commensurate with the specific circumstances as may be necessary" to "halt all inward and outward maritime shipping" and thus ensure implementation of the various sanctions on the former Yugoslav republic [S/Res/787].

Responding to allegations of grave breaches of humanitarian law, including violations of the Geneva Conventions, the Security Council took some other unprecedented actions: It affirmed individual responsibility for grave breaches of these Conventions and demanded that states and humanitarian organizations document violations [S/Res/771]; it established a **"Commission of Experts"** to examine the information they might collect [S/Res/780]; and, shortly after receiving the Commission's "interim report" concluding that grave breaches and other violations of humanitarian law had been committed [S/25274], it decided that the situation constituted a "threat to international peace and security" [S/Res/808; see also S/Res/787]. In February 1993 the Security Council authorized the Secretary-General to draft a proposal for the establishment of an **ad hoc international war crimes tribunal** to prosecute "persons responsible for serious violations of international humanitarian law committed in the territory of the former Yugoslavia since 1991" [S/Res/808].

On May 3, the Secretary-General submitted the requested proposal in the form of a statute for such a tribunal consisting of 34 articles on organizational structure (including composition and election of judges, privileges and immunities, and financial arrangements), applicable law, jurisdiction, territorial and temporal reach, and the relationship with prosecutions by national courts [S/25704]. The accompanying report contends that the urgency of the situation requires establishment of the tribunal as an "enforcement measure under Chapter VII, a subsidiary organ [*sic*] within the terms of Article 29 of the Charter, but one of a judicial nature," avoiding the time-consuming process of a multilateral treaty or General Assembly action [ibid., paras. 19–28]. The report states that

> in assigning to the International Tribunal the task of prosecuting persons responsible for serious violations of international humanitarian law, the Security Council would not be creating or purporting to "legislate" that law. Rather, the International Tribunal would have the task of applying existing international humanitarian law [para. 29].

Among the most significant provisions of the **Statute for the Tribunal** are Articles 2–5, identifying the crimes over which the Tribunal would have jurisdiction, namely, grave breaches of the Geneva Conventions of 1949, violations of the laws or customs of war, genocide, and crimes against humanity; Article 6, providing that personal jurisdiction will extend to the prosecution of natural persons, not states; Article 7, detailing aspects of individual criminal responsibility; Articles 8–10, dealing with issues of concurrent jurisdiction with national courts and with double jeopardy; Article 12, providing for the election by the General Assembly of 11 judges, to be nominated by the Security Council; Article 15, leaving rules of evidence and procedure to be adopted by the Tribunal; Article 16, describing the office of the prosecutor and his/her staff; Articles 18–20, detailing aspects of the investigatory, indictment, and trial stages, with provisions for the "transfer" of accused persons pursuant to a confirmed indictment; Article 21, outlining the rights of the accused, most of them affirming those contained in Article 14 of the International Covenant on Civil and Political Rights; Article 22, providing for victim and witness protection through *in camera* proceedings and anonymity; Article 24, limiting applicable penalties to terms of imprisonment (and excluding the death penalty); Article 31, providing that the Tribunal will sit at The Hague; and Article 32, providing that Tribunal expenses will be borne by the U.N. regular budget under Article 17 of the Charter [ibid.].

The Security Council unanimously approved this statute on May 25, deciding, under Chapter VII, to establish the international Tribunal to prosecute "persons responsible for serious violations of international humanitarian law committed in the territory of the former Yugoslavia between 1 January 1991 and a date to be determined by the Security Council upon the restoration of peace" [S/Res/827]. Significantly, the Council also decided, pursuant to Chapter VII, to require all U.N. members to "cooperate fully" with the Tribunal and take "any measures necessary under their domestic law to implement the present resolution and the Statute, including the obligation of States to comply with requests for assistance or orders issued by a Trial Chamber" [ibid.]. As the United States representative to the Council indicated, the intent is to obligate "every government, including each one in the former Yugoslavia," to "hand over those indicted" [press release USUN 75-(93), 5/25/93]. The Council's resolution anticipates that the Tribunal will take into account states' suggestions concerning appropriate rules of procedure and evidence, and it provides for the continuation of data-gathering by the Commission of Experts pending appointment of a prosecutor [S/Res/827].

With respect to events elsewhere in the world, the Security Council: authorized the Secretary-General to appoint a special representative to help lead **South Africa** through a peaceful post-apartheid transition [S/Res/765 and subsequent resolutions]; continues to exercise supervisory authority over the Secretary-General's and UNTAC's efforts to implement the Paris Agreements in **Cambodia,** including the plan for national elections [see, e.g., S/Res/766, 783, 792, and 810; see also, e.g., S/25719, a progress report by the Secretary-General noting ceasefire and human rights violations, attacks on UNTAC personnel, and other violations of the peace plan]; authorized, with respect to **Somalia,** an urgent airlift operation for humanitarian assistance [S/Res/767], the use of force by the United States to "secure" the environment for humanitarian relief operations [S/Res/794], and, finally, peacebuilding efforts by the Secretary-General and his special representative [S/Res/814]; continues to implement post-Gulf War measures with respect to **Iraq and Kuwait,** including measures having to do with boundary demarcation [see *Issues/47*, pp. 298–300; S/Res/773, 778, and 806]; authorized another special representative and the dispatch of 25 military observers to **Mozambique** (ONUMOZ) at the request of that government [S/Res/782 and 797]; supervised the implementation of peace agreements involving **El Salvador** (including provisions for U.N. factfinders—the Truth Commission) [S/Res/784 and 791]; authorized, under Chapter VII, a "general and complete embargo" on all weapons to **Liberia,** except those destined for the peacekeepers there [S/Res/788 and 813]; supervises "confidence-building" measures in **Cyprus** [S/Res/789] and the implementation of peace accords in **Angola** [S/Res/804 and 811]; condemned **Israel** for the deportation of hundreds of Palestinian civilians [S/Res/799]; authorized the Secretary-General to make the necessary preparations for a referendum on self-determination for the people of **Western Sahara** [S/Res/809]; and fulfilled the request by **Rwanda and Uganda** for deployment of observers at their border and expressed its willingness to assist the Organization of African Unity in implementing a hoped-for agreement between them [S/Res/846].

The Council's actions over the past year obviously demonstrate that Chapter VII action is no longer a rarity; that the Council is making a serious attempt to implement the Secretary-General's recommendation about securing the cooperation of regional organizations under Chapter VIII of the Charter; and that it is already making use of the panoply of measures—preventive diplomacy, peacemaking, peacekeeping, and peacebuilding—advocated by the Secretary-General. Moreover, the United Nations is no longer restricting itself to two deployment models: traditional peacekeeping and the full-scale Chapter VII enforcement action seen in Iraq/Kuwait in 1991.

In a number of situations the Security Council has already acted on the Secretary-General's more flexible agenda for dealing with threats to the peace—by authorizing "forceful" humanitarian intervention in Somalia and in the former Yugoslavia (in the former case, without the consent of a territorial sovereign), by energizing preventive diplomacy efforts by the Secretary-General and regional organizations (Rwanda/Uganda, the former Yugoslavia), and by expanding the concept of peacekeeping and "peace-consolidation" efforts to such degree that the Organization seems at the point of assuming the duties of civil authorities (at least for a time) when charged with overseeing the transition to peace and national elections, as currently in Cambodia.

The impact of this growing body of institutional precedents on the interpretation of the Charter and legal doctrines of express/implied powers remains to be seen but is likely to be significant. Certainly the Council appears to be expanding the scope of the Secretary-General's powers along many, if not all, of the lines suggested in "An Agenda for Peace"—even giving him the authority to draft a statute for a court that would try government officials and others accused of war crimes and assign punishment to them, the first since World War II. The Council also appears to be developing an increasingly broad view of what constitutes a "threat to the peace, breach of the peace or act of aggression"—the determination of which is a prerequisite to taking legally binding action to "maintain or restore international peace and security" under Article 39 of the Charter—since it has found more and more instances in which "international peace and security" are threatened. These have included even a case of unrest within one nation's borders and cases of human rights violations by a government against the country's own nationals.

As was the case when the Council applied Chapter VII to the situation in the Persian Gulf [see *Issues/46*, pp. 246–48] and later to Libya [see *Issues/47*, pp. 301–304], its actions are drawing both praise and concern—concern that it has gone too far (for example, in implementing postwar sanctions and other measures against Iraq), and in one instance charges that it has been too timid (by taking only "fragmentary and limited measures" in former Yugoslavia, which have been ineffective in the face of "aggression," "genocide," and massive forced expulsions of refugees) [see, e.g., comments by Turkey in the Council, as reported in U.N. press release SC/5592, 4/19/93].

Indeed, the growing number of supposedly binding Security Council decisions under challenge by various states—among them Libya and Iraq, and public officials in the former Yugoslavia [see, e.g., *Issues/47*, pp. 299–304, 325–27], is casting doubt on the efficacy of Articles 25 and 41 of the Charter, which give certain Council actions the force of law. And legal scholars and international lawyers may challenge the Council's fidelity to the text of the Charter itself. For example, it is unclear whether the Council acted pursuant to Article 5 (suspension) or Article 6 (expulsion) when it first directed the Assembly to ask Serbia and Montenegro to reapply for U.N. membership, whether that action was intended to resolve matters of state succession as a precondition to membership, whether the action was intended as a transitory arrangement or a permanent disqualification, and whether the intent was to deprive that state of rights to participation in the Organization or only in the Assembly [see S/Res/777 and SC/5471/Rev. 1]. In fact, the confusion was so great that the Secretariat released an explanatory letter indicating that the resolution did not call for either an expulsion or a full-scale suspension but merely prohibited Serbia and Montenegro from participating in the Assembly [A/47/485].

Others might question whether the Council has the legal authority to create an international war crimes tribunal under Chapter VII, even on an ad hoc basis. Its action is also prompting concern among international lawyers that the ad hoc Tribunal may, de facto, constitute a precedent for the structure and jurisdiction of any future permanent international criminal court [see Section 1, "International Law Commission," above] and that, notwithstanding the disclaimers in the Secretary-General's report accompanying the Statute for the Tribunal, it will develop international humanitarian law in ways that differ from existing treaty obligations under the Geneva Conventions. Certainly the draft statute casts doubts about the Tribunal's respect for the rights otherwise guaranteed a criminal defendant—among them the right of confrontation, the right to counsel, and the right against double jeopardy. And it leaves unclear how existing treaty obligations, such as the duty to "prosecute or extradite" under a number of conventions, will relate to the required "transfers" of accused persons to the Tribunal.

More generally, the Security Council's increasing willingness to override claims of "national sovereignty" and "domestic jurisdiction" under Article 2(7) continues to elicit fears among many of the U.N.'s 170-plus members lacking permanent seats on the Council that its actions may conflict with such fundamental legal principles as territorial sovereignty and the equality of states. After all, they say, if the Organization can organize an election, train a nation's domestic police force, and monitor the way domestic institutions treat the country's citizens (as is being done in Cambodia), what is left of sovereignty? Moreover, many have noted, the Chapter VII sanctions that are being applied in more and more situations are often costly to the economies of states that abide by them faithfully yet find it difficult to get the compensation anticipated by Article 50 of the Charter.

During plenary sessions of the 47th General Assembly and in such bodies as the Special Committee on the Charter of the United Nations and on the Strengthening of the Role of the Organization, nonaligned states were particularly vocal about these and other concerns [see Section 3, "Effectiveness of the Organization," below]. They often echoed the Secretary-General's plea (in "An Agenda for Peace") that the Council act consistently rather than in a manner that promotes the interests of particular powerful members. They argued too that the General Assembly, the more "democratic" organ, should have a greater role in peace and security issues, and so too the International Court of Justice. The effect would be to provide a counterweight, or "check," on Council action [see, e.g., comments by Bangladesh, Yemen, and Libya, U.N. press release GA/8378, 10/14/92]. Many of these concerns led the Assembly, acting by consensus, to request the Secretary-General to invite members to submit written comments on the need for more **equitable representation on and an increase in the membership of the Security Council** [A/Res/47/62]. These comments are due by June 30, 1993, and a review of Council membership is on the agenda of the 48th Assembly [ibid.].

As the Security Council continued its absorption with the situation in the former Yugoslavia, the **General Assembly** and its organs turned their attention to the region's problems too. The 47th Session, by a vote of 102–0, with 57 abstentions, approved many of the Council's actions directed at **Serbia and Montenegro,** urged compliance with those Council decisions, reaffirmed Bosnia's inherent right to individual and collective self-defense, condemned "ethnic cleansing" as a "form of genocide," and called for "decisive actions" under Chapter VII, including an exemption of the arms embargo for the Republic of Bosnia and Herzegovina and the recommendation of Chapter VII use of force if there is continued failure to comply with Council decisions [A/Res/47/121]. It also approved (vote: 127–6–26)—and in identical language—the Council's recommendation on Yugoslavia's participation in the United Nations [A/Res/47/1]. The Council's condemnations of **"ethnic cleansing"** were reflected in another Assembly resolution (originating in the Third [Social, Humanitarian, Cultural] Committee), explicitly designating this practice "a grave and serious violation of international humanitarian law" [A/Res/47/80]. The general topic of human rights and humanitarian law violations in the region received extensive Assembly attention as well [see, e.g., A/47/PV.86; see also A/Res/47/30 calling on states to ratify the Protocols to the 1949 Geneva Conventions. For discussions in the Sixth Committee on this issue, see A/C.6/47/SR.6].

On August 14, 1992, at the first emergency Special Session in its history, the Commission on Human Rights requested the appointment of a Special Rapporteur to conduct a first-hand investigation of the **human rights situation in the former Yugoslavia** [Commission on Human Rights, Resolution 1992/S–1/1]; and on February 26, 1993, Special Rapporteur Tadeusz Mazowiecki delivered his latest report to the Commission, which transmitted the report to the Assembly [A/48/92]. Mazowiecki offers a detailed survey of the instances of ethnic cleansing, summary executions, arbitrary detention and maltreatment of prisoners, widespread rape, forced transfers, and attacks on nonmilitary targets of which he found evidence throughout the former Yugoslavia. He also surveys the many international treaties, including the U.N. Charter, violated by these actions and makes numerous proposals for remedying them, including the creation of "security zones" in Bosnia and Herzegovina, authorization to UNPROFOR to intervene in cases of human rights violations, effective international monitoring to verify compliance with human rights standards and permit those forcibly displaced to exercise their right to return to their homes, and the creation of an international war crimes tribunal [ibid., pp. 58–59].

Many other matters dealt with by the Council also found echoes in the General Assembly. The 47th Session, by consensus, supported the Council's decision to deploy U.N. observers to **South Africa** to further the purposes of the 1991 National Peace Accord, and it called upon the Council to continue the mandatory arms embargo against that country [A/Res/47/116A]. Over the dissenting votes of some and abstentions by others, the Assembly also urged states to enact a model law to enforce an oil embargo against South Africa [A/Res/47/116D], urged states to enforce an embargo on products destined for use by that country's "military, police and security services" [A/Res/47/116E], and asked the Security Council to take "appropriate measures" against Israel for its violations of the South African arms embargo [A/Res/47/116F]. By divided votes, with Israel and the United States usually in dissent and some other states choosing to abstain, the Assembly also passed a series of resolutions concerning **Israeli practices affecting Palestinians and other Arabs in the Occupied Territories** [A/Res/47/70A–G], including one that echoed the Council's Resolution 799, with the demand that Israel rescind its "illegal" deportations of Palestinians [A/Res/47/70E]. These resolutions repeatedly affirm that the 1949 Geneva Convention Relative to the Protection of Civilian Persons in Time of War is "applicable to the Arab territories occupied by Israel since 1967, including Jerusalem" and charge "continued and persistent" violations of this Convention [A/Res/47/70A, B].

Prompted by the Secretary-General's "An Agenda for Peace" and by reports on peacekeeping operations prepared by the Secretary-General and by the Special Committee on Peacekeeping Operations, the Assembly made a series of specific proposals for a **comprehensive review of peacekeeping operations in all their aspects,** with special attention to the need to provide the Organization with the resources, both physical and financial, for undertaking the wide variety of operations now under way or anticipated [A/Res/47/71]. That resolution also notes that "preventive peacekeeping"—defined as "the deployment of peacekeeping operations as a deterrent to a possible aggressor"—requires "development and clarification as a helpful tool"; establishes an informal working group, open to all members, to examine "An Agenda for Peace"; and requests that the Special Committee on Peacekeeping Operations consider holding an intersessional meeting to consider the recommendations of "An Agenda for Peace" [ibid.]. The Assembly debate indicated that the "intellectual ferment and expanded activity" surrounding peacekeeping merited this scrutiny. At the same time, some expressed the fear that financial constraints could test the "viability of the whole concept of collective security" and might encourage selective actions and double standards with respect to security threats [U.N. press release GA/SPC/2046, 11/12/92]. A few delegates were of the opinion that "inadequate" U.N. action in Bosnia was actually the result of the Organization's financial crisis [see comments by Malaysia, ibid.]. The Assembly also expressed concern about the **protection of peacekeepers,** urging the Secretary-General to adopt, at the earliest stage of such operations, "status of forces" agreements with the relevant parties to secure rights in accordance with the Convention on the Privileges and Immunities of the United Nations [A/Res/47/72].

As it had during the 46th Session, the Assembly expressed its concern for the **situation of democracy and human rights in Haiti,** again calling for the restoration of the "legitimate" government of President Jean-Bertrand Aristide, "together with the full application of the National Constitution and hence the full observance of human rights in Haiti" [see *Issues/47*, p. 304; A/Res/47/20; see also the Secretary-General's reports on the subject, A/47/599 and A/47/908]. The Assembly also adopted, by consensus, a resolution expressing support for the efforts of the CSCE to remove "foreign military forces" stationed in **Estonia, Latvia, and Lithuania,** and called upon the states concerned to conclude agreements, in line with the basic principles of international law, for an "early, orderly and complete withdrawal" of these forces. The Assembly urged that the Secretary-General use his good offices to this end [A/Res/47/21]. Both items remain on the agenda for the 48th Session.

With Israel, Romania, and the United States voting "against" and 71 other members abstaining, the Assembly called for an end to the **economic, commercial, and financial embargo imposed by the United States against Cuba** [A/Res/47/19]. That resolution asserts that laws and regulations "whose extra-territorial effects affect the sovereignty of other States and the legitimate interests of entities or persons under their jurisdiction, and the freedom of trade and navigation," violate such Charter principles as sovereign equality and nonintervention and noninterference in internal affairs as well as the commercial freedoms "enshrined in many international legal instruments" [ibid.]. It is unclear whether the Assembly majority voting in favor of this resolution meant to suggest that only embargoes authorized by the Council will be deemed legal or that such embargoes are illegal because not authorized by a multilateral authority like the GATT. And it is unclear how this resolution comports with the one the Assembly adopted a month later in which (by a vote of 69–18–64) it expressed concern with "ongoing reports of **serious violations of human rights in Cuba**" as outlined in an interim report filed by a Special Rapporteur appointed by the Commission on Human Rights. The report had indicated that Cuba failed to cooperate with the Commission, and it called upon the government to

> cease the persecution and punishment of citizens for reasons related to freedom of expression and peaceful association, to permit legalization

of independent groups, to respect guarantees of due process, to permit access to the prisons by national independent groups and international humanitarian agencies, to review sentences for crimes of a political nature, and to cease retaliatory measures towards those seeking permission to leave the country [A/Res/47/139].

The resolution on Cuba was only one of many expressing concern with violations of human rights law in a number of countries [see, e.g., A/Res/47/115, A/Res/47/140–147].

As it has during prior sessions, the Assembly reviewed developments in and the prospects for a variety of arms control regimes. It welcomed the 1992 **Convention on the Prohibition of the Development, Production, Stockpiling and Use of Chemical Weapons and on Their Destruction,** urging states to become parties to it [A/Res/47/39]; urged the suspension of all nuclear test explosions through an agreed moratorium, calling on the parties to the **Treaty Banning Nuclear Weapon Tests in the Atmosphere, in Outer Space and Under Water** to participate in an Amendment Conference [A/Res/47/46; the United Kingdom and United States voting against, and 41 states abstaining]; requested that the Conference on Disarmament seek the establishment of an international seismic monitoring network to permit effective monitoring and verification of a **comprehensive nuclear test ban treaty** [A/Res/47/47; the United States in dissent and 4 states abstaining]; urged states to prevent an arms race in outer space and comply with the **Treaty on Principles Governing the Activities of States in the Exploration and Use of Outer Space, including the Moon and Other Celestial Bodies** [A/Res/47/51; Micronesia and the United States abstaining]; affirmed the need for **effective international arrangements to protect non-nuclear weapon states against the use or threat of use of nuclear weapons** [A/Res/47/50; the United Kingdom and United States abstaining]; urged states to become parties to the 1980 **Convention on Prohibitions or Restrictions on the Use of Certain Conventional Weapons Which May Be Deemed to Be Excessively Injurious or to Have Indiscriminate Effects** and related protocols [A/Res/47/56]; and urged Latin American and Caribbean states to take the steps necessary for the entry into force of the **Treaty for the Prohibition of Nuclear Weapons in Latin America and the Caribbean (Treaty of Tlatelolco),** including recent amendments [A/Res/47/61]. All these items reappear on the agenda of the 48th Assembly.

As during the 46th Session, the 47th Assembly called on states to respect the principles of the Charter and international law in the fight against **drug abuse and illicit trafficking** [A/Res/47/98; see also *Issues/47*, p. 306]. Even while combatting drug crimes, the resolution goes on to say, states must respect such principles as the "sovereignty and territorial integrity of states and non-use of force or the threat of force."

The Assembly also recognized that "certain means and methods of warfare may have dire effects on the environment" and urged states to

protect the environment in times of armed conflict by, among other things, respecting the provisions of international law on point, especially the many provisions contained in multilateral treaties under the laws of war, and by incorporating these provisions in military manuals [A/Res/47/37; see also *Issues/47*, pp. 300–301]. It requested that the Secretary-General seek a report on the subject from the International Committee of the Red Cross for consideration at the 48th Session [ibid.]. This innocuous Assembly resolution, adopted by consensus, does not reveal the fundamental division, suggested in Sixth Committee discussions, between states that see shortcomings or gaps in existing law and call for new rules on the subject [see, e.g., comments by Austria, A/C.6/47/SR.8] and those that believe that existing humanitarian law proscribes objectionable conduct [see, e.g., comments by the United States, A/C.6/47/SR.9]. In the U.S. view, new rules are needed only if states adopt excessively narrow readings of existing rules, such as with respect to proportionality. It sees a danger in "unintentionally weakening existing international law by implying that it ha[s] to be strengthened through the elaboration of new law" [ibid.].

Similarly, while both the Assembly and most of those who spoke in the Sixth Committee endorsed the **Protocols Additional to the Geneva Conventions of 1949 relating to the protection of victims of armed conflicts** [A/Res/47/30; A/C.6/47/SR.6], the United States reiterated its long-held position that Protocol I had "fundamental defects which could not be eliminated through either reservations or interpretative declarations." Its representative added that certain provisions in this Protocol "endangered civilian populations and recognized as combatants groups which were not authorized to carry out the obligations imposed by Government," while other provisions were "unacceptable from the military point of view" [A/C.6/47/SR.11].

3. Effectiveness of the Organization

Secretary-General Boutros Boutros-Ghali's first annual **Report on the Work of the Organization** takes a sweeping look at the expanding responsibilities of a United Nations that has never been "so action-oriented, so actively engaged, and so widely expected to respond to needs both immediate and pervasive" [A/47/1, p. 3]. The Secretary-General states that the Organization is in the midst of a "fundamental renewal" and argues that it must apply the "principles of democracy" to itself as well as to the family of nations [ibid., pp. 4, 46]. Among his proposals with special legal implications are the suggestions for implementing the Article 17 duty to pay, some of which are similar to proposals made by his predecessor in the context of peace and security [see discussion of "An Agenda for Peace" in Section 2, "Peace and Security"]. Specifically, his report proposes that interest be charged on unpaid arrearages, that U.N. financial regulations be modified to permit the retention of budgetary surpluses, that the Working Capital Fund be increased, that a temporary Peacekeeping Reserve Fund be established, and that the Secretary-General be permitted to borrow commercially [A/47/1, p. 12]. The Secretary-General also suggests consideration of various nongovernmental sources of funding (and which are likely to prove controversial for precisely that reason), such as a levy on arms sales or on international air travel, authorization for the Organization to borrow from the World Bank and the International Monetary Fund, and general tax exemptions for institutions that contribute to the Organization [ibid. p. 13].

The Secretary-General also makes concrete, by surveying the various kinds of missions that U.N. forces are carrying out around the globe, many of his arguments concerning the changing nature of peacekeeping, noting in particular the Organization's involvement in issues normally associated with national sovereignty—in Cambodia, the former Yugoslavia, Somalia, Angola, and El Salvador [ibid., pp. 30–40].

Recognizing the unpredictable nature of peacekeeping and the increasing demands being placed on the Organization, the Assembly made a bow toward the Secretary-General's financial proposals by approving the establishment of a $150 million **Peacekeeping Reserve Fund** to ensure a "rapid response" to requests for such operations. The Secretary-General would be authorized to advance sums from the fund for unforeseen, new, expanded, or renewed peacekeeping operations, as well as for the start-up costs of new operations [A/Res/47/217]. By separate action, the Assembly invited the Secretary-General to make proposals for "possible systems of incentives," for implementation on or before January 1, 1995, that will "encourage Member States to pay all their assessments in full and on time," and endorsed his proposals for an increase in the working capital fund [A/Res/47/215].

The 47th Assembly had another opportunity to examine some of the underlying issues raised in "An Agenda for Peace" when it discussed the latest report of the **Special Committee on the Charter of the United Nations and on the Strengthening of the Role of the Organization,** which had focused on (1) enhancing cooperation on matters of peace and security between the Organization and regional bodies, (2) providing assistance to third states adversely affected by the application of Chapter VII sanctions, (3) allowing the Secretary-General the authority to seek advisory opinions from the World Court, and (4) elaborating U.N. rules for the conciliation of disputes [A/47/33]. As the United States pointed out during discussion in the Sixth Committee, much of the Secretary-General's "An Agenda for Peace" originated in the work of the Special Committee [A/C.6/47/SR.15, p. 13]; and both the Report of the Special Committee and the Sixth Committee's discussion of it went beyond the official topics on the agenda to still other issues raised in "An Agenda for Peace." Neither the Special Committee's Report nor the discussion in the Sixth Committee suggested agreement with respect to any of these topics, and there was little progress relative to the 46th Session [see *Issues/47*, pp. 313–14].

Regarding the first topic on the Special Committee's agenda, many states welcomed the Russian Federation's "**draft declaration on the improvement of cooperation between the United Nations and regional organizations,**" which proposed a variety of mechanisms to adapt Chapter VIII of the Charter to present-day realities, including information exchanges, liaison missions, regular meetings between the U.N. Secretary-General and the executive heads of regional organizations, and expert-level consultations [A/AC.182/1.72; see also *Issues/47*, p. 314]. Some states, however, noting the wide differences between regional groups and their capabilities, urged caution, greater flexibility, or a change in format (suggesting that perhaps a "handbook" instead of a formal "declaration" was the more appropriate approach) [see comments by, for example, the United Kingdom, Mexico, and Finland, A/C.6/47/SR.15–16; A/47/33, pp. 20–33]. China advised that the question touched on state sovereignty and that aspects of the Russian draft declaration, such as a provision for the involvement of regional organizations in human rights, were unacceptable, on the grounds that the "protection of human rights by a State [falls] essentially within the jurisdiction of that State and [is] not related to international peace and security" [A/C.6/47/SR.17]. Israel based its objections on particular regional organizations' exclusionary practices with respect to some states [ibid.].

There were similarly varying views with respect to the second topic: the need for a more institutionalized process to help third states cope with **Chapter VII sanctions.** The reactions to papers on the subject submitted by a number of delegations were mixed [A/AC.182/L.73; A/47/33, pp. 37–44]. Thus, while Nepal urged creation of a compensatory fund to reimburse states hurt economically by sanctions, the United States and France favored a case-by-case approach [A/C.6/47/SR.14–16]. There was also a difference of opinion about the desirability of giving the **Secretary-General the power to request advisory opinions from the World Court.** The U.N. Legal Counsel had attempted to justify this proposal on various grounds, explaining that "almost all international disputes have some legal component" and that separation of this component would have a "stabilizing and helpful effect" [A/47/33, p. 10]. He had argued further that available alternatives, such as state-to-state dispute settlement or requests for advisory opinions by deliberative bodies like the General Assembly and the Security Council, had drawbacks: The first is an adversarial process, where the positions of the parties tend to become entrenched and the decision is binding, while the second requires a full, public airing of the question to be posed to the Court and is, therefore, inconsistent with the need to defuse tensions. But "if the Secretary-General himself has the competence to request advisory opinions," the Legal Counsel explained, "he would be able to do so in a quiet and discreet manner and without having to involve States not parties to the dispute" [ibid.].

Reactions to this proposal, as reflected in both the Special Committee's Report and in the Sixth Committee, were not wholly favorable, with some states suggesting that Article 96 of the Charter does not authorize such a possibility, since it only anticipates requests from "organs," other states expressing fear that the Secretary-General could use the power in a selective manner based on personal predilections, and still others voicing concern about important unresolved details—such as how one could make a "quiet" submission to the Court and still permit affected states to have a say in the submission, whether the authorization to the Secretary-General would be ad hoc or permanent, and whether the Secretary-General would be free to request such opinions even when the Secretary himself was an interested party [see, e.g., comments by Iran, Spain, Tanzania, the United Kingdom, and Sudan, A/C.6/47/SR.14–16; A/47/33, pp. 11–12].

There have been calls to drop the specific references to "enemy states" in the Charter [A/47/33, p. 5], but even more controversial is the general subject of **Charter revision,** and changes in the composition of the Security Council in particular. A clear line of division is now forming between those who believe that a time when the Charter is finally beginning to work as intended is not the time to consider fundamental changes [see, e.g., Armenia, A/C.6/47/SR.14] and those who seek a radical "democratization" of the Security Council and a better "balance" between it and the Assembly with respect to peace and security issues [see, e.g., Cuba, ibid., and its working paper on the subject, discussed in A/47/33, pp. 45–49].

Those desirous of Charter revisions pointed to changes in the Organization prompted by, among other things, the end of the Cold War, the increase in the number of U.N. members, the development of powerful quasi-sovereign entities (such as the EEC), and the paralyzing potential of the permanent five veto [A/47/33, pp. 4–5]. Germany, for its part, indicated that it would seek a permanent seat should change in the composition of the Council be considered [A/C.6/47/SR.16]. The 47th Session left all these issues on the Special Committee's agenda for further discussion during the 48th Assembly [A/Res/47/38].

4. International Organizations and Host Country Relations

The Secretary-General's annual report on effective measures to enhance **the protection, security, and safety of diplomatic and consular missions and representatives** showed an increase in the number of reported cases of violations of international law governing these premises and persons [A/47/325 and additions]. For the period October 1, 1991–September 18,

1992, there were 82 new cases of violations, including serious violent attacks, compared with 40 and 35 new cases in comparable periods in 1991 and 1990, respectively [ibid.]. Discussion of the report in the Sixth Committee led to uniform condemnation of the acts of violence but no agreement on how to deal with them any more effectively than through greater adherence and strict compliance with relevant international treaties. The Russian Federation, however, argued for considering sanctions in such cases, while Iran suggested that "safety zones" around missions would provide the necessary deterrent [A/C.6/47/SR.11]. A subsequent Assembly resolution condemned these acts of violence; urged states to observe, implement, and enforce the relevant rules of international law and ratify relevant treaties if they had not yet done so; called on states to resolve peacefully any disputes concerning their obligations to missions and to make use of the "good offices" of the Secretary-General for this purpose; and placed the item on the agenda for the 49th Session in 1994 [A/Res/47/31].

Proposals for an **additional protocol on consular functions to the Vienna Convention on Consular Relations**—pending ever since the 45th Session raised the issue of such a protocol to replace existing bilateral arrangements—were tabled in view of objections raised by some states in the Sixth Committee and during informal consultations that present bilateral arrangements were preferable and preserved flexibility [A/Res/47/36; see also A/C.6/47/SR.26 (discussion in the Sixth Committee) and A/C.6/47/L.7 (report on informal consultations)].

As in the past, the attempt by the Assembly majority to extend to those national liberation movements that are recognized as observers to international organizations the **privileges and immunities of diplomatic personnel** did not win the votes of most of the states that are host to international organizations [A/Res/47/29, adopted by a vote of 10–9–34], which have also long opposed the 1975 Vienna Convention on the Representation of States in Their Relations with International Organizations of a Universal Character [see *Issues/46*, pp. 256–57].

During the 47th Assembly, the **Committee on Relations with the Host Country**, established in 1971, focused considerable attention on the continuing problem of **financial indebtedness by missions** to the United Nations [A/47/26 and A/Res/47/35; see also *Issues/47*, pp. 316–17]. The United States, as host state, noted that this issue had become increasingly vexing, had led it to advise diplomats at two permanent missions that they would be directed to leave unless they paid their debts, and "reflected poorly on the entire United Nations community" [A/47/26, p. 9]. The U.N. Legal Counsel, for its part, warned that diplomatic privileges and immunities were not to be abused and used as a means to avoid paying debts [ibid., p. 10]. Switzerland, as host to the U.N. Offices in Geneva, warned that it too would seek reductions in the size of missions that accumulate excessive debts [ibid., p. 11].

The United States announced that it was lifting **travel restrictions on diplomats** from Vietnam, Belarus, the Russian Federation, Georgia, and Ukraine [ibid., pp. 5–7] and answered complaints from Libya regarding a forced reduction in the size of its U.N. mission, which the United States justified under Security Council Resolution 748 [ibid., p. 13; see *Issues/47*, p. 317]. The Committee on Relations with the Host Country also heard complaints from Cuba concerning **protests at its mission** and the U.S. explanation that "there seemed to be a difference of opinion about what constituted democratic process and freedom of speech" [ibid., p. 14].

5. Economic Relations

Resolution 47/15, concerning **foreign economic interests that impede the independence of peoples under colonial domination,** puts in clear relief the continuing North–South divide in the Assembly. Adopted by a vote of 95–34–12, with virtually every developing country in favor and every industrialized nation against, the resolution harkens back to the days of the New International Economic Order and resurrects the language of the Charter of Economic Rights and Duties of States [A/Res/3281 (XXIX), 12/12/74]. Among other things, the 1992 resolution affirms the "inalienable" right of peoples of colonial and non-self-governing territories to dispose of their natural resources as they see fit and proclaims their "permanent sovereignty" over these resources, declares that administering or occupying powers that subordinate this right to "foreign economic and financial interests" violate the U.N. Charter and calls on governments to take legal actions to restrict their nationals and companies accordingly, and condemns transnational corporations and others that make new investments in South Africa, and calls for an embargo on oil supplies and other products to that country. The item appears again on the agenda of the 48th Session.

By contrast, most of the Assembly's five resolutions on the Uruguay Round negotiations for new provisions of the **General Agreement on Tariffs and Trade (GATT)**—calling for prompt, successful conclusions to those multilateral trade negotiations from a variety of perspectives—were adopted by consensus. A "balanced and successful outcome" of the negotiations was deemed necessary for an "open, free, equitable and disciplined trading system" to improve access to all markets for developing-country exports [A/Res/47/178], to promote the pro-development agenda of the U.N. Conference on Trade and Development (UNCTAD) [A/Res/47/183], to help strengthen multilateral trade efforts generally [A/Res/47/184], and to facilitate an expansion of trade in the commodities produced by developing countries [A/Res/47/185; see also Secretary-General's progress report on the Uruguay Round, A/47/410]. Another, related Assembly action—this on "enhanced co-operation towards a **durable solution to the external-debt problems of developing countries**"—also praised the Uruguay Round but drew a dissenting vote by the United States, perhaps because of its call for the "write-off of a significant part of the bilateral official debt by certain donors to the least developed countries" and the cancellation of the "official development assistance debt" of these countries [A/Res/47/198]. That resolution calls too for continued concessional financial assistance to debtor developing countries by the multilateral financial institutions and praises many innovative legal measures to alleviate these states' debts, including debt-for-equity swaps, debt-for-nature swaps, and debt-for-development swaps [ibid.].

The Assembly's agenda contained other legal issues of particular interest to developing states. It endorsed the establishment of an intergovernmental negotiating committee to elaborate an **international convention to combat desertification** among those countries, particularly African states, experiencing serious drought [A/Res/47/188]. The recent U.N. Conference on Environment and Development (UNCED) had proposed the convention, and the goal is to finalize it by June 1994. A special voluntary fund was also established to facilitate the participation in the negotiations of interested developing countries [ibid.]. In accord with another UNCED mandate, the Assembly decided to convene in 1993 an intergovernmental conference to consider the best way to implement the provisions of the U.N. Convention on the Law of the Sea with respect to **straddling fish stocks and highly migratory fish stocks** [A/Res/47/192]. As with the proposed treaty on desertification, a voluntary fund will assist developing-country participation [ibid.]. And in keeping with past practice, the Assembly affirmed the **right to development,** noting that the work of the Commission on Human Rights had entered a "new phase" with respect to this issue and that the question of the relationship between development and enjoyment of other human rights was on the agenda for the 1993 World Conference on Human Rights [A/Res/47/123; see also *Issues/47*, p. 319].

The future of the **Code of Conduct on the Transfer of Technology** is cloudy at best. This effort, begun in 1977 and the focus of six conferences under the auspices of UNCTAD through 1985 and numerous consultations since [see *Issues/46*, p. 258; *Issues/47*, p. 319], reached a stalemate during the eighth session of UNCTAD and did no better during subsequent consultations by UNCTAD's Secretary-General [A/47/636]. Industrialized and developing countries continue to disagree about such basic issues as the exclusive application of national competition laws and the freedom to contract and to choose the applicable law and the forum for dispute settlement [ibid.; *Issues/47*, p. 319]. Only a limited number of governments responded to the latest effort by UNCTAD to solicit views on the subject, and the U.S. response was particularly blunt: It opposed resumption of negotiations, since "there is no basis to believe that there is a 'convergence of views' on the outstanding issues in the draft code of conduct, nor is there likely to be" [A/47/636, p. 7]. The 47th Session of the Assembly opted merely to direct the Secretary-General of UNCTAD to continue consultations and to report to the 48th Session [A/Res/47/182].

In accordance with tradition, the 47th Assembly's review of the latest report of the **U.N. Commission on International Trade Law (UNCITRAL)** culminated in its reaffirmation of UNCITRAL as the "core legal body within the United Nations system in the field of international trade law" [A/Res/47/34; for a note by the Secretariat containing a bibliography of recent writings related to UNCITRAL, see A/CN.9/369]. Perhaps because this was UNCITRAL's 25th anniversary, the Sixth Committee praised UNCITRAL's work more highly than usual, most delegates citing its "efficiency" and its "technical" and "apolitical" work. The representative of Spain suggested that UNCITRAL's success was due to its "judicious choice of issues appropriate to the uniform development of international trade in two main areas—meeting the challenges of technology and devising ways of overcoming the difficulties arising from the differences between countries' legal systems and levels of economic development." What is more, asserted this delegate,

> UNCITRAL's working methods could serve as a model for other United Nations bodies concerned with the development and codification of international law. Its methods were characterized primarily by: (a) a practical approach to the selection of topics and wide participation in that selection; (b) flexibility in the drafting of texts, subordinating the final form to content requirements; (c) close coordination with other organizations specializing in the issues under consideration and concerned with international trade law, thereby avoiding duplication and conflicts; and (d) continued attention to texts already adopted [A/C.6/47/SR.4].

Other countries, however, spoke yet again of the need to ensure that UNCITRAL will promote the interests of poor countries and that its work will be marked by "justice and fairness," rather than by mere efficiency. To this end, there were numerous calls for financial assistance to facilitate the participation of developing countries in UNCITRAL's work [see, e.g., comments by Côte d'Ivoire, China, and Nigeria, A/C.6/47/SR.5]. And, as it has in the past, the Assembly called on the Fifth (Administrative and Budgetary) Committee to consider travel grants for this purpose [A/Res/47/34; A/47/454; and A/C.6/47/4; see also *Issues/47*, p. 320].

Much of the Sixth Committee's attention was directed to UNCITRAL's newly completed **Legal Guide on International Countertrade Transactions,** intended for use by those engaged in the direct exchange or the barter of goods without the use of currency—a particularly significant form of international trade for developing countries [see, e.g., *Issues/47*, p. 322]. The Guide is not intended to encourage or discourage countertrade but only to assist parties to "establish fair and balanced contractual relations when they decide to engage in countertrade" [A/47/17, p. 23], and its 15 chapters are designed to promote a common international approach to underlying legal issues. They cover such subjects as type, quality, and quantity of goods; pricing; participation of third parties; payment; restrictions on resale; liquidated damages and other penalties; security for performance; choice of law; and settlement of disputes [A/CN.9/362 and additions]. In the Sixth Committee, industrialized countries generally recognized the need for the Guide and promised to give it wide distribution but noted that countertrade, which was not wholly in conformity with "free competition," should not be encouraged lest it distort market conditions [see, e.g., comments by Czechoslovakia, Denmark, and the United States, A/C.6/47/SR.4].

At its 25th session, UNCITRAL also completed work on its **Model Law on International Credit Transfers,** which had been sent to governments for comment after adoption in 1991. The Model Law is intended to contribute toward the establishment of a unified legal framework for the increasing number of payments in international trade, particularly those made via high-speed international electronic fund-transfer systems but also including paper-based transfers. After discussion of a number of last-minute revisions—as well as of proposed changes to articles on liability and damages, completion of credit transfer and discharge of obligation, and conflict of laws—the Commission adopted the Model Law and requested that the Secretary-General transmit the text to U.N. member states, together with the *travaux preparatoires* of the 24th and 25th sessions of the Commission, for their consideration when enacting or revising domestic laws [A/47/17, pp. 5–21; for text of Model Law, see ibid., Annex I].

UNCITRAL's chairman proclaimed before the Sixth Committee that the Model Law had surpassed expectations, since it was not merely a set of model rules that might serve as the first draft for any state wishing to consider legislation or a text with alternative formulations but a true "Model Law ready for adoption" containing the collective wisdom of all participants and capable of providing the certainty and uniformity required in this area [A/C.6/47/SR.3]. Industrialized countries in particular agreed with this assessment, and the U.S. representative called the Model Law a "ground breaker" in that it sought to develop legal norms "before, rather than after, conflicts arose between national laws and decisions . . . ; instead of trying to harmonize conflicting legal systems, the Model Law provided the means whereby the United Nations system could anticipate the necessary commercial rules" [A/C.6/47/SR.4]. The representative of India was one of the few dissenting voices, stating that, since the Model Law could be used by a state to regulate purely domestic credit transfers, its incorporation into "any domestic system might disturb the well-settled banking practices and customs of each country" [A/C.6/47/SR.5].

UNCITRAL is also nearing completion of its long-awaited **Model Law on Procurement,** designed to assist states in restructuring or improving their rules governing transactions involving governmental agencies [A/47/17, p. 32; A/CN.9/359; see also *Issues/47*, p. 321]. A draft model law is expected to be submitted to the 26th session of the Commission in 1993 for finalization and adoption, to be followed by a commentary aimed at guiding national bodies that are preparing legislation based on the model law [A/47/17, p. 32]. UNCITRAL's Working Group on International Contract Practices also remains at work on a **Uniform Law on Guarantees and Stand-by Letters of Credit** and is preparing a revised draft of 27 articles of that law [A/47/17, p. 33; A/CN.9/361; see also *Issues/47*, pp. 321–22].

Finally, UNCITRAL's 25th session reviewed the report of the Working Group on International Payments about future work on **electronic data interchange (EDI)**—that is, the formation of international commercial contracts by electronic means [see *Issues/47*, p. 322]. The Working Group had recommended that UNCITRAL facilitate the increased use of EDI by developing model statutory provisions to govern such issues as formation of contracts, risk and liability of commercial partners and of third-party service providers, the definition of standard terms like "writing" and "original," and negotiability and documents of title [A/47/17, p. 30; see also A/CN.9/360]. At the same time, the Working Group had indicated that not all EDI issues could be resolved through a uniform law and that there would be some questions on which legislative unification was premature or inappropriate or which ought to be approached differently, such as through model contractual clauses [ibid.]. In accordance with these recommendations, UNCITRAL entrusted the Working Group, renamed the Working Group on Electronic Data Interchange, to prepare practical legal rules on EDI without making a final decision on the form these rules would take [A/47/17, p. 31].

Pursuant to the Assembly's decision in 1979 that the Secretary-General report to each UNCITRAL session on the development of law in the international trade field [see *Issues/47*, p. 323], the Secretary-General's latest such report focused on **multilateral and bilateral aid agencies' work on the modernization of commercial laws in developing countries** [A/CN.9/364]. The Secretary-General found that such assistance typically takes the form of the service of experts, as well as of funds for the execution of projects, and that this work is focusing on investment laws, intellectual property law, maritime legislation, and commercial law relating to taxation, insurance, customs, procurement, and export/import trade [ibid.].

6. Space Law

The 47th Assembly endorsed the 1992 Report of the **Committee on the Peaceful Uses of Outer Space** [A/47/20] as well as the Legal Subcommittee's ongoing agenda, namely: (1) the review and revision of the newly completed principles relevant to the use of nuclear power sources in outer space; (2) matters relating to the definition and delimitation of outer space; and (3) the legal ramifications of the principle that exploration and utilization should benefit all states, including developing countries [A/Res/47/67]. That resolution also recommended discussion of the possibility of holding a third U.N. Conference on the Exploration and Peaceful Uses of Outer Space and suggested that the Committee on Peaceful Uses of Outer Space take on the subject of space debris and the means of handling it [ibid.; for initial replies of members, provided pursuant to this resolution, on the issue of the problems of collisions of nuclear power sources with space debris, see, e.g., A/AC.105/542 and additions].

By separate resolution and by consensus, the 47th Assembly adopted the **Principles Relevant to the Use of Nuclear Power Sources in Outer Space,** which had been under consideration by a Working Group of the Legal Subcommittee for some time and had been elaborated after recent informal consultations [see, e.g., *Issues/47*, pp. 323–24; A/Res/47/68]. One principle states that activities involving use of such power sources are governed by international law and another provides guidelines and criteria for safe use of such sources, including general goals for radiation protection relating to the design and use of such sources, and indicates limits on the use of nuclear reactors and radioisotope generators. Still other principles call for thorough and comprehensive prelaunch safety assessments, notification of reentry, information exchanges, and mutual assistance. Yet others take up state responsibility, international liability, and dispute settlement [A/Res/47/68]. Several of the provisions follow from the Treaty on Principles Governing the Activities of States in the Exploration and Use of Outer Space, including the Moon and Other Celestial Bodies.

There was no apparent progress on the other two topics on the Outer Space Committee's agenda. States continue to disagree on the need for a legal **definition and delimitation of outer space** [see *Issues/47*, p. 324], and states continue to differ on whether the equitable **utilization of the geostationary orbit** requires the creation of a sui generis legal regime with a system of preferential rights for developing countries and for those countries with no previous access to the orbit [see, e.g., A/47/20, pp. 19–20]. Similarly, some delegations continue to see the third topic, concerning the **exploration and utilization of outer space,** as a mandate to establish a "new international legal framework" within which to address the inequalities between technologically advanced space nations and developing countries and emphasize the need to develop indigenous space capabilities and ensure access to space resources and technology. Still other delegations—usually those of the more industrialized states—continue to see this topic as nothing more than an opportunity for an "exchange of views" [A/47/20, p. 21; see also *Issues/47*, pp. 324–25].

The 47th Assembly also endorsed the ongoing agenda of the Scientific and Technical Subcommittee of the Outer Space Committee, recommending that it give priority to several items that overlap with issues currently before the Legal Subcommittee, including such subjects as the use of nuclear power sources, the physical nature and technical attributes of the geostationary orbit and its utilization, and remote satellite sensing and its application by developing countries [A/Res/47/67].

7. The International Court of Justice

The ICJ, or World Court, is busier than at any time in its history but rendered only a few judgments over the past year.

Perhaps the most publicized action of the Court involves the **Application of the Convention on the Prevention and Punishment of the Crime of Genocide,** resulting from an application by Bosnia and Herzegovina, filed March 20, 1993, instituting proceedings against Yugoslavia (Serbia and Montenegro) under Article IX of the Genocide Convention. The application alleged a wide variety of violations of international law, based on the Genocide Convention, international humanitarian law (including the four Geneva Conventions), the U.N. Charter, human rights law, and customary international law; and it sought, apart from reparations, a determination that Security Council decisions imposing an arms embargo be construed not to impair Bosnia and Herzegovina's inherent right of individual or collective self-defense. The Court held public hearings on April 1–2, 1993, on Bosnia and Herzegovina's separate applications, filed the same day, for provisional measures, rendering its decision on this request on April 8. Here, the Court sidestepped difficult jurisdictional issues concerning the status of the parties as U.N. members and as parties to the Genocide Convention, since these questions need not be determined "definitively" for purposes of provisional relief; found that it had prima facie jurisdiction under the Genocide Convention; and limited itself to allegations arising under that Convention, staying clear of broader issues raised in the application [Order of 4/8/93, paras. 15–35]. Most important, it held, by a vote of 13–1 (Judge Tarassov), that Serbia and Montenegro should

> ensure that any military, paramilitary or irregular armed units which may be directed or supported by it, as well as any organizations and persons which may be subject to its control, direction or influence, do not commit any acts of genocide, of conspiracy to commit genocide, of

> direct and public incitement to commit genocide, or of complicity in genocide, whether directed against the Muslim population of Bosnia and Herzegovina or against any other national, ethnical, racial or religious group [ibid., para. 52].

The Court also determined, unanimously, that neither party should undertake any action that would exacerbate the existing dispute or render any solution more difficult [ibid.]. It rejected the argument that provisional relief would be premature or inappropriate given ongoing Security Council actions in the region, quoting from its decision in *Nicaragua v. United States* to the effect that the Council and the Court exercise complementary but separate functions [ibid., para. 33; *compare* the Court's handling of Libya's request for provisional relief last year. See *Issues/47*, pp. 325–27]. The Court stated that it was only indicating measures to protect rights under the Genocide Convention and was not determining that breaches of that Convention had in fact occurred [para. 46]—although, stated Judge Tarassov in dissent, the order is certainly "open to the interpretation that the Court believes that the Government of the Federal Republic of Yugoslavia is indeed involved in such genocidal acts." Given its decision here, it is probable that subsequent proceedings on the merits will be limited to allegations arising under the Genocide Convention. By order of April 16, 1993, the Court fixed October 15, 1993, as the date for the memorial on the merits by Bosnia-Herzegovina; Serbia-Montenegro has until April 15, 1994, for its countermemorial.

On September 11, 1992, a Chamber of the full Court delivered its judgment in the case of **Land, Island and Maritime Frontier Dispute (El Salvador v. Honduras, Nicaragua Intervening).** The judgment determined the land boundary between Honduras and El Salvador in six disputed sectors, the legal status of three islands in the Gulf of Fonseca, and the legal status of maritime spaces within that Gulf. The Chamber adhered to the parties' view (confirmed by their 1980 Peace Treaty) that, in principle, international boundaries should follow former colonial administrative boundaries, and much of the evidence submitted by the parties related to documents conferring title by the Spanish Crown in disputed areas, or, in the absence of these, evidence of the conduct of administrative authorities as proof of the effective exercise of territorial jurisdiction in the region during the colonial period. The Court based its determinations on the paper record submitted to it and rejected requests for evaluations of evidence *in situ* or for appointments of experts [Communiqué, 9/11/92, p. 11]. Concerning the islands in the Gulf, the Court found that the status of El Tigre, Meanguera, and Meanguerita was in dispute and found, largely on the grounds of effective possession, that the first belongs to Honduras while the other two are part of El Salvador [ibid., pp. 24–27]. With respect to the maritime boundary, the Court found that it was authorized only to "determine their legal situation" and not effect a delimitation, and it stated its view that the Gulf of Fonseca is a historic bay with the character of a closed sea subject to the joint sovereignty (or condominium) of El Salvador, Honduras, and Nicaragua [ibid., pp. 28–33]. It also found that, under the terms by which intervention had been granted to Nicaragua [see *Issues/46*, pp. 266–67], that country had not become a "party" to the proceeding and, accordingly, was not bound by the judgment [ibid., p. 34].

On June 26, 1992, the Court delivered its judgment on the preliminary objections filed by Australia in **Certain Phosphate Lands in Nauru (Nauru v. Australia).** This dispute concerned the "rehabilitation of certain phosphate lands [in Nauru] worked out before Nauruan independence" [Judgment, para. 7]. The Court determined that it had jurisdiction to entertain Nauru's application and that the application was admissible—rejecting in the process a number of Australian objections to jurisdiction (some of which were evocative of those raised unsuccessfully by the United States in *Nicaragua v. United States*): that prior dispute settlement arrangements dating from the time of termination of the trusteeship over Nauru precluded the Court's jurisdiction [ibid., para. 11], that Nauruan authorities had, before acceding to independence, waived all relevant claims [ibid., paras. 12–21], that U.N. termination of the trusteeship precluded any claim [ibid., paras. 22–30], that Nauru delayed too long once it had achieved independence in raising its claim [ibid., paras. 31–36], that Nauru had failed to act consistently and in good faith [ibid., paras. 37–38], and that the claim against Australia could not be adjudicated in the absence of other administrators of the territory of Nauru, namely, New Zealand and the United Kingdom [ibid., paras. 39–55]. The Court agreed, however, to dismiss a portion of Nauru's claim that had been tacked on to the end of Nauru's memorial and was directed at the overseas assets of the British Phosphate Commissioners, ruling that this was essentially a new claim, not part of Nauru's original application [ibid., paras. 58–70]. By an order dated June 29, 1992, the Court fixed March 29, 1993, as the time limit for Australia's countermemorial.

The parties in the **Case Concerning Passage Through the Great Belt** informed the Court that they had reached a settlement in the dispute. This proceeding had been instituted by Finland against Denmark and concerned Denmark's planned construction of a high-level bridge that would prohibit passage of certain vessels through the Great Belt [see *Issues/47*, pp. 329–30]. On September 10, 1992, the Court issued an order recording the discontinuance of the proceedings and removing the case from its docket.

Libya's territorial dispute with Chad, arising from separate notifications to the Court by each of the states in 1990 [see *Issues/46*, p. 268] remains at the pleading stage. The Court, in an order dated April 14, 1992, fixed September 14, 1992, as the time limit for replies by each party. By an order dated January 27, 1993, the Court set the date for hearings as June 7, 1993. The hearings were later postponed until June 14, 1993 [Communiqué, 3/29/93]. The Court's consideration of the merits in the **Case Concerning Questions of the Interpretation and the Application of the 1971 Montreal Convention Arising from the Aerial Incident at Lockerbie (Libya v. United States, Libya v. United Kingdom)** also remains at the pleading stage [for discussion of the Court's determination of provisional measures, see *Issues/47*, pp. 325–27]. An order dated June 19, 1992, fixed December 20, 1993, as the deadline for Libya's memorial and June 20, 1995, for countermemorials by the U.S. and the United Kingdom, respectively.

Also at the pleading stage is Iran's claim against the United States for compensation growing out of the destruction of Iran Airbus A-300B, Flight 655, **Aerial Incident of 3 July 1988** [see *Issues/46*, p. 267]. The Court extended, until September 9, 1992, the time limit for the written observations and submissions of Iran on the preliminary objections that had been filed by the United States [Order, 6/5/92].

In the **Case Concerning Maritime Delimitation and Territorial Questions Between Qatar and Bahrain,** the Court, by order dated June 26, 1992, directed a time limit of September 28, 1992, for the reply of Qatar and a limit of December 29, 1992, for Bahrain's rejoinder. This proceeding concerns "certain existing disputes . . . relating to sovereignty over the Hawar islands, sovereign rights over the shoals of Dibal and Qit'at Jaradah, and the delimitation of the maritime areas of the two states" [A/46/4, p. 18].

Portugal's proceeding against Australia, the **Case Concerning Certain Activities of Australia with Respect to East Timor,** also remains at the pleading stage. The Court, by an order of June 19, 1992, fixed December 1, 1992, as the time limit for the filing of a reply by Portugal and June 1, 1993, as the time limit for the filing of a rejoinder by Australia. Portugal's application, filed on February 22, 1991, claims that the people of East Timor and Portugal suffered serious "legal and moral damage" as a result of an agreement between Australia and Indonesia relating to the exploration and exploitation of certain areas in the continental shelf [see *Issues/46*, p. 269].

Public hearings on the **Case Concerning the Maritime Delimitation in the Area Between Greenland and Jan Mayer (Denmark v. Norway)** [see *Issues/46*, p. 268] began on January 11, 1993, and continued through January 27.

At a meeting held with the President of the Court on October 6, 1992, the parties to the dispute concerning the **maritime delimitation between Guinea and Senegal** stated that some progress had been made in negotiations. The President granted a request to extend the period of negotiations for three months, with a possible extension for three more months. This is the second case to arise out of this dispute [see *Issues/47*, pp.

327–29]. Judgment in the first case was rendered on November 12, 1991 [31 ILM 32 (1992)], at which time the parties stipulated that no time limits should be set for written pleadings pending negotiations of the second case [Communiqué, 10/9/92].

Two additional applications for new cases have been filed with the Court over the past year. On October 23, 1992, Hungary presented the Court with an application concerning the **dispute with the Czech and Slovak Federal Republic over the projected diversion of the Danube.** Hungary is apparently hoping to establish jurisdiction based on consent and has invited the Czech and Slovak Federal Republic (now formally separated into two countries) to accept the jurisdiction of the Court [Communiqué, 10/26/92]. On November 2, 1992, Iran instituted another case against the United States, this time with respect to **the destruction of three offshore oil platforms,** allegedly caused on October 19, 1987, and April 18, 1988, by several U.S. Navy warships. The oil production complexes were owned and operated by the Iranian Oil Company, and Iran claims that the Court has jurisdiction under Article XXI(2) of the Iran-U.S. Treaty of Amity, Economic Relations and Consular Rights of 1955. Its application alleges breaches of the Treaty of Amity as well as of international law and requests reparations [Communiqué, 11/2/92]. On December 4, 1992, the Court issued an order setting May 31, 1993, as the time limit for Iran's memorial and November 30, 1993, as the time limit for the countermemorial of the United States.

A proposal by 21 states of the Ibero-American Conference that the General Assembly request from the ICJ an **advisory opinion concerning the legality of extraterritorial arrests and apprehensions of criminal suspects,** generally assumed to have been prompted by the U.S. Supreme Court's decision in *United States v. Alvarez-Machain* [112 S.Ct. 2188 (1992)], was the subject of lengthy informal consultations [see Virginia Morris and M.-Christiane Bourloyannis, "The Work of the Sixth Committee at the Forty-Seventh Session of the UN General Assembly," 87 *American Journal of International Law* 306 (1993), p. 322]. The Assembly decided to postpone consideration of the issue until the 48th Session, presumably in part to give the new U.S. administration time to consider the matter [ibid.; A/Dec/47/416].

Elected in May 1993 to fill the vacancy on the Court created by the death of Judge Manfred Lachs was Geza Herczegh of Hungary, whose term will expire in February 1994. At last report, 56 states had made declarations recognizing the compulsory jurisdiction of the Court, as contemplated by Article 36(2) and (5) of the Court's statute [A/47/4].

The Secretary-General reported to the 47th Assembly on the progress achieved with respect to the Trust Fund, announced in 1989, to assist states in the settlement of disputes in the Court. According to that report, 34 states have contributed a total of $583,705, and the Secretary-General has now acted on various applications by developing countries for financial assistance [A/47/444]. The Terms of Reference, Guidelines, and Rules established for the Fund provide, among other things, that each request for financial assistance will be referred to a three-person panel of experts for its recommendation [ibid., Annex]. It is anticipated that assistance may be granted for preparation of written pleadings, fees to agents or other necessary personnel, legal research, costs related to oral proceedings, production of technical materials, or costs relating to the execution of judgments (such as demarcation of boundaries) [ibid., para. 9].

8. Other Legal Developments

In what has now become an annual rite demonstrating the membership's lack of agreement on the meaning of Article 2(7) of the Charter, the Assembly passed two contradictory resolutions concerning the degree to which the Organization should become involved in **electoral assistance.** As at the 45th and 46th sessions [see *Issues/46*, pp. 271–72; *Issues/47*, pp. 332–33], the Assembly commended the U.N.'s involvement in electoral assistance, welcoming the establishment of trust funds for electoral observation and for technical electoral assistance [A/Res/47/138, adopted by a vote of 141–0–20]. (The electoral assistance item was "biennialized" and will come up again during the 49th Session in 1994 [ibid.].) The Assembly also affirmed—this, in the traditional second resolution—that the principle of noninterference in internal affairs continues to govern the issue, that there is no "single political system or single model for electoral processes ideally suited to all nations," that all peoples have the right to determine their own political status without "external interference," that activities that attempt "directly or indirectly" to interfere in free electoral processes violate the Charter and the Declaration on Principles of International Law concerning Friendly Relations and Cooperation among States in Accordance with the Charter of the United Nations, and that "there is no universal need for the United Nations to provide electoral assistance to Member States, except in special circumstances such as cases of decolonization" [A/Res/47/130, adopted by a vote of 99–45–16]. This item reappears on the agenda of the 48th Session [ibid.].

As it has during prior sessions, the Assembly encouraged **international cooperation in combatting organized crime** and called on states to implement the guidelines for the prevention and control of organized crime and related model treaties emerging from the Eighth United Nations Congress on the Prevention of Crime and the Treatment of Offenders [A/Res/47/86; and see *Issues/46*, pp. 249–52]. It also invited states to make available to the Secretary-General copies of domestic legislation relating to money laundering; the tracing, seizing, and forfeiture of proceeds of crime; and the monitoring of large-scale cash transactions to assist other states that are considering laws in these areas [ibid.]. Similar priorities were reflected in the Assembly's resolution welcoming the establishment of the U.N.'s **Commission on Crime Prevention and Criminal Justice,** which held its first session in Vienna in 1992 [A/Res/47/91; see also *Issues/47*, pp. 307–308]. The Assembly approved the following program for the Commission on Crime Prevention, which had been designated by ECOSOC:

> (a) National and transnational crime, organized crime, economic crime, including money laundering, and the role of criminal law in the protection of the environment;
> (b) Crime prevention in urban areas, juvenile and violent criminality;
> (c) Efficiency, fairness and improvement in the management and administration of criminal justice and related systems, with due emphasis on the strengthening of national capacities in developing countries for the regular collection, collation, analysis and utilization of data in the development and implementation of appropriate policies [A/Res/47/91].

The Assembly issued several calls for the ratification and implementation of the **U.N. Convention against Illicit Traffic in Narcotic Drugs and Psychotropic Substances** [see A/Res/47/97–102]. And it agreed to hold four high-level plenary meetings during the 48th Session to examine the question of international cooperation to limit drug trafficking with a view to, among other things, encouraging domestic legislation and administrative measures compatible with relevant international treaties and eradicating the links between "terrorist groups, drug traffickers and paramilitary gangs" [A/Res/47/99].

As it has done repeatedly over the years, the Assembly urged states to ratify significant **human rights conventions,** including the Convention on the Prevention and Punishment of the Crime of Genocide [A/Res/47/108]; Convention on the Rights of the Child [A/Res/47/112]; Convention against Torture and Other Cruel, Inhuman or Degrading Treatment or Punishment [A/Res/47/113]; International Convention on the Suppression and Punishment of the Crime of Apartheid [A/Res/47/81]; Convention on the Elimination of All Forms of Discrimination against Women [A/Res/47/94]; International Convention on the Protection of the Rights of All Migrant Workers and Members of Their Families [A/Res/47/110]; and International Convention on the Elimination of All Forms of Racial Discrimination [A/Res/47/78 and 79. See also A/Res/47/111 on the effective implementation of existing human rights instruments and A/Res/47/131 on the need to apply human rights law based on the principles of nonselectivity, impartiality, and objectivity]. As part of its efforts during the **Second Decade to Combat Racism and Racial Discrimination,** the Assembly requested that the Secretary-General finalize draft model laws against racial discrimination to serve as guides for governments considering such legislation [A/Res/47/77]. The Assembly also added to the considerable body of human rights standards two additional detailed declarations—on the **Protection of All Persons From Enforced Disappearance** [A/Res/47/133] and on the **Rights of Persons Belonging to National or Ethnic, Religious and Linguistic Minorities** [A/Res/47/135 Annex].

More controversial was an Assembly effort to reaffirm the "right of self-determination" and, in the process, identify instances in which this right has been infringed. Its resolution on **self-determination and the speedy granting of independence to colonial countries and peoples**—which, among other things, affirms the "national unity and territorial integrity" of the Comoros, condemns "Israeli oppressive measures and the denial of the inalienable rights of the Palestinian people to self-determination," and demands the full application of the mandatory arms embargo against South Africa—drew 22 dissenting votes, mostly from industrialized countries, and 33 abstentions [A/Res/47/82; on the question of Comoros' claim to the island of Mayotte, see *Issues/47*, p. 317]. Similarly controversial was a resolution calling for ratification of the **International Convention against the Recruitment, Use, Financing and Training of Mercenaries,** which expresses concern about the South African government's use of "groups of armed mercenaries against national liberation movements" [A/Res/47/84. Vote: 118–10–36]. A third resolution, affirming the **universal right to self-determination** and requesting that the Commission on Human Rights continue to give the subject special attention, was adopted by consensus [A/Res/47/83].

The Assembly approved the Sixth Committee's program of activities for the second term (1993–94) of the **U.N. Decade of International Law** [A/Res/47/32 and Annex; see also *Issues/47*, pp. 333–34]. That program identifies the goals for the coming year by type of activity: (1) promotion of international law principles, primarily by encouraging adherence to multilateral treaties; (2) promotion of the peaceful settlement of disputes, especially through greater use of the ICJ, regional mechanisms, and arbitration; (3) encouragement of progressive development and codification efforts; and (4) wider dissemination of international law principles, particularly through teaching and research in developing countries [ibid., Annex]. The Sixth Committee's Working Group on the Decade noted some of the topics proposed by states for progressive development and codification, including principles governing collective security (for example, guidelines on the specific rights and duties of competent organs of the United Nations); international legal principles concerning organized crime and terrorism; norms relating to environmental protection; and humanitarian law [A/C.6/47/L.12, p. 4; see also the report of the Secretary-General surveying members' views on the U.N. Decade, A/47/384]. It also proposed convening a five-day U.N. Congress on Public International Law in 1994 or 1995 and began examining the feasibility of holding such a Congress, to be funded through existing resources and voluntary contributions [A/C.6/47/L.12, p. 7].

VII
Finance and Administration

By Anthony Mango

1. The Fifth Committee's Agenda in 1993

The main item on the Fifth Committee's agenda at the 48th Session in 1993 will be the Secretary-General's program budget proposals for the biennium 1994–95. The proposals will reflect the first two phases of the restructuring of the Secretariat, which have already been considered by the General Assembly, together with such additional steps as the Secretary-General may propose. How contentious this item will be depends on the Secretary-General's response to the views expressed by delegations at the 47th Session on the number and allocation of senior-level posts and resources to the various programs and subprograms, and on whether member states will consider that allocation to be compatible with the agreed major priority areas.

Another item that is likely to provoke a long debate is the scale of assessments for the apportionment of the expenses of the United Nations, under which the Assembly will decide on the guidelines to be given to the **Committee on Contributions** in the preparation of the next scale (for 1995–97); the scale itself will be considered by the Assembly in 1994.

The agenda will also include several items discussed at length at the 47th Session, such as the administrative and budgetary aspects of the financing of peacekeeping operations, the review of the efficiency of the administrative and financial functioning of the United Nations, the reports of the Board of Auditors, and improving the Organization's financial situation. Personnel questions are not included in the program of work, but the Fifth Committee will have to attend to unfinished business relating to the common system of salaries and allowances and the pension system, the Joint Inspection Unit, and other matters.

2. U.N. Finances

The Financial Situation: Inaction in the Midst of Crisis

The General Assembly's agenda for its 47th Session included two items on the financial difficulties of the United Nations: "Current financial crisis of the United Nations" and "Financial emergency of the United Nations." The two items were considered jointly by the Fifth Committee, along with the agenda item on the administrative and budgetary aspects of the financing of peacekeeping operations.

In the annex to his report on the financial situation [A/C.5/47/13] the Secretary-General summarized the proposals that he had made to the Assembly at its 46th Session, on which no action had been taken and which were still on the table [see *A Global Agenda: Issues/47,* p. 339] and those made subsequently in his report "An Agenda for Peace." Only 18 member states had met all their financial obligations to the United Nations by September 30, 1992. The amount owed *to* member states, including troop contributors, which could not be paid for lack of resources, was on the order of $800 million. The Secretary-General states that the persistent financial difficulties of the Organization were intrinsically unacceptable because they stemmed from the neglect of their legal obligations by a number of member states; they were also politically incongruous and increasingly damaging to the implementation of mandated programs.

Opening the discussion, the Under-Secretary-General for Administration and Management said that the financial situation of the Organization continued to be a matter of overriding concern. As of October 12, 1992, unpaid assessed contributions totaled some $1.2 billion, of which $550 million was owed for the regular budget and $605 million for assessed peacekeeping operations. During much of 1992 the various peacekeeping operations and, to a lesser extent, regular-budget activities were financed by borrowing from the few accounts in which there had been temporary surpluses. In "An Agenda for Peace" the Secretary-General had referred to the chasm that had developed between the tasks entrusted to the Organization and the financial means provided to carry them out. An **international advisory group on U.N. financing**, consisting of eminent financial and governmental experts from around the world—co-chaired by a former chairman of the U.S. Federal Reserve Board, Paul Volcker, and a retired Deputy Governor of the Japan Development Bank, Mr. Ogata—had been formed to study the problem [A/C.5/47/SR.4, paras. 6–12].

Thirty-nine delegations participated in the debate. As several of them spoke on behalf of groups of countries, the debate reflected the views of approximately a third of the total U.N. membership. Three-quarters of the speakers referred to the Secretary-General's proposals.

Views were divided on the proposal to charge interest on the amounts of assessed contributions that are not paid on time. Twelve speakers supported it, often with reservations; nine (including the United States) opposed it.

The proposal to suspend the Financial Regulations of the United Nations to permit the retention of budgetary surpluses was supported by seven speakers, on the understanding that the suspension would be temporary; three delegations were opposed.

Views were almost equally divided on the proposal to increase the size of the Working Capital Fund; eight delegations were prepared to go along, nine were against it.

There was virtually unanimous support for the establishment of a peacekeeping reserve fund: 25 speakers favored it, and one had reservations (he would have preferred the funding to come from an expanded Working Capital Fund).

The proposal that the Secretary-General be authorized to borrow commercially was endorsed by only one delegation, which did so with reservations; 19 delegations spoke against it.

There was no support for the proposal to establish a U.N. Peace Endowment Fund, with an initial target of $1 billion.

There were only a few references to the additional proposals and ideas contained in "An Agenda for Peace"; most were negative.

While the General Assembly noted with concern that the Board of Auditors had issued a qualified audit opinion on the U.N.'s financial statements for 1990–91, which opinion was subject to the ultimate resolution of unpaid assessed contributions from member states [A/Res/47/211], the only action it took following the prolonged debate on the financial crisis was to establish, effective January 1, 1993, a $150 million **Peacekeeping Reserve Fund** as a cash flow mechanism to ensure that the Organization can respond rapidly to the needs of peacekeeping operations; the initial financing of the Fund was to come from existing accounts (i.e., without requiring additional assessments) [A/Res/47/217]

As to the rest, the General Assembly merely reaffirmed that all member states have the obligation to pay their assessed contributions in full and on time. The Secretary General was asked to report to the 1993 session of the Assembly on the contingency measures he will have taken to address cash shortages. The Assembly also decided to consider the financial situation of the Organization "as and when required" [A/Res/47/215].

Does the failure of the General Assembly to act on the Secretary-General's proposals mean that the financial problems of the United Nations are over? Far from it. Between January 1 and December 31, 1992, unpaid assessed contributions increased by $351.8 million ($61.2 million for the regular budget and $290.6 million for peacekeeping operations) to almost $1,165 million ($500.6 million for the regular budget and $664.3 million for peacekeeping operations—including the $102.3 million for the operation in Somalia, the assessment letters for which were sent out in December 1992).

How does one explain the General Assembly's inaction? The very first speaker in the debate, the representative of Norway, speaking on behalf of the Nordic countries—which, because of the size of their contributions to U.N. voluntary programs, are by far the largest *per capita* contributors to the U.N. system—said that those countries found it hard to understand why the vast majority of the member states failed to pay their assessed contributions to either the regular budget or peacekeeping operations. The same members that were asking the Organization to assume important peacekeeping responsibilities were unwilling to provide it with the financial resources for carrying them out. The members of the Security Council had a special responsibility in that regard. Countries that, like the Nordic countries, faithfully met their financial obligations to the Organization, were coming under mounting domestic pressure as a result of the dramatic increase in appropriations for peacekeeping operations and the sizable amounts outstanding in reimbursement for the peacekeeping troops they had made available to the Organization. With so many states holding back their contributions, countries that had in the past paid in full, on time, and without conditions were less inclined to do so [A/C.5/47/SR.4, paras. 37–38]. The Canadian delegation agreed with the representative of Norway [A/C.5/47/SR.6, para. 4].

The representative of Austria pointed out that nonpayment by some member states was unfair to those states that did pay. In addition, nonpayment of peacekeeping assessments places an additional burden on troop-contributing countries; the withholding of reimbursements to them certainly affects their readiness to support payments to the Organization. Nor has the process of adopting budgetary decisions by consensus increased the willingness of some member states to pay their share of the expenses they had agreed to [A/C.5/47/SR.5, paras. 33 and 36].

Taking the floor on behalf of the 12 countries of the European Community, which account for over 30% of assessed contributions to the regular budget, the United Kingdom representative said that certain states that did not hesitate to call on the good offices of the Organization were at the same time willing to allow its financial situation to deteriorate; they seemed to trust that the Organization would always be financed by the states that met their obligations fully, promptly, and unconditionally. The only answer to the current financial situation, he said, was for all member states to pay their assessed contributions in accordance with their legal obligations under the Charter [A/C.5/47/SR.7, para. 22].

While the spokesmen for West European countries were voicing frustration at their countries' being expected to continue to bail out the United Nations, some Third World delegations saw more sinister motives behind the financial crisis. For instance, the representatives of Cameroon and Nigeria said that some members were using nonpayment of their assessed contributions as a political weapon to influence the Organization and compel it to conduct itself in accordance with their special interests [A/C.5/47/SR.4, para. 46, and SR.7, para. 28]. The representative of Cuba recalled that the crisis originated in 1985, when the main contributor began to hold back part of its contributions to put pressure on other member states. That amounted to political blackmail, he said [A/C.5/47/SR.9, para. 61].

The Malaysian delegation was particularly dismayed that more than half the total arrears was owed by two of the five permanent members of the Security Council (the United States and the Russian Federation—see below) [A/C.5/47/SR.4, para. 50]. The representative of Ghana said that in recent years his delegation had begun to wonder whether (considering all the publicity such last-minute action is sure to generate) it might not be politically advantageous for a member state, particularly a major contributor, to pay all or part of its contribution just as the regular budget and assessed peacekeeping operations were about to run out of money [A/C.5/47/SR.7, para. 37]. The representative of Mexico pointed out that the unilateral withholding of payments as a means of promoting special interests was totally inconsistent with the spirit of the Charter, and that domestic economic conditions could not justify systematic disregard of international obligations [A/C.5/47/SR.9, para. 18].

The representative of Brazil, for his part, said that a contributory factor to the financial crisis was the number of peacekeeping operations, which had strained to the limit the financial capacity of member states to join in the common cause [A/C.5/47/SR.5, para. 21].

It was fairly obvious that in the statements of both the West European and developing-country representatives, responsibility for the financial problems of the United Nations was being laid primarily at the door of the United States, despite the fact that the latter had reduced its indebtedness by almost $86.7 million in the course of 1992, from $407.3 million on January 1 ($266.4 million for the regular budget and $140.9 million for peacekeeping operations) to $320.6 million on December 31 ($239.5 million for the regular budget and $81.1 million for peacekeeping operations). Still, according to U.N. figures, the United States owed at the end of 1992 just under half of the outstanding total contributions to the regular budget.

A major contributing factor to this situation has been the cumulative effect of the **withholding by the United States** for several years of its share of the cost of a few activities with which it disagrees [see *Issues/47*, p. 340]. The United Nations holds that such withholding is inconsistent with Article 17, paragraph 2, of the Charter, which provides that "The expenses of the organization shall be borne by the members as apportioned by the General Assembly." The cumulative total of such withholdings stood at $105.3 million at the end of 1992, including $16.4 million withheld from the 1992 assessment [UNA-USA, *Washington Weekly Report*, XVIII-40]. These withholdings are not included in the five-year arrearage payment plan first announced by the Bush administration.

The situation is further exacerbated by the fact that, instead of paying its annual assessment to the regular budget in full at the beginning of the calendar year, as required under the U.N. Financial Regulations, the United States pays a first installment shortly after October 1 of that year, when its own fiscal year begins. This practice goes back to the Reagan administration in 1981, which sought to minimize the size of the budget deficit by shifting the U.N. system's 1981 assessments into the FY 1982 budget [*Washington Weekly Report*, XVIII-32]. Contributing to the criticism of the United States in the General Assembly has been the fairly transparent manner in which it sometimes seeks to influence a decision by delaying payment of its contributions. For example, there was speculation that payment in December 1992 of a $56.4 million installment of the U.S. assessment under the regular budget was being delayed in order to ensure that the budget outline for 1994–95 would be adopted with zero growth [ibid., XVIII-39].

While the attitude of the United States toward the payment of its assessments continues to worry the membership of the Organization, a new serious threat has emerged to U.N. financial stability in the form of a sharp increase in the amounts owed by the Russian Federation: to the regular budget, from $46 million on January 1, 1992, to $110.1 million on December 31; to peacekeeping, from $126.8 million to $282.2 million. While the United States now pays its peacekeeping assessments without delay, the Russian Federation has run up very large arrears: At the end of 1992 they accounted for half the outstanding assessments for peacekeeping operations. Russia's total debt at the end of 1992 ($392.3 million) was considerably higher than that of the United States ($320.6 million).

Although the regular budget assessments for 1993 became due and payable at the beginning of the year, only 26.4% of those assessments had been paid by March 31 (as against 30.3% in 1992). Thirty countries had paid their regular budget assessments in full by March 31, 1993: Australia, Austria, Bahrain, Belgium, Botswana, Canada, Cyprus, Denmark, Ethiopia, Finland, France, Iceland, Ireland, Jordan, Kuwait, Liechtenstein, Luxembourg, Malaysia, Malta, Micronesia, Myanmar, Namibia, Nepal, Netherlands, New Zealand, Norway, Singapore, Spain, Sri Lanka, and Sweden [ST/ADM/SER.B/408].

The total amount of assessed contributions outstanding as of March 31, 1993, was $2.3 billion. Of that total, unpaid contributions to the regular budget amounted to $1,214.3 million (of which $426.3 million is related to previous years and $788.0 million to 1993 assessments), and unpaid assessments for peacekeeping operations amounted to $1,131.4 million ($500.8 million for previous years and $630.6 million in 1993 assessments).

Even countries that pay their assessed contributions in full during the year to which they relate do not always do it in the first quarter. Therefore, the amount of unpaid contributions for previous years is a fairer criterion. On that basis, the largest amounts are owed by, in descending order, the Russian Federation ($347.2 million, of which $55.6 million is for the regular budget and $291.6 million for peacekeeping operations), the United States ($320.6 million, of which $239.5 million relates to the regular budget and $81.1 million to peacekeeping operations), South Africa ($71.6 million, including $49.0 million for the regular budget and $22.6 million for peacekeeping operations), Ukraine ($47.9 million, of which $17.3 million is for the regular budget and $30.6 million for peacekeeping operations), and Brazil ($32.1 million, including $26.5 million for the regular budget and $5.6 million for peacekeeping).

If unpaid assessments for 1993 are also taken into account, the largest amounts are owed by the United States ($923.2 million: $549.5 million for the regular budget, $373.7 million for peacekeeping operations), followed by the Russian Federation ($473.8 million: $124.1 million for the regular budget, $349.7 million for peacekeeping operations).

It is clear, therefore, that the Organization is still facing a financial crisis, even though the agenda item has been renamed "Improving the financial situation of the United Nations."

Scales of Assessments

The current scale of assessments for the regular budget was approved by the General Assembly on December 20, 1991, after a long debate [see *Issues/47*, pp. 342–46, which also includes a description of the methodology used to construct the scale]. The scale is to be used for apportioning the expenses for 1992, 1993, and 1994 "unless a new scale is approved earlier by the General Assembly on the recommendation of the Committee on Contributions, should the Committee, in accordance with its mandate and the rules of procedure of the General Assembly, so recommend, on the basis of substantial changes in relative capacity to pay, taking account, as appropriate, of representations made by member states and/or its ongoing work on methodology" [A/Res/46/221 A, operative para. 1].

The report that the Committee on Contributions submitted to the General Assembly at its 47th Session [A/47/11] included an account of the discussions in the Committee on various aspects of the methodology. The views in the Committee were divided, and no recommendations to change or adjust the methodology were made to the Assembly.

The Committee did recommend assessment rates for new member states that used to form part of the former USSR and the former Yugoslavia, as well as corresponding reductions in the assessments of successor states, namely, the Russian Federation and "Yugoslavia." (The latter now consists of Serbia and Montenegro, and its participation in the United Nations has been suspended by the General Assembly.) In the process, the Committee also recommended that the assessments of Belarus and Ukraine be adjusted upwards (from 0.31% and 1.18% to, respectively,

0.48% and 1.87%), recalling that the rates for Belarus, Ukraine, and the former USSR throughout their membership in the United Nations had been determined through the distribution among them of the rate calculated for the former Soviet Union as a whole, on the basis of an agreement regarding the proportional strength of their economies. The agreement dated back to 1946 and was never modified, despite the economic changes that had undoubtedly occurred in the meantime. In introducing the report of the Committee, its Chairman said that the Committee viewed its recommendations as an unavoidable transitional step, recognizing that the rates of assessment of the member states formerly constituting the Soviet Union and Yugoslavia might undergo considerable adjustment in the preparation of the next scale of assessments [A/C.5/47/SR.17, para. 61].

The representative of Belarus objected to the proposed increase in his country's assessment on the ground that it constituted a revision of the scale for 1992–94, which had been adopted by consensus [A/C.5/47/SR.17, para. 68]. The representative of Ukraine also did not accept the recommendation of the Committee on Contributions; that recommendation, he said, was inconsistent with the provision of operative paragraph 1 of Resolution 46/221A, which stated that changing the scale would be predicated on substantial changes in relative capacity to pay (see above). The Committee's recommendation was also inconsistent with the scheme of limits, which stipulated that the increase in the assessment of a member state from one scale to the next cannot be greater than 10% [A/C.5/47/SR.18, paras. 8 and 11].

Estonia, Latvia, and Lithuania objected to their assessment rates on the ground that, instead of reflecting their capacity to pay, they were derived from the assessment of the former Soviet Union, which had been distorted by an artificially high exchange rate for the ruble against the U.S. dollar [ibid., para. 3]. Moldova and Azerbaijan also could not accept the assessment rates recommended for them, basically for the same reasons given by the Baltic countries. Croatia and Slovenia likewise felt that their assessment rates were too high.

The representative of Japan, on the other hand, welcomed the principle that the sum of the assessments of new member states acquiring independence from an existing member state plus the adjusted assessment of the latter should not be less than the original assessment rate of that member state [A/C.5/47/SR.24, para. 24].

Following inconclusive informal consultations, the Fifth Committee sought a legal opinion on the approach taken by the Committee on Contributions in arriving at its recommendations on the assessment rates for Belarus and Ukraine. In his legal opinion, Legal Counsel concluded that to treat Belarus and Ukraine, two founding members of the United Nations, as though they were new member states for the purposes of assessment was legally untenable. Nothing in Resolution 46/221 pointed to the admissibility of treating previously assessed members of the Organization belatedly as new member states. Besides, the adoption for the two countries in question of the assessment rates recommended by the Committee on Contributions would be inconsistent with rule 160 of the Assembly's Rules of Procedure. While the Fifth Committee could decide not to apply rule 160 in the case under consideration, he, as Legal Counsel, could not recommend that course [A/C.5/47/SR.38, paras. 6–14].

The conflicting views could not be reconciled in further informal consultations. While there were expressions of sympathy for the plight of the countries whose assessment rates were affected by the recommendations of the Committee on Contributions, the weight of opinion in the Fifth Committee was clearly on the side of those recommendations. Accordingly, the recommendations were put to the vote—the first departure since the Assembly's 43rd Session from the practice of reaching a consensus on questions relating to the regular budget. The recommendations of the Committee on Contributions were adopted by 62 votes in favor, 15 against, with 19 abstentions [A/Dec. 47/456]. In addition to eight countries that had challenged the Committee's recommendations, negative votes were cast by Canada and New Zealand, which felt uneasy at disregarding the legal opinion (see above); by four Nordic countries, which sympathized with the plight of the Baltic countries; and by Turkey, which maintains friendly relations with Azerbaijan. The vote in the plenary of the Assembly was 104 in favor, 16 against, and 34 abstentions.

Many delegations that spoke on the scale of assessments also discussed various technical aspects of the methodology used in constructing the scale. This debate will be joined again at the 48th Session in the fall of 1993, when the Assembly will give the Committee on Contributions guidelines for the next three-year scale (for 1995–97). The discussion promises to be difficult, not only because, as in the past, delegations will be arguing that their countries' assessment rates should be lowered or, at the very least, not raised, but also because the reduced capacity to pay of countries that used to form part of the former Soviet Union and the former Yugoslavia will inevitably result in part of the assessment burden being shifted to other member states.

The costs of *peacekeeping operations* (other than UNFICYP, which is financed by voluntary contributions) are apportioned on the basis of a scale that differs from the scale of assessments for the regular budget. This special scale has been in use for 20 years—each time as "an *ad hoc* arrangement"—since the adoption of Resolution 3101 (XXVIII) on December 11, 1973. That resolution divided the member states into four groups, whose current composition is as follows (the five newest member states had not yet been assigned to any particular groups as of the time of writing):

- **Group A,** consisting of the five permanent members of the Security Council (Britain, China, France, the Russian Federation, and the United States).
- **Group B,** consisting of 22 states, mainly European countries, but also Australia, Canada, Japan, New Zealand, and South Africa.
- **Group C,** consisting of 97 states, mostly from the Third World. The assessment rates of all the states in this group, except for Brazil, are below 1% on the regular-budget scale of assessments, 29 of them being assessed at the "floor rate" of 0.01%.
- **Group D,** consisting of 54 Third World states, all of them assessed at the floor rate.

The countries in group A are assessed, *as a group,* at a rate corresponding to their aggregate rates under the regular-budget scale of assessments, plus 80% of the aggregate assessment of the countries in group C, plus 90% of the aggregate assessment of the countries in group D. The extra assessment burden of group A countries relates to their special responsibilities—and powers—as permanent members of the Security Council.

The countries in group B are assessed, again as a group, at a rate corresponding to the aggregate of their rates on the regular-budget scale.

The countries in groups C and D are assessed, as groups, at rates corresponding to, respectively, 20% and 10% of the aggregates of their rates on the regular-budget scale.

The assessment rates of individual countries are derived from the rate for their group in the proportion that their rate on the regular-budget scale bears to the group aggregate. For example, the aggregate for the group A countries on the current regular-budget scale of assessments is 43.5%; of that aggregate, 25% is the assessment of the United States. Therefore the United States is assessed at $25/43.5 \times 100 = 57.471\%$ of the group's aggregate assessment. As the latter currently corresponds to slightly under 55% of the total, the United States is assessed in 1993 for purposes of peacekeeping operations at a rate of about 31.7% (57.471% of 55).

In a report to the General Assembly at its 47th Session, the Secretary-General addressed what had been perceived by some member states as anomalies in the way in which countries were being assigned to the groups. He suggested an alternative approach, which left unchanged the composition of group A, assigned to group B all countries (other than those in group A) with an average per capita national income in 1980–89 of at least $5,000, and to group C those with an average per capita national income of less than $5,000, except for the least developed countries, all of which (and no others) would be assigned to group D. The methodology for apportioning the costs would remain unchanged [A/47/484].

Fifteen delegations, two of which spoke on behalf of groups of countries, discussed the Secretary-General's suggestions. Seven, mostly representing prosperous countries with small populations, were opposed to the suggestion that all countries with an average per capita national income of $5,000 and above would be assigned to group B. Three delegations (all of them representing Latin American countries) referred to the need to institutionalize the arrangements for the apportionment of peacekeeping expenses (to date the special scale has been applied on each occasion as an ad hoc measure), and stressed the special responsibilities of the permanent members of the Security Council. Two delegations supported the Secretary-General's suggestion, while two others did not agree that average per capita income should be the sole criterion for the assignment of countries to particular groups.

After lengthy informal consultations, the General Assembly decided to request the Chairman of the Fifth Committee to convene an open-ended working group of that Committee to examine the placement of member states into the groups for the apportionment of peacekeeping expenses, with the objective of establishing standard criteria, in order to ensure that the placement is applied in a consistent manner that could be used to allocate member states to the groups for all future peacekeeping operations. The working group is to report to the General Assembly at its 48th Session [A/Res/47/218, Section II].

3. The Expenses of the Organization

The Program Budget for 1992–93

At its 46th Session in 1991, the General Assembly adopted a program budget for the 1992–93 biennium in the amount of $1,940 million net. At its 47th Session it twice revised the approved appropriations to give effect to the first two phases of the restructuring of the Secretariat (see below) and to accommodate additional requirements attributable to decisions taken by competent intergovernmental organs and also the adjustments needed to take account of the differences between actual experience and the earlier assumptions regarding inflation and currency exchange rates. The net increase amounted to $56.5 million, as follows:

	Expenditure	*Income*	*Net*
	$ million	$ million	$ million
Initial appropriations	2,389	449	1,940
1st revision [A/Res/47/220]	2,468	471	1,997
2nd revision [A/Res/47/212B]	2,467.5	471	1,996.5

Further revisions to the 1992–93 budget will be submitted to the Assembly at its 48th Session.

The 1992–93 budget covers the first two years of the medium-term plan for 1992–97. At the 47th Session the Assembly approved changes to that plan in the light of recommendations by the **Committee for Program and Coordination (CPC).** Both in CPC and in the Fifth Committee differences of opinion emerged as to the role of the United Nations in **preventive diplomacy** and in the **electoral process** in individual countries. With reference to the latter, the Secretary-General had proposed the inclusion of a new subprogram entitled "Enhancing the effectiveness of the principle of periodic and genuine elections." The General Assembly decided that the legislative mandate for the subprogram was provided in Resolution 46/137 (which, in operative paragraph 7, had "affirmed the value of the electoral assistance that the United Nations has provided at the request of some member states, in the context of full respect for their sovereignty") [A/Res/47/214, Annex]. The Assembly emphasized the importance of the sectoral, regional, and central intergovernmental bodies in reviewing the plan and its revisions, and regretted the shortage of contributions from those bodies. In this connection reference had been made in the debate to the failure of ECOSOC to provide answers to specific questions regarding the relationship between itself and CPC in the intergovernmental review of the medium-term plan.

The Assembly endorsed the recommendation of CPC that a prototype of a possible new format for the medium-term plan be prepared; the Chairman of CPC, in introducing that Committee's report, had said that the plan, instead of being the main policy document for the Organization, seemed gradually to be becoming irrelevant and to be turning into an instrument for the protection of program managers' domains [A/C.5/47/SR.14, para. 4].

Program Budget Outline for 1994–95

The Fifth Committee considered a program budget outline for 1994–95, which the Secretary-General had submitted pursuant to Resolution 41/213 of December 19, 1986. The purpose of the outline is to provide greater predictability in the resource requirements, promote a greater involvement of member states in the budgetary process, and thereby facilitate the broadest possible agreement on the program budget. When the outline was under consideration in CPC, opinions were divided on whether the concept of zero real growth should be applied. In the Fifth Committee the delegation of Ukraine endorsed the principle of zero budget growth and said that the appropriations for 1994–95 must in no case be higher than the amount of the outline [A/C.5/47/SR.16, para. 18]; and the delegation of Canada expressed the view that the United Nations, like the governments of member states, should no longer assume that it could pass on to the membership automatic adjustments for inflation and currency fluctuations [A/C.5/47/SR.45, para. 8].

Resolution 47/213 reflects a compromise on this point. The Assembly invited the Secretary-General to prepare the proposed program budget for 1994–95 on the basis of a total preliminary estimate of $2,386.4 million (at the initial 1992–93 rates) as recommended by the Advisory Committee on Administrative and Budgetary Questions (ACABQ) (the Secretary-General's estimate was $2,410 million), to be adjusted at revised 1992–93 rates. At the same time, the Assembly reaffirmed the need for a comprehensive and satisfactory solution to the problem of controlling the effects of inflation and currency fluctuations on the U.N. budget.

The level of the contingency fund has been set at 0.75% of the preliminary estimates for 1994–95, to be recosted at 1994–95 rates (the question of the contingency fund is to be reviewed by the Assembly at its 48th Session).

In a separate resolution the Assembly endorsed the proposals of the Secretary-General for a new budget format, designed to present a clearer picture of the budget and to simplify the related methodology, which he had submitted in document A/C.5/47/3, and invited him to continue to improve the presentation [A/Res/47/212, Section III, op. para. 14]. No date has been set for the introduction of the new format.

Peacekeeping Operations

During the first part of its 47th Session, the General Assembly approved the following net appropriations for peacekeeping operations:

Operation	*Period*	*$ million*
U.N. Operation in Somalia	5/1/92–4/30/93	107.9
U.N. Disengagement Observer Force	6/1/92–5/31/93	38.6
U.N. Interim Force in Lebanon	2/1/92–1/31/93	145.7
plus commitment authority (per month)	2/1/93 onwards	11.9
U.N. Iraq-Kuwait Observer Mission	4/9/92–4/30/93	46.9
U.N. Transitional Authority in Cambodia	11/1/92–4/30/93	470.8
plus commitment authority (per month)	5/1/93–7/31/03	235.8
U.N. Protection Force	1/12/92–9/20/93	298.3
plus commitment authority (per month)	2/21/93–9/20/93	46.5
U.N. Angola Verification Mission (commitments)	to 2/28/93	24.2
U.N. Mission for the Referendum in Western Sahara (commitments)	to 2/28/93	6.8

The following additional appropriations were approved at the resumed session in March–April 1993:

Operation	*Period*	*$ million*
U.N. Operation in Somalia	5/1/93–6/30/93	300.0
U.N. Operation in Mozambique	10/15/92–6/30/93	140.0
U.N. Observer Mission in El Salvador	12/1/92–5/31/93	16.0
plus commitment authority (per month)	6/1/93 onwards	2.7

At the time of writing, the General Assembly had not completed its consideration of the expenses of the U.N. Angola Verification Mission and the U.N. Mission for the Referendum in Western Sahara beyond February 28, 1993.

4. Staffing and Administration

Composition of the Secretariat: Geographical Distribution, Recruitment, and Career Development

In Resolution 46/220 of December 20, 1991, on the rationalization of the work of the Fifth Committee and the biennialization of the program of work, the General Assembly decided that personnel questions would be discussed in even-numbered years. As customary, much of the debate in 1992—and a great deal of time in the informal consultations—was devoted to the subitem relating to the **composition of the Secretariat** and, more specifically, to the question of the **geographical distribution of posts.** More than 30 delegations, some of them speaking on behalf of groups of countries, addressed this question.

"The importance of recruiting the staff on as wide a geographical basis as possible" is referred to in Article 101, paragraph 3, of the U.N. Charter. A system of so-called "desirable ranges" of representation of member states in the Secretariat is being applied to give effect to that desideratum. How those "desirable ranges" are to be determined has long been—and continues to be—a contentious issue. Three factors are now taken into account in the calculation: U.N. membership, population, and the country's contribution rate as reflected in the scale of assessments. The current formula assigns a 40% weight to membership, 55% to contribution, and 5% to population. This formula is applied to the so-called "posts subject to geographical distribution" and not to the entire U.N. staff. The groups that are excluded from the calculation constitute staff in the General Service and other locally recruited categories; staff with special language qualifications; the staff of voluntary programs (such as

UNDP, UNICEF, UNRWA, UNHCR), which are not considered part of the Secretariat proper because they have the authority to appoint their own staff, and which are financed wholly or largely from voluntary contributions; and staff on short-term appointments (i.e., serving on contracts of less than a year). In other words, the group to which the geographical distribution formula *does* apply consists essentially of professional and higher posts in the Secretariat proper other than those with special language qualifications. A point to bear in mind in this connection is that broad geographical representation is also to be found in the posts that are *not* considered "subject to geographical distribution." For example, nationals of 53 member states were serving in posts with special language requirements as of June 30, 1992.

The formula referred to in the preceding paragraph, when applied to the total number of posts subject to geographical distribution, yields, for each member state, a number that is regarded as the midpoint of the desirable range for that state. The range itself is determined by applying a flexibility factor upward and downward from the midpoint. (While this factor is supposed to be 15%, the methodology used in the calculation results in a great many member states having a flexibility factor of plus or minus five posts.)

According to the Secretary-General's report on the composition of the Secretariat as of June 30, 1992 [A/47/416], which was considered by the Assembly at its 47th Session, the total number of U.N. staff was 31,127, of whom 13,883 were assigned to the U.N. Secretariat; most of the remaining 17,244 were employed by UNDP, UNHCR, and UNICEF. The number of posts subject to geographical distribution was 2,608. The lowest desirable range (that applied to small countries assessed at the "floor rate" of 0.01%) was 2–14 posts; the largest range (that for the United States) was 328–441.

Countries with nationals in posts subject to geographical distribution in excess of the upper limit of their respective desirable ranges are considered overrepresented. As of June 30, 1992, there were 24 such countries, all but two of them developing countries. The most heavily overrepresented were the Philippines, with 68 nationals in posts subject to geographical distribution as against a desirable range of 5–14, followed by Ethiopia (30 as against 3–14), Chile (28 as against 4–14), and Thailand (27 as against 5–14).

The number of unrepresented member states as of June 30, 1992, was 29; 19 of them were states that had only recently been admitted to membership. Of the remaining ten states, nine had also been unrepresented a year earlier [see *Issues/47*, p. 355] and one entered this category following the departure of both of its nationals serving with the United Nations.

The number of underrepresented states declined by three (one of them being Germany) to 21, as against 24 a year earlier.

The statements made in the debate on the composition of the Secretariat showed how divergent the views of member states are on this question. Countries with large populations (Bangladesh, Brazil, India, Indonesia, Iran, Nigeria, Turkey) urged that greater weight be given to the population factor, while others either sought parity between the weights given to the membership and the contribution factors (Bulgaria) or expressed opposition to any drastic changes in those weights (Hungary). The United States was also opposed to changing the current system for determining desirable ranges, since it had been in use only as of January 1, 1988. Whereas India advocated greater flexibility for the upper and lower limits of the desirable ranges, Bulgaria sought to bring those limits closer to midpoint.

Several countries (India, Libya, Pakistan) felt that some groups of staff that are currently not included in the calculation (e.g., the Field Service, the General Service, civilian posts in peacekeeping missions) should be brought in.

Secondment as a means of improving geographical distribution and introducing new skills was advocated by the representatives of China, Czechoslovakia, New Zealand (speaking also on behalf of Australia and Canada), Oman, Poland, and Ukraine.

The representative of Japan pointed out that desirable ranges were nothing more than a means of achieving equitable geographical distribution. Instead of discussing methodologies, the General Assembly should address the broader question of how to ensure that the Secretariat can strengthen its recruitment policy to achieve that end; of the appointments made in the 12 months up to June 30, 1992, less than 23% had been nationals of unrepresented or underrepresented states [A/C.5/47/SR.17, paras. 40 and 45].

Several delegations referred more specifically to senior posts. The representative of Thailand suggested that a time limit be placed on the terms for senior posts; nationals of some states must not be allowed to have a monopoly over top positions, she said [A/C.5/47/SR.17, para. 46]. The representative of Barbados complained that the Caribbean subregion was completely unrepresented at the Under-Secretary-General (USG) and Assistant Secretary-General (ASG) levels, while the representative of Senegal pointed out that there were no USGs from French-speaking African countries.

Informal consultations over a six-week period failed to produce results, especially with regard to desirable ranges, and the Fifth Committee decided to defer the matter to its resumed session. No progress having been made, it was decided that an open-ended working group would be convened to consider the formula for determining equitable geographical distribution; the outcome is to be reported to the General Assembly at its 48th Session.

In their statements on the composition of the Secretariat, several delegations criticized the **recruitment freeze** that was decreed by the Secretary-General in February 1992 and still remains in effect; those delegations pointed out that the freeze had adversely affected equitable geographical distribution. The General Assembly expressed the hope that the Secretary-General would end the temporary suspension of recruitment as soon as possible [A/Res/47/226, Section I.A, operative para. 5].

In practice, the suspension of recruitment was not absolute. During the 12-month period to June 30, 1992, there were 128 appointments to posts subject to geographical distribution; 36 of those appointed had been successful candidates in **national competitive examinations** for posts at the P-1 and P-2 levels [A/47/416]. The holding of those examinations was generally endorsed in the debate. At the same time, there was criticism of the long delays before appointments were offered to successful candidates, several of whom had in the meantime secured other employment. The delegations of the United States and of Britain, speaking on behalf of the twelve members of the European Community, also wondered whether the examinations were cost-effective, given the relationship between the number of applicants, of successful candidates, and of available posts. The Assembly requested the Secretary-General to expedite the national competitive examination process at the P-1 and P-2 levels, to introduce the process at the P-3 level, and to speed up the recruitment of successful candidates [A/Res/47/226, Section I.A, operative paras. 1–3].

The Assembly also amended the Staff Regulations to make provision for the appointment of **staff on secondment from government service.** It decided that secondment should be based on a tripartite agreement involving the Organization, the government, and the staff member concerned, and that extension of secondment would require the agreement of all three parties [A/Res/47/226, Section I, A.2].

The Fifth Committee also devoted much attention to **career development,** on which the Secretary-General had submitted a special report [A/C.5/47/6] and personally appeared before the Committee. Eighteen delegations referred to this question in their statements.

Although the intention to establish a career development system was announced in a Secretary-General's Bulletin as far back as May 1978, the Organization still does not have such a system. The report by the Secretary-General focuses on the "concept and scope" of a career development scheme and on the action that must be taken to that end by way of human resources planning, the preparation of a skills inventory, the promotion of staff mobility, development and training (the Secretary-General submitted a special report on training in document A/C.5/47/9), career counseling, improved performance evaluation, etc. A pilot project on staff mobility for the administration occupational group is to be carried out in 1993–95. The report refers to obstacles standing in the way of proper career development, notably a "serious retention problem." The report notes that "One major apparent reason is the lack of competitive salaries": The U.N. pay level lagged behind that of the World Bank group and, to an even greater extent, behind the pay scales of the European Coordinated Organizations. Another obstacle identified by the Secretary-General is the rigid and cumbersome classification system. Among the remedies proposed was more recruitment at lower grades and less at the more senior levels to improve promotion prospects, greater flexibility in the management of posts at levels P-2 to P-4, and the introduction of nonpecuniary incentives and motivations.

There was a broad measure of support for the Secretary-General's report on career development and for placing greater emphasis on training. But certain doubts were also expressed. For example, the U.S. delegation questioned whether the United Nations really had a serious retention problem; and it objected to a more flexible use of P-2 to P-4 posts, which might lead to grade creep. The principle behind job classification was equal pay for work of equal difficulty and responsibility [A/C.5/47/SR.19, paras. 13 and 16]. The British delegation, speaking on behalf of the European Community, also expressed doubts about the flexible use of P-2 to P-4 posts. Several delegations, including that of the Russian Federation, referred to the importance of introducing "new blood" at the more senior levels and of balancing the numbers of staff at the professional and higher levels on permanent and on fixed-term contracts.

In Section I B of Resolution 47/226, the General Assembly endorsed the underlying principles in the Secretary-General's reports on career development and on training. At the same time, the Assembly called on the Secretary-General to weed out "dead wood," to encourage staff exchanges between the United Nations and national governments and international organizations, and to examine the possibility and desirability of "achieving appropriate flexibility" between career and fixed-term appointments. Reports on these topics were requested for the 49th Session of the Assembly in 1994.

Recognizing that lack of employment opportunities for spouses had been an obstacle both to recruitment and to mobility of staff, the Assembly, in Section I A.3 of the same resolution, seeks the assistance of the organizations in the U.N. system and of member states in improving those opportunities.

There was a slight overall increase in the **number and percentage of women** in posts subject to geographical distribution, from 759 (29.2%) on June 30, 1991, to 797 (30.6%) a year later. At grades P-1 through P-4 women accounted for 37.6% of the total on June 30, 1992, as against 36.9% a year earlier. There was a substantial increase in the number of women in P-5 and D-1 posts (from 75 to 94 and from 20 to 26, respectively); the number of women in D-2 posts remained unchanged. The region with the highest percentage of women was North America and the Caribbean (44% of the staff from the region in posts subject to geographical distribution), followed by Asia and the Pacific (37.5%); the regions with the lowest percentages were Eastern Europe (10%) and Africa (16.8%). Of the 128 appointed to posts subject to geographical distribution during the 12-month period ending June 30, 1992, 50 (39.1%) were women.

The percentage of women was somewhat higher (34.8%) in posts with special language requirements. Women account for more than half the staff in such posts from North America and the Caribbean, Latin America, and Western Europe, but for only 4% of the language staff from Eastern Europe [A/47/508].

The delegations that referred in their statements to the question of women in the Secretariat welcomed the efforts to increase their number and promotion prospects and urged that those efforts continue and show even greater vigor. In this connection several speakers referred more specifically to the small number of senior posts held by women from their respective regions and subregions. The development of procedures and guidelines to deal with sexual harassment was also welcomed. With regard to the latter point, the United States delegation expressed regret that it had taken so long to issue them [A/C.5/47/SR.19, para. 19].

Several delegations referred to the responsibility of member states for improving the representation of women in the Secretariat and the need for them to put forward more women candidates.

The delegation of the United Kingdom, speaking on behalf of the European Community, pointed out that the status of women in the Secretariat should be promoted through equality of opportunity for all candidates. The representative of Australia, speaking also on behalf of Canada and New Zealand, called for special measures to increase the number of women in senior posts, through outside recruitment if necessary; he proposed that an equal employment opportunity unit, reporting directly to the Secretary-General, be set up with authority over personnel procedures and actions throughout the U.N. system with respect to all posts [A/C.5/47/SR.21, para. 7]. (In putting forward this proposal, the three delegations seem to have overlooked the fact that the Secretary-General's authority does not extend to the personnel policies of the specialized agencies or to those of the major voluntary programs, such as UNDP, UNICEF, and UNFPA).

The resolution that emerged from the informal consultations bears the mark of a compromise between the proponents of "reverse discrimination" benefiting women and of a more gradualist approach. For example, in operative paragraph 6 of the resolution [A/Res/47/226], the Assembly requests the Secretary-General to ensure that "no restriction or discrimination exists in the United Nations in the recruitment, appointment and promotion of men and women." In Section I C of the same resolution, the Secretary-General is requested "to accord high priority to the recruitment and promotion of women to posts subject to geographical distribution, particularly at the senior policy and decision-making levels, in order to achieve the goals set in its resolution 45/239 C" (35% women in professional posts by 1995). At the same time, in the preamble to Section I C, the Secretary-General's intention is noted "to bring the gender balance in policy-level positions as close to 50:50 as possible by the fiftieth anniversary of the U.N." As of June 30, 1992, there were no women among the 19 USGs (one has been appointed since then) and only 1 woman out of 15 ASGs; of the 80 D-2s, 10 were women. Therefore, it is difficult to see how a 50:50 gender balance in policy-level positions can be achieved in the next couple of years, unless there is wholesale dismissal of serving male senior officials or the number of such posts is greatly increased. In Section I C of Resolution 47/226 the Assembly appeals to all member states to identify and nominate more women candidates, especially for senior policy-level and decision-making posts; and the Secretary-General is "encouraged" to improve the role of the Focal Point for Women in the U.N. Secretariat.

Although, as has been stated above, the Assembly will next consider personnel questions in depth in 1994, it decided that it will take up at its 48th Session in 1993 any urgent matter relating to personnel questions the Secretary-General deems necessary.

Restructuring of the Secretariat

The steps taken by the new Secretary-General in 1992 to restructure the Secretariat figured prominently in the deliberations of the Fifth Committee at the 47th Session.

In a note dated February 21, 1992, the Secretary-General announced certain changes that were "intended to consolidate and streamline the Organization's activities into well-defined functional categories" [A/46/882]. The main aspects of that restructuring were:

- The creation of a **Department of Political Affairs,** headed by two USGs, to replace five units (the Office of Political and General Assembly Affairs and Secretariat Services; the Office for Research and the Collection of Information; the Department of Political and Security Council Affairs; the Department of Special Political Questions, Regional Cooperation, Decolonization and Trusteeship; and the Department for Disarmament Affairs).
- The creation of a **Department of Peacekeeping Operations,** headed by a USG and assisted by an ASG, in place of the former Office of Special Political Affairs.

- The creation of a **Department of Economic and Social Development,** headed by a USG, to replace five units (the Office of the Director-General for Development and International Economic Cooperation; the Department of International Economic and Social Affairs; the Department of Technical Cooperation for Development; the Centre for Science and Technology for Development; and the U.N. Centre for Transnational Corporations).
- The creation of a **Department of Humanitarian Affairs,** headed by a USG, incorporating the Office of the U.N. Disaster Relief Coordinator.
- The incorporation of the Department of Conference Services into the **Department of Administration and Management,** headed by a USG and assisted by four ASGs.
- The integration of the Office for Ocean Affairs and the Law of the Sea into the **Office of Legal Affairs,** headed by a USG.

The Secretary-General indicated that the implications of those changes would be presented to the General Assembly in the form of revised program budget estimates for the biennium 1992–93.

The Third World delegations reacted with concern to the changes because they seemed to affect programs to which they attach importance [see *Issues/47*, p. 351].

In Resolution 46/232 of March 2, 1992, the General Assembly requested a report on the programmatic impact and the financial implications of the Secretary-General's initiatives. The revised estimates before the Assembly's 47th Session went beyond the changes outlined in the Secretary-General's original note (see above). Also included were proposals to transfer functions between departments, to move certain functions from one office location to another, and to eliminate additional high-level posts. The Secretary-General proposed to abolish 18 such posts altogether (the post of the Director-General, 7 USG posts, and 10 ASG posts) and to create 5 new ones (all at the ASG level). The restructuring affected more than half the Secretariat's Professional and General Service posts. The U.N. program budget identifies the numbers and levels of posts by program and sometimes also by subprogram. The Secretary-General sought a degree of flexibility in redeploying posts on the grounds that the fundamental principles of program budgeting "were hampered by an excessive rigidity in the administration of the human and financial resources"; he indicated that he had identified a limited number of posts for redeployment and had actually redeployed nine of them; and he proposed that procedures for further redeployment be elaborated as the need arose [A/C.5/47/2 and Corr.1].

In the midst of the Assembly's consideration of the revised estimates, the organizational structure of the Secretariat underwent a further change: The Secretary-General had now decided to divide into three parts the newly created Department of Economic and Social Development. The new departments were named **Department for Policy Coordination and Sustainable Development; Department for Development Support and Management Services;** and **Department for Social Information and Policy Analysis,** all of them headed by USGs (for a net increase of two USG posts). The Secretary-General also proposed the creation of two new ASG-level posts—for the head of the Centre for Human Rights and for the Secretary-General of the Fourth World Conference on Women, to be held in 1995—and the abolition of all four ASG posts in the Department of Administration and Management (i.e., the posts of Controller and of the heads of the Offices of Human Resources Management, General Services, and Conference Services). It was his intention to propose in the future a further redeployment of high-level posts [A/47/753].

The initial revised estimates (those in document A/C.5/47/2 and Corr.1) had been considered by the Committee on Programme and Coordination (CPC). The Committee endorsed the proposed reduction in high-level posts and agreed that the Secretary-General should continue with the restructuring exercise, but it regretted the lack of information on the programmatic aspects of the restructuring and on the norms and procedures for the creation and suppression of posts [A/47/16, Part II, paras. 261 ff.]. The **Advisory Committee on Administrative and Budgetary Questions (ACABQ)** also regretted that no information had been provided by the Secretary-General on the impact of the restructuring on U.N. programs and on the structure and functioning of the new departments and offices. The functional justification for the redeployment of posts was also lacking. In the ACABQ's view such information should have been provided, for it was reasonable to assume that the restructuring process had been preceded by an analysis of what had to be done. As for the proposed flexibility in the treatment of vacant posts, it was not clear to the ACABQ whether the Secretary-General merely sought to ensure more effective use of the current procedures governing the transfer of human and other resources between appropriation sections, or whether he was seeking additional flexibility [A/47/7/Add.1, paras. 13–24].

While there was general agreement in the Fifth Committee that the Secretariat needed to be restructured, the Secretary-General's proposals were met with some skepticism. The warmest support was voiced by developed-country delegations. The representatives of the United Kingdom (speaking on behalf of the European Community), the Russian Federation, and Finland (speaking on behalf of the five Nordic countries) all endorsed the changes reported in the initial revised estimates.

The U.S. delegation, while generally supportive of the first stage of the restructuring, felt that the proposals did not go far enough in reducing the number of senior-level staff and of staff in other categories, nor in addressing fragmentation. Structural changes were inadequate without a radical reform of programs; the failure to restructure programs was especially evident in the area of economic and social affairs [A/C.5/47/SR.14, paras. 26–27].

The reaction of Third World delegations was generally negative, and reflected their concern that lesser priority was being given to activities of importance to developing countries. Thus, the representative of Ghana opposed excessive flexibility in the allocation of the Organization's resources, particularly staff resources, for it could have repercussions on the implementation of programs, and even on the priorities set by the General Assembly. The current rules were sufficiently flexible and there was no need to modify them. Redeploying resources to supposedly higher priority mandates was unacceptable [A/C.5/47/SR.15, paras. 15–17]. The representative of India stressed the need to comply with the provisions of the Financial Regulations; as for the question of greater flexibility, he said that a new mandate should not necessarily have priority over existing ones [A/C.5/47/SR.16, para. 31].

The representatives of Bangladesh and Uganda pointed out that reform was not an end in itself: Its main objective ought to be to increase the Organization's efficiency and cost-effectiveness; the United Nations needed rational criteria for the redeployment of posts. Further, the Secretary-General should explain the programmatic aspect of the restructuring. There was no need to redefine the five priority areas already approved by the General Assembly or to disturb the balance among them. Restructuring should be done within the framework of the Charter and the relevant General Assembly resolutions. A piecemeal approach was not helpful; when reforms continued over a prolonged period, the result was uncertainty, lack of direction, and low staff morale [A/C.5/47/SR. 17, paras. 9–12, SR.20, paras. 44 ff.]

The representative of Cameroon wondered whether the organizational changes were really aimed at ensuring effective implementation of the mandates; his delegation was not prepared to authorize the Secretary-General to transfer or redeploy resources among budget sections without the prior approval of the General Assembly or of the ACABQ, if the Assembly was not in session [A/C.5/47/SR.17, paras. 26–29]. The delegations of China and Pakistan also had reservations about the Secretary-General's request for greater flexibility in the redeployment of resources [A/C.5/47/SR.20, paras. 21, 23–24]. The delegation of Zambia voiced the suspicion that the sequence of the reforms had not been properly thought out; there seemed to be little merit in abolishing posts at the USG level only to recommend the establishment of new ones shortly thereafter [A/C.5/47/SR.20, para. 28].

The representative of Uganda said that the proposed institutional changes carried with them the risk that the influence of the strong might predominate at the expense of the weak. Priorities could be tilted in favor of a few areas at the cost of other, vitally important ones. The maintenance of international peace and security was important, but it seemed that equal importance was not being given to the economic and social areas [A/C.5/47/SR.20, para. 58].

The comments of the representative of Barbados, speaking on behalf of the Caribbean Community, were particularly critical. While the countries of the Community had no difficulty with restructuring or reform per se, he said, they believed that

> it should be based on planning and analysis, and member states and staff should be given some evidence that such was indeed the case. It appeared that member states would be faced with the second phase of the restructuring process even before the report requested in General Assembly Resolution 46/232 had been submitted for consideration. They had hoped that the first phase, which had nullified so many General Assembly resolutions, would have at least been clarified before the second phase was proposed, and that the second and any subsequent phases would have been submitted for consideration by member states before implementation. Many delegations seemed convinced that the seemingly arbitrary decisions taken would lead to greater efficiency, but delegations without the benefit of private briefings had to rely on their powers of observation. What they saw was alarming. It seemed to them that the expected gains in efficiency would prove to be illusory [A/C.5/47/SR.21, para. 17].

Several delegations, from both developed and developing countries, complained of lack of prior consultation with member states. Thus, the delegation of Japan pointed out that instead of merely reporting on what had been done, it was imperative that the Secretary-General submit his plan for reform to the General Assembly and other competent intergovernmental bodies before measures were adopted, particularly when it was a question of abolishing or redefining high-level posts that had been established by those organs or on their recommendation [A/C.5/47/SR.15, para. 22]. The representative of Uganda said that the time had come to restate the relationship between the Secretary-General, as chief administrative officer, and the member states, which must be one of mutual respect based on their respective mandates. It was the role of member states to determine programs and appropriate resources, and to ensure that resources were applied to the programs for which they had been appropriated. Such a role did not represent micromanagement, merely the enforcement of accountability [A/C.5/47/SR.20, para. 52].

The Secretary-General's report on the second phase of the restructuring [A/47/753, see above] elicited mixed reactions. While some delegations viewed it as inaugurating a dialogue between member states and the Secretary-General, others did not. They felt that the General Assembly was being asked to give its approval after the fact, and that such a procedure was unacceptable [A/C.5/47/SR.39].

In Resolution 47/212 of December 23, 1992, the General Assembly stressed that the restructuring of the Secretariat should conform to the objectives and guidelines/principles set out in Resolution 46/232 and should be carried out in close consultation with member states and competent intergovernmental bodies. The Assembly reaffirmed its own role with regard to the structure of the Secretariat, including the creation, suppression, and redeployment of posts financed from the regular budget of the Organization. It requested the Secretary-General to provide comprehensive information on all decisions involving established and temporary high-level posts, including equivalent positions from the regular budget and extrabudgetary resources. The Assembly regretted the absence of information on the programmatic aspects and implications of restructuring, and requested that such information be provided for the resumed 47th Session in the spring of 1993.

The report that the Secretary-General submitted to the resumed session dealt not only with the three-part division of the Department of Economic and Social Development he had set up a few months earlier (see above) but also with the **transfer of certain activities from one duty station to another** [A/C.5/47/88]. Activities pertaining to social development and the advancement of women, involving 59 posts, were proposed for transfer from Vienna to New York; and activities related to the peaceful uses of outer space (16 posts) were proposed for transfer from New York to Vienna. Twenty-seven posts of the World Food Council were proposed for transfer from Rome to New York. A total of 55 posts related to the programs on transnational corporations and science and technology for development were proposed to be redeployed to UNCTAD. The Department of Public Information was to take over library services and publishing activities from the Office of Conference Services in the Department of Administration and Management. It was also proposed that UNDP's Office for Project Services be integrated into the new Department of Development Support and Management Services.

The number of regular-budget high-level posts would be reduced from 48 (28 USGs and 20 ASGs, the number initially approved by the General Assembly at its 46th Session) to 35 (20 USGs and 15 ASGs); 3 of those 35 posts would remain vacant pending the submission of further restructuring proposals.

The CPC was not in session and thus could not comment on the Secretary-General's proposals, but the Fifth Committee did have the benefit of the observations and recommendations of ACABQ. These observations were highly critical. ACABQ held that the Secretary-General's report lacked a context, a long-term concept, or a framework for the whole process of restructuring and for where the restructuring of the Secretariat fits into that process. The report did not demonstrate how the proposed changes would better enable the Secretariat to respond to the relevant intergovernmental decisions and to the program mandates from the member states, or how it would make the Secretariat more responsive, cost-effective, and streamlined. ACABQ identified lacunae in the programmatic justification of the proposed changes; the mandates of the new organizational units were not always given, and the distribution of subprograms and resources among the departments was not shown. Indeed, the internal structures of the new departments had not yet been finalized. With regard to the proposed transfers of functions and posts among duty stations, ACABQ was of the view that the rationale behind those proposals had not been adequately explained, and many questions remained to be addressed. The Committee also raised questions about the proposed changes in the Department of Administration and Management, including the abolition of the four ASG posts (see above), about which it voiced serious misgivings. The ACABQ could not detect a clear rationale or detailed justification for the various proposals involving high-level posts, and it cautioned against the proposed creation of a senior career level above D-2, which could in fact become known as a "second-class ASG." Noting the statement in the Secretary-General's report that he had benefited from the advice of high-level independent experts, ACABQ expressed the view that the report of these experts should have been made available. The Committee cautioned against an overreliance on external consultant expertise, and recommended that the considerable expertise that existed in-house be taken into account [A/47/7/Add.15].

The ACABQ's observations and recommendations were generally endorsed by the General Assembly in its Resolution 47/212B (the summary records of the discussion in the Fifth Committee were not available at the time of writing, thus the views of individual delegations cannot be reported).

In the preamble to that resolution the General Assembly reaffirms both its own functions and powers in considering and approving the budgets of the Organization and, in this context, its role with regard to the structure of the Secretariat and the creation, suppression, and redeployment of posts financed from the regular budget. The Assembly also reaffirms the responsibilities of the Secretary-General as chief administrative officer of the Organization. The Assembly recalls the Financial Regulations and Rules and the Regulations Governing Program Planning, the Program Aspects of the Budget, the Monitoring of Implementation and the Methods of Evaluation, and reaffirms the priorities set out in the current medium-term plan.

These preambular paragraphs put the Secretary-General on notice that any reorganization proposals must involve full consultations with member states, and that he would not be allowed to redeploy resources within the approved program budget in a manner that could be seen as interfering with approved priority activities.

In Section I of the resolution, the Assembly approved the Secretary-General's request for the transfer of resources among program budget sections to give effect to the restructuring of the Secretariat, along with most of his proposals regarding high-level posts. At the same time, the Secretary-General was requested to reconsider his proposal to abolish the four ASG-level posts of the Controller and the heads of the Offices of Human Resources Management, General Services, and Conference Services. He was also asked to reconsider his proposal to abolish the USG-level post of the head of the U.N. Centre for Human Settlements (Habitat), taking into account the views of the competent intergovernmental organs. He was requested to agree with the Director-General of GATT on a prompt appointment of the Executive Director of the UNCTAD/GATT International Trade Centre at its present level; the Secretary-General had proposed that the post be downgraded from ASG to D-2.

In Section II the 47th General Assembly emphasized inter alia that the restructuring of the Secretariat should be carried out in accordance with the guidance given by the Assembly, and reiterated the need for the full and effective implementation of all programs and subprograms as set out in the current medium-term plan.

Much of the resolution, which has 29 operative paragraphs, consists of noting various assurances given by the Secretary-General and of requests or invitations to him to take steps to meet the various concerns expressed by delegations and the observations of ACABQ. All these steps are to be reflected in his program budget proposals for 1994–95, which the Assembly is to consider at its 48th Session in the fall of 1993. The tenor of the debate at the forthcoming session will depend, therefore, on the extent to which the Secretary-General responds to requests that have been addressed to him.

Questions of Audit and Control

Concern over the adequacy of budgetary and other controls loomed large in the Fifth Committee's deliberations at the 47th Session.

The reports on the accounts for 1990–91 submitted by the **Board of Auditors** drew attention to various shortcomings in the management of the resources of the United Nations and its related funds and programs, including cases of expenditures exceeding allotments and of lapses in the application of rules and procedures governing the appointment of experts and consultants, deficiencies in the procurement system (including frequent exceptions to the rule mandating competitive bidding), and slack control over non-expendable property. The Board's reports also referred to several cases of fraud. The Board found that internal audit operations needed to be expanded and strengthened; it also felt that participation of internal auditors in committees dealing with recruitment, promotion, and grievances diminished their independence [A/47/5 and Add. 1–8].

The U.S. delegation—the first to take the floor in the debate on this item—called for an expanded audit of the 1990–91 accounts; the Assembly should await its results before it could approve the accounts for the biennium. The serious deficiencies identified by the Board suggested that the potential existed for widespread fraud and abuse with regard to various staff entitlements. Fundamental changes were needed in the Secretariat's approach to the internal audit function. The Director of Internal Audit should report directly to the Secretary-General; the resources of the Internal Audit Division should be strengthened, and its reports should be made available to ACABQ. The U.S. delegation was in favor of the **establishment of an Inspector-General for the U.N. system** [A/C.5/47/SR.6, paras. 21–37].

In a subsequent intervention, the U.S. representative said that the series of articles in *The Washington Post* on the United Nations had had an enormous impact in U.S. government circles. Unless the instances of mismanagement described by the Board were immediately corrected, the capacity of the United Nations to respond to global problems and the capacity of its supporters to provide the necessary resources would be undermined [A/C.5/47/SR.22, para. 1].

The United Nations, followed by UNDP, had established a mechanism for confidential notification by staff members of any case of fraud or presumptive fraud involving improper use of funds [A/47/510]. The U.S. delegation expressed disappointment at the Secretary-General's response to the Assembly's request for information on the implementation of the confidential reporting system [A/C.5/47/SR.12, para. 57].

The representative of the United Kingdom, speaking on behalf of the European Community, said that it was unacceptable that problems of long standing, repeatedly criticized by the Board of Auditors, still remained unresolved. As for the Board's comments on consultants, experts, and temporary assistance, which made "depressing reading," there were two possibilities: Either the existing provisions were inappropriate, in which case they should be reviewed, or they were adequate, in which case exceptions should be few in number. The situation with regard to procurement had become untenable. The European Community agreed that there was need for effective internal audit arrangements. The dedication of U.N. staff was not in question, but management issues had to be addressed [A/C.5/47/SR.10, paras. 9–22].

The Canadian delegation found the financial statements inadequate and called for the appointment of a consultant to propose a set of accounting standards. A regime ensuring respect for the principle of accountability within the U.N. system was required; management must enforce its own rules with regard to internal control. The creation of a post of Inspector-General would serve no purpose if management continued not to heed the recommendations made. The delegation called on U.N. organizations immediately to strengthen the independence of their internal audit services, to provide them with appropriate staff resources, and to ensure that those to whom internal audit reports were addressed would be held accountable for implementing their recommendations [A/C.5/47/SR.10, paras. 26–31].

The Nordic countries also called for strengthening the internal audit functions, as well as the oversight functions of the intergovernmental bodies, starting with the General Assembly. Immediate corrective action should be taken to deal with shortcomings in property control, and with failure to apply the rules calling for competitive bidding [ibid., paras. 32–29].

The representative of Argentina, speaking on behalf of 14 Central and South American countries in addition to his own, said that the cases of the misuse of funds noted by the auditors were exceptional, and should not tarnish the reputation of the thousands of staff members who carried out their functions conscientiously. Member states should not use such cases as an excuse for not meeting their financial obligations [ibid., para. 60].

The representative of Japan endorsed the U.S. suggestion that the Board undertake an expanded audit of the 1990–91 accounts [A/C.5/47/SR.11, para. 54].

Responding to the debate, the Chairman of the Board of Auditors said that there was no need to reexamine the 1990–91 accounts; the Board had had full access to all the information and records it needed, and had been able to form an opinion on the U.N. financial statements. With regard to the internal audit function, the Board considered it inappropriate for internal audit reports to be provided to others than management [A/C.5/47/SR.12, paras. 68 and 72].

In a resolution of 23 operative paragraphs [A/Res/47/211] the General Assembly approved all the recommendations and conclusions of the Board of Auditors and the related comments of ACABQ. It requested the Secretary-General and the executive heads of U.N. organizations and programs:

(a) to strengthen budgetary control, in order to avoid over-expenditure of approved budgets or allotments;
(b) to make purchasing goods and services more cost-effective and transparent, notably by reducing the number of exceptions to competitive bidding;
(c) to give priority attention to compliance with the recommendations on the hiring, remuneration, and performance evaluation of experts, consultants, and short-term staff;

(d) to enhance the effectiveness of the control over staff allowances and benefits; and

(e) to tighten control over the inventory of non-expendable property.

The Secretary-General and the executive heads were also encouraged to take urgent steps to strengthen the independence and effectiveness of the internal audit function, and to accelerate their efforts to develop common accounting standards, which should be applied in preparing the financial statements for the period ending December 31, 1993. The Secretary-General was requested to submit proposals for establishing legal and effective mechanisms to obtain recovery of misappropriated funds, and for seeking criminal prosecution of those who have committed fraud. Lastly, the Assembly called the Secretary-General's attention to the implications that the findings of the Board of Auditors about the management of the Organization may have for the image of the United Nations. Among several requests addressed to the Board of Auditors was one to expand its audit coverage of all peacekeeping operations without reducing the coverage of regular-budget and extrabudgetary activities. The Secretary-General was requested to report to the General Assembly at its 48th Session on the action he will have taken.

In two other resolutions [A/Res/47/214, section V; A/Res/47/212/B, Section III, para. 24] the Secretary-General was requested to establish a system of responsibility and accountability of program managers, and to report thereon to the Assembly at its 48th Session.

In a separate decision, the Assembly requested the Secretary-General to review the operation and effectiveness of all the specialized administrative and budgetary support units of the Secretariat, and to submit a report thereon at the Assembly's 48th Session. It also decided to consider not later than at its 49th Session the roles and coverage of the coordination, administration, and budgetary subsidiary bodies, including ACABQ, the U.N. Board of Auditors, the Joint Inspection Unit (JIU), and the CPC, with a view to improving the effectiveness of its oversight and coordination mechanisms [A/Dec. 47/454].

The Fifth Committee's program of work for 1992 included an item on the **Joint Inspection Unit,** a body whose effectiveness and the relevance of whose reports had been questioned over the years by some delegations. The discussion of the item was perfunctory; of the few delegations that took part in it, several represented countries whose nationals were serving members of the Unit, and the comments on the Unit's work were generally complimentary. In Resolution 47/201 the Assembly decided to resume consideration of the item at its 48th Session.

Respect for the Privileges and Immunities of International Officials

The Fifth Committee had before it a report by the Secretary-General [A/C.5/47/14] containing a consolidated list, as of June 30, 1992, of staff members under arrest and detention or missing and with respect to whom the United Nations and its specialized agencies and related organizations had been unable to exercise fully their right to protection. The list contained 45 names (as against 78 names a year earlier). Some of the persons concerned had been missing or in detention for years; however, two of the long-standing cases had been resolved with the release of two staff members of the U.N. Relief and Works Agency for Palestine Refugees (UNRWA), one of whom had been detained since 1982, the other since 1988.

The relative improvement in the situation was ascribed by the Secretary-General to fewer incidents involving UNRWA staff members. Nonetheless, UNRWA staff continue to account for most of the cases: 38 out of the 45 listed in the Secretary-General's report. During the 12 months to June 30, 1992, 66 UNRWA staff had been arrested or detained; 51 of them had subsequently been released without charge or trial, and 5 had been sentenced to various terms of imprisonment. In no case had UNRWA received adequate and timely information on the reasons for the arrests and detentions. UNRWA had been unable to visit staff in detention in Jordan, Lebanon, the Syrian Arab Republic, and, in several cases, staff detained by the Israeli authorities. UNRWA had also continued to experience difficulties with the movement of staff into and out of the West Bank and the Gaza Strip.

The representative of Israel argued that the persons concerned had been detained under the laws applied in the administered areas as a result of their involvement in illegal activities, and that they were granted all requisite facilities [A/C.5/47/SR.22, paras. 11–15]. The Director of Personnel responded that UNRWA had repeatedly but unsuccessfully requested information from the Israeli authorities about the reasons for the detention of staff members, and declared that UNRWA did not employ staff who had been involved in acts of violence or incitement to violence [A/C.5/47/SR.25, para. 3].

The dispute with Sudan over the tax imposed on international officials of Sudanese nationality when they renewed their passports [see *Issues/47*, p. 361] and with Hungary over the taxation of the salaries and emoluments of locally recruited staff of the U.N. High Commissioner for Refugees (UNHCR) had been resolved satisfactorily.

As a consequence of the increased demands on the U.N. system for peacekeeping and humanitarian missions, often in areas of military confrontation, staff members had found themselves serving in areas where the security situation is tenuous at best. Eleven lost their lives in the first nine months of 1992: three staff of UNICEF, two each of UNHCR and UNRWA, and one each of FAO/WFP, ICAO, the U.N. Centre for Human Settlements, and UNESCO.

Addressing the Fifth Committee on this issue, the Secretary-General said that member states should respect and strictly enforce the international legal instruments and undertakings that were meant to protect U.N. staff in the performance of their functions. Member states should be prudent and responsible when calling for increased U.N. involvement. He could not permit staff to take on responsibilities that could not be performed within a context of acceptable security. He had recommended that the Security Council consider what action, including collective measures agreed in advance, should be taken toward those who put U.N. personnel in danger or caused their death [A/C.5/47/SR.21, para. 63].

The delegations that spoke to this question shared the Secretary-General's concern for the safety and security of U.N. staff, and stressed the responsibility of the states in their respective territories. The representative of Japan called for a plan to provide generous compensation for the families of staff members who lost their lives while serving with peacekeeping or humanitarian missions; consideration should be given in this connection to augmenting the current compensation scheme through additional private insurance [A/C.5/47/SR.17, para. 39]. The U.S. representative said that staff members who are arrested or detained and subsequently released should be provided with rehabilitation facilities with a view to their reintegration into the U.N. community.

On the other hand, the representative of Senegal pointed out that the privileges and immunities of staff members applied only within the framework of activities connected with their functional powers and status; a tendentious presentation of the incidents should be avoided and the views of the member states concerned should be reflected in the Secretary-General's reports. He recalled that the various concerns had been clearly stated by the General Assembly in its Resolution 45/240 [A/C.5/47/SR.22, para. 8]. The representative of Sierra Leone also referred to the obligation of staff to obey the laws of their host country [ibid., para. 36].

In the informal consultations, the question was raised whether respect for the privileges and immunities of international officials should be considered as a separate item of the Assembly's agenda or whether it should remain a subitem under "Personnel questions." No agreement could be reached on this point.

In Resolution 47/28 the General Assembly inter alia took note "with grave concern" of the report submitted by the Secretary-General; it strongly deplored the increasing number of fatalities; it condemned and deplored the disregard for Article 105 of the Charter displayed by some member states; it reminded host countries of their responsibility for the safety of peacekeeping and all U.N. personnel on their territory; and strongly affirmed that disregard for the privileges and immunities of officials has always constituted one of the main obstacles to the implementation of the missions and programs of the Organization.

Updated information on the situation of U.N. staff with special regard to violations of their privileges and immunities will be submitted to the Assembly at its 1993 Session.

The Common System

The reports of the **International Civil Service Commission (ICSC)** and **U.N. Joint Staff Pension Board** were considered jointly by the Fifth Committee at the 47th Session.

A major topic discussed by the two bodies was the methodology for determining pensionable remuneration for staff in the General Service and other locally recruited categories. Both ICSC and the Pension Board had already dealt with that question in their reports to the 46th Session of the Assembly, without reaching a consensus [see *Issues/47*, pp. 368–70], a fact that was noted by the Assembly in Section II of Resolution 46/192. After further study, the two bodies agreed that one of the two alternative methods identified for further consideration, namely relating General Service pensions to best prevailing practices in the various localities, would be too complex and should not be pursued. Accordingly, ICSC decided that the remaining alternative, under which pensions would be related to the salaries paid to the staff while in service (the so-called "income replacement" approach), should be selected. However, no agreement could be reached in the Pension Board where the participant-elected members wanted the current methodology to be retained because it yielded higher pensions. For the same reason the representatives of the staff associations had withdrawn from participation in the ICSC sessions. It should be noted in this connection that the "income replacement" approach is already applied in calculating the scale of pensionable remuneration for participants in the Professional and higher categories [ibid., p. 371]. The remaining recommendations of ICSC and the Pension Board were technical in nature.

Most delegations in the Fifth Committee confined themselves to generally supporting the recommendations of the two bodies. Only the French delegation discussed staff remuneration in a broader context, stating that the Fifth Committee must go beyond purely technical considerations; remuneration could not be considered without regard to career development and staffing policies. There was no direct and exclusive correlation between remuneration and personnel costs. More competent, better paid, and more motivated staff could generate significant management economies, as had long been recognized in the private sector and some civil services. By contrast, errors at the higher levels could have important budgetary implications and serious repercussions on the discharge of mandates. There were indications that the U.N. system did not offer sufficiently competitive conditions of service. The real question was whether a general decline had indeed occurred, or whether recruitment and retention difficulties were due to specific problems that could be addressed on their own. Any systematic bias affecting comparisons with the comparator civil service should be eliminated. The main competitors should be identified, disparities in remuneration assessed, and note taken of trends regarding the geographical origin of those seeking employment, the response to vacancy notices, and retention. Armed with the facts, ICSC would be able to address the question of restoring competitiveness through a comprehensive approach [A/C.5/47/SR. 35, paras. 1–8].

The representative of Tunisia, for his part, stressed that ICSC must maintain its impartiality and be immune to pressure. Its working methods and rules of procedure could not be amended or interpreted according to the wishes of some delegations. It would be useful to consider means of ensuring the Commission's independence, including financial [A/C.5/47/SR.29, para. 12].

In the resolution on the report of ICSC [A/Res/47/216], the General Assembly reaffirmed its own central role with regard to the conditions of service for the U.N. common system as a whole, and the role of the Commission as the independent technical body responsible to the Assembly for the regulation and coordination of those conditions. The Assembly noted with regret that the International Telecommunication Union (ITU) had made a further payment of the special post allowance to its staff despite the views against such action expressed in General Assembly Resolution 46/191, Section II. It also regretted the suspension of the participation of the staff bodies in the work of the Commission. Responding to doubts about whether the **U.S. civil service** was still the highest paid civil service with which the U.N. common system conditions of service should be compared in accordance with the so-called **Noblemaire principle,** the General Assembly reiterated its request to the commission to complete the first phase of its study designed to identify the highest paid civil service, and to report thereon at the Assembly's 49th Session; and it invited the Commission also to study all aspects of the application of the Noblemaire principle with a view to ensuring the competitiveness of the U.N. common system. It also endorsed in principle the Commission's suggestion for the introduction of special occupational rates, and requested the Commission to submit recommendations at the Assembly's 48th Session.

Consideration of the conditions of service of USGs and ASGs and of equivalent levels, including the question of their representation allowances (on which there was no unanimity, because some delegations asked that such officials account for their representation expenses, lest the representation allowance simply become an addition to salary), was deferred until "the earliest possible opportunity."

In the resolution on the pension system [A/Res/47/203] the General Assembly endorsed the conclusions of the Board and of ICSC that the methodology for determining the pensionable remuneration of staff in the General Service and other locally recruited categories should relate the levels of pensionable remuneration and consequent pensions to salaries while in service (i.e., it endorsed the "income replacement" approach) and requested that recommendations on this subject be submitted at the 48th Session. With regard to pensionable remuneration and pensions of ungraded officials, including the executive heads of the member organizations of the fund other than the Secretary-General of the United Nations [see *Issues/47th*, pp. 372–73], the General Assembly decided to convey to the governing bodies of those member organizations its view that their ungraded officials should be participants in the fund so as to ensure systemwide comparability. However, the relevant articles of the fund's regulations will not be amended until 1994 so as to allow the governing bodies to consider the matter. The Board was also asked to continue to consider economy measures, including in particular a change of the "120% cap" provision under the two-track adjustment system [ibid., pp. 370–71]. Thus, the pensionable remuneration of staff in the General Service and related categories is likely to be the only pension matter considered by the General Assembly in 1993.

Index